HAMAS

AZZAM TAMIMI

HAMAS

A HISTORY FROM WITHIN

OLIVE
BRANCH
PRESS

An imprint of Interlink Publishing Group, Inc.
www.interlinkbooks.com

First published in 2007 by

OLIVE BRANCH PRESS
An imprint of Interlink Publishing Group, Inc.
46 Crosby Street
Northampton, Massachusetts 01060
www.interlinkbooks.com

Library of Congress Cataloging-in-Publication Data
Tamimi, Azzam.
Hamas : a history / by Azzam Tamimi.
    p. cm.
Includes bibliographical references and index.
ISBN 978-1-56656-689-6 (pbk.)
1. Harakat al-Muqawamah al-Islamiyah--History. 2. Islam and politics. I. Title.

JQ1830.A98H3778 2007
324.25695'3083--dc22

2007006828

Cover image: A Hamas supporter holds a copy of the Quran during a rally in front of the Palestinian parliament in Gaza City. (AP Photo/Khalil Hamra) © 2007 The Associated Press. All rights reserved.

Book design by Juliana Spear

Printed and bound in the United States of America

To request our complete 40-page full-color catalog, please call us toll free at 1-800-238-LINK, visit our website at www.interlinkbooks.com, or write to Interlink Publishing, 46 Crosby Street, Northampton, MA 01060
e-mail: info@interlinkbooks.com

CONTENTS

Acknowledgments

THIS BOOK COULD NOT HAVE BEEN RESEARCHED AND WRITTEN WITHOUT two fellowships that I was granted by two prestigious universities in Japan. The first fellowship was awarded to me by Kyoto University, where I was visiting professor at the Graduate School of Asian and African Area Studies for six months from 1 April to 30 September 2004. While at Kyoto, I had the great pleasure of being hosted by Professor Yasushi Kosugi, professor of the study of the Islamic world, who provided me with invaluable assistance. The second fellowship was granted by Nagoya University, where I was visiting fellow at the Graduate School of International Development for three months from 1 January to 31 March 2006. At Nagoya my host was my very dear friend, the school's dean, Professor Hisae Nakanishi, whose support I could not have managed without. I am equally grateful to the academic and administrative staff and postgraduate students at both universities, who spared no effort to make my stay comfortable and worthwhile.

I am most grateful to friends and colleagues who read different parts of the manuscript and provided me with valuable comments and insightful feedback. Many thanks to Ramzy Baroud, veteran Arab-American journalist and author; Gabrielle Rifkind, human security consultant, process director of the Middle East Policy Initiative Forum and member of the Oxford Research Group; and Dr. Mohammad Nazari Ismail, associate professor and head of the Department of Business Policy and Strategy, the Faculty of Business and Accounting at the University of Malaysia.

I offer my profound gratitude to my very dear friend Alastair Crooke of Conflicts Forum for his advice and for providing the foreword to this book.

Last but not least, my dear wife Rifqah deserves all the credit for her support and patience.

A.T.

Foreword

Beirut, 13 August 2006

AS I WRITE, THE UN RESOLUTION DESIGNED TO RESOLVE THE CONFLICT in Lebanon has yet to take force. But, even as the fate of South Lebanon has yet to be determined, it is plain that that events here will have a far-reaching impact. That impact is already evident in the way movements such as Hezbollah and Hamas have seized the imagination of Muslims everywhere. It is certain too that the ripples from Lebanon will extend far beyond the sphere of public opinion, and that we may be at the edge of more profound changes — even if we cannot be certain what these changes will entail.

It is also clear from the language used in the West and particularly in the United States in relation to this conflict that there exists a deep misunderstanding of what movements such as Hezbollah and Hamas represent. This parallels the misreading of the ground that gave rise to the ill-conceived "Global War on Terror," which has sought to conflate movements such Hamas with al-Qaeda, a conflation that — while it might suit some policymakers interested only in promoting like-minded pro-Western Arab "moderates" — does extreme violence to the truth.

By deliberately propagating and perpetuating the untruth that moderate Islamist movements such as Hamas are no different from al-Qaeda revolutionaries who believe that to build a new society you have to burn it down first, the West deepens the prospect of a wider conflict between it and the prevalent currents of politics in the region. The conflation risks real conflict — with potentially disastrous consequences — by placing the West at odds with movements such as Hamas that symbolize for many

Muslims the hope for real reform and a better society. In this condition of profound misunderstanding, a book that helps to explain Hamas and to address these flaws of Western analysis is more than important — it is vital. Dr. Tamimi's deep knowledge of wider political Islam permits him to address Hamas within a wider optic as well as to write authoritatively on a subject with which he has great familiarity. Unlike so many "experts," here is a real expert.

Hamas stands in the vanguard of movements reflecting a sense of deep Muslim discontent with the present world order as it impacts directly on their societies. Many Muslims resent also the hegemony that seeks to impose the Western cultural template as unique in presenting the universal values of freedom, justice, and good governance. Islamists espouse and proclaim these values, but reject the idea that the West enjoys some sort of cultural copyright on how these values should be implemented, how they should be made a part of everyday life. Furthermore, Hamas would contest that the West as it is presently configured has much to teach Muslims about the values of justice (in the wider sense), ethical governance, or respect for others. Both Hamas and Hezbollah endorse free elections, but perceive the West to be highly selective in its enthusiasm for "freedom."

Hamas, of course, also stands for armed resistance. For the West this is troublesome: Westerners can understand that Islamism is the politicization of Muslim discontent at the present world order, but the use of violence by a non-state actor seems peculiarly threatening to our susceptibilities. To us, the use of violence threatens a descent into chaos; it strikes at the European certainties formed since our own "Christian caliphate" came to an end with the Treaty of Westphalia. At this point, our caliphate of the Holy Roman Empire broke up into separate nation-states; Church was separated from the state, and religion, at least in theory, became the preserve of the personal domain alone. This was a pivotal moment in European history, which we perceive as a necessary building block for the Enlightenment as well as for the growth of reason and secularism and the progress of science. This mindset has dominated European thought for the last 200 years. It has become synonymous with modernity itself for most Westerners.

It has not been the case that Western governments abhor violence per se: Iraq, Afghanistan, and now Lebanon attest to that; but we see the Westphalian structure of nation-states as the only framework for the "legitimate" use of violence. States may practice violence; but when movements use it, it seems to threaten traditional certainties — the same traditional certainties that underpin the Enlightenment. At bottom, movements such as Hamas seem to challenge our Westphalian certainties. Of course for Islamists recent history carries a different message. The nation-state has none of the benevolent associations that we couple to the Enlightenment. For most Arabs the drawing of national boundaries was recent, was imposed — with few benevolent associations and little "enlightenment."

When the West contemplates a movement such as Hamas that seems to contradict our basic Enlightenment certainties, its first demand is that it should renounce violence, disarm, and espouse party politics.

Implicit in this stipulation is that movements such as Hamas should acquiesce to our certainties. Our invariable pre-condition, before even talking, is that they must engage on our terms. "Legitimate" violence, we insist, must remain only in the hands of state actors — however discredited they may be. Our demand also implies that these movements should recognize statements about the world order that perpetuate and position the West as owner of the template for the operational implementation of modernity. This is the crux — for Hamas to accommodate to our template is tantamount to its acquiescence in the prevailing world order that seeks to impose the terms for a Palestinian state on a basis that the Palestinians view to be manifestly unjust. Hamas also sees the demand to play only by the Western rules as an exercise in power designed to "domesticate" them, and to force a backing down in the face of Western hegemony. Acquiescence denies the movement both its authority and legitimacy: accommodation therefore is not an option — hence the need to remain an armed force in the face of Western and Israeli hostility.

The challenge to Western and Israeli hegemony should not be confused with being anti-Western. Hamas is not anti-Western. Nor should Hamas's challenge to our presumed copyright on the socioeconomic organization of modernity imply any virulent anti-modernism. Rather, Hamas seeks to fashion a just social and political order in Palestine as opposed to an environment of oppression and exploitation that is based on the hegemony of the West. It believes that it has better answers to fashioning a Palestinian political future than can be offered by the West.

In doing this, Hamas, like other Islamist movements, believes that new Islamist political thinking can only be undertaken by disengaging from the received historical and philosophical perspectives of the West.

The challenge posed by a movement such as Hamas should be understood to be intellectual as much as military. Hamas views armed action as just one tool that can be used to achieve its objectives, and its predominance is perceived not as an essential ingredient of its philosophy, but as a requisite in the face of almost universal hostility and an occupation that it is pledged to end. I believe Dr. Tamimi's book will go a long way toward helping us to gain the courage to examine this challenge to some of our cultural certainties and icons and to respond reflectively rather than with our customary defensiveness.

Alastair Crooke
Conflicts Forum

Introduction

WHEN THIS BOOK WAS COMMISSIONED IN 2003, THERE WAS LITTLE TO suggest that less than three years later the Islamic Resistance Movement in Palestine (Hamas) would achieve a sweeping victory in one of the most unusual democratic exercises ever allowed to take place in the Arabic-speaking world. Notwithstanding later developments, many observers at the time already saw Hamas, which was formed in December 1987, as a major player in the Palestinian arena. As the peace process between the Palestinians and the Israelis ground to a halt, the slow, though painful, war of attrition raging between the two sides has seemed to center increasingly on the role of Hamas and its impact on Middle Eastern politics on a local, regional, and global scale.

There therefore appeared to be a need for a book that would give an account of this rapidly growing movement and the phases of its development. A few books had already been published in English about Hamas. Almost all of these, however, apart from Khalid Hroub's *Hamas: Political Thought and Practice*,[1] had been written from an Israeli perspective, relying heavily on data obtained from security and intelligence files. As authentic a narrative as possible of the events that led to the rise and predominance of Hamas seemed therefore to be called for, to enable an English readership to understand how the movement sees itself and the world around it. Such an insight is rarely communicated to the non–Arabic-speaking world.

A good illustration of how Hamas has been presented to Western readers is the recent book by Matthew Levitt, who, at the time of publication in 2006, was deputy assistant secretary for intelligence and analysis at the US Treasury Department. *Hamas: Politics, Charity, and Terrorism in the Service of Jihad* depicts Hamas as a terrorist organization that uses "its extensive charitable and educational work to promote its foremost aim: driving Israel into the sea." Hamas's reputable charity activities are condemned as a mere device to recruit new soldiers to its "holy war" against Israel. The movement's sponsored mosques, schools, orphanages, and sports organizations are portrayed as "integral parts of an overarching apparatus of terror."[2] Any view of Hamas that conflicts with this stereotypical image has been brushed away as ill informed or biased. A critical review of Levitt's work by Steven Erlanger, the Jerusalem bureau chief of the *New York Times*,[3] was unashamedly denounced by Barry Rubin, director of the Global Research in International Affairs Center in Israel, as "a shocking anti-Israel diatribe."[4] Rubin suggested that Erlanger was an unfair reporter, with an inadequate understanding of the contemporary issues he was covering. He insisted that Hamas itself and its main supporters held their views because of their desire to wipe Israel off the map, rather than due to anger at Israel's presence in the West Bank and the Gaza Strip. Rubin's own stated view was that "Hamas believes that continuing to fight Israel, ignoring Israeli concessions and ensuring that peace fails, is the best way to build support for an Islamist revolution among Palestinians." In a judgment fully representative of the prevalent image of Hamas held in Israel and the United States, Rubin characterizes Hamas as a racist, terrorist group with genocidal intentions against the Israeli people.

Hamas: A History from Within is an attempt to redress the imbalance in contemporary literature on Hamas. An accurate account of Hamas's origins will be provided. Analysis of the beliefs and values of Hamas will distinguish between what is essential in its position and what is marginal, with an examination of how the thinking of its leaders and ideologues has evolved over the years. Hamas's reaction to challenges will be discussed, together with how it has dealt with its friends and foes, and its ability to recover from seemingly fatal setbacks. Finally, an explanation will be offered of how Hamas has grown to constitute a convincing alternative in the minds of many Palestinians to the former symbols of their struggle, the Palestine Liberation Organization (the PLO) and the Fatah movement. Al-Fatah, the faction headed by the late Yasir Arafat, is the backbone of the PLO, which maintained a monopoly on Palestinian struggle and activism through several decades before Hamas's birth.

The difference between this book and most others written about Hamas is that it discusses Hamas in a global context rather than placing it exclusively within the context of Israel. Hamas is an organization of Arabs and Muslims who happen to be Palestinian, and who perceive themselves as the immediate victims of a plot hatched by an unjust world order that saw fit to create a Jewish state in the very heart of the Arab and Muslim lands. More immediately, they perceive the Israelis as the oppressors who have dispossessed them and have persecuted them for generations. While attending primarily to local concerns, the activities of Hamas possess regional as well as global implications and consequences. The struggle against Israel is one of several elements that inform the thinking of the movement and instruct its activism, but is by no means the only one. Hamas, which had its origins in al-Ikhwan al-Muslimun (the Muslim Brotherhood), grew out of a social project motivated by philanthropy and dedicated to charity.

The Muslim Brotherhood is a movement loathed and feared in some quarters, but loved and supported by millions of Arabs and admired by many more millions of Muslims around the world. It is respected by many non-Muslims who have studied it or come to know it well either through the writings of its leaders or through communicating with them directly. Best characterized by its adherents as a comprehensive reform movement, the Ikhwan was Egyptian in its origins but has since grown into a global network. The mother organization was founded in 1928 by Hassan al-Banna (1906–1949) in the Egyptian town of al-Isma'iliyah, where he taught at a primary school not far from the headquarters of the British occupying forces. Combining elements of spirituality acquired from al-Banna's association with the Hasafiyah Sufi order with the pristine monotheistic teachings of Islam, he learned from the Salafi school of Muhammad Rashid Rida (1865–1935) — a disciple and close associate of Muhammad Abduh (1849–1905) — the project had a great popular appeal. Soon after its birth, the Ikhwan movement grew rapidly within Egypt and beyond it. Inside Egypt, it had four branches in 1929, 15 in 1932, 300 by 1938, and more than 2000 in 1948. By 1945, it had half a million active members in Egypt alone. Between 1946 and 1948, branches of the Ikhwan were opened in Palestine, Sudan, Iraq, and Syria.

3

Al-Banna's genius was manifest in his ability to take to the masses the concerns of the intellectuals of his time and to transform into a grassroots movement the elitist projects of the reformists that preceded him. He did not work in the mosques, for those who frequented the mosques were not his target. Nor did he work within cultural clubs or other elite meeting places. His field of activity lay in the popular cafés and meeting places, where he reiterated in simpler, more direct terms the calls for reform made by reformers of the 19th century. On colonialism, he echoed Jamal al-Din al-Afghani (1838–1897) and Mustafa Kamil (1874–1908). On *riba* (usury), he took his cue from Muhammad Abduh and Muhammad Rashid Rida. Mustafa Kamil shaped his view of the influence of foreign business, while Abduh and Rida formed his ideas on intellectual chaos and the loss of moral values. Jamal al-Din al-Afghani and Shakib Arsalan (1869–1946) were the inspiration for his condemnation for blind imitation of the West, and Shakib Arsalan prompted his critique of manmade laws that fail to curb crime or deter criminals. Muhammad Abduh was the origin of his thoughts on the mismanagement of education. Finally, on the signs of desperation and loss of will manifest within the Muslim community, he took inspiration from Arsalan and Kamil.

Al-Banna blamed partisan divisions for the intensification of the problems already suffered by the umma as the result of backwardness and colonialism. His priority was to alert the people of Egypt to the importance of unity and cohesion. He warned that as long as the umma was fragmented and drowned in disputes, it would never be able to confront the threat of colonial hegemony. His message was not confined to Egypt but transcended it to spread throughout the entire Muslim world, much of which was under foreign occupation at the time. He held the European powers responsible for "dismembering the Islamic Empire and annihilating the Islamic State and erasing it from the list of powerful living nations."[5] His movement's long-term goals were, first, to free the Islamic homeland from all foreign authority; and second, to establish an Islamic state within this Islamic homeland. Neither objective could be achieved, however, without initially attending to the more immediate needs of society. Al-Banna's project was, above all, an endeavor to "rehabilitate" the umma, beginning with the individual, then going on to the family, and culminating with society as a whole, all through a process of gradual reform.

These two same goals have been pursued, using the same methodology of gradual reform, by offshoots of the Ikhwan across the Arab region, including Palestine, where the Palestinian Ikhwan took root immediately after the end of World War II. The Palestinian Ikhwan initially opened a few local branches in Gaza. However, on 6 May 1946, its structure neared completion with the official inauguration of the movement's Central Office in Jerusalem in the presence of local dignitaries, as well as guests who came from Cairo to represent the mother movement in Egypt. The creation of Israel in two-thirds of Palestine in 1948 led to the split of the Palestinian Ikhwan into two separate organizations. One of these was in Gaza, which came under Egyptian military rule, and the other was in the West Bank, which was annexed to Transjordan and in due course became part of the Hashemite Kingdom of Jordan. This book begins from the point in 1967 when the Israeli occupation of the remaining third of Palestine created an opportunity for the Ikhwan to revive and reunite.

Chapter One, "The Beginnings," opens with a brief description of the incident that sparked the intifada on 8 December 1987 and the circumstances that led to the birth of Hamas soon afterward. The chapter then looks at the preceding two decades to give this event an appropriate context. From 1967 to 1977, the Ikhwan of Palestine were busy putting their house in order, uniting their ranks, and regaining some of the ground they had lost to the secular nationalist movements that gained their popularity from mounting resistance against the Israeli occupation. Inside Palestine, the Ikhwan leadership was being challenged to take a stand against the Israeli occupation. Outside Palestine, the Palestinian student communities, especially in Egypt and Kuwait, played a significant role in revolutionizing the thinking within the movement as a whole.

Chapter Two, "From Da'wah To Jihad," takes up the story from 1977. This was when the Palestinian Ikhwan began to plan the launch of their own resistance project, which saw the light ten years later with the outbreak of the intifada. This decade saw the creation of major institutions, such as the al-Mujamma' al-Islami and the Islamic University, which provided Palestinian society with essential services in the social, medical, and educational spheres and helped significantly to increase the movement's standing and enhance its popularity.

5

Chapter Three, "An All-Out War," recounts some of the major events that affected Hamas from the immediate aftermath of the start of the intifada in the early days of 1988 up to the announcement of the Oslo Agreement between the PLO and Israel in 1993. This was the period when Israel cracked down heavily on Hamas, arresting wave after wave of its leaders and activists and deporting hundreds of them to Lebanon. The merciless Israeli campaign against the movement prompted its leadership to transfer all executive powers to the Palestinian Ikhwan outside Palestine. This move was intended primarily to protect the organization from total collapse under the impact of the Israeli onslaught. It was in these circumstances that the Hamas military wing, the Martyr Izzadin al-Qassam Brigades, came into existence as a response to the brutality of Israeli occupation troops.

Chapter Four, entitled "Into Jordan," tells how the Hamas leadership transferred to Jordan following the invasion of Kuwait by Saddam Hussein in 1990. Initially the Jordanians tolerated the clandestine Hamas operation, but the Gulf war climate of popular mobilization in response to the perceived threat of an imminent Israeli invasion soon ended, and Hamas activists were arrested or forced underground or out of the country. The Jordanians reconsidered the value they had placed on Hamas's support in their rivalry with the PLO. The Wadi Araba peace agreement between Jordan and Israel, together with mounting pressure on the Jordanian authorities, led to the scaling down of the Hamas operation and the removal from the country of its non-Jordanian leaders. Two other developments are discussed in some detail in this chapter. The first of these is the arrest of the leading Hamas figure Musa Abu Marzuq at Kennedy Airport in New York and his subsequent detention. Jordan, however, had no choice but to take back Marzuq two years later. The second issue is the growing rift between the Hamas leadership in Jordan and the Jordanian Ikhwan.

Chapter Five, "The Mish'al Affair," tells the story of the botched Israeli assassination attempt on the life of the Hamas leader Khalid Mish'al. The Israeli adventure in the event brought unexpected dividends for Hamas. To rescue their special relationship with Jordan, the Israelis agreed not only to spare the life of Mish'al but also to release Hamas's founder, Sheikh Ahmad Yassin, from detention. Sheikh Yassin had an opportunity to tour several Arab and Muslim countries, garnering support for the movement. Despite a brief thaw in relations between Hamas and Jordan, however, the crisis soon deepened due to mounting pressure on Jordan from the US, Israel, and the Palestinian National Authority.

Chapter Six, entitled "Out Of Jordan," recounts the events that led to the complete removal of Hamas from Jordan. Following the death of King Hussein in January 1999, the Jordanian regime seemed to lose interest entirely in Hamas. Jordanian hostility toward Hamas began while the organization's senior leadership was on a visit to Tehran in the summer of 1999. The deteriorating relationship between Hamas and the Jordanian Ikhwan catalyzed the eclipse of the Hamas operation in Jordan, with the closure of its offices and the deportation of its leaders. The Hamas Political Bureau moved to Damascus, where the Syrian authorities granted it space and protection.

Chapter Seven of the book, "The Liberation Ideology of Hamas," deals with the position of Hamas concerning the Jews and the State of Israel, as well as the military tactics appropriate for the struggle, including the use of suicide bombings or "martyrdom operations." The chapter shows how Hamas's political discourse on these and other issues has evolved significantly since its Charter was first published in the summer of 1988. The Charter has been both problematic and embarrassing and has been cited more by the critics of the movement than by its spokesmen. What this chapter seeks to show is that from the outset the Charter has never been an accurate reflection of either the philosophy or the political standpoint of the movement. After subjecting the Charter to a critique, the chapter discusses in some detail the concept of *hudna*, a truce or cease-fire agreement offered by Hamas to the Israelis as early as 1994.

Chapter Eight, "Jihad and Martyrdom," concerns the debate on the issue of martyrdom within contemporary Islamic political thought. This is of direct relevance to Hamas, whose military wing has employed "martyrdom operations" as a weapon in the struggle against Israeli occupation. The chapter begins with an explanation of the concepts of *jihad* and *qital*, placing both within a historical context before discussing their relevance to contemporary Muslim life. As the chapter illustrates, the debate about martyrdom is more a matter of politics than of jurisprudence. There are a number of controversies. First, there is the question of whether the act is a contemptible suicide or a noble self-sacrifice; second, there is the issue of what is a legitimate target and what is not; and third, there is the debate over whether the tactic serves or harms the cause.

Chapter Nine, "Hamas, the PLO, and the Palestinian Authority," discusses the attitude toward Hamas of its main rival within the Palestinian arena, the Fatah movement. Hamas was from the outset perceived as a grave danger, and al-Fatah's leadership, which had also led the PLO and then became the leadership of the Palestinian Authority (PA), sought in a variety of ways to undermine it. Sometimes, the leaders of Fatah have behaved almost as if Hamas did not exist, while at other times they have taken action against it, aiming either to contain or to liquidate it.

Chapter Ten, entitled "Hamas in Government," starts from the aftermath of Arafat's death in November 2004. It gives an account of the developments leading up to the legislative elections of January 2006 and of the consequences of Hamas's sweeping victory. The chapter provides readers with an insight into the steps taken by Hamas's opponents, including the Israelis, the Americans, and some of the leaders of Fatah, to attempt to oblige it to abandon the leadership of the Palestinian Authority, which it had democratically inherited from Fatah.

Chapter Eleven, entitled "Toward the Next Intifada?," covers the ongoing power struggle between Fatah and Hamas following Hamas's electoral victory, which resulted eventually in the formation of a national unity government on 17 March 2007 after negotiations in Mecca. Hamas was not ultimately required to yield to international conditions in forming the national unity government, and thus continued to refuse to recognize Israel; nevertheless, immediately following the agreement, Hamas leader Khalid Mish'al made the movement's first unequivocal statement about its willingness to accept a Palestinian state confined to the territories captured by Israel in 1967. This series of landmark events did not, however, result in an end to international sanctions or anything more than a temporary respite in factional conflict. The escalating violence in the Gaza Strip resulted, in June 2007, in Hamas taking full military control; in response, President Abbas dissolved the national unity government, and the divide between Fatah and Hamas seemed nearly insurmountable. Around the world all eyes turned toward Gaza as it faced a humanitarian crisis grown increasingly desperate through years of siege.

The book concludes with six appendices, which may throw further light on some of the issues raised by its eleven chapters. The first of these is a document entitled "This is What We Struggle for." This is the text of a memorandum drafted by the Hamas Political Bureau in English in the late 1990s at the request of Western diplomats in the Jordanian capital Amman. The second, entitled "The Islamic Resistance Movement (Hamas)," is another memorandum, this time originally drafted in Arabic by the Hamas Political Bureau in 2000, just before the eruption of the second intifada, to explain the position of the movement on the various issues. The third appendix is the text of an article by Khalid Mish'al, the head of the Hamas Political Bureau. Under the title "We Will Not Sell Our People or Principles for Foreign Aid," this was published in the *Guardian* on 31 January 2006. The fourth appendix is a further article that appeared on the same day in the *Washington Post*. Authored by the deputy head of the Hamas Political Bureau, Musa Abu Marzuq, the article is entitled "What Hamas Is Seeking." The fifth appendix is an article by the Palestinian Prime Minister Isma'il Haniyah. Entitled "A Just Peace or No Peace," it appeared in the *Guardian* on 31 March 2006. The sixth and final appendix is the text of the election manifesto of Hamas's "Change and Reform" List for the legislative elections held on 25 January 2006.

In the English-speaking world, the story this book seeks to tell has hitherto been little heard. It is the sincere hope of the author that the book will provide the public with a more accurate description of what Hamas is and what it stands for. Those in academia, the media, or political authority who are interested in seeing an end to the conflict in the Middle East, or are working for this outcome, will hopefully find here a valuable contribution to this enterprise.

ONE

THE BEGINNINGS

Our preparations continued, with our efforts and the efforts of our brothers,
for years and years. Throughout that time we gathered,
observed and waited until the moment to move arrived.[1]

—Sheikh Ahmad Yassin

REPORTING FROM THE GAZA STRIP ON WEDNESDAY, 9 DECEMBER 1987,
an Associated Press reporter described how Israeli soldiers opened fire
"on bottle-throwing Arab protesters in a wave of violence triggered by a
traffic accident." What the agency described as a traffic accident was to
the Palestinians nothing less than a deliberate act of murder. The incident
had taken place the previous evening, when three Palestinian workers
were killed and seven others injured as the driver of an Israeli military
tractor-trailer ploughed head-on into two vans carrying the workers, on
their way back home from Israel. This "traffic accident" was the single
event from which flowed all the momentous changes that took place in
Palestine in the subsequent years.

On the night of 9 December, following an eventful day, the seven
men who made up the senior leadership of al-Ikhwan al-Muslimun (the
Muslim Brotherhood — henceforth referred to as the Ikhwan) in Gaza
held an emergency meeting. These were Sheikh Ahmad Yassin, Dr. Abd
al-Aziz al-Rantisi, Salah Shihadah, Abd al-Fattah Dukhan, Muhammad
Sham'ah, Ibrahim al-Yazuri, and 'Isa al-Nashar.[2] Earlier in the day, they
had instructed staff and students at the Islamic University, one of their
most important institutions in the Gaza Strip, to close down at noon and
stage a general strike. In response, people assembled around al-Shifa hospital in what became a massive rally. Until the evening, many could still
be seen lining up outside the hospital for their turn to donate blood. At

their meeting that night, the seven Ikhwan leaders took the historic decision to transform the Ikhwan organization in Palestine into a resistance movement that was to be known as Harakat al-Muqawamah al-Islamiyah (the Islamic Resistance Movement) [HAMAS]. Dr. Abd al-Aziz al-Rantisi immediately drafted the first communiqué. This was released to the press on 14 December, which therefore became the day on which Hamas officially came into being. For ten years Sheikh Yassin and his "brothers" had been preparing for this moment, though they had no prior warning that what they had planned for so long would come at this specific time or in this particular fashion.

Life in the Gaza Strip had grown increasingly unbearable since 1977, when in June, Israel's right-wing Likud party came to power for the first time. In November that same year, the Egyptian President Anwar al-Sadat visited Jerusalem to address the Knesset (Israel's parliament), thus striking a major blow to Palestinian hopes that their elder sister, Egypt, might play any role in rescuing them from oppression and liberating their land from occupation. Since long before Sadat's rise to power, most Palestinians had anticipated that Egypt would set them free. This had been the promise of Sadat's predecessor Gamal Abd al-Nasir: a promise abruptly broken by a regime that was interested only in recovering Sinai back from Israel, which had occupied it ten years earlier.

Paradoxically, since they fell under Israeli occupation in 1967, the Palestinians of Gaza had enjoyed a relative economic boom. Palestinian workers could with relative ease cross into Israel and earn good money for a day's work, of which there was plenty. Meanwhile, Israelis would come to the Gaza Strip to shop: in this undeclared free-trade zone, not subjected to taxation or duties, the prices were seductive. Undoubtedly, the defeat of the Arab armies in 1967, which led to the capture of what remained of Palestine by the Israelis, was in a number of ways a blessing in disguise.[3] While the Gaza Strip succumbed to Israeli occupation, it was freed from the oppressive regime of Egypt's President Gamal Abd al-Nasir.[4] In addition, Gaza became accessible from the West Bank and both areas were opened to Israeli citizens of Arab origin, who saw this as an opportunity for "family reunion."[5]

What gradually soured the prosperity that Israeli occupation seemed to bring to the lands occupied in 1967 was the humiliation to which Palestinian workers were subjected. Palestinian workers who crossed the

"Green Line" into Israel left behind their dignity and self-respect. Israeli society needed the laborers but despised them for being "the other"; they were seen as different, subhuman, and not worthy of respect. At the same time, the mere presence of these workers in their midst was an agonizing daily reminder to the Israelis of the fact that they were living on land stolen a few decades earlier from the parents or grandparents of these wretched Palestinians. The indignation and frustration of the Palestinians were fueled by the rise in Palestinian nationalism[6] as well as by the breeze of Islamic revivalism that was beginning to be felt. Both national and Islamic leaders discouraged Palestinians from "cohabiting" with their oppressors, encouraging, if not resistance, at least boycott. Above all, the Islamic leaders were concerned that workers would inevitably come under the influence of what they saw as the lax and promiscuous customs of Israeli society. In the meantime, however, sporadic resistance activities mounted by members of Palestinian resistance groups, such as Fatah and the People's Front for the Liberation of Palestine (PFLP), from within the "territories" or from across the borders, drew severe and frequently collective punitive measures. The Israeli occupation authorities mounted draconian security operations and carried out arbitrary arrests, particularly against the populations of the refugee camps in both the West Bank and Gaza. While in detention and under interrogation, Palestinians would be subjected to both physical and psychological torture, which often left permanent physical and mental scars.

This had been the atmosphere in Palestine when Egypt's President Anwar al-Sadat shocked the world with his 1977 journey to Jerusalem, which paved the way for the Camp David Accords. The signature of these in turn led to the peace treaty between Israel and Egypt, which was signed on 26 March 1979 in the presence of President Jimmy Carter, on the White House lawn in Washington, DC. Ironically, this peace was made between Egypt, historically regarded by Israel as its principal adversary in the Arab world, and the first Israeli right-wing Likud government under the leadership of Menachem Begin. Likud's supporters in general took the view that the borders of the state of Israel should be those supposed to have been bequeathed to the Jews by divine right, namely from the Nile to the Euphrates. As the achievement of peace with Egypt was celebrated, the Palestinian issue was relegated to the back burner. In the meantime Israel continued to deal crushing blows one after another to the Palestinian nationalist resistance, thus weakening the factions encompassed by the PLO.

The coming to power of the Likud government signaled a major change for the people of Gaza.[7] It was this government that authorized the establishment of the first Jewish settlements in the Gaza Strip, already one of the world's most densely populated pieces of territory. Apart from the frustration felt by the Palestinians over the neutralization of Egypt in the Arab–Israeli conflict, the people of Gaza appeared to have been singled out to pay the price for the peace process. Having withdrawn their troops and settlers from Sinai, the Israelis deployed more soldiers in the Gaza Strip. Despite the peace with Egypt, the Israelis did not amend their conscription policy and there was nowhere else to deploy new conscripts than in the occupied territories. Prior to the implementation of the peace treaty between Israel and Egypt, Israel's de facto frontier with Egypt was far away from Gaza. However, in the new era of Israeli–Egyptian peace, Gaza became the border, and it was here that Israel's frontier forces were massively deployed.

Gradually, the humiliation to which Palestinian workers were subjected in the Israeli labor market was extended to the residents of Gaza as a whole. In a policy initiated by Ariel Sharon, who in 1981 became Defense Minister of Israel in the Likud cabinet, Israeli paratroopers — known to the Palestinians as the "red berets" — were deployed with instructions to intimidate and humiliate Arabs suspected of giving assistance to the resistance. It became a common practice for Israeli troops manning checkpoints inside the occupied territories to stop Arab passers-by, especially university and high-school students, who were held at gunpoint and subjected to verbal and physical abuse for no obvious reason other than to demonstrate who was in charge. Eventually, Gaza became in effect a huge prison. It was no longer easy for a resident of Gaza to travel to Egypt, and soon afterward inhabitants of the Gaza Strip were banned altogether from traveling to Jordan. Israeli restrictions on workers meant that fewer men and women could earn a living in the lucrative Israeli labor market. One humiliating alternative was to earn a living by working in the construction of Jewish settlements built on land illegally expropriated from the Arabs themselves. Life became increasingly unbearable, and an explosion lay ahead.

The list of factors that precipitated the December 1987 intifada (uprising) is a long one, but these were not necessarily the same factors that led to the emergence of Hamas, despite the simultaneity of the two occurrences. The leaders of the Ikhwan in Gaza simply made use of the surge in the frustration and anger of the people of the Strip to bring about the transformation of their organization into a resistance movement. Few members of the organization knew that the decision to effect such a transformation had taken place as long as ten years before. Even fewer people might have been aware that the decision was taken in coordination by the many wings of the Palestinian Ikhwan, in Gaza and the West Bank as well as in Jordan and elsewhere in the diaspora.

The war of June 1967 shamed the Arabs and won new territories for Israel, including the Gaza Strip, the West Bank, Sinai, and the Golan Heights. Throughout the following decade, the Ikhwan across the Arab world reaped the fruits of what was seen as the scandalous failure of Arab nationalism. After the death of Abd al-Nasir in 1970, Ikhwan leaders and members who had long been held in Egyptian prisons were released. This gave the Ikhwan an advantage over other organizations competing with them to recruit new members, in a climate made favorable by the Islamic resurgence triggered by the 1967 defeat.[8] In Palestine, young men, some of them young teenagers, flooded the ranks of the Ikhwan. Most of the recruits came from within the student community.

The revival of the Ikhwan in Gaza resulted from the efforts of a few dedicated men. These saw ignorance and a lack of commitment to Islam as the greatest threat to their community. In the view of the leaders of the Ikhwan, the systematic suppression of Islamic activism under Egypt's rule was at fault, and Israel was the real beneficiary. The inability of the people of Gaza to resist the corrupting policies of the Israeli occupation authorities alarmed the Islamist leaders. Only a morality based on Islam could equip a jobless or penniless inhabitant of Gaza to say no to an Israeli officer offering him or her a comfortable life, a good job, or a permit to travel abroad for employment or education in exchange for collaborating with the authorities. At the same time, Israel was simply unable to control the occupied territories without collaboration from some Palestinians. The Israelis had a deliberate policy of converting as many Palestinians as possible into informers, into spies against their own people, or at least into beneficiaries of the occupation, so that they would do all they could to preserve the status quo. The tools used by Israel to recruit or blackmail collaborators were money, drugs, sex, and intimidation, as well as the temptation of material benefits to mitigate the deprivations suffered by a population under siege. The Islamists embarked on a long-term project to shield the people of Gaza from these menaces, spearheaded by a quadriplegic school teacher by the name of Ahmad Yassin.

Ahmad Yassin was born in June 1936 in the village of al-Jurah, near the modern city of Ashkelon, less than a year after Sheikh Izzadin al-Qassam[9] led the first armed revolution against foreign occupation troops in Palestine. This was the year of the Great Strike staged by the Palestinians in protest against British pro-Zionist policies, which lasted for six months, from May to October 1936. Yassin was a mere boy of twelve when the Nakba (the catastrophe) of 1948 obliged his mother to flee with her children, as part of the general exodus. Palestinians from the village of al-Jurah, as from numerous other villages and towns, fled from what they feared was imminent death at the hands of Zionist armed militiamen who sought to create an exclusively Jewish state in Palestine.[10]

Ahmad Yassin's father, Isma'il, died when Ahmad was three years old. He was destined to grow up fatherless and homeless in a refugee camp in the Gaza Strip. Just a stone's throw away, at his former home in al-Jurah, Jewish immigrants from Europe had settled, claiming to have returned to the land their ancestors had left 2,000 years earlier. Like hundreds of thousands of other Palestinians, the Yassin family was made to suffer, ostensibly because of a divine covenant granted to the Israelis by their God. He would later come to believe that his country was stolen from his people for purely worldly political reasons: religion had nothing to do with it. Until his family was forced out of al-Jurah, Ahmad Yassin had enjoyed nothing more than playing on the seashore, just 200 yards from his home.[11] He observed from the top of a nearby hill the British and then the Egyptian troops as they moved past al-Jurah. Highly dramatic developments were anticipated, and soon the news of Zionist massacres of Palestinians, began to arrive, instilling horror in the hearts and the minds of the villagers.[12] His family joined others in expressing their anger at the Arab armies. They had arrived promising to fight against the Zionists, save Palestine, and rescue the Palestinians. However, they only disarmed the people, claiming that they alone were capable of taking the action that was required. Their promise was never fulfilled; indeed, they played a part in bringing the catastrophe to pass.[13]

The pain of homelessness was exacerbated by poverty. Food handouts from the Egyptian troops stationed in Gaza helped at times. Nevertheless, the young Yassin was compelled to take a year off from school from 1949 to 1950 to work as a waiter in a restaurant in order to feed the seven members of his fatherless family. Then catastrophe struck. At the age of sixteen he fell on his back in an accident while he was playing sports, seriously injuring the vertebrae of his neck. Afterward his condition continued to deteriorate, until he lost his ability to walk. However, his immobility did not prevent him from pursuing a career in education, which brought him into direct contact with the people, especially with the young generation.

After he finished his education in June 1958, he was offered a place to study for a degree in Cairo, but could not afford to go. He worked as a teacher, hoping to be able one day to go to university, and visited Cairo a number of times, seeking treatment for his injury. He almost accomplished his dream when he was accepted in 1964 by 'Ain Shams University in Cairo. He made a brief visit to Egypt to complete his registration formalities and, apparently after studying in Gaza as an external student, he returned to sit an examination in 1965. Later in 1965, however, his hopes were dashed after his return home by the Egyptian security services, then in control of Gaza. On 18 December 1965, he was detained on suspicion of affiliation to the Ikhwan, who had been subjected to a campaign of persecution for more than a decade by the regime of Abd al-Nasir. After a month of solitary confinement in Gaza's Central Prison, to which he was subjected despite his physical disability, he was released after investigations proved him innocent of the "crime." He was, however, banned from traveling to Cairo. This experience had a lasting impact on him. He had never been affiliated to the Ikhwan in Egypt, but had come under their influence. In 1966 or 1967, he formally joined the Ikhwan, to which he became devoted, hating the injustice done to them. He later recalled: "That one-month ordeal deepened my hatred for injustice and taught me that the legitimacy of any authority must be based on justice and on sanctifying the right of a human being to live in dignity and freedom."[14]

Yassin's adherence to the Ikhwan was a gesture of defiance. A world of difference distinguished the early 1960s from the previous decade. In the early 1950s, joining the Ikhwan had been the fashionable thing to do. The group's bravery and sacrifices during the 1948 struggle to prevent the Zionists from seizing Palestine and turning it into a Jewish state were still vivid in the minds of the people of both Gaza and the West Bank. However, from 1954 onwards, as Abd al-Nasir's regime in Egypt turned against them and began to suppress them, fewer and fewer people wanted to have anything to do with the Ikhwan. Instead, Arab nationalism was on the rise. Aided by Abd al-Nasir's powerful and far-reaching propaganda machine, Arabism presented itself as a progressive alternative to a decadent and reactionary Ikhwan movement that was blamed for all the ills of the past and the present. By the late sixties, scarcely any distinguished figures of authority or credibility publicly identified themselves with the Ikhwan in Palestine. Many such figures had already gone to other countries in search of better living conditions or in pursuit of personal safety. In addition, the Ikhwan had begun to lose some of their best members to the Fatah movement, dedicated to the national liberation of Palestine, which was founded in 1957.[15] The ambition of the Fatah leaders at the time was to assimilate the entire Palestinian Ikhwan organization into their newly founded movement. They believed the Ikhwan no longer served any purpose and that their incorporation could provide Fatah's nascent project with a major boost at a time when it also faced some hostility from Abd al-Nasir.[16]

Few people would have predicted that a quadriplegic young man like Ahmad Yassin would live to lead a massive transformation in the lives of the Palestinians, not only within the Gaza Strip but also in Palestine as a whole and beyond. From the outset, he had his eyes set on resisting occupation. He knew, however, that there could be little resistance without stamina and organization. As he has said himself, he had for many years held the belief that resistance to occupation required arduous preparations. He was approached in 1965 by the Fatah movement when it launched its struggle against Israel in the hope of embroiling the Arab countries in a war with the Zionist state. He was invited to join but refused, insisting that in his view the Arab countries were neither ready nor willing to fight. He saw no point in drawing them into a duel that was most certainly going to end in their defeat, and could subsequently lead to more loss of territory to the Israelis.[17]

It was not long before he was proved right, on a number of occasions. The first came when Fatah mounted an attack from the Gaza Strip on an Israeli bus to the east of Deir al-Balah. The Egyptian authorities, who were in control of Gaza, responded by arresting and imprisoning those suspected of mounting the attack. Egypt was unwilling to be drawn into a war it knew it could not win. At the time the Egyptian government accused the Ikhwan of seeking to embarrass Egypt and to force an internationalization of the Gaza Strip. Although the Ikhwan had nothing to do with the attack, its perpetrators had originally been Ikhwan members who had been induced to join Fatah, whose founders, apart from Yasir Arafat, had all been former members of the Ikhwan.[18]

The second occasion on which Ahmad Yassin was proved right was in the June 1967 war. This was a confrontation with Israel unwanted by the Arab states, including Egypt, which lost miserably. The skepticism expressed by Ahmad Yassin during the days leading up to the war surprised many of his contemporaries. Egypt, in his opinion, was simply not ready for war, and Abd al-Nasir's stratagem of ordering the evacuation of UN peacekeepers from Sinai would cost him dearly. He could see from the condition of the Egyptian troops deployed in Gaza that they were totally unprepared. They were given no specific instructions and had no clear objective. Many of them were reservists, called in precipitately and hurriedly deployed. He also feared that Israel might deal a fatal blow to the Egyptian air force, leaving the Egyptian army stranded like a lame duck in the Sinai desert.

This was exactly what happened. As the Egyptian troops were being heavily defeated by the Israelis, Abd al-Nasir's propaganda machine claimed that Egypt had the upper hand and was heading toward decisive victory. Eventually, Israeli troops not only entered Gaza and the West Bank but also advanced as far as the Suez Canal, while also capturing the insurmountable Syrian Golan Heights, all in a matter of six days. The defeat was most shocking to those who had blind faith in the Egyptian leadership: they had hoped that Palestine would be liberated by Gamal Abd al-Nasir, the hero of Arab nationalism. Only afterward did many recall with utter dismay the announcement Abd al-Nasir had made two years earlier in an address before the Palestine National Council in Cairo: "If I told you I had a plan to liberate Palestine I'd be lying to you."[19]

After the 1967 war, Sheikh Yassin, as he had by now become known, saw the people of Gaza gradually wake up from their shock only to acquiesce in the new reality. They seemed to have no option but to accept the status quo. Many of them sought to satisfy their daily needs by doing business with the occupation authority rather than resisting it. They felt they had no choice but to return to their jobs and be paid for them by the new authorities. Sheikh Yassin lamented the situation but understood it: "The people had no food. Day after day they started accepting the reality and decided to go back to their jobs. If only we had a good organization then we would have organized ourselves and boycotted the occupation. But we had no organization, there were no guarantees for the protection of the people, and the people did not know what to do."[20]

He himself had to weigh his options. Before the occupation of Gaza, he had been working as a teacher. When it was announced that schools would reopen and that teachers should report for work, he asked himself: "Would I be supporting the occupation by teaching or would I be serving my people?"[21] Sheikh Yassin's misgivings stemmed from the fact that the occupation authority was supposed to be boycotted and not served.[22] He decided that he would be serving his people, and therefore decided, together with his colleagues, to go back to work. It was through his profession as a teacher that he undertook the project of transforming Palestinian society in Gaza. Indeed, some of his students grew up to be leaders of the Islamic movement in the Gaza Strip; they were the products of Islamic revival, referred to at times as Islamic resurgence, a process that took root in society in the early 1970s and was led by Sheikh Yassin.

Israel's occupation of the Gaza Strip and the West Bank following the naksa paradoxically provided a window of opportunity for Sheikh Yassin, who was able for the first time to travel throughout the whole of historic Palestine. This enabled him to communicate his wisdom and knowledge to the forgotten Arabs of Israel, those Palestinians who had been allowed to remain within the territories occupied in 1948 within which Israel was established. Links were also forged with the Palestinians of the West Bank and soon even with the Palestinians in the diaspora. However, his most formidable task was to persuade an extremely skeptical population that the Ikhwan was a worthwhile movement. Its reputation had been tarnished and its credibility severely damaged by the Egyptian Nasirist media, with the result that it was not attractive to the people of Palestine. A combination of propaganda, intimidation, and suppression discouraged individuals from associating themselves with it.

The Ikhwan of the West Bank were popularly viewed even more unfavorably than were their brothers in Gaza. The West Bank had been part of Jordan, and therefore subject to the direct rule of the Hashemites, since the creation of Israel in 1948. The Ikhwan seemed to have entered into an undeclared pact with the Hashemite regime. In exchange for legal status, they apparently contributed to the maintenance of the stability of the Jordanian regime by guarding society against undesirable influences deemed to be harmful, including communism, championed then by the Soviet Union, and Arab nationalism, promoted at that time by Egypt's President Abd al-Nasir. While the latter was perceived as patriotic and anti-imperialist, many Palestinians saw the Hashemite regime as a lackey of the United States and a collaborator with Israel. So, while the Ikhwan of the West Bank had registered offices and functioned openly, they had difficulty attracting much popular support or sympathy. In the 1950s and 1960s, the West Bank Ikhwan were perceived as an undemocratic and elitist organization. This was an image very different from that of the Ikhwan in Egypt during the movement's formative years in the 1930s and 1940s. As the principal force of criticism against the Egyptian regime, they defended the poor and the oppressed, spoke out against foreign influence, and raised the banner of liberation from colonialism.

In Gaza, Sheikh Yassin was one of only a few figures who identified themselves publicly with the Ikhwan. For this reason, when he led the Friday prayers at the Northern Camp mosque, young men in the congregation began to go to other mosques for fear of being accused of sympathy with him or his group. To attain his goal, the Sheikh needed to reconstruct the movement, which had been driven underground by years of persecution. In the aftermath of the 1965 Nasirist purge, many of the leading figures had either been detained or had already fled Gaza to other Arab countries to escape harassment and lead a dignified and comfortable life. Sheikh Yassin identified ten Brothers (Ikhwan cadres) from Gaza and Jerusalem and invited them to a meeting to discuss re-launching the Ikhwan. Not all of them were enthusiastic or optimistic: in fact, soon afterward some of them left the territories in pursuit of jobs elsewhere in the "Arab homeland."

Nevertheless, the process got underway, beginning in the mosques. Most of those attracted to the activity of the Ikhwan were young men, mostly students in their later teens. This was the generation that grew up at the time of the 1967 defeat, many of whom had become disillusioned with Nasirism and the claims of Arab nationalism. On the other hand, others who had been followers of Abd al-Nasir continued to idolize him until he died and even afterward. For a decade or so, the movement revived by Sheikh Yassin focused primarily on instilling Islamic values and ethics in the hearts and minds of the young. Unlike the former Nasirist administration in Gaza, the Israeli occupation authorities did not object to this seemingly benign religious activity. Israel's concern lay elsewhere, in hunting down the nationalist resistance elements that posed an immediate threat to their authority. Sheikh Yassin and his group, which included veteran Ikhwan figures such as Abd al-Fattah Dukhan and Hasan Sham'ah, who were also teachers, had neither the ability nor the willingness at that time to engage in resistance.

Sheikh Yassin's view was that much remained to be done before resistance could be mounted. Through his public lectures and his teaching in schools, he succeeded in rallying around himself a core of committed followers, drawn from among the high-school students who had initially been attracted to Nasirism but had deserted it in the aftermath of the June 1967 war. Their initial response to the defeat was to seek solace in religion, which seemed to present an alternative to failed nationalism. The Ikhwan simply provided the vehicle. The very first group of young men to cluster around the sheikh and seek his guidance included Ibrahim al-Maqadmah, Isma'il Abu Shanab, Abd al-Aziz Awdah, Fathi al-Shiqaqi, and Musa Abu Marzuq.[23] All of these later studied in Egypt, playing an active role in the organization of the Palestinian Islamic student community there. In varying degrees, they initiated or took part in the debate about the priorities of the Islamic movement with regards to the Palestinian issue.

The Egyptian Connection

Preceding Israel's occupation of the Gaza Strip and the West Bank in 1967, Palestinian students who successfully completed their high-school studies went abroad in pursuit of further education. There were no local universities, and most of those who had been high flyers at secondary school enrolled at universities in Egypt to study medicine, engineering, or science subjects. Egypt set aside places in its universities for Palestinian students. A specific quota was allocated to students from the Gaza Strip, another for those from the West Bank, and a third for those resident outside Palestine, in what has become known as the Palestinian diaspora.

For a number of years after the occupation of Gaza and the West Bank, however, the intake of Palestinian students was suspended because their return to their homes could not be guaranteed. The Egyptian authorities, as well as the Palestinians themselves, were fearful that Israel might not allow the students to return after the completion of their studies. In the academic year 1970–1971, the intake of Palestinian students by Egyptian universities was resumed, thanks to a deal brokered by the International Red Cross. Egypt agreed to accept the students, provided Israel would allow them back; the Red Cross guaranteed their safe return to their homes during summer vacations and when they ultimately completed their courses. Apparently this arrangement was encouraged by Israel, as part of what became known as the "open bridges" policy. This was the plan to maintain a controlled flow of people and merchandise across the Jordan River from the West Bank to Jordan.[24] For the Gaza Strip, the policy served primarily to defuse the pressure that had built up as a result of the accumulation of those who finished high school in the thousands every year but could not be absorbed locally either into further education or the job market.[25] These high-school graduates posed a serious threat to Israel because they were potential recruits for the resistance.

Sheikh Ahmad Yassin had earlier considered sending some of his students to Egypt to study at the Egyptian military academy. Egypt permitted Palestinian students from Gaza to join the academy, but with the suspension of the intake of Palestinian students, only those who had completed their high-school studies within Egypt itself could benefit from this facility. A young Ikhwan recruit by the name of Musa Abu Marzuq was selected by Sheikh Ahmad Yassin to leave the Gaza Strip and relocate to Egypt one year before finishing his secondary education, in order to complete it there and thus be eligible for entry into the military academy. Things went according to plan until just before Abu Marzuq finished his high-school education in Egypt, when the Egyptian government announced new regulations allowing Gaza students once more to travel to Egypt and awarding them scholarships for both undergraduate and postgraduate education. At the same time, however, Egypt ceased to allow Palestinian students to join the military academy. Abu Marzuq was told he might still be able to enter the academy if he were to apply through the PLO, an option he preferred not to take. Instead, he joined the faculty of engineering.[26]

Like his Ikhwan peers, Musa Abu Marzuq was born and raised in a refugee camp. He was born in 1951, in a tent provided by the United Nations in a refugee camp in Rafah. He was his mother's sixth child, and the first to be born in exile, to a family that eventually numbered five sons and five daughters. After Palestine was re-united by virtue of Israel's expansion in the aftermath of the June 1967 war, he visited Yubnah, the village from which his parents were driven in 1948. In the village, halfway between Jaffa and Gaza, his elder brother Mahmud showed him the remains of the family house where his five elder siblings had been born. The building that had housed the school still stood, but it had been taken over by a Jewish charity, providing social services to Jewish homeless women. Before it was cleansed of its Palestinian inhabitants, Yubnah had a population of 15,000 and was one of the biggest villages in the Jaffa region.[27]

On his arrival in Egypt, Abu Marzuq joined a small Palestinian Ikhwan circle with no formal ties with the local Egyptian Ikhwan organization, which was in any case still underground after the Nasirist repression. He maintained his links with this circle until its other more senior members left Egypt after finishing their studies. This coincided with the arrival in Egypt of the first batch of Palestinian Ikhwan students, following the resumption of Palestinian student intake by Egyptian universities. The leader of the group was Abd al-Aziz Awdah, one of the earlier recruits to the Ikhwan and a close associate of Sheikh Ahmad Yassin. Initially, the Ikhwan students were only a small minority among the total population of Palestinian students. Most of the 700–800 students arriving in Egypt every year were affiliated, or at least sympathized, with the nationalist camp, led by the PLO. Gradually, however, the balance began to change. As the Ikhwan students rapidly increased in numbers, they needed organization. They formed a committee to take responsibility for the administration of the affairs of the students and the maintenance of liaison with the leadership in Gaza. Among the members of this committee were Abu Marzuq, Awdah, and a third student by the name of Ali Shakshak.

The Palestinian Ikhwan students arrived in Egypt at the time when one of the most painful chapters in modern Palestinian history was unfolding in Jordan: what the Palestinians refer to as Black September. This was the culmination of mounting tension between the Hashemite regime and the PLO. For more than three years, the PLO had been augmenting its military presence in Jordan and its use of Jordanian territory to launch attacks against Israel. Pressure had been mounting on King Hussein, not only from the US and Israel but also from circles within his own regime, to act against the PLO, which was seen as building a state within the state and was thus perceived as a threat to the Hashemite throne. Events were brought to a boiling point on 6 September 1970 with the hijacking of four passenger planes by members of the Popular Front for the Liberation of Palestine (PFLP), a left-wing constituent member of the PLO. The hijackers flew three of the planes to Dawson's Field in Jordan, a disused airfield controlled by the PLO not far from the Jordanian capital Amman, and one to Cairo. While the passengers and crews escaped unharmed, the planes were blown up. Throughout September the Jordanian military continued its operations to push the PLO out of Jordan. Many thousands of PLO resistance fighters, Jordanian troops, and civilians were killed, although the actual figures continue to be disputed. The PLO forces initially retreated to northern Jordan but within ten months they were driven out of the country completely. With nowhere else to go, they reestablished themselves in Lebanon. This dark and costly episode proved Sheikh Yassin's vision once more to be accurate. He had always dreaded the consequences of forcing weak, unprepared, and unwilling Arab regimes into a confrontation with Israel. The mere fact of the PLO's presence in Jordan, even disregarding the excesses it committed and its violations of Jordanian sovereignty, inevitably put the Hashemite regime on a collision course with Israel.

The fate of the PLO in Jordan dominated the discussions among the Palestinian students in Egypt. The September events deepened the divide among the Palestinians into two distinct camps. The nationalists, who were affiliates of the PLO, blamed the problem entirely on Jordan. Meanwhile, the Islamists, who were for the most part affiliated with the Ikhwan, were more philosophical in their analysis, distributing the blame equally between the Jordanian regime and the PLO.[28] The events seemed also to reinforce the Islamists' conviction that their priority should be the reform of the Arab political system and the establishment of a strong and independent Islamic state capable of leading the liberation struggle against Israel.

At the same time, Egypt was also in crisis. Gamal Abd al-Nasir, the nation's self-proclaimed father figure, died on 29 September 1970. His autocratic rule had lasted since he and his fellow Free Officers toppled the monarchy in July 1952. Although the crushing defeat suffered by his regime in the war with Israel in 1967 had weakened him, forcing him to make a number of concessions to Egypt's student and labor movements, it was not until his death that tangible forms of opposition made their appearance. The post-Nasir era saw secular communist and socialist forces give way to a rapidly spreading Islamic trend that manifested itself primarily on university campuses. The policies adopted by Nasir's comrade and successor Anwar al-Sadat may have assisted this tendency. Calling himself "The Believing President," Sadat shunned the secular, socialist, and nationalist position of his predecessor, throwing himself instead into the fold of Islam, on which he built his image and based his claim to political legitimacy. The arrival of the Palestinian students in Egypt coincided with these significant changes, which entailed among other things the lifting of restrictions on student activism.

Many of the Islamic students were high achievers in their high schools and had won scholarships to study prestigious subjects such as medicine and engineering. At one time they numbered about 300, distributed among a number of universities across Egypt. Under the leadership of Abd al-Aziz Awdah, they were organized into a number of circles, including several in Cairo, two in Mansurah, one in Shbin el-Kum, one in Zaqaziq, and four in Alexandria. In the autumn of 1971, a newcomer joined the Palestinian Ikhwan students. This was Bashir Nafi,[29] who came to Egypt to study veterinary medicine. Although born and brought up in the Rafah refugee camp in Gaza, he arrived from Jordan, where he had been since the aftermath of the 1967 war. His family then sent him to

Amman to stay with his uncle, a medical doctor also called Bashir Nafi, where he completed his secondary-school education. Bashir Nafi soon joined the Ikhwan and became a prominent student figure within the organization. While in Jordan he was recruited by Fatah but he changed his allegiance soon after arriving in Egypt. Having become disillusioned with the PLO in the aftermath of the September 1970 tragedy, he thought that the Ikhwan offered a better alternative. What swayed Nafi to join the Ikhwan was Sayyid Qutb's book, *Ma'alim fi al-tariq* (*Milestones*), brought to his attention by Ali Shakshak. Shakshak had brought Nafi some gifts from his family after paying a visit to his own family home in Rafah, and their meeting afforded an opportunity for a lengthy and serious discussion between the two about the Ikhwan and the future of the Palestinian issue. On this occasion, Shakshak gave Nafi a copy of Qutb's book, which fascinated him and changed his ideas.[30]

Simultaneously the Egyptian student groups known as Al-Jama'at al-Islamiyyah (Islamic associations) began to emerge at Egypt's universities. A decade later, some of the members of these student groups became leading second-generation Egyptian Ikhwan figures. They included names such as Abdul Mun'im Abul-Futuh and Issam al-Iryan, who had forged links with the Palestinian Ikhwan, purely as Islamic activists, long before they themselves had become members of the Egyptian Ikhwan. At this period, a number of Jordanian Ikhwan members had also been pursuing their postgraduate studies in Egypt. These included such well-known names as Abdullah Azzam, Fadl Abbas, and Ahmad Nawfal, who were also in communication with the Palestinian Ikhwan group. This was also the time when Ikhwan prisoners began to be released from Egyptian jails. They included some Palestinians, foremost among whom was Abd al-Rahman Barud, who was jailed in 1965 while he was a PhD student in Egypt.[31]

In 1973, Egypt saw the arrival of a number of figures later to be prominent in the Palestinian movement, such as Fathi al-Shiqaqi, who like Awdah was very close to Sheikh Ahmad Yassin and was one of his early recruits. Later arrivals also included Ibrahim al-Maqadmah and Salah Shihadah.[32] About a year later Abd al-Aziz Awdah was expelled from the Ikhwan for misconduct, after an internal investigation and a hearing chaired by al-Maqadmah, his junior. Bashir Nafi, who had been a close associate of Awdah, also left the Ikhwan, presumably out of sympathy with him. Officially, however, the Ikhwan, never expelled Nafi or intended to do so. They maintain that he left of his own choosing.[33]

One of the issues that preoccupied the Islamic students in Egypt at the time was the need to improve the way in which the Ikhwan were organized and administered. Some of them objected to the way they were subjected to the discipline of local Ikhwan circles when they returned home during the summer vacation. They felt that the issues discussed within these local groups did not rise to the intellectual level attained by the students in Egypt, nor were they appropriate in the light of the challenge facing the Palestinians under occupation. One of the issues raised pertained to the status of the students' organization in Egypt, whether it was autonomous or merely an extension of that in Gaza. In addition, the students felt a need to define their positions regarding the Palestinian question, which up to that time did not seem to feature largely in the thinking of the Ikhwan's leadership in Gaza. Summer after summer, as students at home for vacation spent the warm nights sitting on the beach discussing these issues, a discontented faction began to distinguish itself from the rest of the group.

Fathi al-Shiqaqi, a staunch Ikhwan loyalist, emerged as the leader of this trend, which derived its inspiration from a paper authored by a Syrian postgraduate student by the name of Tawfiq al-Tayyib.[34] Entitled "Al-Hal al-Islami ma ba'da al-nakbatayn" (The Islamic solution after the two catastrophes), this came to the students in Egypt from Germany where al-Tayyib was preparing his doctorate in philosophy. Within its 21 pages, including endnotes, was embodied a revolution in Islamic thinking. In his introduction, the author starts with the question of the significance of 5 June 1967 in the history of Islam. On this date, Israel captured the West Bank from Jordan, including East Jerusalem, where al-Aqsa, Islam's third holiest mosque, is located. The 1967 war dealt a fatal blow to Arab nationalism and triggered an Islamic resurgence. Al-Tayyib goes on to consider the loss of Jerusalem as a consequence of the Arab defeat. Should it be equated with the fall of Jerusalem to the Crusaders in 1099, or with the loss of Cordova to the Spaniards in 1237, or the ransacking of Baghdad by the Mongols in 1285? None of those major past events are seen by al-Tayyib as having had a significant impact on the world of Islam. In contrast, the fall of Jerusalem in 1967 represented the pinnacle of a profound and continuing onslaught on Muslims and Islamic civilization, so that this event was to be seen as more catastrophic than all previous disasters. According to al-Tayyib, the course of events on 5 June 1967 "has brought our umma and our faith face to face with their fate, which will be either existence or extinction. This umma will either live or die; our culture will either live on or vanish. Islam as a faith and the Arabs as a people are facing their destiny, and the decisive factor is Palestine."[35] His conclusion was that Palestine was indeed Islam's foremost cause and should therefore be the first priority of the Islamic movement. The fate of Islam and that of the Islamic movement, the writer asserted, are inseparable from the fate of Palestine.[36]

Meanwhile, Islamic political thought had come to be dominated by an excessive emphasis on the Islamic state, whose re-establishment was seen as the main priority. The Ikhwan subscribed to this conviction and argued that Palestine could only be liberated from the Zionists by a strong Islamic state, but they also insisted that this was conditional upon a strong Islamic society, which in turn must consist of conscientious, enlightened, observant, and well-trained Muslim individuals. The loss of Palestine was seen as a symptom, or a consequence, of the loss of the Islamic caliphate, which itself had been the victim of Muslim decline and of the departure of Muslims from the true path of Islam. The caliphate, therefore, had to be reinstated for the symptoms of Islam's sickness to disappear, but this could only be achieved through a gradual and long-term process of reform, of the individual, the family, and the entire community.[37]

Ironically, this standpoint on Palestine had not been the Ikhwan's original position. In the months leading up to the creation of the State of Israel in Palestine in 1948, the Ikhwan sent hundreds of volunteers from Egypt, Syria, Lebanon, Yemen, Jordan, and other places to fight against the Zionist forces in Palestine. The new way of thinking had evolved out of the crisis that afflicted the Ikhwan across the Arab world as a consequence of the persecution they suffered at the hands of despotic secular nationalist regimes, which arrogated authority to themselves and sought to base their legitimacy on the Palestinian question. For much of the 1950s and 1960s, Islamic and nationalist trends competed and quarreled, with Palestine at the core of ongoing debates. The fiercest of these debates took place within the universities between students who espoused the two opposing trends. The debate focused mainly on how the Arabs could best resist the Zionist project, which all agreed was the biggest threat. The Islamists insisted that the liberation of Palestine would only occur after Islam had been adopted as a way of life, so that participation in any effort to liberate Palestine undertaken by an un-Islamic regime would be unthinkable.[38] They questioned in particular the legitimacy of jihad under the leadership of secular nationalist regimes such as that of Abd al-Nasir in Egypt and the Ba'th in Syria. These regimes had been perceived as waging war against Islam and were thus considered to be in the service of the Zionists themselves. Not surprisingly, when some of the Ikhwan were motivated to join the Palestinian resistance against Israel in the late 1960s they insisted on setting up their own separate bases in the Jordan Valley. In practice, however, they had no option, for political and logistical reasons, but to fight under the umbrella of Fatah, the PLO's main faction.

Controversy among the Palestinian Ikhwan students in Egypt was fueled further when some of them were approached in the mid-1970s by members of Fatah to persuade them to join the "Islamic wing" of the organization, known as Fatah al-Islami (Islamic Fatah). A Fatah member from the Khizindar family came to Cairo from Beirut to challenge the position of the Ikhwan students on the basis of their own philosophy. The Ikhwan had always avowed that jihad and *istishad* (the seeking of martyrdom) were their most sublime wishes.[39] When they were asked, why not take part in the struggle and thus accomplish their wishes, their answer was that they would never fight under a secular nationalist banner. In addition, they argued that the emergence of an Islamic wing within Fatah was intended only to absorb the Islamists and assimilate them rather than recognize them as an autonomous entity.[40]

The Kuwaiti Connection

During the same period, the Palestinian Ikhwan in Kuwait had their own problems. The emergence of Fatah and other PLO factions as the champions of Palestinian rights and the leaders of the struggle for liberation constituted a serious challenge to the Palestinian Islamists. Kuwait had since the late 1950s played host to an increasing number of Palestinians who, like many Arabs and Asians, were attracted by its fast-growing economy and rapid development. Compared to its much larger and richer neighbor Saudi Arabia, Kuwait was more open and a much more comfortable place to live. In the aftermath of the 1967 war, it saw an influx of Palestinian professionals and laborers, in most cases accompanied by their families, from the West Bank, the Gaza Strip, and Jordan. Some of the early Palestinian professionals who arrived in Kuwait in the later 1950s were members of the Ikhwan. Some were fleeing Nasirist persecution in Gaza and Egypt; others were young graduates who had just finished their education in Egyptian universities and were looking for good jobs so as to support their families at home.

In the late 1950s, Kuwait was also where the nucleus was formed that less than a decade later gave birth to al-Fatah.[41] Similarly, in the late 1970s, it provided a safe haven for the founding of the Palestinian Ikhwan student movement, which played a pivotal role in paving the way for the emergence of Hamas toward the end of the 1980s. The early 1970s were the years of Islamic revival, when young men and women were being attracted to the ideas of religion in increasing numbers. In Kuwait, as in other places, the defeat of Nasirism revitalized the Ikhwan. The group saw an opportunity in the readiness of the public to question Arab nationalism and its claims. It benefited from the arrival in Kuwait of a number of Egyptian scholars and activists who had just been released from prison in the aftermath of the death of Egypt's President Gamal Abd al-Nasir in 1970. One such scholar was Hassan Ayyub, who rallied to himself hundreds of admirers with a thirst and hunger for Islamic knowledge and spirituality that turned them into faithful disciples. His weekly lectures attracted large crowds and were recorded on audiocassettes to be distributed across the country and beyond. There seemed to be no issue on which he was not well versed. He lectured on history, theology, jurisprudence, and philosophy. Soon afterward, he began to publish a series of books on Islamic theological and jurisprudential matters as well as on contemporary issues of a sociopolitical nature.

Despite having been originally a member of the Ikhwan and having been imprisoned for years in Egypt for that reason, Sheikh Ayyub did not appear to approve of the idea of the existence of an Ikhwan organization in Kuwait. He believed the era of the Ikhwan was over and that it was time to think of another way forward, and for the construction of a new platform. His following developed into an independent faction, and he encouraged the Palestinians among them to involve themselves in the effort to liberate their country. Several Palestinian organizations in Kuwait sought his endorsement, while delegations from al-Fatah and even from the more left-wing PFLP (the Popular Front for the Liberation of Palestine) visited him, looking for some way to exploit his enthusiasm for jihad in Palestine.

At this time, the Palestinian Ikhwan in Kuwait, as elsewhere, were concerned principally with the education and training of their members and supporters so as to shield them from what they deemed to be alien and hostile ideologies and sociopolitical trends. The issue that mattered most for them was the rescue of the individual, the family, and the community as a whole from the onslaught of Western ideas, whether liberal or Marxist. The Islamic rehabilitation of the Muslim individual, the Muslim family, and consequently the Muslim society were deemed to be the answer to all problems, including the occupation of Palestine by the Jews.[42]

Two principal factors appear to have prevented the Palestinian Ikhwan from engaging in the national effort for Palestine. On the one hand they were apprehensive of the prospect of losing their Islamic identity. They saw this happen to the founders of al-Fatah who were all, apart from Yasir Arafat, members of the Ikhwan but ended up sloughing off their Islamic ideology in favor of secular nationalism. On the other hand, the Ikhwan lost the confidence, and perhaps also the ability, to distinguish between more and less important issues. The persecution from which they suffered, or that undergone by their brothers in Egypt and other countries in the region, drove them to direct their attention inward, toward themselves. Because of this, they became unable to recognize important national concerns as Islamic issues that deserved their attention. Their primary concern had been to establish, preserve, and express an Islamic identity as a means toward the achievement of the pan-Islamic project.[43] That tendency may well have been aided by the fact that in most Arab countries the movement had been forced underground. Ikhwan members argued that nothing could be accomplished without the establishment of an Islamic order. This was an idea not far removed from that espoused by members of Hizb al-Tahrir.[44] They pointed to earlier failures, citing especially the Egyptian Ikhwan's experience prior to their clash with Nasir.

It was ironic that the Ikhwan, who sent hundreds of volunteers to prevent the fall of Palestine into Zionist hands in 1948, had by the early 1970s begun to rationalize their abstention from the jihad in Palestine. What happened in Palestine, they would argue, was nothing other than a symptom of the sickness that afflicted the umma, which had been weakened by the lack of religious observance. The most drastic consequence of wandering away from the path of Islam, they explained, had been the collapse of the project to consolidate an Islamic civilization, which in turn enabled the enemies of Islam to occupy Muslim lands, including Palestine. The solution, it was explained, would be to return to Islam and establish its law and its standards. Only then would the umma be in a position to face its external enemies, whether in Palestine or elsewhere.[45]

Sheikh Hassan Ayyub rejected this logic and ridiculed those that defended it. His ability to rally many Palestinians to him alarmed the Palestinian Ikhwan, forcing them to re-think their discourse and strategy. As they did so, they discovered how faulty, and even dangerous, their claims had been. The phenomenon of Islamic revival had broken the monopoly of organized groups on activities promoting awareness of Islam. At the same time, however, it provided these groups with a dose of confidence that shattered the barriers of fear and anxiety. The days when only the adherents of the Ikhwan showed signs of religious awareness were gone: society as a whole was becoming increasingly religious and observance of Islamic values and standards was increasingly becoming the norm rather than the exception. The Palestinian Ikhwan saw that any delay in espousing the cause of liberating their homeland from Israeli occupation might be likely to cost them their credibility and nullify their achievements.

Students and young people in general made up the section of the population most influenced by the Islamic revival. This was the generation in which the potential for recruitment was greatest and competition at its most intense between the various ideological and political factions. In the 1970s, the Ikhwan, like other groups, began to target high-school students, recruiting them and instructing them to form Islamic student societies that in turn attracted publicity and promoted further recruitment. However, their greatest success was in the mosques, where mosque committees would be set up to look after the youth and to provide them with social, recreational, and educational services. The establishment of a student section within the organization of the Palestinian

Ikhwan in Kuwait in the mid-1970s was a historical turning point. It was a timely move, which coincided with the entry into Kuwait University of the first batch of young Ikhwan members who had been recruited even before leaving their high schools. One of these young recruits was Khalid Mish'al, who today is the head of Hamas's Political Bureau.

Khalid Mish'al was born in 1956, in the West Bank village of Silwad near Ramallah. He lived there for eleven years, until 1967, when he was obliged to leave home and settle in Jordan. Soon afterward, young Khalid left Jordan for Kuwait, where his father had lived and worked since before 1967. In 1970, after completing his primary education, he went to the prestigious Abdullah al-Salim Secondary School, which was open only to high-achieving pupils, and which was in the early 1970s a hotbed of intense political and ideological activities. In his second year at al-Salim school he was recruited by the Ikhwan, of which he became a serious and dedicated member. After completing his school education, he was admitted to Kuwait University, where he studied for a BSc degree in physics.

Kuwait University had an active branch of the General Union of Palestinian Students (GUPS), which had been under the absolute control of the al-Fatah movement. Though the Islamists had initially shunned the GUPS, they decided in 1977 to join it and contest its leadership election. This coincided with the visit to Jerusalem by Egypt's President Anwar al-Sadat, to appeal for an end to the Palestinian conflict. Khalid Mish'al and his colleagues formed a list for the GUPS election under the title of al-Haqq (truth), which launched a campaign that focused primarily on two issues: the war in Lebanon and its impact on the Palestinian cause; and Sadat's visit to the Israeli Knesset in Jerusalem and its repercussions.

However, it proved impossible to work from within the GUPS. The Islamists felt constantly hamstrung and concluded they would never be allowed to put their ideas into practice. By 1980, two years after Khalid Mish'al's graduation from Kuwait University, his juniors decided to leave the GUPS and form their own Palestinian association within the university. Kuwait's Islamic Association of Palestinian Students was one of several such student associations set up by the Palestinian Ikhwan around the world as platforms for Palestinian students who did not wish to join the PLO-dominated GUPS. Among the most active of these associations were those set up in the early 1980s in the US, the United Kingdom, and other European countries where Palestinian students had been pursuing their studies. Many of these students had already lost their faith in the PLO. They were disillusioned with the PLO leadership, which seemed intent on settling for much less than the dream with which Palestinian youth had grown up, namely the liberation of Palestine from the river to the sea, and the return of all the refugees to their homes.

TWO

From Da'wah to Jihad

*I had a personal desire, and I was motivated, to launch the battle as early as
1967. However, whenever we studied the circumstances and
assessed the resources we found them insufficient and had to postpone.
Then we would study the case once more then postpone again.*[1]

—Sheikh Ahmad Yassin

THE EARLY 1970S WERE TOUGH YEARS FOR SHEIKH YASSIN AND HIS IKHWAN
comrades in the Gaza Strip. They were obliged to work in a hostile environment, characterized by the prevalence of a strong Arab nationalist
sentiment and the increasing popularity of leftist groups engaged in guerrilla warfare against Israeli occupation forces. Faith in Arab nationalism
began to waver, however, as Israel cracked down on the groups fighting
against it, killing, deporting, or imprisoning activists. The result was that
the Ikhwan's insistence on the work of peaceful *da'wah* (preaching) increasingly seemed to make sense to the population.

From the beginning, Sheikh Yassin suspected the October 1973 war
between Egypt and Israel was merely a maneuver to pave the way for
peace-making with Israel. The sheikh was once more proved right in
his assessment of the readiness, or lack of it, of the neighboring Arab
countries to liberate Palestine. However, the Palestinians were equally
unprepared. They lacked the necessary logistic and financial support from
their brethren across the Arab world. In addition, Israel had been able to
infiltrate numerous collaborators into their ranks, thus rendering resistance almost impossible.[2] The credo of the Ikhwan was that the sickness of
Palestinian society was such that it needed to be cured before it was fit to
resist, and that there was no better medicine than a return to Islam.

35

Islamic Society

In 1967, after working for nearly a decade from their own homes and in the mosques, the Ikhwan deemed the situation appropriate for the launch of their first public platform. This was al-Jam'iyah al-Islamiyah (the Islamic Society), whose objective was to conduct educational, recreational, and sporting programs for the youth. The Israelis did not see this association as any kind of threat, and granted the Ikhwan a license for its establishment. Run from a room in al-Shati' (beach) Mosque, the society's activities included sports, recreational trips, scouting activities, and public lectures on religious and social issues.

Meanwhile, from his base at al-Abbas Mosque, Sheikh Yassin succeeded in collecting enough money from donors to reprint the last volume of Sayyid Qutb's Qur'anic exegesis, entitled *Fi dhilal al-Qur'an* (In the shade of the Qur'an). To ensure that it gained the widest possible circulation, and especially to encourage students to read it, he divided it into five separate sections, printing 2,000 copies of each. This project helped change the way the Ikhwan was perceived in Gaza. Qutb, as a leading Egyptian Ikhwan figure and himself a victim of Nasir's oppressive regime, was introduced to the readers both as a revolutionary fighting for justice and as a scholar of the highest standing.[3]

Encouraged by what they had achieved so far, the Ikhwan decided to set up a new institution that became known as al-Mujamma' al-Islami (the Islamic Center). Initiated around 1976, this project, linked to a mosque, was initially intended to provide social, medical, and educational services to the community in Jawrat al-Shams, to the south of Gaza City. The building was funded by donations collected from the wealthier Palestinians of the West Bank, and once construction was complete, an application for a license to operate was lodged with the Israeli occupation authorities. The Israelis issued the necessary licence, which, however, a few days later, they revoked. It later emerged that a prominent Palestinian figure in Gaza had advised the Israeli authorities to withdraw the license because of a personal dispute with the project committee over his own role in it. This prominent Palestinian, believed to have links to the Israelis, resented the committee's choice of Sheikh Yassin as general secretary of the Center over himself. After repeated appeals, and through the good offices of another prominent Palestinian figure, who seemingly also had connections with Israel, the Israeli authorities re-issued the license and the Center was opened. Al-Mujamma' (the Center) had a much wider scope than al-Jam'iyah (the Society) and its objectives included the provision of a variety of social services and the establishment of mosques, kindergartens, schools, and clinics across the Gaza Strip. The services and facilities provided by the Center proved so popular that a branch was soon opened in Khan Yunis.

The Palestinian Islamists may be viewed as pioneers in the way they transformed their intellectual and ideological discourse into practical programs providing services to the public through voluntary institutions. Their brethren elsewhere in the Arab world had, for decades, been denied such opportunities because the majority of the Arab countries had imposed restrictions on any form of nongovernmental activity linking religion and education or of a voluntary and charitable nature. Postcolonial governments across the region had an existential interest in suppressing civil institutions in order to maintain their tight control over the population and their monopoly on the disposal of resources. Sadly, they sought to justify their oppressive practices principally in the name of confronting imperialism and Zionism and the liberation of Palestine. The incompetence of government-owned and government-run public service institutions was invariably blamed on the need to observe austerity because public funding was being channeled toward the war effort against Israel. The Palestinians were themselves the victims of the same oppressive climate when Gaza was under Egyptian rule and the West Bank under Jordanian rule.

The irony was that the situation changed in the aftermath of the 1967 war and the Israeli occupation. Israel opted to revive certain aspects of archaic Ottoman law in its administration of the affairs of the Arab populations in the West Bank and Gaza. This permitted the creation of voluntary or nongovernmental organizations such as charitable, educational, and other forms of privately funded service institutions. This was a fortunate development for the Palestinians under occupation. For the first ten years of occupation, from 1967 to 1977, the Israeli occupation authorities pursued a policy of "non-intervention" drawn up and supervised by Moshe Dayan, then minister of defense in the Labor government. The intention was to be responsive to Palestinian wishes, allowing them the freedom to enjoy their nonpolitical institutions as far as these institutions remained consistent with Israeli rule and posed no threat to it. Though this permissive atmosphere benefited all groups that had set up and were running civil society institutions, groups based on religion particularly profited. Experience has shown that in a Muslim society, in such a climate of freedom, even if limitations are placed upon it, no political, intellectual, or ideological group can compete with the potential ability of religion-based NGOs to serve the community. The provision of services to the public, and the collection of the necessary funds, are in themselves acts of worship central to Islamic faith, and a practical implementation of the requirements of Islam's third most important pillar, zakat,[4] the giving of alms.

On the basis of the Society and the Center, the Ikhwan succeeded in more than doubling the number of mosques under their authority. In general, each mosque featured a kindergarten and a Qur'anic school, while some mosques also had their own medical clinics. Mobile units provided free medical services to the public, which visited rural areas regularly. In each area, on a particular day, Ikhwan medical specialists in the different branches of medicine would provide free medical consultations on a voluntary basis. Meanwhile, Ikhwan pharmacists would dispense medicine at cost or lower. There was also a day when boys could be circumcised without charge and the Ikhwan would organize and pay for the customary celebrations. Activities expanded rapidly, limited only by the availability of funds. There was therefore a need for systematic fundraising to maintain a steady flow, with accounts kept of what had been collected, and what had been spent, by whom, how, and where. This led to a mushrooming of zakat committees across the territories, with each committee working from or in association with the neighborhood mosque. These same zakat committees later became the principal recipients and dispensers of donations sent from abroad by Ikhwan branches that had set up their own fundraising networks to support the Palestinians under occupation.[5]

Islamic University

By 1978, as an increasing number of highly qualified Ikhwan graduates returned from abroad after finishing their studies in Egypt and elsewhere, the idea of setting up a university in Gaza was mooted. Since the early 1970s, the West Bank had seen the establishment of universities, some of them created through the transformation of particular high schools and colleges. The first initiative was taken in 1972 by Birzeit College, which announced a plan to upgrade itself into a university with the launch of a four-year program leading to bachelors' degrees in arts and sciences. In 1975 Birzeit College changed its name and became "Birzeit University," holding its first graduation ceremony on 11 July 1976. The second institution to become a fully fledged university was Bethlehem University of the Holy Land, a Catholic Christian coeducational institution of higher learning. Founded in 1973, this institution traces its roots to 1893, when the De La Salle Christian Brothers opened schools in Bethlehem, Jerusalem, Jaffa, and Nazareth, as well as in Jordan, Lebanon, Egypt, and Turkey. Al-Najah University in Nablus, which had originally been established as al-Najah School in 1918, was founded in 1977. Al-Khalil (Hebron) University came to being in 1980 as a result of the upgrading of the Shari'ah College, which had been set up in 1971. In addition to Islamic studies, the university soon expanded its scope to include various science and arts disciplines.

The first university to be established in the Gaza Strip was the Islamic University. Its founding board members were mainly members of the Ikhwan who were also involved with the al-Mujamma' al-Islami (the Islamic Center), at the time presided over by Sheikh Yassin. The birth of the university was attended by some difficulties. The local Fatah organization, which was already beset by anxiety over the growing influence of the Ikhwan in Gaza, was prepared to go to any lengths to prevent the project from coming to fruition, unless Fatah was wholly able to control it. To avert the potential threat to their project, the Ikhwan asked the PLO Chairman and Fatah leader Yassir Arafat to endorse the founding document of the university and to issue a decree appointing a founding committee. He may not have been aware that at least half of the membership of the committee were leading Ikhwan figures from Palestine and Jordan, while the other half consisted of Fatah officials selected for their sympathy toward the Ikhwan.[6] On the other hand, the PLO chairman may have intended to gain the confidence and support of the Ikhwan by offering them a concession. He had always entertained the idea that he was the father of the nation and the leader of the entire Palestinian people, including the Islamists. The latter, however, actually never accepted his leadership, despite his insistence when meeting them that he had once himself been a member of the Ikhwan.

The first few years of the university were fraught with serious disputes, initially within the founding committee and then within the board of trustees. One of the major points of disagreement was over who would fill the position of president of the university. The Ikhwan wanted one of their number, while Arafat would not settle for anything less than one of his own supporters. At times arguments spilled over on to the streets of Gaza in the form of violence between the partisans of Fatah and members of the Ikhwan. The Ikhwan leadership, however, was determined to impose its full authority and to maintain total control of the university, even if its only recourse was to respond in kind to intimidation and violence.[7] The founding of the Islamic University in Gaza was an important landmark in the history of the Islamic movement in Palestine. It took to new heights the movement's ability to reach out to the community and provided much needed services in employment, training, and education. The effect was to bring enormous prestige to the Ikhwan and to reinforce their role as a leading influence in the Gaza Strip. At the same time, it afforded the Islamic movement a unique opportunity to celebrate its significant dates by embodying them in a university calendar to which all students had to adhere. The university attracted thousands of students, both men and women, from around the Gaza Strip and the West Bank, and in the years that followed provided a high quality of education combined with an Islamic orientation. This gave Palestinian society an unprecedented preparation for its massive popular uprising against the Israeli occupation.

Outside Palestine, the endeavor to bring the Islamic University project to fruition generated a sense of responsibility for providing it with the necessary financial, political, and moral support. The Ikhwan among the Palestinian diaspora, in Jordan, Kuwait, Saudi Arabia, and the rest of the Gulf, closed ranks in a new unity. Until 1978, any Palestinian member of the Ikhwan who hailed from the West Bank, which was of course under Jordanian rule until 1967, would be affiliated with the Jordan-based organization. Those from the Gaza Strip would be members of the Palestinian-led organization. In 1978, the product of unification was an organization entitled Tanzim Bilad al-Sham (the organization of the land of Greater Syria) under the leadership of the Amman-based Jordanian Ikhwan leader Abd al-Rahman Khalifah. The name implied that the organization covered all the lands forming part of the historical Greater Syria, namely Syria, Lebanon, Jordan, and Palestine. It was felt, however, that unification, though a step in the right direction, was insufficient on its own as a response to the rapid and dramatic developments in and around Palestine. The Palestinian members of the new organization therefore pressed for the creation of a body within the Tanzim Bilad al-Sham specifically to support the needs of the Palestinian Ikhwan inside the territories. A "Palestine Committee" was created for this purpose by the first *shura* (board) meeting of the Tanzim to be convened after unification of the various Ikhwan branches took place.

The year 1979 saw a significant broadening of the Ikhwan's support, with the recruitment of new members across the region. The Ikhwan's appeal and popularity were boosted by the revival of their mother organization in Egypt. The imprisoned leaders of the Egyptian Ikhwan had been released in the early 1970s, and some of them had been traveling, both within the Arab world and elsewhere. The freed Egyptian Ikhwan leaders were perceived as heroes who had withstood years of persecution, resisting all pressure to relinquish their principles or renounce their affiliation. In the eyes of many young men and women in the Muslim world, they were contemporary reflections of the very first generation of Muslims in the years after the death of the Prophet Muhammad, who had persevered in their endeavors so that Islam might succeed and spread. The Palestinian Ikhwan students, whether in Kuwait or in the West, had read the writings of leading Ikhwan figures such as Hassan al-Banna, Abd al-Qadir Awdah, and Sayyid Qutb. These Palestinians were particularly thrilled to meet men who had known these almost legendary figures, in order to hear from them directly about the Ikhwan and its founders.

1979 was also a year of momentous events on the international scene. Ayatollah Khomeini led the revolution in Iran that deposed the pro-American and pro-Israel regime of the Shah. Khomeini abolished the monarchy, installing an Islamic Republic that expressed itself in an anti-Israel and anti-American rhetoric that was music to the ears of the Palestinian public. The same year saw the launch of the jihad to liberate Afghanistan from Soviet occupation. Islamic Iran's defiance of the "Great Satan," as it characterized the United States, together with the inspiring stories of the victories of the jihad in Afghanistan, inflamed sentiments on the streets of Gaza and the West Bank just as they did elsewhere in the Muslim world. In the meantime, however, the Palestinians' own project of national resistance was faltering. Throughout the 1970s, the PLO had showed signs of fatigue under the pressure of regional and international politics and had been increasingly plagued by corruption and mismanagement. The PLO had begun to display a tendency to plunge into fatal political gambles, and an inclination toward costly compromises that fell well short of the declared national aspirations of the Palestinian people. In 1982, Israel invaded Lebanon, following seven years of intermittent civil conflict in that country. Israeli forces advanced all the way to the Lebanese capital Beirut, resulting in the eventual eviction of the PLO from Lebanon. While Beirut was under siege by the Israeli forces, commanded by Israel's then Defense Minister Ariel Sharon, between 2,000 and 3,000 unprotected and unarmed Palestinian civilians in the Sabra and Shatila camps were massacred by Israel's ally, the Christian Lebanese Forces.[8] Palestinian populations across the world felt a suffocating sense of anger, impotence, and frustration.

Amid all these dramatic events, pressure was mounting on the Ikhwan in Palestine to take action on behalf of their cause. Their social reform program had seemed to absorb all their efforts at a time when developments in and around Palestine called for a more drastic response. Having successfully outflanked the nationalist and leftist forces within Palestinian society, the Islamists now faced the criticism that while others had been making sacrifices resisting occupation they had restricted themselves to social and educational services. Their detractors went so far as to accuse them of brokering a deal with the occupation authorities, which is why activities were tolerated and their projects licensed. The Islamists' enemies embarked on old-fashioned Nasir-style propaganda, labeling the Ikhwan as the invention of Britain or the United States, or as lackeys of the Zionists.

Islamic Jihad

The Ikhwan's predicament deepened further with the founding of Islamic Jihad, an organization formed in the early 1980s in Gaza by Fathi
al-Shiqaqi. Al-Shiqaqi had been expelled from the Ikhwan while studying in Cairo in 1979, ostensibly because he had written and published a
pamphlet entitled *Al-Khumayni: al-hal al-Islami wal-badil* (Khomeini: the
Islamic solution and the alternative) despite an order from the Ikhwan's
leadership banning him from doing so. It seems possible that his expulsion had more to do with his critique of the Ikhwan's lack of a strategy
for armed struggle to liberate Palestine than his pro-Khomeini book. The
official discourse of the Ikhwan at the time did not prioritize Palestine
over other Islamic issues. Al-Shiqaqi, on the other hand, believed that
Palestine was the "mother" of all causes, and should therefore be the central cause of the Islamic movement, a position that only began to feature
in the official discourse of the Ikhwan a decade later. It transpired, however, that al-Shiqaqi had actually been setting up a new Islamic organization, whose members were recruited from within the Ikhwan as well as
from without. This would seem to offer a better explanation of why the
Ikhwan washed their hands of him. One of his first recruits from outside
the Ikhwan was Abdallah Ramadan Shallah, who was later to succeed him
in leading the Islamic Jihad movement after his assassination in 1995.
Other early recruits included some of the current leaders of Islamic Jihad
in Palestine, such as Khadr Habib, Nafidh Azzam, and Abdullah al-Shami.
For years, al-Shiqaqi's movement was called al-Tal'i' al-Islamiyah (the
Islamic vanguards): the name Islamic Jihad was not adopted until the
mid-1980s.[9]

After returning to Gaza in 1981, al-Shiqaqi continued to seek recruits
for his project and soon clashed with the Ikhwan, which had by now
grown into a formidable network of mosques and civil institutions, run
or supervised by a new generation of activists. Some of these were also
recent graduates from Egypt, such as Salah Shihadah, Isma'il Abu Shanab,
Ibrahim al-Maqadmah, and 'Isa al-Nashar. Al-Shiqaqi knew he could not
compete with the Ikhwan's program. In fact, he was not particularly
interested in competing with them in the areas of education and social
welfare, at which they excelled. Where he did wish to offer competition
was in the area where he always believed they had abandoned one of

their prime responsibilities: the jihad to liberate Palestine. He soon had a sizeable following, and this led the Israelis to identify him as a potential threat. His first brief period of imprisonment in 1983 acquainted him with a number of individuals from various organizational backgrounds who had been jailed for their resistance activities. Such men, who had experience in the struggle and had received some training, were potential recruits for al-Shiqaqi's project.

In the meantime, a group of Islamic-oriented members of Fatah had independently embarked on a campaign of resistance against the Israeli occupation. Operating from hideouts in the West Bank, this organization, Saraya al-Jihad al-Islami, sought to revive armed resistance against the Israeli occupation forces and against the Jewish settlers inside the territories. The PLO leadership, which was increasingly convinced that there could be a peaceful settlement, and had been embroiled in internal Arab feuds, had little to do with this project, though at times it took credit for the operations mounted by the group. Saraya al-Jihad achieved notoriety on Friday, 2 May 1980, when several of its armed fighters opened fire from rooftops on a column of Jewish settlers from the nearby Jewish settlement of Kiryat Arba as they entered the city of Hebron, killing six of them and wounding seventeen.[10] Al-Shiqaqi succeeded in forging an alliance with Saraya al-Jihad, whose leaders had extensive contacts with other Palestinian groups within Palestine and abroad. These included Abdullah Azzam, a member of the Ikhwan, who led the Arab contingent in the Afghan jihad from his base in the Pakistani city of Peshawar.[11] Saraya al-Jihad's daring attacks on Israeli targets stunned Arabs and Israelis alike. One of its most famous operations was the al-Buraq (Wailing Wall) operation mounted on 15 October 1986 against Israeli military personnel visiting the site, which killed one Israeli and wounded around seventy.[12]

From 1979 to 1981, throughout the network of the Ikhwan organization inside Gaza and the West Bank, the younger members, who were electrified by Saraya al-Jihad's resistance operations, voiced one persistent question: "Why are we not involved in the military resistance to occupation?" Little was known at the time about a plan to engage in military action that had already been drawn up, during that same period of soul-searching, by Sheikh Ahmad Yassin, as the leader of the Ikhwan in Gaza. Clearly, the Ikhwan, or at least some of its leaders, could no longer withstand the pressure from within their own ranks and the mounting skepticism of Palestinian society as a whole. They had also begun to suffer, perhaps, from a growing sense of guilt on their own part over their inaction. The project, which was kept secret to the extent that many Ikhwan leaders in Gaza and the West Bank were caught off guard when news of it broke, seems first to have been conceived in 1980, when the official discourse of the Ikhwan still favored waiting for some outside power to come to the rescue of the Palestinians. The Ikhwan still saw their main task as that of caring for the individual and the community inside Palestine, building whatever civic institutions might assist in accomplishing the mission. The liberation of Palestine, it was maintained, was too great a task, which only the power of an Islamic state could undertake. The establishment of that Islamic state was the project on which other Ikhwan movements elsewhere in the Arab world had, supposedly, been working.

It is now known that Palestinian Ikhwan members in the diaspora had also been pressing for military action. Their efforts were assisted by the unification of their organizations at the end of the 1970s, a project that reached its culmination in the historic conference convened secretly in Amman in 1983. Representatives of the Palestinian Ikhwan attended from within Palestine, both from the Gaza Strip and the West Bank, as well as from Jordan, Kuwait, Saudi Arabia, the other Gulf countries, Europe, and the United States. The purpose of the meeting was to lay the cornerstone for what became known as the Islamic "global project for Palestine," a project proposed to the conference by the delegates from Kuwait.[13] At this conference, a unanimous decision was taken to give financial and logistic support to the effort of the Ikhwan in Palestine to wage jihad. Meanwhile, quite independently, the Palestine Committee, at times referred to as the "Inside Committee," headed by the Amman-based Secretary of the Tanzim Bilad al-Sham Executive Office, received a sum of $70,000, raised by the Kuwaiti branch. This was to be delivered to the Ikhwan in Gaza to fund their first jihad project, to which the committee had, in confidence, given its backing. The money was to be used for the purchase of weapons and ammunition and to send a number of individuals to Amman to receive military training.[14]

Only Sheikh Ahmad Yassin and a very close circle of his associates were aware of this project, plans for which were finalized in 1982. Other members of the Gaza Executive Committee of the Ikhwan were not informed. Outside Palestine, no one knew about the plan apart from those directly involved in the Palestine Committee, whose role was to provide the funds and the facilities to train the Gazans in Jordan. A group of Ikhwan members from Gaza came to Jordan, received the necessary training, and returned to Gaza to form the first cell in the Ikhwan's military apparatus. Sheikh Yassin set up two separate systems for the purchase of arms, which were readily available for sale in Israel and usually originated with the Israeli army. Israeli officers and soldiers would steal weapons and sell them on the black market. Those who did this were generally doing it to support their drug addictions. However, the Ikhwan members who were assigned the task of procuring the weapons by way of one of these two routes lacked experience and took insufficient precautions. Consequently, they fell into a trap set up for them by collaborators, and were tricked into buying weapons from Israeli agents. The plan was uncovered, and those who were interrogated by the Israelis, under severe torture, divulged the names of their superiors. Initially Sheikh Yassin believed the arrests were the result of some accident, but he soon saw that those targeted were progressively higher in the ladder of responsibility. If the process was allowed to continue, he concluded, the Israelis would eventually reach him. Only two people knew of his involvement: those who headed the two weapons-purchasing networks. He immediately ordered these two men to leave the country. One of them, Dr. Ahmad al-Milh, fled successfully to Yemen, where he has since remained. The other, Dr. Ibrahim al-Maqadmah, could not find a way to leave. He was arrested and confessed under torture that Sheikh Yassin was the ringleader. Sheikh Yassin was immediately arrested.

At the time, rumors were circulating in Gaza to the effect that the Ikhwan had been buying weapons in order to use them against their opponents in the other Palestinian factions. The Ikhwan had already made powerful enemies in the ranks of Fatah and the left wing of the Palestinian nationalist movement. These rumors found ready credence, owing to the tension that gripped Gaza at the time, following the dispute over the Islamic University. However, on 15 April 1984, an Israeli military court found Sheikh Yassin guilty of plotting to destroy the State of Israel and sentenced him to thirteeen years imprisonment. Ibrahim al-Maqadmah was sentenced to, and served, eight years. A key figure in the plot was

Salah Shihadah, whom the court was unable to convict because he would not confess. Nevertheless, the Israelis continued to suspect his involvement and he spent two years in administrative detention. The Israeli authorities were able to seize half the weapons the Ikhwan had bought and stored. However, the other half, purchased through the second network, which had not been broken, remained hidden. These arms were used in part some two years later when military actions were taken against Israel's collaborators ahead of the eruption of the intifada in 1987.

Less than a year later, on 20 May 1985, Sheikh Ahmad Yassin was released from prison in an exchange of prisoners negotiated between Israel and Ahmad Jibril, the leader of the Popular Front for the Liberation of Palestine–General Command (PFLP-GC). The exchange brought the release of 1,150 Palestinians in exchange for three Israeli soldiers held by the PFLP. The general perception at the time was that this was the result of an unauthorized personal initiative taken by the Sheikh, without the consent of the other leaders of the Ikhwan. In Ikhwan circles across Palestine the debate over the value of the armed struggle continued. Many Ikhwan leaders, especially in the West Bank, claimed that the failure of Sheikh Ahmad Yassin's bid to mount military action vindicated their long-held position that it was futile to pursue this path. It was simply impossible to defeat Israel by a local resistance effort, they maintained. The opponents of action pointed out that Israel receives extensive support from the United States and Western Europe, and that the Arab countries bordering Palestine had revealed themselves as utterly ineffectual. Therefore, they argued, a jihad against Israel would result only in the destruction of the achievements of the Islamic movement, without the liberation of so much as an inch of the occupied land.

However, from 1982 onwards, as a growing number of young recruits came from those pursuing their education in local West Bank universities, two groups were gradually becoming distinct. The first of these consisted of the generation of those who had studied in Jordan in the 1970s. By the 1980s, these had become the movement's leaders and were still influenced by the school of thought that prevailed in Jordan, which believed in waiting with a kind of Messianic fatalism for the emergence of the Islamic state that would lead the jihad to liberate Palestine. The affiliates of the Jordanian school of thought were mostly the older members of the Ikhwan. The age factor, combined with their lack of contact with events

47

on the ground, inclined them to remain entrenched in their wait-and-see position. They were slow to recognize the threat that they would lose credibility because of their inaction, and that they would lose recruits because of the enormous pressure suffered by the younger members of the Ikhwan. Frequent fights occurred on campus in the years from 1981 to 1984. While most of these fights were over the exercise of authority on campus, the nationalist and leftist students would use the occasion to taunt the Islamists for their supposedly unpatriotic attitude.

The second trend comprised the younger members of the Ikhwan, who were locally educated. Galvanized by the Iranian revolution and the jihad in Afghanistan, they were the ones who had been obliged to inter- act on campus with students from nationalist and leftist trends, arguing and on occasion even fighting with them. The members of this group were discontented with waiting and their patience was exhausted. More than anything else, these youths were dismayed by the disparity between theory and practice. They had been taught within the Ikhwan that the movement's mission, from the moment of its establishment by Hassan al-Banna in Egypt in 1928, was to fight injustice, resist imperialism, and wage the jihad to liberate Palestine. In front of their eyes, however, they saw only the spectacle of their movement's inaction. At the same time, al-Shiqaqi's Islamic Jihad was taking the initiative in performing the duty of jihad, and was consequently winning credibility and respect, while also gaining more ground inside and outside the universities. It appeared to these young members of the Ikhwan that every single political group in Palestine had espoused the cause of jihad, save their own. As time passed, the position of the Ikhwan, which continued to discourage participation in any form of protest activities, became indefensible. Ikhwan students could find no response to make when bullied or ridiculed by their coun- terparts in the nationalist and leftist organizations for the inaction of the Islamic movement. Worse still was the feeling that while the nationalists and leftists did battle with the Israelis on the streets of Palestine's towns and camps the Islamists "took the safest route home where they stayed indoors like the harem."[15]

Despite its failure, however, Sheikh Yassin's bid to take military action against the occupation did succeed in giving a boost to the morale of the younger generation of the Ikhwan, and forced a change in attitude and in policy. Some of the emerging young leaders of the Ikhwan in the West

Bank had become convinced of the need for change, and pressed hard for it. In addition to being motivated by local factors, they were influenced by some of their colleagues who had come from the Gaza Strip to study in the West Bank. These included Isma'il Abu Shanab, who studied at al-Najah University. The Ikhwan of Gaza were more willing to mount a struggle against the Israelis: they suffered more from the occupation and had been less influenced by the Jordanian school of thought. The Ikhwan leadership eventually gave permission to confront the Israelis. In June 1986, the Islamic faction at Birzeit University announced from loudspeakers on campus that a rally to protest against Israeli atrocities had been organized and that all students were urged to join in. The rally was suppressed by Israeli troops, with 22 casualties including two fatalities,[16] giving the Islamic movement martyrs to take pride in and to boast about.

This was just the beginning of the flood. From then on Ikhwan members were not only allowed, but also encouraged, to take part in or stage protests against the occupation. A few years later, the student leaders who had succeeded in forcing this change of policy were to graduate, assuming various leadership responsibilities within the Islamic movement from the late 1980s onward.

In implementation of the resolutions of the Amman 1983 conference, the Palestinian Ikhwan of Kuwait, Jordan, and Saudi Arabia drew up a comprehensive plan for financial, political, and logistical support. By this time, Palestinian Islamists from Palestine, Jordan, Kuwait, Saudi Arabia, and the other Gulf states who were studying in the United Kingdom and the United States had set up various Islamic associations in aid of Palestine. The self-imposed tasks of these associations included the provision of care for Palestinian students, making every possible resource to which they had access available to their brethren in Palestine. They established safe, effective, and serviceable channels of communication between Palestine and the outside world, set up charities, published journals and books, and formed think tanks, all of which provided invaluable assistance to the Palestinian Islamic movement. In late 1985 the Palestine Committee set up a specialized body, called Jihaz Filastin (the Palestine apparatus), responsible for coordinating the activities of the various institutions set up around the world by the Palestinian Ikhwan and overseeing the creation of further institutions that might be needed. This "Jihaz" was

49

the nucleus out of which grew the global network that later provided the logistical support for Hamas. Three of the Jihaz's central figures were to become senior Hamas leaders in the 1990s. The first was Khalid Mish'al, who had been living in Kuwait. Musa Abu Marzuq had moved to the United States to pursue his postgraduate studies before returning to the Gaza Strip to work at the Islamic University, of whose board he was a founding member. The third, Ibrahim Ghosheh, became Hamas's first official spokesperson outside Palestine, shuttling between Kuwait and Jordan until Saddam Hussein's invasion of Kuwait in August 1990.

Meanwhile, Sheikh Ahmad Yassin and his immediate group continued their activities. In public, the Sheikh said at this stage that he had learned from the movement's recent experience that it was too early to think of military action and that more work was still needed in the field of *tarbiyah* (education and training). In private, he pressed for the reconstruction of the military apparatus that had been inaugurated before his imprisonment, setting 17 November 1987 as the date for launching the jihad campaign. He commissioned Salah Shihadah to form a new organization, known as al-Mujahidun al-Filastiniyun (the Palestinian Mujahidin). This military organization's main mission was to attack Israeli soldiers and Jewish settlers in the Gaza Strip. He also commissioned Yahya al-Sinwar and Rawhi Mushtaha[17] to form a security organization to be called Majd (glory), whose principal task was to apprehend, prosecute, and execute Palestinian collaborators working for Israel. Neither organization achieved much prior to the outbreak of the intifada, despite some attempts that ended in failure or went unnoticed.

In the lead-up to the intifada, Islamic Jihad captured the imagination of the Palestinians and attracted the attention of outside observers with a succession of daring actions against the Israelis. On 15 May 1987, six of its members escaped from Gaza Central Prison. On 2 August 1987, an Islamic Jihad member assassinated Captain Ron Tal, commander of the military police in the Gaza Strip, in his car in the main street in Gaza City. On 6 October 1987, four Islamic Jihad members opened fire on an Israeli army patrol in al-Shuja'iyah district of Gaza City, killing one Israeli soldier with the loss of one of their own fighters. Overall, however, though there were moments of daring defiance, there were also moments of utter despair, while a cloud of profound tension hung over the Gaza Strip and the West Bank. The population under occupation felt abandoned and under siege, more than ever before. Feelings of anxiety were mingled with feelings of anticipation. The mood was one of apprehension, as if some change was on the way, though no one knew what it was or could tell whether it would be good or bad. Some resigned themselves to their fate, feeling that nothing worse could happen than what was already taking place. Others anticipated a massive explosion. It did not take long for the latter to be proved right.

THREE

AN ALL-OUT WAR

We should break their hands and legs.[1]

This Government will fight any manifestation of violence and terror, and will neither permit nor allow either Hamas or Islamic Jihad to harm citizens of the State of Israel — and it will take all legal steps at its disposal, to battle murderous terrorist organizations.[2]

—Yitzhak Rabin

The intifada will go on and the suffering of the Palestinian people will continue. But so will our absolute determination to pursue the struggle.[3]

—Sheikh Ahmad Yassin

NO ONE TOOK THE DECISION TO IGNITE THE INTIFADA ON 8 DECEMBER 1987; it was triggered by an accident, which in turn set off the spontaneous explosion of anger by the masses. However, it was an explosion anticipated by the Palestinian Ikhwan, for which they had been preparing since at least 1983. The day the intifada began, the institutions created by the Ikhwan inside and outside Palestine came into action, with each performing the tasks assigned to it. The Ikhwan had no option except to seize the occasion. They needed to exploit it to the limit of their ability, in order to reinstate themselves as leaders of the jihad to liberate Palestine. Had they not done so, it would have meant the demise of their movement. In addition, only the Ikhwan had the intention, the will, the infrastructure and the global logistical support to keep the flame of the intifada alight for as long as it could be maintained.

For the Ikhwan, now acting under the name of Hamas, the intifada was a gift from heaven. They were determined to end the occupation, and to ensure that this would be only the beginning of a long-term jihad. They mobilized their members, employing the network of mosques and other institutions under their control, foremost among which was the Islamic University. They called for civil disobedience and organized rallies, which almost invariably culminated in stone-throwing at Israeli troops, burning the Israeli flag, and setting up improvised road blocks with burning tires. The intifada was an explosion of anger in the face of the occupation, sparked off by the dreadful and inhumane conditions endured by the Palestinians for many years and the humiliation and degradation to which they had been subjected. However, the Ikhwan's slogans were not confined to demands for the end of the occupation. They went further, also demanding the abolition of the State of Israel. Most of the demonstrators had been refugees, and their real homes were not the squalid and wretched UN camps of Gaza or the West Bank but the hundreds of towns and villages that once stood where Israel exists today.

These Palestinians became refugees when the Zionists invaded their towns and villages. What the Palestinians call the Nakba (the catastrophe) refers to the events of 1948, which led to their dispossession and to the creation of the Jewish state on their land. Between 1947 and 1949, some 750,000 Palestinians became refugees; most were expelled in accordance with a Zionist plan to cleanse the country of non-Jews. The official Israeli position holds that the refugees fled at the orders of Arab political and military leaders. However, according to Israeli military intelligence, at least 75 percent of the refugees left as the result of Zionist or Israeli military actions, psychological campaigns aimed at frightening Palestinians into leaving, and direct expulsions. Cases of mass expulsions during and after the military operations of 1948–49 are well-documented, together with massacres and atrocities that led to large-scale Palestinian flight.[4]

When the intifada began, the PLO leadership in Tunis was caught off guard. Yasir Arafat and his advisers were engaged in promoting their image to the world as peacemakers. Meanwhile, the world's leading power, the United States, was insisting that as a precondition for peace the PLO should first recognize Israel's right to exist and renounce all forms of violence. The PLO leaders had very good reasons to capitalize on the intifada, which seemed to provide the PLO with an opportunity. Their goal from the outset was to seize control of the intifada, and to reap whatever dividends the popular uprising might bring them to help promote their own project. They were desperate, above all, to obtain recognition from the United States of the PLO's status as the "sole legitimate representative" of the Palestinian people, with whom alone peace was to be negotiated. From this sprang the decision to mobilize PLO members and supporters inside Palestine to compete with the Ikhwan in fueling the intifada and in the business of making the occupation of Gaza and the West Bank a daily nightmare for the Israelis.

Israel was also caught off guard. Believing at first that the intifada was merely an expression of anger that would abate in a day or two, like many other such eruptions that had preceded it, they soon found otherwise. They found themselves fighting an entire unarmed population in the narrow streets and alleys of the Gaza Strip, the most densely populated piece of land on the face of the earth. Clearly panicked and confused, they ordered the closure of the Islamic University in Gaza. They failed, however, to understand that this would only inflame the intifada further, since it released more young men to be available on the streets to throw stones and engage in other forms of protest. For the Israelis, no tactic seemed to work. Acts of brutality against demonstrators – many of them women and children – only had the effect of expanding the circle of anger and drawing in more protestors. Many Palestinian laborers working at Israeli factories and farms began to heed the calls for boycott. In consequence, they either stayed at home or joined the protesters. The loudspeakers of the mosque minarets filled the air with Qur'anic recitations and *nashid* (a form of patriotic singing without accompanying music), as well as giving out announcements alerting the public to the occurrence of activities or confrontations, or appealing for aid of one sort or another. Within days, the intifada spread from Jabalya to Khan Yunis, then to the al-Shati' (beach) Camp in Gaza, and then to the other camps all the way to Rafah in the far south. In short order, the intifada also took hold in the refugee camps of the West Bank. The first West Bank camp to rise was Balatah Camp in Nablus.

At this moment, the Ikhwan was able to reap the dividend of its decision in the early 1980s to unify its organizations around the world.

Since the 1980s, the Ikhwan in the Gaza Strip and the West Bank had locally been under the command of a council of elected representatives drawn from the Gaza Strip and from the northern, central, and southern regions of the West Bank. The senior leadership council was convened immediately after the eruption of the intifada to ensure the effective management and coordination of its activities throughout the territories. The state of siege imposed by the Israelis on Palestinian refugee camps, where much of the action was taking place, prompted Sheikh Yassin to propose steps to restore a degree of calm, prompted by the feeling that the people might not be able to absorb further collective punishment. However, the measures adopted by the Israeli occupation forces, including a shoot-to-kill policy against unarmed demonstrators and the brutal beating of teenagers caught throwing stones, only infuriated the people, making them want more confrontations with the Israeli occupation troops, rather than less.[5] The intifada began with peaceful protests whose weapons were symbolic: no more than stones and bare chests. The spectacle of unarmed civilians, including children and women, being shot at, and the rate at which Israeli brutality was escalating, brought on to the scene the first Molotov cocktails and other forms of more violent reaction.

Initially, the Israelis were not sure who was orchestrating the unrest. However, they suspected that Sheikh Yassin and his organization had a part in it. He was given a warning by Israel, and threatened with deportation to South Lebanon. He insisted that he bore no responsibility for what was happening. When summoned to the Saraya (the headquarters of the Israeli occupation authority in Gaza) to be asked about the role the mosques appeared to be playing in the agitation, he continued to maintain his total innocence.[6] When the first Hamas communiqué was distributed on 14 December 1987, it was unsigned, bearing only the name of the "The Islamic Resistance Movement" abbreviated to the Arabic letters "h," "m," and "s."[7] The Israelis therefore targeted public figures and outspoken critics of Israel within the Ikhwan. The first prominent Ikhwan personality to be arrested, less than a month after the intifada started, was Khalil al-Quqa, director of the Islamic Society of al-Shati' (beach) Camp.[8] Dr. Abd al-Aziz al-Rantisi, a founding member of Hamas, was detained on 15 January 1988.[9] The leaders of the Hamas security apparatus, Majd, were both arrested soon afterward: Yahya al-Sinwar on 20 January 1988 and Rawhi Mushtaha on 13 February 1988.

The Israelis had been seeking an opportunity to attach the blame for the intifada to the Hamas leadership. A window of opportunity seemed to present itself in August 1988, when Hamas published its Charter, in which it declared a jihad that would continue until Palestine was liberated in its entirety and the State of Israel was eliminated.[10] In the meantime, an individual from Jerusalem, detained in connection with a completely unrelated matter, confessed under torture that he had sent money to Ibrahim al-Yazuri, a co-founder of Hamas, to fund the activities of the intifada. Al-Yazuri was arrested and divulged under further torture the names of the top leaders in the various regions of the Gaza Strip among whom funds were distributed. As the picture became clearer, the Israelies prepared to act. In August 1988, they initiated their first mass detention campaign against Hamas leaders and activists. The leadership of the movement had anticipated that such a course of events might take place, and had taken some precautions. A shadow leadership was set up, so there would be no leadership vacuum if the Israelis were to carry out mass arrests. In less than two months, 120 senior figures were rounded up, including all the founding members of Hamas apart from Sheikh Yassin. Al-Rantisi was now joined in detention by his fellow Hamas co-founders Salah Shihadah, Ibrahim al-Yazuri, Muhammad Sham'ah, Abd al-Fattah Dukhan, and 'Isa al-Nashar. Despite admissions on the part of some of these detainees that Sheikh Yassin was the founder and head of the movement, the Israelis decided to allow him his continued freedom; they were eager to find out more about his activities and to monitor his movements and communications. They put him under 24-hour surveillance, in the hope of unraveling the network he had so successfully constructed in the three years since his release from prison.

By chance, these mass arrests coincided with the arrest of the members of two Hamas military cells that had been operating in Jabalya and in Beit Hanun. These two cells had targeted some collaborators. But they were between them also responsible for five attacks against Israeli patrols in the West Bank and Gaza, using homemade explosive devices. As if in celebration, the operations were carried out on the day of Id al-Adha, which fell that year on 24 July 1988.[11] The members of the two cells were identified, arrested, and prosecuted, but seemingly no connection was immediately made between them and the Hamas leaders detained around the same time. Later, Salah Shihadah seems to have been suspected of responsibility for organizing the cells.

A Near-Fatal Blow

The Hamas shadow leadership took over the task of managing the daily activities of the intifada, while Sheikh Yassin and his close aides in the military wing began to construct a new military cell they referred to as "Cell 101." This cell was led by Muhammad al-Sharatiha, who was selected partly because of his existing experience but mainly because of his reputed robustness under severe interrogation. The leadership devised a means of communicating with him that maintained their confidentiality. This was the "dead spot" technique, where anonymous messages are left in a location of which the recipient is informed just before collection. Al-Sharatiha was instructed to identify suitable individuals for recruitment and report their identities to his contact via the dead spot so that they could be cleared for security before contact was made with them. The intention was to avoid recruiting collaborators.

Unlike the activists of the nationalist movement, these Islamic recruits brought with them little apart from zeal, determination, and longing for martyrdom; they had neither training nor experience. Much of what they attempted at this stage either failed completely or had a very limited effect, but they were apparently able to learn quickly. Their first target was an Israeli contractor who was drilling a well in al-Shaykh Radwan area in Gaza. The man was well trained in martial arts and succeeded in escaping safely from his attackers. The second mission was to fire on a Jewish settlement using an antiquated rifle, seemingly with little effect. However, their third and fourth operations were serious enough to provoke a major reaction in Israel. These operations prompted a decision by Israel to declare an all-out war on Hamas.

On 16 February 1989, members of the new military cell travelled to Israel and kidnapped Sergeant Avi Sasportas, who was hitchhiking from his base to his home in Ashdod. Not knowing what to do with him, they killed him and buried his body. Then, on 3 May 1989, they kidnapped Sergeant Ilan Sa'adon, who was hitchhiking near Ashkelon. He was also killed and buried. During the search for Sa'adon, the Israelis found Sasportas's body not far from where he had been kidnapped. Sa'adon's body was not recovered until seven years later, after Israel received intelligence reports regarding its location. The car used in the latter operation had an Israeli license plate because it was a stolen car purchased on the black market in Israel. The Israeli authorities identified the car and traced it to a location close to where the leader of the cell had been living. Rather than dispose of it, the cell members had rashly retained the car in case they needed to travel to Israel again on some future occasion. After the Israeli authorities discovered the missing soldiers had been kidnapped, the members of the military cell fled and were eventually smuggled to safety outside Palestine, except for al-Sharatiha, who was arrested. Under interrogation and torture he divulged the name of an acquaintance he suspected had been his "dead spot" liaison man. This individual was in turn arrested and tortured until he confessed to receiving money and instructions from Sheikh Ahmad Yassin himself.[12] Sheikh Yassin was immediately arrested. This was when the Israelis launched their second and more extensive mass arrest campaign against Hamas, in which they rounded up some 1,500 members of the organization across the Gaza Strip and the West Bank.

Here is how Sheikh Yassin described his arrest on 18 May 1989 and his subsequent interrogation:

I was at home. The curfew, which would daily be enforced from 9 pm to around dawn, just in time for the laborers to go to work, had just started. I had some guests at my house who had rushed to go back to their own homes before the start of the curfew. The Israeli army surrounded the house at five past nine in the evening. Some of the soldiers jumped over the wall while others stayed in their vehicles. It seemed as if a whole battalion had been deployed just to arrest me. Some intelligence officers came to me and said, "We need you for a short while." I said, "Yes, but let me put some clothes on." So I put on some clothes and was taken out in my wheelchair. They said, "Where is your son?" I said, "Here he is." They said, "Let him come with you, so as to help you." That was my son Abdulhamid who had just turned sixteen and had just been issued with an identity card. They took me in and put me in a cell where they sat me down. They began immediately to shout abuse at me, swearing, spitting into my face and slapping me. They brought a tray and started banging it over my head; they squeezed my neck veins and pushed upward to cause maximum pain. They then started hammering my chest and continued to slap it until it turned blue. Then *they dragged in my son, who was supposed to be there to serve me; they threw him on the floor in front of me and four of them jumped on him. One of them squeezed his neck as if to strangle him, another beat him, a third yelled abuse at him. All the while my son was shouting underneath them. They kept beating him in front of me saying, "Have mercy on your child; confess and that will be the end of the story. Hamas is finished, it is over; there is no point denying your role in it. Give us what you have for the sake of your son." I said to them, "I have nothing to say." They went away for a couple of hours, then came back with my son and began once more to beat him. Again, they sat over him and hurt him severely. So severe was the torture that he almost died. They then took him away. For four days I was deprived of sleep and was forced to remain in my chair while interrogators took turns every two or three hours in questioning me. Finally, I lost consciousness and fell off the chair. When I woke up they brought me the brothers who were detained because of their involvement in the military case. Salah [Shihadah] came first and said, "I came to you and took from you $2,500 and that is all I have to say." Then I was brought the other brothers who had been responsible for interrogating collaborators. They said, "We came to you and obtained a fatwa from you that it was permissible to kill the collaborators." They seemed to want me to know that this was all they had confessed to. The Israelis were all the while standing and listening. They were eager to know who would lead the movement after me. I said to them this was a grass roots organization; you remove the tip and a new tip will grow out of the base. I concluded that there was no point in denying my share of responsibility: the statements implicating me were sufficient to prosecute me anyway. I confessed that I did issue a fatwa legalizing the execution of collaborators and that I had a right as a Palestinian to rise against occupation.*[13]

The mass detentions decapitated Hamas: all of its first- and second-ranking officials were detained. The Israeli campaign almost succeeded in annihilating the movement. However, Israel's crackdown revealed for the first time the extent of Hamas's military capacity, indicating that the movement had been preparing it for years.[14] Israel's action caused concern to those Palestinians who ran the Jihaz outside Palestine. The previous year had seen the transformation of the Jihaz into the hierarchical leadership structure it now has. At the apex of this is a representative council, called in Arabic the Istishari (the consultative council). Below this is an elected executive committee, in Arabic the Tanfidhi (the executive committee), which in turn supervised several specialized committees whose remit was to provide the logistic support required by Hamas. Despite its representative capacity, the members of the Istishari are not directly elected. Their appointment to the council is recommended by the sectors they represent. The idea is for the Palestinian Ikhwan inside the West Bank and the Gaza Strip to be represented, as well as those in the various locations where they exist in sizeable numbers in the diaspora.

In the aftermath of this blow to the movement in 1989, the Tanfidhi turned to Musa Abu Marzuq, who had been studying for his doctorate in the United States, asking him to return at once to Gaza, where he was already a frequent visitor. His task would be to salvage what he could of the severely damaged organization. He had been a close associate of Sheikh Ahmad Yassin and was therefore regarded by the membership of Hamas not as an intruder but as one of the organization's loyal sons. Once back in Gaza, Abu Marzuq, known as Abu Omar, found few people to work with. Most of the senior members on whom he would have been able to depend, or whom he had personally known, had been arrested. Sayyid Abu Musamih was one of the few senior figures left at liberty and Abu Marzuq was obliged to rely on him. Most of the others he was able to contact had played no more than a marginal role in the movement before the crisis struck. Nevertheless, he had to contrive what he could with what was available to him, with the dearth of senior figures members left at liberty. Anticipating that many of those presently detained would in a few months time be released, Abu Marzuq set up a new provisional structure for the movement and took his leave. In fact, many of the 1,500 rounded up in May were freed after six months or so because the Israelis deemed them harmless.

This was a significant turning point in the history of Hamas. A crucial new feature was that, under the new structure, the "inside" had now come under the control of the "outside," whose role was no longer restricted to providing support. Until mid-1989 the "outside" provided funding, logistics, and advice. Henceforth, however, it became the central command and the point of reference. In addition to rebuilding the organization, a further element in Abu Marzuq's mission was to devise a formula to ensure that the movement would not totally collapse should it be subjected to any future onslaught similar to the one by which it had just been devastated.[15] Had the movement's leadership continued to be inside

Palestine, Israel could easily have broken its back, using mass arrests and other repressive measures to inflict irreparable damage on its ability to operate. Working from the relative safety of world capitals in which various Hamas decision-making centers were now situated, such as Kuwait, Amman, London, and Washington, the leadership had the time and space to respond calmly to eventualities. The presence of senior Hamas leaders outside Palestine shielded the movement not only against potentially fatal measures on the part of the Israelis, but also against moves by the PLO. The PLO constantly attempted to compromise lower-ranking members of Hamas, through intimidation or by offering inducements, at times when the senior Hamas leaders were in detention, as was often the case.

In the wake of the Abu Marzuq mission, and the system he established, the restructuring of the movement after every setback became a matter of routine. The Israelis launched campaigns of mass arrests almost annually. The campaigns of 1990, 1991, and 1992 were on a large scale, but the effects were not as devastating as they might have been, and the reconstruction not as difficult, because of the effectiveness of the strategy devised by Abu Marzuq. With a new and more resilient structure in place, and with a seemingly inexhaustible supply of recruits, Hamas was able easily to recover after every apparently terminal blow. The Israelis were oblivious to the fact that whenever they hit Hamas, and no matter how hard they hit it, they only earned it further popular sympathy and support. They apparently failed to take into account that their actions contributed to the emergence of Hamas as a credible alternative to the PLO. The most intensive campaigns against the movement took place just at the time when the PLO was making history by revoking its own Charter and abandoning its constituency. In December 1988, Yasir Arafat declared to the world that "the PLO has accepted Israel's right to exist, will participate in an international peace conference on the basis of UN Resolutions 242 and 338, and rejects terrorism in all its forms." The explicit implication of this concession on the part of the PLO leadership was the forfeiture of the right of return of the Palestinian refugees. By forfeiting this right, the PLO immediately gained the recognition of the United States and its Western allies, but lost credibility in the eyes of millions of Palestinian refugees inside and outside Palestine who had been waiting for half a century to return home. The PLO's loss, clearly, was Hamas's gain.

The War of the Knives

More than a mere restructuring was required to resuscitate Hamas's military capacity, however. Here, Israel unwittingly made a major contribution. Conditions were worsening for the Palestinians every day. On 8 October 1990, 22 Palestinians were killed and more than 200 were wounded when Israeli troops stormed into al-Haram al-Sharif (the compound of the Aqsa Mosque in Jerusalem), firing on Muslim worshippers. The Muslims had gathered inside the Haram to foil a plot by a group of Jewish extremists known as the "Temple Mount Faithful,"[16] to lay what they said was to be the cornerstone of the Third Temple. On the same day, infuriated by the news of the massacre, 'Amir Sa'ud Abu Sarhan, who was said to be close to Hamas, stabbed three Israeli soldiers to death in Jerusalem, and wounded a fourth. This was the beginning of what became known as the "war of the knives." The last straw for the Israelis came on 14 December 1990, with a further knife attack on a group of Israelis working in an aluminium factory in Jaffa by two Arabs from Gaza who had crossed the Green Line earlier in the day. The attackers, Marwan al-Zayigh and Ashraf al-Ba'luji, left on the wall of the factory a declaration of responsibility in the name of Hamas, stating that the action was meant to commemorate the second anniversary of the birth of the movement. They succeeded in escaping and went hiding, thus becoming the first *mutaradun* (fugitives). They were soon to be joined by hundreds of Palestinian young men, wanted by the Israelis for a variety of terrorism charges ranging from stone throwing to murder.

On 4 December 1990, the day of the stabbing in Jaffa, the Israelis launched a massive campaign against what remained of Hamas. Throughout the West Bank and Gaza, they arrested no less than 1,700 people suspected of membership or of any kind of affiliation to the movement. Among those arrested were the members of the new leadership put in place by Musa Abu Marzuq during his 1989 visit. The West Bank was harder hit this time than previously because the two attackers in the aluminium factory were believed to have been sheltered by Hamas members there. Despite the extent of the Israeli campaign, Hamas on this occasion took less time to recover. With the overall control of the movement now in the hands of its leaders abroad, little disruption occurred. In addition, the leadership on the outside was boosted by the arrival of four main

Hamas figures from the inside. After a brief period of detention, Imad al-Alami, Fadl al-Zahhar, Mustapha al-Qanu', and Mustafa al-Liddawi were deported to Lebanon. They soon assumed senior positions of responsibility within Hamas's institutions abroad.[17]

Meanwhile, Sheikh Ahmad Yassin faced trial in an Israeli military court. After a series of hearings that began in early 1990, he was eventually sentenced on 16 October 1991 to one life term plus 15 years. The court decided he was guilty of all charges in the indictment submitted by the military prosecutor.[18] He maintained his innocence of the kidnappings and killings of the two Israeli soldiers, but took responsibility for founding Hamas. Two weeks earlier, Muhammad al-Sharatiha, who was then aged 34, was sentenced to three life terms plus thirty years for his role in kidnapping and killing the two soldiers. One of the unforeseen outcomes of the Israeli onslaught on Hamas was the swelling of the ranks of the *mutaradun*, fugitives who were obliged to flee the country if they could, or if they could not, to go underground for as long as they were able. Those who were in hiding usually felt that since they had already lost their freedom, they had nothing more to lose. Their general practice was to form small groups to mount attacks on Israeli targets, or to improvise whatever attacks they could on an individual basis. It was out of this phenomenon that Hamas's military wing, Kata'ib al-Shahid Izzadin al-Qassam (the Martyr Izzadin al-Qassam Brigades) was born. The brigades were not an extension of al-Mujahidun al-Filastiniyun, but an entirely new creation, set up and led by a much younger generation of Hamas activists whose motive was to take revenge for Israel's ruthless repression of Hamas. The Israelis had already apprehended the founding members of the Mujahidun, and some of them had received very long sentences. Meanwhile, the inspiration of the Mujahidun long antedated the intifada and the movement was seen as the result of plans laid as long ago as the early 1980s. It was conceived as an Islamic version of the struggle waged over decades by the Palestinian nationalist movement. In contrast, the Qassam Brigades were a product of the intifada itself, and had come into being as a reaction to Israel's mounting repression of what had begun as a peaceful protest. Initially, the intifada had been merely a series of exercises in civil disobedience, intended to oblige the Israeli occupation authorities to treat the Palestinians more humanely. However, the disproportionate scale of the Israeli response to the intifada was what provoked the young victims of Israeli brutality to take retaliatory action of a more violent nature.

The "war of the knives," waged under the banner of the Martyr Iz-zadin al-Qassam Brigades, continued unabated until December 1992, when the brigades inaugurated what Hamas called the "war of the seven days." On 7 December 1992, an armed cell operating in Gaza ambushed an Israeli army patrol on the road from al-Shuja'iyah to Beit Lahia, kill-ing three soldiers. On 12 December, another armed cell operating in Hebron ambushed an Israeli patrol, killing three more soldiers. Early on 13 December, a third cell kidnapped Sergeant-Major Nissim Toledano of the Israeli Border Police, aged 29, as he was travelling from his home in Lod to his posting in the West Bank city of Ramallah. The Hamas cell took their hostage to a safe location, while two masked men delivered a message to the Ramallah office of the International Red Cross at around 11 AM, demanding the following concessions in exchange for the safe return of the hostage:

1. Strict adherence by the Israeli authorities to the specified deadline (9 PM the same day), failing which the hostage would be executed;
2. The release of Sheikh Ahmad Yassin in the presence of a representative of the International Red Cross and the presence of the ambassadors of Egypt, France, Sweden, and Turkey, before whom the Israeli authori-ties would pledge that they would not re-arrest the Sheikh;
3. Live coverage by Israeli television of the release of Sheikh Ahmad Yassin and the Israeli pledge made before the ambassadors in exchange for freeing the kidnapped soldier.

During the ten hours that preceded the deadline of the ultimatum, the Israelis implemented a state of emergency unprecedented since the war with Egypt of October 1973. They attempted to play for time in the hope the kidnappers might be identified, or the hideout where the hostage was being kept be discovered. For the first time ever, Hamas received global media coverage and worldwide attention. In a last-ditch attempt to influence the kidnappers, the Israeli authorities interviewed Sheikh Ahmad Yassin on Israeli television in the hope that he would appeal for the release of the hostage.

This interview gave Hamas a publicity bonanza it had never antici-pated. The Sheikh, who was visibly ill because of his disabilities, appealed to the kidnappers to keep the soldier alive but pressed the Israelis to meet their demands. For the first time in his life, and in the life of Hamas, Sheikh Yassin was able to speak directly to the Israeli public and to the wider world, albeit very briefly, about his movement's position regarding the conflict between Israel and the Palestinians. Excerpts from the transcript of the Israeli TV interview follow:

Interviewer: An armed group has kidnapped a policeman and is demanding your release; what is your opinion of this?

Sheikh Yassin: No man would refuse freedom and no man demands to be shackled. I believe that any incarcerated person, especially in these political circumstances of ours, has the right to be freed.

Interviewer: What if they kill the policeman?

Sheikh Yassin: I would advise against it, so the authorities can be given a chance to meet the demands of these people.

Interviewer: In principle, what would be your position concerning the killing of this policeman?

Sheikh Yassin: The killing of the policeman, the killing of the Palestinian and the killing of the soldier are all part of a cycle created by the occupation. When the causes are removed all these problems will be solved.

Interviewer: And what about the incident of the kidnapping of this policeman?

Sheikh Yassin: Is this an incident taking place in isolation? It is part of this cycle; every day people on both sides are killed. When we alter the circumstances of occupation all of this will end automatically.

Interviewer: What if they kill the policeman?

Sheikh Yassin: I do not agree that they should kill him. A kidnapper has objectives and will, naturally, demand that his objectives be fulfilled. The authorities should look into these objectives and accomplish them.

Interviewer: How do you see the power of Hamas today in the occupied territories?

Sheikh Yassin: From here I have no view: how can I observe when I am confined?

Interviewer: From what you hear from visitors and prisoners?

Sheikh Yassin: What I hear from the media is that the Hamas movement is getting bigger and bigger.

Interviewer: What does that indicate?

Sheikh Yassin: It indicates that the Islamic solution is the alternative.

Interviewer: What about the peace process and the Washington talks?[19]

Sheikh Yassin: Not a single Palestinian rejects peace. Every Palestinian loves peace. However, the peace you desire is different from the one I desire. Each one has a means and a way for peace.

Interviewer: How do you see the negotiations taking place today?

Sheikh Yassin: Thus far they have achieved nothing. I expected right from the start that they would be unable to achieve anything because of the lack of balance.[20]

The Israelis refused to meet any demands, and Toledano was executed. His body was found on 15 December 1992 dumped in a ditch close to the West Bank Jewish settlement of Maaleh Adumim along the Jericho road. Israeli Prime Minister Yitzhak Rabin convened an emergency cabinet meeting, and on 16 December he announced that harsh measures would immediately be taken against Hamas. By 17 December, almost 2,000 Palestinians had been arrested, along with 415 Hamas and Islamic Jihad leaders. Some of these had recently been detained, others were brought from prisons where they had been in detention for some time, and yet others were brought straight from their homes. All were put on coaches and driven straight to the border with Lebanon, where they were dumped in a freezing no man's land just outside the self-declared Israeli security zone. The place was called, ironically, Marj al-Zuhur: "Meadow of Flowers."

Worldwide Publicity

The entire world watched on television as the deportees, blindfolded and handcuffed, with their hands tied behind their backs, remained confined to their seats in the coaches, which were parked for up to 24 hours at the de facto border with Lebanon. Their agony was prolonged by the efforts of well-meaning people in Israel who sought a ruling from the Israeli High Court in the hope of forcing the Israeli government to stop the deportation. The hearing began at 5 AM before three judges, only to conclude after fourteen hours with an endorsement of the government's decision. The deportees were transported to the Zumriyeh crossing point at the northernmost point of what was then the Israeli-imposed security zone in the south of Lebanon. The Lebanese army prevented the deportees from continuing north. Meanwhile, Israel pushed them across the border, insisting that it was no longer responsible for them on the grounds that they were in territory controlled by Lebanon. On a freezing December night, 415 Palestinians were left in the open in an inhospitable terrain covered with snow. Most of them, if not all, had already suffered severe bruising to their hands from the handcuffs and were suffering from a variety of gastrointestinal disorders triggered by the cold weather and the agonizing wait.

It was probably not long before the Israeli establishment began to regret its blunder. The Israelis wanted to punish Hamas but ended up rewarding it. Only a few days earlier Israel was portrayed as the victim of Palestinian terrorism. Now it was being condemned for its breach of international law and particularly of articles 33 and 49 of the Fourth Geneva Convention.[21] Even Israel's staunch ally the United States was obliged to express disapproval. On 18 December 1992, the UN Security Council unanimously adopted resolution 799, in which the council strongly condemned "the action taken by Israel, the occupying Power, to deport hundreds of Palestinian civilians." The resolution went on to express "its firm opposition to any such deportation by Israel," and demanded "that Israel, the occupying Power, ensure the safe and immediate return to the occupied territories of all those deported."

Marj al-Zuhur, a barren piece of land probably never before inhabited, became in the course of a few days the site of a camp that attracted the world's sympathy and drew extensive media attention. Journalists and television crews flocked to the scene from around the globe. With ages ranging between 16 and 67, the deportees were the cream of their society. Seventeen of them were university lecturers with doctorates; eleven were medical doctors, some of them senior specialists; fourteen were engineers; thirty-six were businessmen; and five were journalists. One hundred and nine were university students, many of them postgraduate students. And finally, 208 were imams from various mosques. Of course, at the individual level, every one of the deportees suffered physical and psychological torment. They were uprooted from their own communities and banished from their families and loved ones. It was also true that after each mass detention or mass deportation campaign a leadership vacuum ensued and the Hamas movement was severely shaken. But this only happened momentarily: on each occasion the inevitable outcome was the ascent of a new generation of leaders who, despite their lack of experience, would soon learn and even excel. In a sense this was a factor that distinguished Hamas from other Palestinian factions in the territories. Hamas as a movement seemed to make gains out of its losses, as it had done in each of its earlier setbacks. On this occasion, it turned the temporary exile of hundreds of its top leaders and activists to its advantage.

Under the leadership of Dr. Abd al-Aziz al-Rantisi, the deportees refused to move forward from the spot where they had been dumped. They even tried to walk back toward Israel, but the Israelis fired on them. They set up a camp and called it Mukhayyam al-Awdah (the camp of return). Had they agreed to go to Beirut, and from there to various other parts of the Arab world, their fate would have been sealed: they would never have returned. This was what the Israelis wished to happen. Instead, they defied the Israeli government and gave the world no option other than to be aware day by day of their fate. Including as they did so many academics and students, the deportees set up a university that they named after the great Islamic scholar Ibn Taymiyah.[22] In no time the camp became a hub of constant activity.

At Marj al-Zuhur, the leaders of Hamas on the inside and the outside were able to meet freely for the first time, taking the opportunity to work together to put the movement's house in order. The temporary exile itself turned out to be a blessing in disguise. Not only did the inside meet the outside: some of those on the inside encountered each other for the first time in years. They had not been able to see each other inside the territories because of the Israeli collective punishment that routinely imposed a state of siege on towns, villages, and camps, isolating entire communities. In addition, many of the deportees had been denied the freedom to move freely not only across Palestine but within their own locations. The leading figures on the inside and the outside seized the opportunity to discuss and refine their ideas and conclusions. For once, they had ample time to overcome whatever disagreements there might have been in their philosophies and policies. If the barriers of occupation had previously prevented them from communicating with each other, they were now able to exchange ideas with clarity and confidence. The sojourn in South Lebanon was also an opportunity to survey the human resources available to the movement in the territories, and thus to restructure the leadership on the inside in the aftermath of the series of crises that had marked the past two years. It was also an occasion to establish cooperation among charities inside and outside Palestine. Finally, the greatest opportunity of all was that for military training. Hamas was inundated with offers to train its young deportees in a variety of combat techniques, including the manufacture of explosives from old mines and from readily available chemicals.[23]

Before this crisis, which had begun with the kidnapping of the two Israeli soldiers, the name of Hamas had rarely been mentioned anywhere in the international media. There had been little interest in what it stood for or what it sought to achieve. Now, journalists and researchers from many countries around the world were filing reports, writing stories, or filming documentaries for news outlets about the movement, which had emerged into international prominence so rapidly and so unexpectedly. Some deportees, such as Dr. Abd al-Aziz al-Rantisi, Dr. Mahmud al-Zahhar, and Professor Aziz Duwayk, appeared regularly on TV news channels. Professor Duwayk was a guest on Christmas night on the CNN show Larry King Live, an opportunity he used to convey his Christmas best wishes to the Christian world. At the same time, however, he drew attention to the fact that he and his brethren were obliged to spend Christmas in a makeshift camp in sub-zero temperatures away from their families and loved ones. For the first time, Hamas was able to get its message across to individuals, organizations, and governments all over the world. In the Palestinian context, the movement forged fresh links with various Palestinian organization and factions. At the Arab level, it established contacts throughout the Arab world, both at governmental and nongovernmental levels. And in the international sphere, it was able to communicate with individuals and institutions within or associated with the United Nations and the European Union.[24]

On 15 August 1993, after eight months of exile, the deportees accepted an Israeli proposal that would permit the immediate return of nearly half of them to the occupied Palestinian territories, with the remainder returning in December. In early September, 181 of them returned. Most

went back to their homes, but some were held in Israeli prisons or detention centers. On 14 December 1993, following the signing of the Declaration of Principles by Israel and the PLO on 13 September 1993, the
remaining deportees were returned to the occupied Palestinian territory.
Once again, however, some were imprisoned or detained.

FOUR

INTO JORDAN

Not a healthy relationship: a relationship with inertia.[1]

—Khalid Mish'al

The Loss of Kuwait

When Saddam Hussein sent his troops into Kuwait on 2 August 1990, many Kuwait residents were out of the country, seeking relief from its scorching heat in lands with cooler and more compassionate climates. Among those who had come to the Jordanian capital Amman that summer, to enjoy the moderate weather and to meet friends and relatives from around the world, were some of the leading figures within the nascent Palestinian Hamas movement. Kuwait had hitherto been their main base of operation. The many support committees set up since the start of the intifada in 1987 were either situated in Kuwait or supervised from there. It did not take long for these Palestinians to realize that Saddam's adventure had dealt their project a very heavy blow.

Kuwait had been a safe haven and a comfortable place in which to live and work. It was the Arab country by far the most conducive to a political movement's ability to conduct its business securely and in confidence. Its inhabitants enjoyed more freedom than in any other country in the region and the intellectual elite within its population were highly sympathetic to Arab national causes, especially that of Palestine. In addition, Kuwait had one of the largest and most prosperous Palestinian populations outside Palestine and Jordan. Almost half a million Palestinians lived there, many with prestigious, secure, and well-paid jobs. Thousands of families in

Palestine and in the refugee camps of Jordan, Syria, and Lebanon literally depended on remittances from their sons and daughters working
in Kuwait. Throughout the 1980s, the Palestinian Ikhwan had become
so popular a cause that a large portion of the funds raised by Kuwaiti
NGOs for Palestine was channeled through the charities set up by them.
The overwhelmingly religious population of Kuwait saw Hamas, when it
emerged, as the real alternative to a corrupt and bankrupt PLO.[2]

After the invasion, however, many people lost their jobs, and Palestinians who had been out of the country during the invasion found they were
not permitted to return. Kuwait suspected many of its Palestinian residents of collaborating with Saddam Hussein, and life in Kuwait became
increasingly difficult. Faced with the new reality, Hamas leaders had no
option but to set up a fresh operation in Jordan. There, the Hashemite
monarchy had opted to support Saddam Hussein, in a position that was
not at all out of line with the popular sentiment in Jordan. The Jordanian
people did not see Saddam Hussein as an aggressor who had seized a
neighboring country and had torn it apart, but as someone who was defying the US and Israel. The Ikhwan of Jordan, empowered by the sizeable
share of seats in the Jordanian parliament they had won in the elections of
November 1989, led the protests against threats by the US to intervene
against Iraq. They also played a leading role in establishing a pan-Islamic
delegation whose mission was to mediate between Saudi Arabia and Iraq
in the hope of resolving the crisis peacefully.

The Ikhwan in Jordan lent their full support to their dispossessed
brothers from Hamas, placing their own offices at Hamas's disposal
until Hamas could set up their own new headquarters. Jordan had its
advantages for Hamas. Soon, it seemed that the loss of Kuwait had been
compensated for by the acquisition of a new location, logistically and
demographically more conducive to Hamas's purposes. In Jordan, the
Hamas operatives were a stone's throw from the actual theater of operations in Palestine. A majority of Jordanians were themselves originally
Palestinians, of Palestinian origin, or had direct links with Palestine.
There would be no shortage of recruits should the movement need more
operatives. The Jordanians were overwhelmingly supportive of the Palestinian cause, regarding it as their own. In addition, Jordan was one of
the few Arab countries where qualified and experienced personnel in all

fields were available, whose first priority would be to serve the Palestinian cause.

The members of the Tanfidhi, the Hamas executive office that ran the operations outside Palestine, had mostly lived and worked in Kuwait until the Iraqi invasion. After the move to Amman, their first task was to reassemble their former staff, or to recruit new personnel from within the ranks of the Jordanian Ikhwan. Hamas would only employ operatives who were already Ikhwan members, and only after they passed its own process of screening. The senior figure in the Tanfidhi was Musa Abu Marzuq, who was still residing in the United States. He moved to Amman in September 1990 to be with the rest of the group. After his return from a brief trip abroad about a month later, the Jordanian authorities denied him entry because he was not a Jordanian national and had no residence permit. He and his colleagues had intended to benefit from the prevalent circumstances in Jordan to assemble in one place all the officials in charge of the support committees attached to the Tanfidhi, and there could be no better location than across the river from Palestine. The exclusion of Abu Marzuq indicated that the authorities in Jordan had begun to monitor the activities of Hamas in their capital. Abu Marzuq had no option other than to return to the United States.

However, the climate in Jordan was in general highly propitious for the kind of operation Hamas intended to undertake. As the construction of the US-led coalition neared completion and the attack on Iraq appeared imminent, the atmosphere in Jordan became more favorable to the idea of jihad. There was a virtual state of emergency because of the perceived threat to Jordan from Israel. The population was encouraged to acquire arms for self-defense in the event that the anticipated war drew in Israel, which would consequently involve Jordan, sandwiched as it was between Israel and Iraq. The Jordanian army opened its training camps to the public and deployed its ground-to-air missiles along its western frontiers. Despite the danger looming on the horizon, there was euphoria and excitement that perhaps at last the country was about to engage the Israelis in real conflict. It was hard to find a Jordanian who was not spoiling for a fight with Israel.

Working clandestinely from the offices of the Jordanian Ikhwan in Amman, and with the knowledge of no more than a handful of top local Ikhwan leaders, Hamas set up an arms procurement committee.

73

The committee's task was to purchase weapons and store them until circumstances allowed them to be smuggled into Palestine for use there by Hamas. The logic was simply that, since people all around were arming themselves and seeking military training, the best use should be made of such a golden opportunity. However, the honeymoon between Hamas and Jordan soon ended. In the early hours of 17 January 1991, the US-led alliance of close to 30 countries launched air attacks, initiating "Operation Desert Storm," whose objective was to liberate Kuwait from the Iraqi troops. The land assault began on 24 February. By 28 February, the Iraqi troops had been pushed back into Iraq and were in full flight when a ceasefire was declared by the US. On 3 March, the war was ended with an agreement between the Iraqi and Allied commanders. An atmosphere of gloom and doom replaced the euphoria and excitement. The humiliating defeat of Iraq dealt a painful blow to Jordanians and Palestinians alike. It was not that Saddam was believed when he claimed he could win a war with the United States. Many people, however, including of course Saddam himself as well as King Hussein of Jordan, continued to the last minute to indulge in wishful thinking that perhaps the Americans would never attack.

Normality soon returned. The margin of freedom permitted by the authorities while the people were being mobilized gradually shrank. The Jordanian intelligence services resumed their activities, which had apparently been suspended while the war mentality that had prevailed over the previous few months persisted. No sooner did the war in the Gulf end than the authorities in Jordan uncovered the network of Hamas members who had been buying and stockpiling weapons. Eleven Hamas operatives were arrested and detained. Sensing danger, some of the main figures in the Tanfidhi left the country immediately. At Musa Abu Marzuq's suggestion, some of those working closely with the political committee traveled to Washington, DC, to join him. His deputy Khalid Mish'al, who was in charge of logistic support for Hamas inside Palestine, went to London, which he made his base of operations for several months.

Hosting Hamas

Meanwhile, the Jordanian Ikhwan, who held five ministries in the Jordanian cabinet and were in their second year of powersharing,[3] endeavored

74

to secure the release of the arrested Hamas operatives, many of whom had in any case been recruited from within the local Ikhwan organization. Their objective was to defuse the crisis that had ensued between themselves and the Hashemite regime because of the confrontation between Hamas and the Jordanian authorities. The former leader of the Ikhwan's parliamentary group, the late Ahmad Qutaysh al-Azaydah, one of the most highly respected and most popular figures in Jordan, arranged for Ibrahim Ghosheh, the Hamas representative in Amman, to meet the Prime Minister Zayd bin Shakir. At the meeting, Ghosheh requested the release of the detainees.[4] A week later, Ghosheh discussed the problem with Mustafa al-Qaysi, the director of the Jordanian General Intelligence Directorate (GID). Al-Qaysi raised the issue of the discovery of arms stockpiles, pointing out that this was a serious matter. Ghosheh explained that these were arms procured in 1991, when the former Prime Minister Mudar Badran called on every Jordanian citizen to be armed to defend the country in the event that it came under attack or was invaded. He assured al-Qaysi that there had never been any intention to harm Jordan in any way, that Hamas would never intervene in Jordanian domestic affairs, and that the weapons were intended for use only inside Palestine.[5] Consequently, a royal pardon was issued in 1992 and the eleven Hamas detainees were released.

By the end of 1992, both the PLO leadership and the Jordanian authorities had concluded that Hamas had become a power that had to be taken seriously. This was at a moment when Israel had virtually declared war on the movement. The PLO asked for a meeting with the leadership of Hamas outside Palestine, while the Jordanians welcomed the good offices of an Arab politician close to Hamas to initiate contacts and open up talks with the movement to discuss its presence in the country. The PLO's approach, which suggested that Yasir Arafat himself would be heading their side of the talks, prompted the Tanfidhi to create a new structure, al-Maktab al-Siyasi (the Political Bureau), with Abu Marzuq as its head, in order to parallel the structure of the PLO's leadership.[6] It is significant that these developments might not have occurred had it not been for the crisis of the deportees in South Lebanon, which began in late December 1992 and boosted the popularity and authority of Hamas inside Palestine and across the region.

In early 1993, a meeting was arranged between al-Qaysi and Muhammad Nazzal, a Jordanian national and a leading figure in the Tanfidhi,
who had settled in Jordan following the loss of Kuwait.[7] The Jordanians
agreed that they would now accept that the purchase and stockpiling of
arms by Hamas during the period of crisis that preceded the Gulf war
was innocent, and that the arms were intended only for operations inside
the occupied territories. Al-Qaysi confirmed that Jordan was confident it
had not been the intended target, and, speaking on behalf of the authorities, expressed the desire to open a new phase of relations with Hamas.
He added that Jordan would permit Hamas's recently created Political
Bureau to establish its headquarters in Amman. Nazzal asked if it would
therefore be possible to allow Musa Abu Marzuq, the head of the bureau, and his fellow bureau member Imad al-Alami, who until then had
been Hamas's representative in Iran, to reside in Jordan. The Jordanians
agreed that both men, neither of whom was a Jordanian national, would
be welcome. Nazzal was informed that Hamas would be allowed to engage in political and media-related activities, but that no military activity
would be permitted either within Jordan or across its borders against
Israel.[8] In Hamas's view, this seemed a reasonable deal.

When Musa Abu Marzuq and Imad al-Alami arrived in the country, a
meeting to ratify the agreement was held in al-Qaysi's office at the GID
headquarters in Abdali in central Amman. Abu Marzuq, al-Alami, Nazzal,
and Ghosheh represented Hamas, while al-Qaysi and his deputy Samih
al-Battikhi spoke for Jordan. The Hamas team was told that a meeting
would soon be arranged for them with Prime Minister Zayd bin Shakir.
The Jordanians seemed keen to give a political dimension to the relationship, rather than confining it to the realm of security. In due course, the
prime minister together with his deputy, Dhawqan al-Hindawi, received
the four representatives of Hamas at his office. The prime minister welcomed his guests and expressed satisfaction that an agreement had been
concluded between the two sides, informing them that the king himself
had instructed him to "bless" the deal. This was an unwritten gentlemen's
agreement. Both sides accepted that should either side wish to change
any of its terms it must give advance notice to the other. Two channels
of communication between Hamas and the Jordanian authorities were
agreed upon. One of these was to be between Muhammad Nazzal, in
his capacity as the Hamas representative in Jordan, and al-Qaysi. The

second, at a lower level, would be between Nazzal's secretary, Isam al-Najjar, and a Jordanian intelligence official, Amjad al-Hadid.[9]

The Jordanians believed the new arrangement would bring substantial benefits. On the one hand, the authorities wished to ensure that Hamas, which clearly enjoyed massive popularity in Jordan, would pose no threat. The regime was anxious to avert any repetition of the scenario of the late 1960s, when its clash with the PLO culminated in the events of September 1970. It therefore sought to guarantee that Jordan's western frontier would not be used for military operations against Israel. To draw Hamas into a friendly relationship and sanction its presence in the country appeared the best option. The nationalist sentiments of over-zealous Jordanian youths, who might otherwise be tempted to carry out attacks of their own against Israel, would, it was hoped, be satisfied by the presence of Hamas in Jordan. In addition, Jordan wished to have a card to play in its continuing competition with the PLO, which was at the time holding out blandishments to Hamas and seeking cooperation with it. King Hussein anticipated that Hamas, which was gaining rapidly in strength, would soon pose a serious challenge to the PLO and might in time provide a credible alternative. He was confident, on the basis of his long and comfortable working relationship with the Ikhwan of Jordan, that he could count on the Ikhwan to ensure that Hamas would not seek in any way to undermine his own authority.

The Hamas leadership accepted the conditions stipulated in the deal because it judged that the opportunity to establish a permanent Hamas presence in Jordan was worth the price. In fact, the agreement with Jordan is still regarded by Hamas leaders as having been one of the most important accomplishments in the early history of the movement.[10] From that time on, Hamas, whose leadership on the inside was repeatedly ravaged by mass detention and mass deportation, for the first time had a headquarters with an address, and a leadership whose figures were identifiable and able to be contacted. For the Hamas leadership, the arrangement represented a transformation from the condition of having no location to that of possessing a well-defined geography with a well-resourced decision-making center. It was a transition from secrecy to openness, and from an existence eked out underground to an overt presence.

77

The Jordanian move encouraged other governments that had been eager to communicate with the movement to take steps of their own. The co-location of all the members of Hamas's Political Bureau in Amman was particularly helpful in opening up channels and building bridges with other countries. For some time, the movement had maintained some degree of presence in a number of capitals, but had an official existence only in Khartoum and Tehran. Thanks to the initiative on Jordan's part, Hamas was soon invited to establish official representation in Syria, Lebanon, and Yemen. It also made useful contacts with the governments of Saudi Arabia, the Gulf states, and the Arab Maghreb countries of North Africa. Senior Hamas officials made unofficial visits to these countries on a number of occasions. Hamas also opened a channel of communications with Egypt, while diplomats from an array of foreign embassies in Amman, including those of the United States and several Western European countries, began to open channels of communication with it.

For a while, things went well for Hamas in Jordan. However, in the autumn of 1993, Hamas officials began to notice a change in the attitude of their Jordanian counterparts.[11] On 13 September 1993, the PLO and Israel signed the Oslo Agreement on the White House lawn, a startling event that few would have anticipated only a few weeks earlier. The Palestinians and the Israelis shocked the world with the revelation that they had been talking secretly in Oslo, and that they had reached agreement on a Declaration of Principles. Before this event, Jordan had been growing increasingly pessimistic about the chance of any meaningful deal emerging from the negotiations being held by the joint Jordanian–Palestinian team and the Israeli negotiators in Washington within the framework of the bilateral talks. Once a deal was signed between the PLO and Israel, the Jordanians had to become resigned to a new reality. Bitter about what they perceived to be a betrayal on the part of the PLO, they pushed forward along their own track of negotiations with Israel. Undoubtedly, however, reaching a peace deal with Israel would necessitate a revision of their agreement with Hamas. Additionally, Jordan was subjected regularly to various levels of pressure from the United States, Israel, and the PLO to curtail the activities of Hamas on its soil.

As if to pave the way for a reversal of policy, the Jordanians began to harass Hamas operatives. They seemed intent on bringing Hamas's officials to realize that their activities were being monitored and that, perhaps, their presence was no longer welcomed. Senior Hamas officials traveling in and out of the country began to be subjected to thorough searches, with the consequent feeling they were being treated with disrespect. Evidently, the Jordanians were slowly absolving themselves from the terms of their unwritten pact with Hamas.

Falling Out With Jordan

The first major sign of a real crack in the relationship occurred soon after Hamas's military wing, the Izzadin al-Qassam Brigades, claimed responsibility for the bombing in Afula on 6 April 1994 that killed 8 Israelis and wounded 44. The brigades promised four further attacks, in retaliation for the massacre perpetrated by Baruch Goldstein, an American Jewish settler from the Kiryat Arba settlement on the outskirts of Hebron. Goldstein killed 29 Muslims and injured approximately 100 as they performed the dawn prayers at Hebron's Ibrahimi Mosque on 25 February, which in that year fell on the fifteenth day of the Islamic fasting month of Ramadan. A week later, on 13 April, the brigades struck again, with a bombing at Hadera killing 5 Israelis and wounding 30. Journalists contacted Muhammad Nazzal, the Hamas representative in Jordan, asking him to comment about the threat by the brigades that more attacks of the same kind were on the way. He was quoted as saying that the bombings were part of the response to the Ibrahimi Mosque massacre, and that according to the brigades there would be five such operations in all. In Israel, Shimon Peres, then Israel's foreign minister, protested against Nazzal's statement and demanded that Jordan, which had been negotiating a peace settlement with Israel, should prevent Hamas members from making such pronouncements on its soil.

On Thursday, 14 April, both Nazzal and Ghosheh were summoned to the Jordanian Interior Ministry. The interior minister, Salamah Hammad, told them angrily that the statement made to the press by Nazzal was inappropriate, and that no claim of responsibility for military operations inside Israel should ever be made from within Jordan. The following day, despite it being a Friday, the two Hamas officials were summoned to the Amman Police Department where the interior minister was awaiting them. He informed them that matters had reached a serious level, that Jordan was being subjected to pressure, and that they should immediately surrender their passports to the authorities. The two Hamas officials were given the impression that their lives were in danger. They were told to report any suspicious activity they might observe to a security agent whose name and direct contact number were given to them. An officer accompanied them to their homes to collect their passports, which were returned to them after a short interval.[12]

Tension between Hamas and the Jordanian authorities continued to be exacerbated by a succession of major events on the world stage. First, Jordan and Israel signed the Washington Declaration on 25 July 1994, thus paving the way for the peace treaty between the two countries to be signed on 26 October. Although senior Jordanian officials assured the Hamas leaders in Amman that the treaty would have no repercussions on them, the Hamas leadership suspected that the signature of the treaty signaled the beginning of the end of their sojourn in the country. A number of Hamas officials met Mustafa al-Qaysi to express their concern that the Wadi Araba Treaty between Jordan and Israel appeared to be a prelude to the termination of Hamas's presence in Jordan. Al-Qaysi responded that they had nothing to worry about, so long as their activities, as agreed, were confined to political and media-related matters.

The treaty stipulated explicitly that "the two parties will refrain from any acts of belligerency or hostility, will ensure that no threats of violence against the other party originate from within their territory, and will undertake to take necessary and effective measures to prevent acts of terrorism. They will also refrain from joining any coalition whose objectives include military aggression against the other party ... [and] will abstain from hostile propaganda and will repeal all discriminatory references and expressions of hostility in their respective legislation."[13] Hamas had pledged, and had never broken its promise, not to mount any military action against Israel from Jordanian soil. Nevertheless, Israel, the United States, and, by the summer of 1994, the Palestinian Authority missed no opportunity to interpret any activity on the part of Hamas in Jordan, even a press statement, as an act of hostility against Israel that would undermine international efforts to make peace.

King Hussein was genuinely keen to maintain the presence of Hamas in Jordan because he continued to believe it could be useful to him in terms of regional politics. Apparently, he was confident that Hamas did not pose a threat to law and order in his country, and therefore wished to grasp the opportunity to be seen as making a remarkable contribution to the ongoing peace process by containing Hamas and "domesticating" it. He was soon to discover, however, that this was an impossible mission. The pressure exerted on Jordan by Israel and the United States reached a peak when, on 11 October 1994, the Izzadin al-Qassam Brigades claimed responsibility for the kidnapping two days earlier of Nachshon Vaxman, an Israeli soldier from the Golani Infantry Brigade. The kidnappers, led by Salah Jadallah, a resident of Gaza City, barricaded themselves and their hostage inside a house in the village of Bir Nabala near the West Bank city of Ramallah, demanding the release of Palestinian prisoners in exchange for the safe return of the soldier. The list of prisoners whose release they wanted included Sheikh Ahmad Yassin and two Hezbollah hostages in Israeli detention, Abd al-Karim Ubayd and Mustapha al-Dirani. King Hussein believed he could persuade the Hamas leaders in Amman to secure the release of the soldier. To his utter disappointment, they had neither the will nor the ability to intervene.

In any case, there was little time for negotiations. On the basis of intelligence communicated to them by the Palestinian Authority about the location of the hideout, the Israelis started immediately to plan a rescue operation. The kidnappers had made a video showing Vaxman in his military uniform with his weapon and identity card, which they sent to a local journalist via their contacts in Gaza. When the tape was broadcast, the Palestinian Authority arrested the journalist and interrogated him, extracting from him information that led them to the house in Bir Nabala. The Israeli government deliberately gave the impression it was preparing to meet the demands of the hostages, even claiming that the detainees had already been put on buses and were heading toward the Erez checkpoint in Gaza. According to Sheikh Yassin, the Israelis considered taking him to the hideout in the hope that he might persuade the kidnappers to release their hostage. However, the plan was abandoned for fear that the kidnappers might decide to execute the hostage on seeing the Sheikh. The al-Qassam operation had been intended from the start to be transformed, if and when necessary, into a martyrdom operation. The al-Qassam fighters were determined to succeed in their mission or die. In fact, the Israelis had already decided to use force to free their hostage, and on 14 October, an Israeli Special Forces unit was sent in to rescue him. The raid ended with the killing of the hostage, his kidnappers, and the Israeli Special Unit's commander.[14]

The Palestinian Authority (PA), which Israel expected would assume full responsibility after the arrival in Gaza in July 1994 of its president Yasir Arafat, is believed to have played a crucial role in encouraging both Israel and the United States to target Hamas in Jordan. In response to censure for their failure to fulfill their Oslo obligation of reining in "terrorists" and preventing attacks on Israel, PA officials attempted to divert the blame onto Jordan. The PA's line was that it was doing its best to halt the violence against Israel, but that its efforts were being undermined by the continued hospitality given by Jordan to Hamas's senior leadership, who, it was alleged, exercised control over military operations from their safe haven in Amman.[15] The Palestinian Authority and its President Yasir Arafat went so far as to accuse Jordan of authorizing Hamas military operations against Israeli targets. They claimed this formed part of a deal between Jordan and Hamas to thwart the Palestinian Authority, as a prelude to the recovery by Jordan of control over the West Bank, to which Jordan might even be thinking of adding the Gaza Strip as a bonus. The Americans and the Israelis found it difficult to accept that Jordan could remain faithful to its peace treaty with Israel while still hosting Hamas.[16]

The Abu Marzuq Affair

In early May 1995, the Jordanian Interior Minister Salamah Hammad summoned the members of Hamas's Political bureau for urgent discussions. A meeting took place between Khalid Mish'al, deputy head of the Political Bureau, and three other bureau members: Muhammad Nazzal, Ibrahim Ghosheh, and Imad al-Alami. For whatever reason, Abu Marzuq had intuited what the purpose of the meeting with the Jordanians would be, and had therefore declined to attend. This was Mish'al's first official meeting with the Jordanians. Up to this point, he had maintained a very low profile, carrying out his duties discreetly while staying out of the public eye. The minister received his guests cordially, but informed them that the two non-Jordanian members of the Hamas Political Bureau, Abu Marzuq and al-Alami, would have to leave Jordan by the end of the month. The decision to expel Abu Marzuq and al-Alami was connected to the visit to Amman two weeks earlier of a senior envoy from Yasir Arafat, Abd al-Razaq al-Yahya. In mid-April 1995, Arafat had sent al-Yahya from Ramallah to meet the Hamas leadership in Amman. His mission was to request that Hamas order an end to all forms of violence in Palestine, since continued violence was impeding progress and undermining the Palestinian Authority's endeavor to make territorial gains. The Hamas leaders said they were unable to agree.[17] Subsequently, Hamas asked a number of influential figures in the Jordanian hierarchy to intercede with the authorities, but none were able to influence the decision to expel the two Hamas leaders. The Jordanian government's view was that only by taking this drastic step could it gain relief from the increasing pressure put on it by the United States and Israel. It would have been unthinkable, on the other hand, for Jordan to ask the Jordanian nationals within Hamas to leave the country. This would have been a source of great shame, which King Hussein would have found unacceptable.

A number of incidents irritating to Hamas had taken place since the beginning of the year, starting less than two months after Jordan signed its peace treaty with Israel. The most ominous of these incidents was a clash with the GID over the treatment of a Hamas operative who had been arrested as he arrived from abroad. It should be said that some Hamas officials conceded that the movement had erred in not informing the authorities about the arrival of a new recruit to their operation in Jordan.[18] The operative himself made matters worse by denying under interrogation that he was a member of Hamas, insisting that he had nothing to do with the movement. Isam al-Najjar, the Hamas liaison officer with the GID, who now reported to Musa Abu Marzuq rather than Muhammad Nazzal, was sent to the GID to speak to the detained Hamas operative. His GID counterpart, Amjad al-Hadid, told him he would be allowed to meet with his detained Hamas colleague provided he instructed him to cooperate with his GID interrogators. Al-Najjar agreed and was therefore allowed to see the new arrival. To the horror of the intelligence officer, and before his eyes, al-Najjar did the exact opposite of what he had promised to do: he told the Hamas operative that "Abu Marzuq sends his greetings to you and tells you not to cooperate with these guys." The meeting was immediately terminated and so was further contact between the GID and Hamas's Political Bureau. Following the decision to expel Abu Marzuq from Amman, the GID sought to punish al-Najjar for what they considered an act of betrayal. They ordered him to surrender his passport and family card, and threatened to downgrade him from the status of a full Jordanian citizen to that of a temporary resident with a limited two-year permit. He refused to hand over his documents and was jailed for two nights. The crisis was resolved after the intervention of senior government and Ikhwan officials, but only temporarily. Clearly, the attitudes of the Hamas members involved in this case were anything but wise. If the Jordanian authorities needed a pretext for expelling Abu Marzuq, this incident would have provided one.

On 31 May 1995, Musa Abu Marzuq and Imad al-Alami left Jordan, the first for Yemen and the second for Syria. For more than six weeks Abu Marzuq considered his options. After he left Yemen, he visited a number of countries, including the United Arab Emirates, Iran, Egypt, Sudan, and Syria. The difficulty was for him to find a suitable place for his family. The governments of some of the countries he visited told him that they could not accept him because of his leading position in Hamas. The UAE would not issue his family a residence permit, despite the fact that he himself had permission to reside there, which was in effect tantamount to a refusal.[19] Syria welcomed him as it had also welcomed his colleague al-Alami. However, Abu Marzuq believed that by far the best option for him was to return to the US, where he had previously lived comfortably and prosperously for seventeen years. Only a short while earlier, he had paid a visit to the United States and had found there was apparently no objection to his presence. He and his family had green cards, permitting them to live and work there, and his children, some of whom were American citizens, were at home in the country. Constant movement from one place to another, at a time when his children were growing up and needed stability, had been exhausting for his family. However, his Hamas Political Bureau colleagues unanimously demurred, telling him that in view of the recent hostility of the US to Hamas, returning there was not an option for him. Their view was that it was not rational to go to the United States when its government had earlier in the year designated Hamas a terrorist organization, and had made transactions with it a criminal offense.[20] Abu Marzuq, on the other hand, insisted that his instinct was that if he went to the US all would turn out well. Clearly his instinct failed him. His comrades had feared the worst, and the worst happened.

On his arrival at New York's Kennedy Airport with his family on 25 July 1995, Musa Abu Marzuq was arrested by the FBI.

Undoubtedly, Abu Marzuq's detention was a major blow and an embarrassment for Hamas, placing it in some difficulty. His colleagues in the leadership found his decision to fly to New York indefensible. Many Hamas supporters were impelled to ask why he had not anticipated what might happen.[21] Nonetheless, the movement spared no effort in demanding his immediate release, and alerted the US administration to the serious repercussions that could ensue should Abu Marzuq be handed over to Israel. Hamas, now led by Khalid Mish'al, engaged in a series of public relations and damage limitation measures. Hamas's leaders mobilized their supporters to protest against Abu Marzuq's detention, writing memos and letters to a number of leading politicians and diplomats. On 28 July 1995, they addressed letters to President Clinton, to the US attorney general, and to King Hassan II of Morocco. On 31 July 1995, they sent another letter to the Reverend Jesse Jackson. On 1 August 1995, they wrote to the secretary-general of the Arab League and the Organization of the Islamic Conference. Letters were also sent to an array of personalities and organizations around the world as the crisis continued.

After Abu Marzuq's arrest and incarceration, it seemed as if the American authorities did not know exactly what to charge him with. His immigration status was legitimate, and there was no illegal activity within the US of which he could be accused. The Israelis did not know about the arrest until later. Apparently, however, they had neither demanded the arrest of the Hamas leader nor even considered it an option. Abu Marzuq was initially told he was being held on suspicion of his involvement in activities relating to a foreign terrorist organization, though Hamas was in fact not designated as such an organization until October 1997.[22] It transpired soon afterwards that some elements within the American administration wished to give Israel the opportunity to extradite him. Abu Marzuq believes that the CIA was not in agreement with the measures taken by the FBI against him. He maintains that the CIA knew from the outset that the US had no case against him, but that pro-Israel elements within the FBI were hoping to do a favor for their friends in Israel.[23]

On 28 September 1995, Israel in fact handed the American authorities an official request for extradition, supported with documents totaling more than 950 pages detailing the charges against Abu Marzuq, that Israel wished to bring. His lawyers denounced the proceedings against him as politically motivated, describing them as lacking the minimum requirements of judicial independence and due process of law. The judge presiding over the case, whom the defense lawyers accused of being pro-Israeli, ruled that Abu Marzuq should be extradited to Israel. He was refused the right to appear in court to rebut Israel's allegations against him, and his defense lawyers were denied the opportunity to call their own witnesses. Abu Marzuq appealed against the decision but his appeal was rejected.

Meanwhile, the Jordanian authorities continued to harass Hamas activists in Jordan, apparently aiming to induce more of those who remained, who by now consisted entirely of Jordanian citizens, to leave the country voluntarily. Hamas Political Bureau member Sami Khatir was arrested on 25 December 1995 while walking to his office. He was taken to his house, which was thoroughly searched; his documents and money were seized, and he was detained. During the same period, another Political Bureau member, Izzat al-Rishiq (known by his *nom de guerre* of Abd al-Aziz al-Umari) was also briefly detained.

However, in due course Israel embarrassed its ally, the US government, when it decided that it did not want to extradite Abu Marzuq after all. What triggered the shift in Israel's position was the change of government there. Abu Marzuq suspected that the changing political climate in Israel that had brought about the downfall of the Labor government would work in his favor. Against the advice of his lawyers, he withdrew his appeal against the extradition ruling and, in an official submission dated 28 January 1997, demanded that he be handed over to Israel immediately. His instinct was correct: the Israelis no longer wanted him.[24] On 29 May 1996 the Labor leader Shimon Peres lost the election to Likud's Binyamin Netanyahu, who campaigned against the Rabin-Peres peace program with the slogan "Peace with Security." In his attitude to Hamas, Netanyahu appeared to have learned a lesson from errors of judgment made by his predecessor. Peres had paid a heavy price for ordering the liquidation of Hamas's military commander Yahya Ayyash (the Engineer). Ayyash's assassination on 5 January 1996 triggered a wave of retaliatory bombings between 25 February and 4 March 1996, killing 60 Israelis and wounding many more in West Jerusalem, Ashkelon, and Tel Aviv.[25] Netanyahu was keen to avoid provoking Hamas and therefore reasoned that to continue with the extradition of Abu Marzuq was liable to prove costly. At the very least, he feared it would undermine his efforts to fulfil his electoral promise.

On 3 April 1997, Israel withdrew its extradition request. The US authorities were left with no option but to release Abu Marzuq and deport him. There was one small problem: where was he to go? In a desperate bid to save face, the Americans sent FBI Director Louis Freeh to request permission for Abu Marzuq to go to either Egypt or Jordan, the only two Arab countries that had peace treaties with Israel. Freeh's mission was to ask whichever country would accept Abu Marzuq to accept a set of conditions the Americans wished to stipulate for his release. He was to be barred from visiting Libya, Syria, Iraq, Sudan, and Iran, and had to remain in his new country of residence for at least six months from his date of arrival. He would also be expected to make a statement condemning terrorism; and, finally, he was expected to refrain from political activity. Egypt and Jordan both turned down the offer, saying they did not believe Abu Marzuq would accept any of these conditions and that they had no power to force him to do so. Indeed, Abu Marzuq refused all four conditions but was nevertheless eventually released unconditionally. Continued pressure on Jordan, however, bore fruit, and King Hussein of Jordan agreed to take him back. On 5 May 1997 Abu Marzuq was flown to Amman in a private jet and delivered to the Jordanian authorities.

Jordan had expelled Abu Marzuq in May 1995 as the result of pressure from the United States and Israel, and had passed intelligence information about his activities during his stay in the country to the Americans prior to his detention in New York. Now, ironically, it was Jordan that succumbed to American pressure to take him back. The new director of the General Intelligence Department, Samih al-Battikhi, al-Qaysi's former deputy, who had been appointed on 5 February 1996, could not conceal his anger at Abu Marzuq's return. The first time he met Abu Marzuq, he made it clear to him that he had a month to find another country in which to live. However, when Abu Marzuq visited King Hussein to thank him for his offer of hospitality, in the company of Jordanian Ikhwan parliamentarian Bassam al-'Umush, al-'Umush informed the king that Samih al-Battikhi had given Abu Marzuq a month's notice to quit the country.[26] The king, in the tradition of an Arab tribal chief, told Abu Marzuq that he was in his own country and that he did not have to search for another home. The same hospitality was extended to Abu Marzuq's wife and children, who joined him soon afterward.

Abu Marzuq's release and his arrival in Amman as a guest of the king relieved somewhat the atmosphere of discord that had prevailed as a result of the rapidly deteriorating relationship between Hamas and the Jordanian regime. The past year in particular had not been pleasant for Hamas. Matters had taken a turn for the worse when al-Battikhi was appointed director of the GID. Al-Battikhi had replaced his former superior, al-Qaysi, at the request of Abd al-Karim al-Kabariti, appointed prime minister by the king in early February. Al-Battikhi's critics accused him of having a personal grudge against Islamists in general and Hamas in particular. He went further than any previous director of the GID in the extent of his action against the Islamic movement. His appointment should be put into perspective, however; al-Battikhi had taken charge of the GID in the aftermath of Israel's assassination of Hamas's military commander Yahya Ayyash and the ensuing campaign of bombing against Israel. President Clinton had immediately summoned the top leaders of some 30 countries from the region and beyond, including 13 Arab states, to an emergency summit conference at Sharm al-Sheikh in Egypt to coordinate international efforts to save the peace process from total collapse.

"The Summit of the Peacemakers" on 13 March 1996 was said to have three fundamental objectives. These were to enhance the peace process, to promote security, and to combat terror. In a concluding joint statement on behalf of the participants in the summit, President Clinton announced that they:

... expressed their full support for the Middle East peace process and their determination that this process continue in order to accomplish a just, lasting and comprehensive peace in the region; affirmed their determination to promote security and stability and to prevent the enemies of peace from achieving their ultimate objective of destroying the real opportunity for peace in the Middle East; re-emphasized their strong condemnation of all acts of terror in all its abhorrent forms – whatever its motivation and whoever its perpetrator, including recent attacks in Israel – considering them alien to the moral and spiritual values shared by all peoples of the region, and reaffirmed their intention to stand staunchly against all such acts and to urge all governments to join them in this condemnation and opposition.

He went on to say:

88

To that end we decided to: – Support the Israeli–Palestinian agreements, the continuation of the negotiating process, and to politically and economically re-inforce it; – Enhance the security situation for both with special attention to the current and pressing economic needs of the Palestinians; – Support the continu-ation of the negotiating process in order to achieve a comprehensive settlement; – Work together to promote security and stability in the region by developing effective and practical means of cooperation and further assistance; –Promote coordination of efforts to stop acts of terror on bilateral, regional and interna-tional levels, ensuring instigators of such acts are brought to justice; – Support efforts by all parties to prevent their territories from being used for terrorist purposes and prevent terrorist organizations from engaging in recruitment, supplying arms, or fundraising; – Exert maximum efforts to identify and de-termine the sources of financing for these groups and to cooperate in cutting them off – Provide training, equipment and other forms of support to those taking steps against groups using violence and terror to undermine peace, se-curity or stability....[27]

Observers could not help but conclude that the summit was nothing but a declaration of a war on Hamas, in which Jordan was a key participant whose role in this war would be highly appreciated and closely monitored.

Apparently, in the light of this declaration and Jordan's adherence to it, Samih al-Battikhi, as the new head of the GID, was only doing his job. His attack on Hamas had a number of aspects. First, he authorized his men to harass, intimidate, and frustrate the Hamas leadership and those identified as members of or suspected of associating with the movement. Suspects were intensively interrogated in a bid to assemble as complete a picture as possible of Hamas's operations and support institutions not only locally but also at the global level. Many of these emerged from their interrogations with the impression that the intelligence gathered was not intended exclusively for local consumption. In the light of the Sharm al-Sheikh meeting, this was only to be expected. Hamas sources maintained that at least 100 men suspected of working for the movement were detained and interrogated in 1996 and 1997.[28]

A further tactic employed by al-Battikhi was to silence Hamas officials and prevent them from talking to the media. On occasion, however, they had no choice but to speak out, in defiance of the ban. In late May 1996, the Palestinian Authority arrested hundreds of Hamas members in the West Bank and Gaza, meanwhile putting pressure on the Hamas spokesman in Gaza, Mahmud al-Zahhar, to call for an end to "martyrdom operations," which he agreed to say were a mistake. Khalid Mish'al, who had already become head of the Political Bureau, but whose appointment had not as yet been made public,[29] instructed Ibrahim Ghosheh, Hamas's official spokesman, to issue a statement saying that Hamas's position had not changed and that al-Zahhar was speaking under duress. Al-Battikhi telephoned Ghosheh, verbally abused him, and threatened him that he would be arrested if he spoke again to the media.[30] He did speak again, and was indeed arrested. On 4 September 1997, three explosions in Jerusalem, claimed by Hamas, killed 8 Israelis and wounded more than 170. Reuters contacted Ghosheh for clarification and he affirmed that the Palestinian people had the right to resist occupation. Ghosheh was then detained at the GID headquarters for fifteen days, during which he was totally isolated from the outside world and subjected to intensive daily questioning by up to four interrogators at once.[31]

The Creation of Tension between Hamas and the Jordanian Ikhwan

The Jordanian intelligence chief also schemed to create a rift between Hamas and the Jordanian Ikhwan. This would have had no hope of success had it not been for the crisis the Ikhwan in Jordan were themselves undergoing. A fierce internal power struggle was raging within the Ikhwan, which at that particular moment took the form of disagreement over whether to participate in or boycott the 1997 elections in Jordan. After an internal conference in early 1996, followed by a plebiscite of the membership, the leadership decided to boycott the elections. Three reasons were put forward in favor of the boycott. The first was the government's insistence on applying the election law as amended in 1993, which limited the number of constituencies in which the Ikhwan could stand and debarred them from forging alliances with other political groups. Because of the amendment, the parliamentary share of the Islamic Action Front (IAF), which the Ikhwan had established as their political party in 1992, was reduced from 22 seats in 1989 to 16 seats in 1993. The share of all opposition groups in parliament was halved from 70 percent to 35 percent. The second reason was the wide-scale rigging of which the government was accused during the 1993 election, especially in al-Zarqa Province, one of the strongholds of the Ikhwan. The third and most important reason was the October 1994 Wadi Araba Peace treaty between

Jordan and Israel. The Ikhwan vehemently opposed the treaty but could do nothing about it apart from expressing their objection in the form of boycotting the parliamentary elections.

In reality, the dispute was over more than just this: it was also about power and influence. The Islamic Action Front had begun to pose a serious threat to the authority of the Ikhwan's leadership as represented by its Executive Office. Though there was a degree of overlap, the leaders of the IAF were no longer directly involved in running the Ikhwan itself, although some of them were at various times also members of the Executive Office. Through their political and media activities, the IAF members acquired a level of prestige in the eyes of the public that the Ikhwan had never achieved. Many IAF figures became political celebrities and understandably became the envy of their brethren. Few members of the Executive Office could hide their ambition to share in this fame. Some, however, disliked the fact that the IAF was taking all the credit while the members of the executive office remained hidden from the public eye. For the first time in the history of the Jordanian Ikhwan, the organization effectively had two competing leaderships. The only way the IAF could be brought under control, and its growing power checked, was to sideline it. If the IAF leaders were not permitted to take part in the elections, they would have no public role. This is believed to be one reason the Executive Office pressed hard for an electoral boycott. The other reason was linked to an ongoing internal feud between two groups within the Ikhwan, which became known as the hawks and the doves. The current leadership of the Ikhwan contained predominantly doveish elements, who were accused by the more hawkish members of a tendency toward compromise with the regime and of diluting the values and principles upon which the movement was founded. The hawks, on the other hand, some of whom were theologians and renowned public speakers, had always identified themselves with the Palestinian cause. When Hamas came to Jordan, the Ikhwan hawks pretended to be its guardians, using their ostensible association with it as a source of legitimacy and credibility and eventually as a weapon in their rivalry with the Ikhwan doves.

Hamas's leadership in Jordan, which already had much on its mind, kept clear of all these rivalries. However, it was involuntarily pulled into the dispute because of what seemed to be becoming an argument about priorities. Hamas officials gave the IAF credit for being at the forefront of defending Hamas, and for directing criticism at the Jordanian government for its negative attitude toward Hamas. They suspected, however, that the Ikhwan were gradually being taken over by a tendency whose philosophy was that their organization should focus more on local issues rather than issues of an international nature, including Palestine. This perception alarmed Hamas; never before had any Ikhwan leader in Jordan dared to relegate the Palestinian issue even to second place, let alone demote it to a low position in their list of priorities. The deputy leader of the Ikhwan, Imad Abu Dayyah, was suspected of leading this tendency, whose argument was that since Hamas's field of operation was in the occupied territories, its leadership should be inside Palestine, not in Jordan. Some Ikhwan commentators expressed the opinion that the leaders of Hamas in Jordan should decide whether they wanted to be Palestinian or Jordanian. If the former, then their place should be inside Palestine, but if the latter, they should cease to operate as Hamas from within Jordan.

Such ideas must have been music to the ears of GID director Samih al-Battikhi. They provided him with the incentive to continue with his machinations against Hamas. On 31 August 1996, he instructed his subordinate Amjad al-Hadid to telephone his former Hamas contact Isam al-Najjar to say that al-Hadid wished to see him to give him a message. They had not met for nearly fifteen months since the squabble over the Hamas operative who had arrived unannounced from abroad. Al-Najjar thought that the subject would probably be the resumption of relations between the two sides. He consulted Khalid Mish'al, who said he should keep the appointment in order to find out what the Jordanians wanted. What happened next is disputed. According to al-Najjar's original account, when he arrived at the GID he was arrested and detained for several days, and was released only when two Ikhwan members of parliament, Abdullah al-Akaylah and Bassam al-Umush, appealed to the GID director himself to let him go. Al-Najjar then went to see Khalid Mish'al, breaking down in tears as he described to him what had happened at the GID. He alleged that he was placed in solitary confinement and ill-treated. He claimed he was brought urine to drink and was told it was Amjad al-Hadid's urine. He also claimed that GID agents had smeared his head and body with his own excrement, after tampering with the toilet in his cell to cause a blockage. He was finally forced to kiss the hand of Amjad al-Hadid, and was photographed while doing so. The picture was posted on the ceiling of his cell.[32]

Alarmed and disgusted by what he had heard, Mish'al made a report to Hamas's Political Bureau about al-Najjar's experience. The bureau decided the Ikhwan's Executive Office should be informed. The Executive Office requested a more detailed report and some of its members suggested that the story should be released to the media. Mish'al asked al-Najjar to write a full account. Al-Najjar begged that the matter not be taken further because al-Hadid had warned him that, if any details were leaked to the public, the next time he was detained he would not be released without a permanent physical disability. With a promise that the entire Ikhwan leadership would stand behind him, so that the GID could not harm him further after his story was revealed, al-Najjar was persuaded to write down his account. The report was given to Hilmi al-Asmar, chief editor of the Ikhwan's weekly newspaper, *Assabeel*, and was published on the front page. The account was also sent to a number of well-placed people in the country, including Crown Prince Hassan, who was at the time deputizing for the king during his absence abroad. On the day the story was published, the GID arrested Hilmi al-Asmar at his home. They went also to the home of Isam al-Najjar to arrest him but could not find him. He had already gone into hiding. Hamas then sought and obtained an assurance from Prime Minister Abd al-Karim al-Kabariti that al-Najjar would not be further pursued or harassed by the GID, and should therefore be able to resume his normal life.

Al-Najjar's life never returned to normality. Though the GID did not harass him further, he began to encounter difficulties with his Hamas superiors and colleagues. He started to complain that his superiors had involved him in an unnecessary confrontation with the GID. In the version of events al-Najjar insisted on at this time, Musa Abu Marzuq, as head of Hamas's Political Bureau, had instructed him to tell the detained Hamas operative not to cooperate with his GID interrogators, the event that had begun his troubles. In addition, the current head of the Political Bureau, Khalid Mish'al, had encouraged him to go to see Amjad al-Hadid, which was the occasion of his more recent unpleasant experience. He also blamed Mish'al for insisting that he write the report about his experience in detention and for having it published. His repeated complaints aroused the hostility of the Hamas staff in Amman, whose criticism of him soon turned to threats. To resolve the problem and contain al-Najjar's grievances, the Hamas leadership offered to pay his expenses to go abroad to undertake postgraduate studies. When he refused this, they offered to help him find a good job in one of the Gulf states. He did not want to leave the country, so they found him a position at the newly founded Ikhwan University at Zarqa. Initially, he accepted this offer but then changed his mind and turned it down. Hamas officials concluded he was intent on causing trouble, and their only remaining option was to bring him before an internal Hamas tribunal.

This conduct on the part of Isam al-Najjar gave rise to puzzlement and speculation among Hamas members and in Ikhwan circles. Some thought it was possible that perhaps his entire story was a fabrication. Others suggested that he had been recruited by the GID, and that both his detention and his story of the torture to which he had been subjected were no more than a ploy to cover his mission, which was to cause a split between Hamas and the Ikhwan. Muhammad Nazzal, however, took a different view. He knew al-Najjar quite well because they had worked together a good deal and were both originally residents of Kuwait. Nazzal believed that al-Najjar's persecution story was genuine, and that he might subsequently have been subjected to further pressure from the GID to collaborate. Another possibility was that he might have been motivated by an urge to retaliate against Hamas for allowing such things to happen to him.

An internal Hamas tribunal was set up to hear the charges and countercharges. Al-Najjar was found guilty of fomenting sedition; his membership of Hamas was suspended for a year; and it was ruled that he would be denied future promotion within the organization's hierarchy. He took his case to the assistant secretary of the Jordanian Ikhwan's Executive Office, Yahya Shaqra, whom he told that he had highly sensitive information that the leadership of the Ikhwan should know. When asked what that information was, he said that what he had written earlier about the GID torturing him while in detention was entirely baseless. In effect, he confessed that he had simply made everything up. Shocked by the revelation Shaqra asked him why he had made the allegations in the first place. Al-Najjar then alleged that Khalid Mish'al had ordered him to do so. Al-Najjar went on to say that Mish'al had told him after his release

94

from GID detention that Hamas had a plan to discredit the GID before launching a public campaign against it. As part of this plan, Mish'al had asked al-Najjar to make his allegations of torture against the GID. Referring to the leadership of Hamas, al-Najjar then said to Shaqra that he had highly classified information that would "expose these people for what they are." Intrigued by what he heard, Shaqra promised al-Najjar a hearing before the Ikhwan's Executive Office.

Without returning to the Hamas leadership, or letting Mish'al know, a highly secret Ikhwan committee was set up to investigate al-Najjar's allegations. Headed by Ikhwan deputy leader Imad Abu Dayyah, the committee also included Ikhwan Executive Office members Salim al-Falahat and Haytham Abu al-Raghib, in addition to Yahya Shaqra. When Mish'al learned of this development, he immediately contacted the members of the Ikhwan Executive Office. Mish'al categorically denied the allegations made against him, insisting that al-Najjar was lying and protesting against the Ikhwan's decision to embark on an investigation without referring the matter to him and his colleagues in Hamas. The Ikhwan Executive Office did not accept his protest and continued with their inquiries.

Strictly speaking, the Hamas officials in Jordan were members of the Jordanian Ikhwan, and were supposed to be accountable to its leadership. What should have been a routine matter had turned into a major crisis because for almost five years neither Hamas nor the Ikhwan had paid attention to the rapid transformation undergone by Hamas and to the implications of the change on the relationship between the two organizations. In practice, it was no longer possible for the Ikhwan of Jordan to impose its will on Hamas, which had rapidly become a fully fledged organization within itself. Both sides needed to reconsider their relationship, which could no longer be one of patronage. Perhaps relations between the two needed to be more of a fraternal nature. On the one hand, the Jordanian Ikhwan leaders saw themselves as the ultimate source of authority, viewing those working for Hamas in the country, such as Mish'al and his colleagues, as members of a department within the overall body of the Ikhwan. However, these men did not see themselves as such. They had constituted the senior leadership of Hamas since 1989 and wielded their own authority. On the other hand, while Mish'al and his friends behaved in a highly autonomous way when it suited them, they still believed they had the right to make use of the Ikhwan's premises and facilities and to recruit whomever they wished from within the ranks of the Jordanian Ikhwan. Seen from the Jordanian side, the Hamas leaders were behaving as if their needs and problems had priority over all others. It was a mutual error of judgment to leave issues of authority and jurisdiction unresolved for so long. Inevitably a barrier of misunderstanding arose between the two sides and a climate of mistrust prevailed within the organization as a whole.

Ikhwan leaders such as Abu Dayyah, who agonized over the question of authority, truly believed that an opportunity had opened up inside Palestine for his brothers within Hamas. He did not hesitate to tell Mish'al and his Hamas colleagues that it would be better for them to return to Palestine while the Palestinian Authority was still in its infancy. His view was that they could influence the course of events if they transferred the leadership of Hamas back to Gaza and the West Bank before the Palestinian Authority developed into a powerful entity. However, he was unable to appreciate that there was no practical way for this to happen. He was overly optimistic, believing that Israel would simply allow Hamas to return. He failed to understand that the Palestinian Authority had a degree of influence over who entered or left. He also failed to see that it was the shift of Hamas's leadership from Gaza to the diaspora in 1989 that had saved the movement from total destruction by Israel and its collaborators.

In such a climate it was not difficult for al-Najjar to convince some of the Ikhwan leaders that Hamas had a plan to infiltrate their own organization. He claimed that he had seen an internal Hamas document entitled "The Plan to Infiltrate the Ikhwan." He cited as evidence a series of documents that were circulated in the country while he was in detention at the GID. He claimed that these documents, attacking the Ikhwan's Executive Office, were written and disseminated by the Hamas leaders in Jordan. When the documents first appeared, signed only "Kawadir al-Ikhwan al-Muslimin" (the Ikhwan cadres), the Ikhwan had concluded they were the work of the GID. Al-Najjar also accused Muhammad Nazzal of leaking stories to the press about the internal affairs of the Ikhwan in Jordan. The Ikhwan attempted to maintain absolute secrecy while conducting their investigations. Some of the witnesses brought before them by al-Najjar had been working for Hamas and wanted their involvement to remain secret. However, Hamas's Political Bureau became aware of

what was taking place. The Ikhwan investigation coincided with the holding of an appeals tribunal to hear the objections made by both al-Najjar
and the Hamas leadership against the verdict of the previous tribunal.
Hamas thought the sentence against al-Najjar was too lenient, while al-
Najjar believed he should not have been indicted in the first place. With
new evidence against al-Najjar before it, the appeals tribunal decided he
should be expelled completely from the movement and denied all rights.
The appeal judges were of the opinion that al-Najjar had committed a
major offense by lying about his treatment by the GID. If Mish'al had
told him to lie, something the court was in any case convinced never
happened, al-Najjar should not have listened to him.

The leaders of the Ikhwan, who had promised to protect al-Najjar
while their investigation continued, were infuriated by Hamas's decision
to expel him, and decided to allow him to retain his Ikhwan membership
irrespective of what Hamas might decide. They also criticized the Hamas
tribunal for ruling that al-Najjar should be denied his rights. The Ikhwan
took the view that even if al-Najjar was in the wrong, the best option was
to contain him rather than provoke him further. Al-Najjar was also suspected of disseminating written statements about the internal affairs of
Hamas that revealed confidential information, of publicizing the names of
members and leaders who had not been known to the public, and of accusing senior Hamas leaders of corruption. Certain Hamas leaders were
forced to defend themselves. As a result of the allegations, they were
obliged to produce documents to prove that their houses, which they
were accused of buying with money belonging to Hamas, were actually
purchased with their own money or that of their spouses.

The murky environment created by these allegations encouraged various disgruntled Ikhwan members, who had previously worked for Hamas
and had left following some dispute or other, to become involved in the
affair. One such example was Ibrahim Gharaybah, who had formerly
been a close associate of the Ikhwan deputy leader Abu Dayyah. Gharaybah published numerous articles in the local and regional Arabic press
that criticized or even denounced the Hamas leadership in Jordan. He
had been employed for a short while by a Hamas media project in Jordan,
but his employment was terminated when it was felt he was failing to
perform his functions. He initially published his articles under pseudo-
nyms, but later signed them with his own name. His friend Abu Dayyah

repeatedly asked him to stop, since those who were aware of the friendship between them had begun to suspect that Gharaybah might be expressing Abu Dayyah's views. Eventually, Gharaybah was expelled from the Ikhwan for refusing to halt his activities. As in the case of al-Najjar, many believed Gharaybah's principal objective was to retaliate against his former superiors. In his articles, he insistently argued that Hamas should exist only to the west of the Jordan River, where it properly belonged.

Some leading Ikhwan figures, however, chose to believe the scurrilous allegations made against the Hamas leaders in Jordan and made reference to them when arguing the case for what they believed Hamas's priorities should be. The affair could no longer be confined within the closed circles of Hamas and the Ikhwan, and awareness of it soon spread to a wider public both within Jordan and beyond. In the end, the affair served to accelerate the deterioration of the relationship between Hamas and the Ikhwan. It also provided, though only for a short period, ammunition for those who wished the Ikhwan to recover the political ground taken from it in Jordan by Hamas. It appears, therefore, that the plot initially hatched by GID Director Samih al-Battikhi had achieved at least some of its intended objectives.

FIVE

THE MISH'AL AFFAIR

I send my greetings to the entire Palestinian people; I want to inform them that I am coming to Gaza in the near future.[1]

—Sheikh Ahmad Yassin

I can see the glory of the Arabs shining in your eyes.[2]

—Abdullah Ibn Abd al-Aziz

A Blessing in Disguise

Sheikh Ahmad Yassin had just entered his ninth year of detention when his wife came to visit him on the morning of Tuesday, 30 September 1997. This was to be a fateful day for the sheikh. For some time, he had been allowed visits from his family, relatives, and friends. However, the Israeli authorities had soon forbidden all visitors except for his wife and daughters. It was not easy for them to visit him frequently: sometimes they were only able to come every six months or so. As he became increasingly deaf, he had to communicate with his wife via a third person when she visited, so that nothing they said to each other could be private. On this occasion, he seemed to have had enough of this uncomfortable arrangement. No longer able to bear the pain and the humiliation of having to speak to his wife through the intermediary of a prison guard, he told her never to visit him again. She wept as she returned home. Later the same day, his lawyer arrived to show him a petition the lawyer had prepared for his release. The sheikh understood that the petition bore the signatures of 40 Knesset members demanding his release from prison because of his worsening health condition. He told the lawyer not to pin his hopes on approaches of such a kind, since if he were ever to be released it would be despite the Israelis and not because of them.[3]

The sheikh was counting neither the years nor the days. His sentence was life plus fifteen years. Without a divine miracle, he believed he might never see the world outside his prison cell again. Soon after his incarceration he decided there was no better occupation than to learn the Qur'an by heart. This is something most Islamic prisoners undertake, in pursuit of comfort, peace of mind, and reward in the world to come. He had memorized the entire Qur'an by the end of 1990. He then busied himself by studying a 23-volume encyclopedia of Islamic jurisprudence entitled *Al-Majmu'*.[4] He followed that with the study of a number of basic works on Islamic history and Arabic grammar. In the intervals between his studies, he would perform his *salat* (prayer) and *dhikr* (remembering and glorifying God).[5] He passed hours with his *salat*, reciting four *ajza'* (parts) of the Qur'an each day in the course of his *nawafil* (optional prayers).[6] Until mid-September 1995, he was held at Kfar Yuna prison at Beit Lid in the district of Tulkarm. He was then moved to Tel Mond prison near Kfar Saba, also in the district of Tulkarm, remaining there until the first week of January 1996, when he was moved to a hospital for treatment for pneumonia.

The members and sympathizers of Hamas never ceased to demand the release of the sheikh. To mobilize public opinion in support of this objective they launched the "International Campaign for the Release of Sheikh Ahmad Yassin." This was run by Hamas's media office in Amman and arranged events on 18 May each year in various parts of the Arab world and elsewhere to mark the anniversary of the sheikh's detention. There were real concerns that due to the deteriorating state of his health the sheikh might die in prison. It was clear that the main causes of his decline were abuse during interrogation and unwholesome prison conditions. In a bid to put pressure on the Israelis to free him, senior Hamas figures in the Gaza Strip repeatedly threatened that, should the sheikh die inside the Israeli prison, Israel would suffer a wave of revenge attacks more severe than anything it had seen before. Israel's politicians, however, were not in a frame of mind to listen. Motivated by purely partisan political calculations, they were unwilling even to heed the advice of their own senior intelligence officers, who repeatedly recommended that Sheikh

Yassin should be set free. Their concern was that his death in detention would be the spark for another intifada. In addition, some Israelis were encouraged by what seemed to them the relatively moderate attitude taken by the sheikh toward Arafat's Palestinian Authority. They believed that Sheikh Yassin's release would strengthen the moderate trend within Hamas and could eventually isolate the supposedly more hard-line leadership abroad.[7]

While in prison, Sheikh Yassin had some awareness of what was happening on the outside. Two pairs of fellow Hamas prisoners, working in alternation, provided physical care for him. Each pair of prisoners would serve him for 45 days. When each new team took over, messages would be exchanged. The Hamas leadership chose those who were to assist Sheikh Yassin, by agreement with the prison authorities, after some initial misgivings on the authorities' part. The prisoners of each Palestinian faction elected their own leadership inside the prison, which administered their affairs to the extent the Israelis would permit. The Israeli prison authorities wanted to select Sheikh Yassin's aides but he rejected this, and so did the Hamas prison leadership. The sheikh was uncomfortable with strangers, and the Hamas leadership within the prison was anxious to ensure that those who were with him were trustworthy.

Like the other prisoners, Sheikh Yassin had access to radio and television, though only Israeli channels were allowed. He gathered some information from the news, and the Israeli authorities themselves informed him of other developments. At times of crisis, the Israelis sometimes approached him, hoping he might intervene to stop the violence. In December 1994, the prison authorities allowed Sheikh Yassin a visit from Sheikh Abdullah Nimr Darwish of the Islamic Movement in Israel and Dr. Ahmad Tibi, Yasir Arafat's special adviser. These two visitors, clearly acting at the behest of the Israeli authorities, had come to seek the sheikh's help in locating the body of the Israeli soldier Ilan Sa'adon who had been kidnapped and killed by Hamas fighters in May 1989.

From time to time, the Israeli authorities tried to persuade Sheikh Yassin to appear on television and speak to the press about the need to end the violence. In response he would say: "I oppose the killing of civilians; I do not support it." But he would add: "It is you who force us to do it. You start the killing and retaliation follows. So, stay away from our civilians and we shall stay away from yours." If questioned about the targeting of civilians he would say: "What makes you so sure that civilians were targeted? Perhaps the attacker meant to carry the bomb to a military barracks but it went off on the bus before he arrived." On one occasion, he was asked about the double bombing at Beit Lid on 22 January 1995. This had been so close to where he was held at Kfar Yuna Prison that he heard the explosion from his prison cell. Twenty-two Israeli soldiers were killed and 59 others were wounded.[8] He said: "By Allah, how sad I am." He was asked: "In what way are you sad?" He said: "I am sad because the bloodshed is not over." When they asked him to make an appeal to end these operations, he replied: "But this would not make sense. You should stop the killing first, and then every other killing will stop. Let's keep the civilians out of it. If you agree, we are ready. But do you want me to tell my own people to stop while you are not stopping? That would be illogical."[9] Once, in conversation with Israeli intelligence officers, he proposed a long-term cease-fire of the kind called a *hudna* (truce). This was in 1994, after Hamas launched a campaign of martyrdom operations in retaliation for the massacre of Muslim worshippers in Hebron. The sheikh suggested that the killing could end if the Israelis agreed to a list of conditions. First, they had to cease killing Palestinians. Secondly, they should withdraw to the 1967 borders, thus restoring the West Bank and the Gaza Strip to the Palestinians. Thirdly, they should release all Palestinian prisoners detained in their jails. Fourthly, they should dismantle all the settlements built in the West Bank and Gaza since 1967. If these conditions were met, then, he suggested, Hamas would sign a cease-fire agreement that could last as long as 15, 20, or even 30 years.

Sheikh Yassin had become aware that, since his imprisonment, Hamas had grown enormously. Its military wing, the Izzadin al-Qassam Brigades, had become sophisticated and formidable. However, it had also faced fierce opposition, on a local, regional, and international scale. He was aware that 1996 had been Hamas's toughest year by far since its creation. In both Jordan and Palestine, the movement had taken severe punishment. The death of Yahya Ayyash in January had been a blow, and President Clinton's Sharm al-Sheikh summit of world leaders in March had amounted to a declaration of war on Hamas. In response to the summit, the security forces of the Palestinian Authority, under the command of Muhammad Dahlan in Gaza and Jibril al-Rajub in the West Bank, had begun to detain Hamas's leaders and activists. In Jordan, the authorities cracked down on the movement's leaders and institutions. Finally, the internal crisis and power struggle within the Jordanian Ikhwan took its toll on their ability to support their Hamas brethren.

On that Tuesday, 30 September, at about 8:30 PM, a prison guard asked Sheikh Yassin's two companions to take him upstairs to the office. At first his companions claimed he was not well enough to go and suggested that whoever wished to speak to the sheikh should come to him. The guards insisted, however, until the sheikh felt he ought to find out what the matter was. In the office were three high-ranking police officers and two senior army officers, who made him an astounding offer. They said: "You have a sweet opportunity to go home; do you accept?" "Of course I do," he replied. They went on: "King Hussein has made an approach to Netanyahu: they have agreed that you can go to Jordan, and then whatever you and the king agree on will happen." Sheikh Yassin responded: "No, I only agree to go home. To go to Jordan to work something out with the king will not do; I do not accept." The Israelis seemed eager to release him and did their best to convince him that he need not worry. He still had no idea why this was happening, and was not anxious to ask. The Israelis wanted to put nothing in writing. They claimed that because he would be dealing with the king, he had nothing to fear. Sheikh Yassin insisted. After three hours of wrangling they gave in to his demand and signed their names to a pledge that he would be returned home, after a brief visit to Jordan for a medical check-up and treatment. He then asked for his two companions to be released with him: one of them had finished three years of his sentence of twelve years, and the other had completed five years out of eight. The Israelis agreed to release one of them, Ra'id Balbul, which Sheikh Yassin accepted.

A Jordanian army helicopter flew the sheikh and his companion to the al-Hussein Medical Center in Amman, where he arrived at around two in the morning. Despite the lateness of the hour, he found King Hussein and Prime Minister Abd al-Salam al-Majali waiting for him, with a number of senior Jordanian officials and some representatives of Hamas. He learned later from Hamas officials in Amman that King Hussein had demanded his release. The king had been profoundly angered by the assassination attempt made on the life of Hamas Political Bureau Chief Khalid Mish'al five days earlier in Amman by two Israeli Mossad agents.

Mossad's Botched Adventure

In the early hours of Thursday, 25 September 1997, two Hyundai saloon cars left the Israeli embassy compound in the Rabiyah district of Amman. Their destination was the residence of Khalid Mish'al in Shumaysani. The first car, with a green license plate signifying that the vehicle was a rented car, carried a team of four members of the Israeli Kidon unit.[10] The team consisted of a driver, a guard and two hit men, John Kendall, aged 28, and Barry Beads, 36. The two assassins had entered Jordan a day earlier, traveling on Canadian passports. The second car, with a diplomatic license plate, carried a support team of four Mossad agents, including a medical doctor. The two cars waited until Mish'al left his residence at around 10 AM, in his chauffeur-driven car, with his bodyguard, Muhammad Abu Sayf, and three of his children. Thursday was the first day of the weekend break in Jordan, so the children were not at school. Mish'al's children accompanied their father to his office at the Shamiyah Building in Wasfi al-Tal Street, and were to have been taken from there to the barber for haircuts.

The hired car followed Mish'al all the way to his office while the other car headed toward Makkah Street nearby. As Mish'al left the car and walked toward the entrance of the building, Kendall and Beads rushed up behind him. One of them was carrying a device disguised as a bandage on his hand, and apparently did not notice Mish'al's bodyguard, who was still in the car. The agent carrying the device dashed up to Mish'al, pointing it at his left ear. Mish'al reported later that it felt like an electric shock. It was not clear at the time what exactly the device was. Mish'al survived the attack, and Abu Sayf pursued the two Mossad agents. Meanwhile Mish'al's driver took him quickly up to his office.

Abu Sayf succeeded in apprehending the Israeli agents, after a tough fight and with the help of passersby. He was assisted by Sa'd Na'im al-Khatib, an officer in the Palestine Liberation Army stationed in Jordan, who happened to be close by as the two Israeli agents tried to make their escape. Abu Sayf was bleeding profusely, having been hit on the head with a metal object by one of the agents. The two agents were handed over to the Jordanian police.[11] Abu Sayf told the officer in charge that they were Israeli agents who had attempted to assassinate Khalid Mish'al, the Political Bureau chief of Hamas. The officer sent Abu Sayf by ambulance to al-Hussein Medical Center for treatment. On his way he called Khalid Mish'al's office on his mobile telephone, confirming that he had arrested the two agents and that they were now in police custody.

Meanwhile, Khalid Mish'al sent his children home with the driver and asked an employee to drive him to the home of Muhammad Nazzal, the Hamas representative in Jordan, who had already been alerted and had immediately rushed home. Nazzal immediately summoned the other members of the Political Bureau to an emergency meeting at his house. Nazzal decided to issue a press statement and called Randa Habib, a correspondent with the French news agency (AFP), who in turn contacted the Jordanian information minister, Samir Mutawi'. Mutawi' claimed to know nothing about the incident but promised to make enquiries. He called Habib shortly afterward, and denied that any such incident had taken place, claiming that an argument between Khalid Mish'al and two Canadian tourists who were shopping had developed into a squabble when Mish'al's bodyguard Abu Sayf had begun to harass them. However, AFP carried a statement released by Muhammad Nazzal confirming the assassination attempt.[12] This report soon reached the GID director, Samih al-Battikhi, who purported to be enraged by what he insisted were Hamas's false allegations. Al-Battikhi immediately contacted Musa Abu Marzuq to protest against what Nazzal had said, calling Nazzal a liar. He insisted that according to his own sources what had happened was nothing but an argument between Mish'al's staff and the supposed Canadian tourists.

At Muhammad Nazzal's house, Mish'al described to his colleagues what had happened to him. He said the two men attacked him from behind using what seemed to him to be some kind of sophisticated device. The device did not touch him but made a loud booming sound in his ear, which began to ring. As he described to his Hamas comrades how his whole body had shivered as if subjected to an electric shock, he began to feel dizzy and sick. Realizing that something was seriously wrong with him, his colleagues immediately rushed him to the Islamic Hospital in Amman. He arrived at the hospital at around 1:20 PM, where he began to lose consciousness. Tests conducted on him showed little, except that the level of oxygen in his blood continued to fall, even though he was being given a continuous flow of oxygen. The news of the attack on him had already spread across the country, and leading figures from different political groups including the Jordanian Ikhwan began to arrive at the hospital to see him. The Ikhwan leader, Dr. Abdullah al-'Akaylah, who was also a member of the Jordanian Parliament, began to make calls to senior government officials urging them to inform the king.

While these dramatic events rapidly unfurled, the hit men in police custody continued to claim they were Canadian tourists who had simply been minding their own business when Abu Sayf attacked them without provocation. The police officer in charge, following standard procedure, telephoned the Canadian legation in Amman to report the incident, requesting the immediate presence of a Canadian consular representative. When the diplomat arrived at the police station both he and the police officer were astounded by the insolence of the two detainees. They showed no courtesy to the Canadian representative and refused to accept his offer of assistance, though they continued to maintain that they were Canadian citizens. In view of Abu Sayf's original statement, which he had reconfirmed when he returned to the police station from the hospital, the police officer had his own suspicions regarding the two men. He therefore reported the incident to his superiors at the Interior Ministry, who placed the two men in the custody of the GID for further investigation.

The ranking Mossad official in Amman had been aware of the plot and had been directly involved in its planning and execution. He had already learned from the support unit, whose members had fled the scene to take refuge inside the Israeli embassy, that the mission had gone wrong and that the two agents had been arrested. He telephoned Samih al-Battikhi to tell him that the two men in his custody were his agents and that they should not be harmed. He added that the Israeli government would be in touch with King Hussein shortly.[13] When the affair was brought to the attention of the king, he immediately took charge. The two detained Mossad agents had by then confessed and admitted they had used some kind of poison with the intention of killing Mish'al. King Hussein ordered Mish'al to be transferred to al-Hussein Medical Center, where a team of highly qualified doctors attempted to diagnose his condition and investigate its causes. He also summoned a specialist from the Mayo Clinic in the United States, where he himself had been a patient receiving treatment for cancer. In addition, he informed US President Bill Clinton of what Israel had attempted to do on his country's soil, despite the peace treaty between the two countries. He asked President Clinton to insist that Israel disclose the nature of the poison used in the assassination attempt and provide whatever antidote to it might exist.

Although the Mossad hit men were close enough easily to have shot Mish'al dead, the plan had been to eliminate him silently and without creating an international incident. He was supposed to collapse and die mysteriously. The intention was that a message would be delivered to Hamas, while Israel would have continued to deny responsibility. However, through attempting to avoid an international incident, the Israelis had become involved in another situation of a very embarrassing nature. Israel's aim was now to minimize as much as possible the damage to its relations with Jordan while securing the release and safe return of its agents. Their prolonged detention and interrogation by the Jordanians would probably uncover the local support network for Mossad's operation inside Jordan. The Americans responded to King Hussein's request by insisting that the Israelis should send the antidote to save Mish'al's life. Without this antidote, he could not have survived for long. The effect of the poison was such that without a mechanical ventilator the victim's lungs would collapse the moment he fell asleep or lost consciousness.

On 30 September, five days after the attempt on Mish'al's life, King Hussein addressed a mass rally in the Jordanian city of Zarqa. In his speech, he called on Israeli Prime Minister Binyamin Netanyahu to "come up with a creative initiative and rebuild the bridges of mutual trust by releasing Sheikh Ahmad Yassin and other Palestinian prisoners" held in Israeli detention. In less than 24 hours, the sheikh was on Jordanian soil.[14] While in Jordan, Sheikh Yassin became the focus of world media attention. The episode placed Hamas once more in the spotlight, as well as dampening down for a while the tension that had sprung up between Hamas and the Jordanian regime. Some Hamas leaders consider that the failed Israeli assassination attempt salvaged Jordanian–Hamas relations, which had been on the verge of total collapse. Relations between Hamas and the Palestinian Authority also improved, although initially the Palestinian Authority was jealous because King Hussein had succeeded in securing the release of Sheikh Yassin while it had not been able to do so. The negative outcome, as far as the Palestinian Authority was concerned, was the boost given to Hamas, at a time when the PA and Fatah had striven for two years to marginalize it. On 2 October, the Palestinian President, Yasir Arafat, who had previously been under intense Israeli and American pressure to crack down on Hamas, flew to Amman, where, accompanied by King Hussein, he visited Sheikh Yassin in his hospital room in the presence of several members of Hamas's Political Bureau.[15]

Although grateful for King Hussein's initiative, which had freed the founder of their movement, the Hamas leaders in Jordan were entirely taken by surprise. They had not been consulted over any deal involving the release of Sheikh Yassin. Initially, Jordanian officials denied that there was a deal, insisting that the Mossad agents would be tried in Amman in accordance with Jordanian law for the attempted murder of a Jordanian citizen. However, it became clear that a deal had in fact been made when the Israelis insisted that Sheikh Yassin would not be allowed to return to Gaza unless the two Israeli agents were released. Unknown to Hamas, however, was the fact that King Hussein had been seeking to improve the terms of his initial deal with the Israelis over the affair. Israel accused him of reneging on the original arrangement by asking for the release of other senior Hamas officials held in Israeli jails. Israel refused this, insisting that such a move would only increase the threat of terrorism and at the same time further undermine Israel's demand that the Palestinian Authority crack down on Hamas.

On 5 October, the government of Israeli Prime Minister Binyamin Netanyahu issued the first public statement in which it admitted responsibility for the botched assassination attempt in Amman. However, the statement also defended the Israeli government's "obligation to protect the lives of its citizens, and to fight terror without compromise." As more details emerged, Netanyahu was said by press reports to have approved the assassination plan, which had been devised by Mossad. Israeli government officials were infuriated by a story that appeared in the *Times* of London, alleging that Netanyahu had insisted on the assassination attempt over the objections of Mossad officials. According to the *Times*, Netanyahu wanted revenge for the Hamas bombings and did not particularly care which Hamas official was assassinated. Netanyahu's aides vehemently denied the story, though it only confirmed a statement made on 4 November by the Mossad chief, Danny Yatom. Yatom told an Israeli parliamentary commission of inquiry into the bungled operation that Prime Minister Netanyahu had played a direct role in the attempt to assassinate Mish'al. In his eight hours of testimony, Yatom put the blame on the prime minister for the failed operation, maintaining that Netanyahu had ordered Mossad to assassinate the Hamas leader against Mossad's advice. According to Israeli television, Yatom told the subcommittee of the Knesset Foreign Affairs and Defense Committee that he had been opposed to the plan. Yatom said that he had personally favored a different target in a different continent. However, Prime Minister Netanyahu, Defense Minister Yitzhak Mordechai, and Shin Bet chief Ami Ayalon had decided to target Mish'al because he was a "more qualitative target."[16] According to the Israeli television report, Yatom was annoyed that others were deciding his operational priorities and assessing the merit of his targets.

Nevertheless, on Monday, 16 February 1998, the three-man panel appointed to investigate what had become the most embarrassing affair in Mossad's history cleared Netanyahu of blame for the bungled assassination. The official inquiry into the incident placed much of the blame for the failure of the attack on Mossad, and described the assassination plot as amateurish. On 24 February, Netanyahu accepted the resignation of Danny Yatom, who had been the head of Mossad for two years.[17] It is noteworthy that the Israeli parliamentary investigation was prompted only by the failure of the operation. Its focus was on why the operation failed rather than why it was authorized or who authorized it. In other words, as far as Israel's political establishment was concerned, there was nothing morally wrong with assassinating Mish'al, provided the operation could have remained secret, with no repercussions for Israel. The operation was justified by the simple fact that Khalid Mish'al was, as he was described by the inquiry, "a top-level Hamas leader with direct responsibility for murdering Israelis." Press reports in Israel quoted Cabinet Secretary Danny Naveh, a top aide to Netanyahu, as saying the operation was justified. Naveh added: "It is the responsibility of the government of Israel to protect the lives of its citizens and to fight uncompromisingly against terrorism. Mish'al is regarded as the number one figure in Hamas, responsible for the murder of innocent Israelis." Israeli politicians said they were assured by Mossad that Mish'al had given the order for the two bombings in Jerusalem on 30 July and 4 September 1997, which killed 21 people and for which Hamas claimed responsibility.

Despite Israel's admission of responsibility for the failed assassination attempt, the Jordanian authorities released the two Israeli agents. A Jordanian statement said that "the investigations of the two persons who attacked Khalid Mish'al had proved nothing. No evidence or material proof against them had been found, so they were released and had left Jordan." On the afternoon of 6 October 1997, two Jordanian army helicopters took off from western Amman. One, from al-Hussein Medical Center, flew Sheikh Ahmad Yassin to Gaza. The other, from the nearby GID headquarters, took the two Mossad agents to Tel Aviv. Forty other Palestinian and Jordanian prisoners were freed from Israeli detention as part of the deal.[18] Some Hamas leaders felt that Jordan could have got a better deal, perhaps freeing hundreds of Palestinian prisoners. Others maintained that the Mossad agents should have been prosecuted rather than released. However, the courage, bravery, and wisdom with which King Hussein handled the affair was acknowledged and appreciated throughout the movement.[19]

Several factors had come together to arouse King Hussein's anger and to prompt him to take such decisive action. First, the king wanted all parties to know that Israel's attempt to assassinate Mish'al on Jordanian soil was a serious affront. Apart from being a Jordanian citizen, Mish'al was in the country in accordance with an agreement concluded with Hamas. The king considered the release of Sheikh Yassin a suitable response to Israel's bid to exploit its relationship with Jordan. The so-called warm peace between Israel and Jordan, as distinct from the cold peace that existed between Israel and the rest of the countries in the region, was all that had made the operation feasible. The king also took the view that, out of prison, Sheikh Yassin was more likely to influence Hamas to moderate its position. In prison, his continued incarceration only served to bolster the intransigence of the supposed extremists within Hamas who had been leading the movement since Sheikh Yassin was imprisoned.

A second consideration for the king was that he calculated that if he did not act decisively and firmly, further similar incidents might take place, with grave consequences to the reputation of Jordan as a stable and secure country in the region. He wished to avert any possibility that his country might be destabilized through becoming a battlefield between Israel and Hamas. This was a particular concern in the light of a statement released in the name of Hamas in the aftermath of the assassination attempt that Israel had now extended the battleground beyond Palestine. Thirdly, the king was concerned that if he did not act swiftly against Israel, relations between Jordan and the Palestinians might suffer. The consequences of any such deterioration had the potential to be as serious as the events of Black September and the war between the PLO and Jordan in 1970. By being both firm and decisive, the King silenced rumors claiming that perhaps certain Jordanian official circles might even have been involved in or have known beforehand about the plot. These rumors were prompted by the dismissive response of GID Director Samih al-Battikhi on the first day of the attack.

Yassin's World Tour

Mish'al's miraculous escape and Sheikh Yassin's unanticipated release were seen by Hamas members and supporters as two precious gifts from heaven. Sheikh Yassin returned to Gaza to see for himself what, in his absence, had become of the movement he founded. He found that he was widely regarded no longer as merely the leader of Hamas but also the symbol of resistance and defiance for millions of Palestinians who felt betrayed by the PLO leadership. The rallies organized to celebrate his return home amounted in effect to a plebiscite on the leading position he and his movement had assumed in the Palestinian struggle for liberation from occupation.

The ailments from which the sheikh suffered had grown worse in the eight-and-a-half years he had spent in prison. The leaders of Hamas in Jordan arranged for him to receive treatment in Egypt and then to travel to Saudi Arabia in time for the pilgrimage season. He left Gaza for Cairo on 19 February 1998 and moved on to Jeddah in Saudi Arabia on 4 March. The Egyptian authorities strictly controlled his stay at the al-Galaa Hospital in Cairo. He was permitted no visitors or telephone calls. Egypt's attitude toward Islamists in general and those affiliated to the Muslim Brotherhood in particular was anything but friendly. Unsurprisingly, Sheikh Yassin was anxious to leave. In Saudi Arabia, in addition to performing the hajj, Sheikh Yassin had the opportunity to meet many dignitaries from around the world and to hold talks with his fellow Hamas leaders in the Palestinian diaspora. This was a golden opportunity to strengthen ties between the inside and the outside, to resolve problems and address issues.

The Sheikh had already been aware of the structure and activities of Hamas outside Palestine, but this was his first opportunity to learn the details directly from the members of the Hamas Political Bureau in

Jordan, who joined him for the hajj. He concluded from the discussion that the inside and the outside complemented each other well, and that the inside would be unable to function without the movement's outside component. The outside had provided logistical support, raising funds, establishing political relations, carrying out publicity and promotional activities, and mobilizing the Arab and Muslim masses.[20] Since the Palestinian Authority had come into existence, as the product of the Oslo Accords of 1993, several attempts had been made to drive a wedge between the two wings of Hamas. Israel, the Palestinian Authority, and Jordan had all been active players in this game. The release of Sheikh Yassin ended all speculations as to a rift, and had the effect of consolidating relations between inside and outside.

After performing the rites of the pilgrimage, Sheikh Yassin was received by the acting ruler of Saudi Arabia, Crown Prince Abdullah. The prince showed great respect and evident admiration for the sheikh. He is reported to have said that he could see "the glory of the Arabs" shining in the sheikh's eyes.[21] Immediately afterward, Sheikh Yassin was inundated with invitations from governments in the region. In mid-April 1998, he left Saudi Arabia for Qatar, where he was treated as a guest of honor and received by the amir and top government officials. During his stay, he began to record his "testimony" for the Aljazeera Arabic satellite channel and made several press statements.[22] On 25 April, he criticized the Palestinian Authority for being subservient to Israel and the United States. In an interview with a television station in Qatar, he said the PA did not represent the interests of the Palestinian people but that Hamas had chosen to avoid confrontation with it while continuing its struggle against Israel.

Sheikh Yassin's harsh words for the PA reflected a profound irritation that dated from the aftermath of his departure from Gaza, when a crisis arose between Hamas and the PA. The reason for this was the mysterious assassination of the senior commander of the Izzadin al-Qassam Brigades, Muhyiddin al-Sharif, on 29 March 1998.[23] The PA hastily accused al-Sharif's own comrades within Hamas of liquidating him over some financial dispute. A number of Hamas activists were arrested and tortured to make them confess to the killing of their colleague. The PA failed to indict any of them and could not substantiate its allegations against Hamas.[24] In turn, Hamas accused Israel of assassinating al-Sharif, with the assistance of some elements within the PA. Leaflets to this effect were distributed in various parts of the territories, especially within the Islamic University in Gaza, and al-Najah and Birzeit Universities in the West Bank. The PA responded with raids on the three universities to seize publicity material. Several student leaders who sympathized with Hamas were arrested, and some were tortured. On 9 April the senior Hamas leader Dr. Abd al-Aziz al-Rantisi was detained and a day later another Hamas leader, Dr. Ibrahim al-Maqadmah, was detained when his house was raided.

On 28 April, Sheikh Yassin arrived in Tehran for what was virtually a state visit to the Islamic Republic of Iran. Received by its highest leadership, he praised "Iran's support for the Palestinians' struggle against Israel." He was quoted in the international media as saying that the Palestinians would not cease to fight Israel until their lands were liberated. In the first week of May, after his visit to Iran, he went to the United Arab Emirates. This coincided with the conclusion on 5 May of peace talks in London, attended by Yasir Arafat and Binyamin Netanyahu and hosted by British Prime Minister Tony Blair and US Secretary of State Madeleine Albright. These talks made little progress and were dismissed by Sheikh Yassin as futile "because of the bias displayed by Britain and the United States." He said the London talks were designed to waste time and mislead international public opinion. His statements in Doha, Tehran, and Abu Dhabi could not have come at a worst time for Arafat, who had already been angered by the successful public relations exercise in which Hamas was engaged. The respect and hospitality Sheikh Yassin was receiving from various governments and the attention he had from the international media annoyed Arafat.

It transpired soon afterward that Arafat had attempted to curtail Sheikh Yassin's tour. The Muslim community of South Africa exposed Arafat's machinations. A number of Muslim groups in South Africa had invited Sheikh Yassin to visit the country. He was due to arrive in Johannesburg on Friday, 8 May 1998, and travel to Cape Town on Sunday, 10 May, as the guest of Muslim organizations in the country, including the Muslim Judicial Council. The proposal that he should visit South Africa had been mooted when he met two Muslim South African cabinet ministers in Saudi Arabia during the hajj. Yasir Arafat's personal friendship with the leaders of South Africa's ruling African National Council enabled him to block the project. On 10 May, while visiting Kuwait, Sheikh Yassin was informed that the South African government had barred him from the country. His response was that he continued to respect the South African president, Nelson Mandela, and would be happy to visit the country on another occasion. The BBC quoted a spokesman for the South African government admitting that the Palestinian Authority had expressed its reservations to South Africa over the proposed visit by Sheikh Yassin.

Iraq, Jordan, and Lebanon were the three other countries that succumbed to pressure from Arafat and denied Sheikh Yassin entry. The political leaders of those countries may well in fact have been anxious about the long-term impact of Sheikh Yassin's visit, and may simply have seized on Arafat's approach as an excuse to ban the Hamas leader. Jordan and Lebanon had large Palestinian populations that were eager to meet the sheikh, and could have become restive under his influence. Iraq's Palestinian population was also sizeable. The refugees in particular saw in the small quadriplegic figure of the half-blind, half-deaf, and wheelchair-bound sheikh an image of their own suffering and defiance. They had languished, rotting in their camps, hoping that one day they could return to the homes from which they or their parents were driven half a century ago. Sheikh Yassin's persistence and determination in the face of his personal adversity made the dream of return seem more realizable.

Elsewhere, however, the Sheikh found a welcome. In Kuwait, Arafat had no influence. Kuwaitis in general loathed Arafat because of his support for Saddam Hussein's invasion in 1990. Hundreds of thousands of Palestinians were expelled from Kuwait at the end of the Gulf war in 1991. In this oil-rich emirate, Sheikh Yassin held talks with the ruler Sheikh Jabir al-Ahmad al-Sabah, and the Crown Prince Sheikh Sa'd al-Abdallah al-Sabah. The sheikh offered to mediate with Iraq to secure the release of Kuwaiti detainees in Iraq, but the Iraqis refused his offer.

In Yemen, the next stop in Sheikh Yassin's tour, the situation was more delicate. On 17 May 1998, he was received by President Ali Abdullah Salih, who was a good friend of Yasir Arafat. The Yemeni leader called for unity among the Palestinians, adding that factional disputes would only benefit Israel. Clearly, President Ali Abdullah Salih was aware of the tension between Hamas and the Palestinian Authority over the sheikh's tour. Sheikh Yassin used the occasion to reiterate Hamas's determination to continue its struggle until the Palestinian people achieved their legitimate rights. Many thousands of Yemenis and Palestinians living in Yemen attended a rally in honor of Sheikh Yassin. The sheikh also received a delegation from the women's section of the Yemeni Islamic movement, who came to pledge their homage and express support. On Thursday, 21 May 1998, Sheikh Yassin arrived in Damascus, where the Syrian authorities received him graciously. He spoke at a rally attended by many thousands of Palestinian refugees, telling them that all the countries he had visited so far had expressed their support for Hamas's struggle to liberate Palestine.

The last leg of Sheikh Yassin's four-month circuit was in Sudan, where he arrived on 30 May. The speaker of the Sudanese parliament, Hasan al-Turabi, acclaimed him as representing "the pulse of the Islamic jihad for the restoration of the rights of the Palestinian people." During his one-week official visit he was received by the Sudanese leadership and also had ample time to meet with fellow Hamas leaders, who came from Jordan and elsewhere outside Palestine to hold discussions with him on organizational matters. His visit to Sudan was prolonged by two weeks to give him sufficient time for these talks.

With his tour of the Arab world complete, problems began to emerge when Sheikh Yassin wished to return to Palestine as he had been promised. The Egyptian authorities refused to grant him an entry visa to Egypt, because they were uncertain whether the Israelis would allow him back into Gaza. The Egyptians did not wish to find him permanently resident as a deportee on their soil. The Israeli government, meanwhile, was attempting to decide whether it would be more dangerous for Israel to allow the sheikh back in or to ban him from returning. In the end, the latter option was deemed the more dangerous; Sheikh Yassin's extremely successful public relations tour had only served to increase his already immense prestige. Prime Minister Netanyahu decided it would be better to confine the sheikh to the Gaza Strip, where he would be less able to boost the global influence of Hamas than if he were to continue his tour of Arab and Islamic countries. On Monday, 22 June 1998, Sheikh Yassin was allowed to enter Egypt, where he was admitted once more to Cairo's al-Galaa Hospital for medical tests. As before, the authorities strictly supervised him, allowing no visitors or telephone calls. On 24 June 1998, four months and five days from his departure date in February, he finally returned to Gaza by way of the Rafah crossing.

Both the leaders of Israel and many outside observers speculated that the main purpose of Sheikh Yassin's tour had been to raise funds. The sheikh's aides and other Hamas figures in Gaza and in Jordan maintained that this was not so. Dr. Mahmud al-Zahhar described the allegations as "Israeli propaganda." Speaking to journalists following his arrival in Gaza, Sheikh Yassin said he had been dismayed by this speculation. He said that the countries he had visited had invited him, and that the original purpose of his journey to Egypt was to receive medical treatment. He added that he had used his tour to highlight the plight of the Palestinian people and to ask for support for them. He emphatically denied he had been raising funds, adding: "I did not ask for any money; I asked only for vigorous support from those I met." Most of the countries that received him would have been embarrassed if he had attempted to raise funds, given the delicate status of Hamas in the context of the global consensus against terrorism. Only a year earlier, the leaders of most of the countries visited by Sheikh Yassin had been in Sharm al-Sheikh, listening to President Clinton dictating the new rules of engagement in the Middle East. Hamas had topped the agenda at that meeting as a proscribed terrorist organization.

Though Sheikh Yassin maintained that his tour had not been deliberately intended to raise funds, it in fact released a torrent of financial support for Hamas. This was how the royal family in Saudi Arabia, the sheikhs of Qatar and Kuwait, the rulers of the United Arab Emirates, and the leaders of Iran expressed their sympathy and support for a movement they admired and respected. Hamas's image had been hugely enhanced by the movement's steadfastness in recent years in the face of an American-led global campaign against it. In the face of would-be crushing blows, Hamas had refused to modify its stance in the slightest toward compliance. From the first mass arrests of its members in 1988 to the attempted assassination of Khalid Mish'al nine years later, Hamas continued to embody that revival of Arab glory that Crown Prince Abdullah Ibn Abd al-Aziz saw in the face of Sheikh Ahmad Yassin. Speaking privately, where their words would not be reported to the US administration, most Arab and Muslim leaders, though they could do little, would express sentiments of the utmost respect for Hamas.

The other factor that served and still serves Hamas well is the reputation of its leaders and activists among the Palestinians for asceticism, altruism, dedication, and honesty. This is not a political strategy but an attitude that lies at the heart of Islamic values. If this attitude has political utility, it is an incidental effect and not its objective. The plight of the Palestinians, whom Hamas endeavors to help, has far-reaching political ramifications and is the result of a profound political problem. Hamas's altruism is motivated by the principle that the world belongs to God, that He gives wealth to whom He wishes and denies wealth to whom He wishes, and that all those that earn wealth in this life shall be brought to account on the Day of Judgment. Such a doctrine renders personal wealth a burden rather than a benefit. The true benefit, therefore, would be to spend more in order to help those in need. Not only does this offer relief from the burden of wealth, but in reality brings unlimited rewards. Hamas's embodiment of this ethic offers reassurance to donors that their money is in good hands. For example, when Sheikh Yassin returned to Gaza, his Hamas comrades suggested a monthly stipend for him equivalent to one thousand US$1,000. He refused to take more than the equivalent of $600 because he believed he did not need more to live comfortably. Sheikh Yassin's example was followed throughout the ranks of the movement. No one joins Hamas to make money or has become rich by virtue of their position within it.

Finally, donors were aware that only a small fraction of the money raised by Hamas would be used for military purposes. Most of the money raised would be channeled toward the social and educational institutions that, together with the United Nations Relief and Works Agency (UN-RWA) and a handful of NGOs, shouldered the burden of keeping some semblance of Palestinian society in existence. Hamas had established and run a range of educational institutions ranging from kindergarten to the university, as well as healthcare institutions from small rural clinics up to the multi-disciplinary general hospital, and social institutions from orphanages to vocational training centers. All of these institutions rendered their services to the public free of charge. The movement also established an extensive network of charities that delivered urgent assistance to hundreds of families who had been left without breadwinners. In contrast, senior Palestinian Authority officials were seen to be paid unreasonably high sums. Meanwhile, ever larger numbers were employed in the expanding security services, whose task was to control the occupied Palestinians on behalf of Israel. Additionally, the PA also maintained a vast bureaucracy, which secured the loyalty of its employees by lifting them above the breadline at which most Palestinians existed, and at the same time served to increase the disparity of economic means between Palestinians.

SIX

OUT OF JORDAN

We did not choose to leave Jordan... We were deported... We were taken from prison in shackles straight to the airport and onto the plane.[1]

—Khalid Mish'al

Even if you were to abandon me in the alleys of Bangkok, I should not put my name to such a humiliating statement.[2]

—Ibrahim Ghosheh

Wye River

On 23 October 1998, when Yasir Arafat and Binyamin Netanyahu signed a deal they had negotiated over nine days at the Wye River summit, the peace process between the Palestinian Authority and Israel had been virtually in suspense for more than a year and a half. The deal was brokered by the United States, whose president, Bill Clinton, attended many of its rounds of negotiations and finally witnessed the signing of the memorandum, at which King Hussein of Jordan was also present. The talks opened on 15 October but little progress was made until 20 October. At this stage, the obstacles had seemed insurmountable. Yasir Arafat was under pressure from the Americans to agree to a series of radical measures to stem Palestinian terrorism, which was Israel's condition for any further redeployment. Fearing the collapse of the talks, President Clinton sought the assistance of King Hussein, who had been in the United States since July, undergoing chemotherapy treatment for cancer at the Mayo Clinic in Minnesota. The Americans trusted that the king could "help bring home to the two delegations the importance of taking the tough choices for peace."[3] Finally, it was agreed that the PA would step up its efforts against alleged terrorists and confiscate illegal weapons, as well as removing phraseology explicitly hostile to the existence of Israel from the Palestinian National Covenant. In exchange Israel would agree to redeploy from a further 13 percent of the West Bank, release several hundred Palestinian prisoners, allow the Palestinian airport in Gaza to open, and provide safe passage for Palestinians to move between the West Bank and the Gaza Strip.[4]

The Jordanians celebrated the deal as their own, regarding King Hussein's effort to bring the two parties to an agreement as pivotal. When Hamas declared its opposition to the agreement, saying that if implemented it would be likely to stir up internal conflict between the Palestinians, the Jordanians were, unsurprisingly, deeply offended. King Hussein was personally upset when Sheikh Ahmad Yassin, for whose release from Israeli detention he took the credit, described the signature of the Wye River Memorandum as an act of treason, and suggested it would cost the Palestinians more than they would gain. Sheikh Yassin went on to issue a warning that any new measures against Hamas would be likely to restrict only temporarily the activities of its military wing, the Izzadin al-Qassam Brigades.

Hamas's criticism of the deal could not have come at a worse time. Relations between Hamas and Jordan were already under enormous strain. In addition, the PA had for some time been pressing Jordan to take action against the Hamas leaders in Amman, whom they believed to be the main obstacle preventing them from containing Hamas inside the West Bank and the Gaza Strip. In April 1998, while Sheikh Yassin was on his tour of Arab and Islamic countries, King Hussein received a formal complaint, by no means the first, from Yasir Arafat. Arafat drew attention to reports in the Jordanian media that quoted statements by the Hamas leaders in Jordan about the dispute between Hamas and the Palestinian Authority over the assassination of Muhyiddin al-Sharif.[5] King Hussein subsequently sent a letter to Prime Minister Abd al-Salam al-Majali in which he referred to "attempts by the local media to sabotage relations between Jordan and the Palestinian Authority." In an indirect ultimatum to Hamas, the King's letter re-emphasized Jordan's full recognition of the PA as the sole legitimate representative of the Palestinian people and Jordan's wholehearted support for Palestinian national aspirations.

After signing its own peace treaty with Israel, Jordan had ceased to allow Hamas spokesmen in Jordan to issue statements about its military activities inside Palestine. The PA had striven to obtain a similar ban on Hamas statements pertaining to its PA affairs. During the Muhyiddin al-Sharif affair, Arafat and his aides were angered by what they saw as Jordan's refusal to support their version of who was responsible for the murder of al-Sharif in late March 1998. King Hussein's letter to his prime minister was intended not only to silence Hamas spokesmen in Jordan but also to rebuke Jordanian officials who had earlier said the kingdom would not interfere in internal Palestinian politics. The message was apparently also meant to be leaked to the local press, who had failed to be convinced by the Palestinian Authority's version of the story.

Soon after the signature of the Wye River Memorandum, the leaders of Hamas in Jordan sensed a marked change in the attitude of the Jordanian authorities toward them. In hindsight, Wye River represented a watershed: it signaled the beginning of the end of the Hamas presence in Jordan. An early indication of this change came when the Hamas spokesman, Ibrahim Ghosheh, was summoned to the GID to be questioned about remarks he was quoted by the press as making at a seminar organized by the Jordanian Ikhwan at their headquarters in Amman. He was interrogated by GID Deputy Director Sa'd Khayr, who was furious that Ghosheh had criticized the Wye River deal despite earlier warnings to Hamas members in Jordan not to make any public statements about it. Ghosheh's defense was that he had supposed the meeting was private and that he was unaware that journalists were present.[6]

The renewed harassment of the leaders and activists of Hamas in Amman by the authorities prompted Khalid Mish'al, the head of Hamas's Political Bureau, to express his concern. He himself had a taste of this harassment when on 31 October 1998 he was stopped at the Jordanian frontier on his way to Damascus. He was obliged to return to Amman after being held for more than an hour, while he was treated discourteously and threatened that if he went to Damascus he would not to be allowed back into Jordan. He had intended to take part in a meeting of Palestinian factions in Damascus to discuss the repercussions of the Wye River agreement. In the same week, the Jordanian authorities also prevented Muhammad Nazzal, then the Hamas representative in Jordan, from leaving the country. He had intended to travel to Doha, where he had been invited to take part in a live discussion on Aljazeera TV on the security aspects of the Wye River agreement.[7] In a statement in November 1998 to the Jordanian weekly *Al-Urdun*, Khalid Mish'al complained that some members of the Hamas leadership in Jordan had been subjected to a campaign of harassment since the signing of the Wye River Memorandum. He also disclosed the threats made to prevent the return of Hamas leaders if they traveled outside the country.[8] In December, Khalid Mish'al, Ibrahim Ghosheh, and Musa Abu Marzuq were prevented from flying to Damascus, where they had been due to attend a major conference on 12 and 13 December. This had been organized as a protest against the meeting in Gaza scheduled for 14 December, when President Clinton was to address the Palestine National Council at a meeting convened to repeal the articles of the Palestinian National Charter denying Israel's right to exist.

During the same period, rumors circulated to the effect that Hamas's Political Bureau had decided to transfer its offices and staff from Amman to Damascus. The newspaper *Al-Quds*, which is published in the West Bank, quoted anonymous sources as saying that Musa Abu Marzuq had already held talks with Syrian officials in Damascus who had given Hamas the green light for the transfer. Khalid Mish'al denied there was any such intention. In a statement to the Jordanian weekly *Al-Majd,* he said: "I am a Jordanian. I do not ever think of leaving the homeland."[9]

A Fraternal Crisis

In fact, more people than Khalid Mish'al might have imagined were already querying the appropriateness of Hamas's link with Jordan. These included some members of the Ikhwan's senior leadership. After Mish'al was prevented from traveling to Damascus, he convened an emergency meeting with the Jordanian Ikhwan to discuss the issue. This took place at the house of Abd al-Majid Dhunaybat, the Ikhwan's senior figure (al-Muraqib al-'Amm). For the Ikhwan, Executive Office members Haytham Abu al-Raghib and the Dhunaybat's deputy, Imad Abu Dayyah, attended. On Hamas's side, Mish'al was accompanied by Muhammad Nazzal and Ibrahim Ghosheh. The Hamas officials were dismayed when Imad Abu

Dayyah told them that in his view it was time for the movement to reconsider its activities outside Palestine. He suggested that the leadership should return to the inside, since it no longer needed to remain in exile. He said that a new reality was crystallizing inside Palestine, and a political entity was under construction there, whether people liked it or not. It was therefore essential for Hamas's leadership to be inside rather than outside Palestine. He went on to stress that it was no longer acceptable that Jordanian citizens should lead a Palestinian organization and that those leaders of Hamas who had dual status as Jordanians and Palestinians should decide where their loyalties lay. It was time to choose whether to be Jordanian or Palestinian. Since none of the Ikhwan leaders present dissented from Abu Dayyah's formulation, the Hamas delegation was obliged to conclude that this was now the Ikhwan's official position.[10] For the Hamas group, it was a shock to hear such language from a leading member of the Ikhwan, an organization that had played a pivotal role in creating Hamas and in supporting it. However, during much of the 1990s, a group had been forming within the Jordanian Ikhwan that favored an effective separation between the Palestinian Ikhwan, or Hamas, and the Jordanian Ikhwan. This faction welcomed the apparent success of the peace process, which held out the promise of Palestinian statehood. When the Wye River Memorandum was signed, this faction believed that the direction of events was toward the early establishment of Palestinian statehood, so that the Hamas leadership no longer needed to remain in Jordan.

From the beginning of 1999, Hamas's operation in Jordan gradually lost its backing from the Jordanian Ikhwan. GID Director al-Battikhi's plan to drive a wedge between the Ikhwan and Hamas seemed to have worked well. Ibrahim Ghosheh reported that senior Islamic Action Front officials began to show discomfort whenever he passed through their office, which he shared. One IAF official reportedly complained that Khalid Mish'al was causing embarrassment. GID Director Samih al-Battikhi had told a number of senior IAF members that Mish'al had been planning military operations against Israel from his office in Amman. It appeared to Ghosheh that some IAF figures "believed Al-Battikhi, and were being taken in by his schemes."[11] King Hussein was terminally ill with cancer, and al-Battikhi was emerging as the most powerful man in Jordan. It was rumored that he played a pivotal role in the reshuffle within the royal family, when King Hussein's eldest son Prince Abdullah replaced the king's brother, Prince Hassan, as heir to the throne. For some months following the death of King Hussein on 7 February 1999, al-Battikhi seemed to almost have a free hand to run the country.[12]

Binyamin Netanyahu's defeat by Ehud Barak in the Israeli election of 17 May 1999 was seen in some Palestinian circles as ushering in new hopes for peace and reconciliation. Barak was a candidate as much favored by the PA as by his own Israeli supporters. The PA genuinely believed that Barak was an apostle of peace, whose mission was to end the conflict. It was, after all, in anticipation of his arrival, and after considerable pressure from the Americans, that Yasir Arafat decided to put on hold the declaration of Palestinian statehood he had previously set for 4 May 1999. In hindsight, it can be conjectured that Barak's election prompted Jordan's decision to clear the way for the PA by silencing Hamas in Jordan for good. All that remained was the question of how and when.

For several months, the PA, Israel, and the United States had been putting pressure on the Jordanian government in this direction. Meanwhile the Jordanian authorities had been attempting to make use of the Jordanian Ikhwan to achieve their anti-Hamas goal. A number of mysterious maneuvers took place in the summer of 1999. A further series of messages signed by the supposed "Hamas Cadres" was published in the local press, which were in effect a smear campaign against the leadership of Hamas in Jordan. Hamas suspected that these four press releases, one of which was given prominence in a leading daily newspaper, might have been the work of Isam al-Najjar, whom the movement had earlier expelled because of the major rift he caused between Hamas and the Jordanian Ikhwan. Hamas leaders also thought the GID might have been directly involved in the orchestration of a campaign to discredit the Hamas Political Bureau in prelude to a final onslaught. The main theme of the smear campaign was that the Hamas leaders in Jordan were corrupt and authoritarian. Because many of them had known each other in Kuwait before Saddam Hussein's invasion in 1990, they were accused of nepotism and of centralizing power in the hands of a small group that excluded outsiders. As in previous leaks to the media, perhaps from the same sources, the names of certain Hamas activists who had hitherto been unknown to the public were published in the press. Some of these activists were also members of the Jordanian Ikhwan. The revelations aggravated further the hostility between the Ikhwan and Hamas, which had been accused by some Ikhwan leaders, as well as by GID officials, of recruiting Ikhwan members with the objective of infiltrating the Ikhwan and eventually running it for their own purposes. Finally, in July, an article appeared in *Al-Masa'iyah*, Jordan's evening newspaper, which said that Hamas had refused to change its ways and would therefore be expelled from Jordan.[13]

The Onslaught

Toward the end of July 1999, Ibrahim Ghosheh was summoned to the GID. When he arrived, he was surprised to be given an unusually friendly reception. He was even given a permit to park his car inside the courtyard of the GID building. To his puzzlement, a GID official asked him why members of Hamas's Political Bureau had not been visiting Iran. "Is there a problem between you and Iran?" he was asked. The significance of this visit by Ghosheh to the GID, and the implication of the question put to him, would become clear a month later. On 28 August 1999, the three senior Hamas officials in Jordan—Khalid Mish'al, Musa Abu Marzuq, and Ibrahim Ghosheh—in fact began a planned official visit to the Islamic Republic of Iran. It appeared that this was the moment for which the GID had been waiting.[14] Two days after the Hamas group had left Jordan, at 3 PM on Monday, 30 August, Jordanian security agents raided and closed down several Hamas offices in Amman, and 16 people working for the movement were arrested for questioning. The doors of the offices were sealed to prevent further access to them.

Five Hamas offices were raided simultaneously. One of these was that of a public relations company called the Contemporary Center for Information and Consultancy, which was used as a base by Muhammad Nazzal, the Hamas representative in Jordan. The second was that of Musa Abu Marzuq, who, since his release from US custody in May 1997, had been the deputy head of Hamas's Political Bureau. The third office belonged to Ibrahim Ghosheh, the movement's official spokesman. The fourth was that of Khalid Mish'al, the head of the Political Bureau, which was actually at his own house, fortified and placed under surveillance since the attempt on his life by Mossad in 1997. The fifth office was that of *Filastin al-Muslimah*, the monthly magazine that was Hamas's official organ. This was also the headquarters of the Hamas media operation, headed by Political Bureau member Izzat al-Rishiq. All the offices were subjected to a thorough search lasting several hours, and documents, computers, discs, and electronic storage facilities were seized. All personnel present at the time were detained. Muhammad Nazzal has provided an account of events:

When the offices were raided I was at home busy arranging things at my new residence. Izzat [al-Rishiq] was not in his office either. I was eating lunch when my secretary called. I was at a new house and he did not know its telephone number, so he called me on the mobile phone of someone who was with me. He said that the State Security Tribunal general prosecutor was there and wanted me to come. I said: "Why does he need me there?" He replied: "Because there is a warrant to search the office and they want you to be here as you are the owner." I had misgivings: why would they insist on my presence? I was getting ready had not yet decided whether to go or not when the brethren called to tell me that all our offices had been raided. I realized this was not just a matter of searching the premises, and decided that it would be better not to go in person, so as to leave myself some room for movement and time to think. I decided that if I went I would surely be detained. Then a GID officer called me on the same number and spoke to me aggressively. He insisted I should be there, as if I did not come the office could not be searched but would remain occupied indefinitely by the security agents. I was not deceived, as I knew already they were search-ing the other offices while the brethren were away in Tehran. All they wanted was to arrest me. Now we know that their plan was to arrest and detain all the members of the Political Bureau before expelling them from Jordan. As for the staff, they took them hostage. They were remanded in custody until those who were still on the run had been arrested and those outside Jordan had been advised not to return.[15]

On 31 August the authorities issued arrest warrants for the six senior Jor-dan-based Hamas leaders, the three in Tehran plus the three who were still in Amman: Muhammad Nazzal, Sami Khatir, and Izzat al-Rishiq. Sami Khatir was arrested on the day of the raid, while Nazzal and al-Rishiq went into hiding. The government announced that the six men were wanted for belonging to an illegal organization. The measure an-gered both Hamas and the Jordanian Ikhwan. In Gaza City, Sheikh Yassin condemned the action, noting that it came days before US Secretary of State Madeleine Albright's visit to the region. He described it as part of a campaign "to pressure Hamas to join the process of political settlement, which we regard as intended to damage the Palestinian cause, and protect Israeli interests in the area." He called on Jordan's King Abdullah to "halt this campaign, and work at consolidating brotherly ties with Hamas, and the Palestinian people, for the good of the Palestinian cause as a whole." In Amman, the Jordanian Ikhwan organization issued a press release condemning the raids and describing the crackdown as an insult to "the feelings of Jordanians, Arabs and Muslims who consider Hamas to be the vanguard of the Arab nation in fighting the occupation."

Imad al-Alami, another Political Bureau member currently based in Damascus, joined the three Hamas leaders stranded in Tehran for emergency talks. They were unanimously of the opinion that they had no option but to return to Amman. Their first priority was to clear their names. The Jordanian authorities had claimed they were engaged in illegal activities in Jordan, and that arms had been found in their possession.[16] Unless they went back, they argued, the accusations would stick to them forever and they would be treated as fugitive miscreants, despite having committed no crime. To reassure them they were making the right decision, they decided to consult more broadly. Mish'al, Abu Marzuq, and al-Alami therefore flew to Damascus, while Ghosheh remained in Tehran.

Meanwhile, Muhammad Nazzal, who was in hiding, communicated with his colleagues in Tehran, who advised him to surrender to the authorities together with Izzat al-Rishiq. He did not like the idea and voiced his objection to it, but eventually agreed provided it could be done in what he described as "a dignified manner." On Saturday, 4 September, he and al-Rishiq agreed to meet at the Ikhwan's head office in Amman, where a rally in support of Hamas was being organized. The idea was for him to deliver a speech and then be arrested. This plan was devised in consultation with Abd al-Majid Dhunaybat, al-Muraqib al-'Amm of the Ikhwan, and the Ikhwan secretary-general, Jamil Abu Bakr.

When Nazzal and al-Rishiq arrived at the rally, other members of the Ikhwan's Executive Office, including Imad Abu Dayyah and Salim al-Falahat, objected to Nazzal's request to make a speech because "such a step would amount to a blatant provocation of the government and the regime." This was a further demonstration of the division among the Jordanian Ikhwan leaders on how to deal with the crisis. Abu Dayyah and al-Falahat seemed to wield great influence and were easily able to rally the rest of the members of the Executive Office behind them. They ruled

that Nazzal and his colleague were welcome to sit in the crowd without making any statement. The two Hamas men refused this and took
their leave, as secretly as they had come, undetected by the GID security
agents. The two then went their separate ways and for many months
afterward saw each other only rarely. Nazzal called Mish'al to tell him
about the failure of their scheme, suggesting that it would be best for the
time being if he and al-Rishiq remained underground.[17]

In Damascus, constant consultations took place involving members of
the Hamas Shura Council, the movement's highest authority, and representatives of the Jordanian Ikhwan, who either traveled to Damascus
or spoke by telephone from Amman. Despite a strongly worded statement issued by the Jordanian Ikhwan condemning the government's action against Hamas, the leadership of the Ikhwan tried to avoid a direct
confrontation with the regime. In the early days of the crisis, they told
the three Hamas leaders stranded in Tehran to make their own decision
as to what they wanted to do. However, when it became clear that the
three had made up their minds to return to Jordan, the Ikhwan leadership
asked them to wait and not to act hastily. A Jordanian Ikhwan mission
to Damascus then tried to dissuade the three from taking "such a drastic
action whose consequences could be grave." The Ikhwan still hoped to
persuade the Jordanian authorities to resolve the issue amicably.

On one occasion, Nazzal and al-Rishiq met the members of the
Ikhwan Executive Office in a secret location in Amman to hold further
discussions over the issue of the return of the three Hamas leaders from
Tehran. Throughout seven hours of discussions, the Executive Office
members remained resolute that the three should not return, insisting
that they should stay in Tehran until the Ikhwan was able to resolve the
problem with the government through dialogue. Nazzal and al-Rishiq
agreed to this in principle, but suggested that was not possible to go on
in this way indefinitely and that a time limit should be set. Imad Abu
Dayyah, however, who took a leading part in the meeting, did not think
it was appropriate to set a time limit because the issue needed delicate
handling. The Hamas brethren might have been excused for suspecting
that his aim was to leave time to seal Hamas's fate in Jordan while the
three senior Hamas men remained out of the country.[18] In contrast to this
approach, most of those who sympathized with Hamas, both in Jordan
and elsewhere in the world, were of the opinion that returning to Jordan

was not only the best option but the only one.[19] It had become clear by this time that the Jordanian authorities were not interested in having those who were in Tehran arrested and brought back. On the contrary, they hoped that the arrest warrants against them would keep them out of Jordan for good. Finally, in a last bid to obstruct the return of the three Hamas leaders, the Ikhwan Executive Office in Amman convened an emergency meeting of the Ikhwan's Shura Council, the Ikhwan's highest authority. The Council voted by a slim majority to ask Mish'al and his two comrades to stay outside the country.

This came too late, however. On 21 September 1999, three weeks after the closure of their offices in the Jordanian capital, the three Hamas leaders and the four staff members who had accompanied them left Tehran for Amman via Dubai, arriving at Queen Alia International Airport the following morning. GID agents were waiting for them. They were escorted into a detention area, where they were separated, arrested, and handed over to the police. A state of emergency was declared at the airport, and the public were denied access. Hundreds of sympathizers and family members had driven toward the airport to receive the Hamas leaders upon arrival but were refused entry.[20]

Musa Abu Marzuq was immediately deported, as he was not a Jordanian citizen.[21] The rest were driven, with their hands tightly cuffed behind their backs, to the military court in the Marka district of Amman. From the airport they took a circuitous route across the countryside to evade the press and the public. In Marka, they were brought before a military prosecutor, Mahmud Ubaydat. Asked if they wished to appoint a lawyer, they named Salih al-Armuti. They spent their first night in detention in the cells of the central police station in Amman. The following day they were returned to the same court, where Ubaydat informed them that they were accused of belonging to an illegal organization and of the illegal possession of arms. In addition to al-Armuti, a team of lawyers volunteered to defend the group, including Hani al-Khasawnah, Zuhayr Abu al-Raghib, and Ahmad Bishat. The session in court was stormy and unproductive. No crimes had been committed by any of the detainees and it was difficult for the prosecution to make a case against them.[22]

The affair was, indeed, one of the most bizarre and embarrassing Jordan had ever witnessed. The government was on one side, and popular feeling was on the other. It was not even the result of a government decision but a scheme devised by the GID, which had calculated that the Hamas men would simply stay away from Jordan, and that would be the end of the matter. Now that they had returned, the GID could not decide what its next move should be. The irony was that arrest warrants had been issued for the three, but when they returned voluntarily and gave themselves up, they were accused of undermining the integrity of the state by their return. For their part, their intention was to give the state a chance to prosecute them, if any evidence against them existed. In the meantime, Musa Abu Marzuq established himself in the Syrian capital, Damascus, where he discussed the crisis with other Palestinian groups in Syria and communicated with politicians and community leaders across the Arab world, hoping to bring pressure to bear on the Jordanians. Hamas's policy was to conduct itself as if the arrests and the closure of the offices had not been ordered by King Abdullah, but by the GID, hoping that the king might step in and reverse the decision. The movement even wrote to the king, explaining that the presence of its Political Bureau in Jordan, and all its related activities, were part of a deal concluded with the Jordanian government during the reign of King Hussein. Hamas, they insisted, did not in any way seek to harm Jordanian interests.

For nearly two months, Mish'al, Ghosheh, and their four Hamas companions were held at the correctional facility at al-Juwaydah in southern Amman. In a wing of their own, they were separated from the rest of the inmates. The prison guards were friendly, and some were even sympathetic and supportive. Every morning they would receive the two semi-official daily newspapers *Al-Ra'y* and *Al-Dustur*, both of which represented the government's position. They had no access to other publications, apart from some old books. Such publications as the daily *Al-Arab al-Yawm* and the weekly Jordanian newspapers that sympathized with Hamas were not permitted. They were not allowed a radio, but had a TV set. This, however, was under the control of the prison guards and received only Jordan's main government channel. They passed their nights in metal double bunks, seemingly designed to make sleeping highly uncomfortable.[23]

The group turned their prison into a religious encampment. From the time they woke up early in the morning for *salat al-fajr* (the dawn prayer) until they went to bed after performing *salat al-'isha* (the last of the five daily prayers), they followed a daily program of physical exercise,

Qur'anic recitation, study circles, and recreation. Every night after performing *salat al-'isha*, each of them would get into bed to prepare for the daily quiz game. They divided themselves into two teams to compete in general knowledge and poetry. In comparison to their incarceration in the GID cells, this was a much more dignified environment. They were allowed visits twice a week. The Political Bureau members were permitted to meet their visitors in the office of the prison governor, while their companions could talk to theirs through the barrier fence. All the other Hamas members detained during that period, including Political Bureau member Sami Khatir, were held at Qafqafa Prison, near the northern Jordanian city of Irbid.

After almost two weeks, the group went on hunger strike to demand their release. This followed a second appearance before the military court in Marka, where two further charges were added to their charge sheet that potentially carried the death penalty. The news of their hunger strike reached the outside world through visiting relatives. After three days, three of the companions were taken to al-Hussein Medical Center in Amman for emergency treatment.[24] On Friday, 15 October, hundreds of Palestinians at the al-Wihdat refugee camp near Amman held a demonstration in solidarity with the hunger strikers to demand the release of the Hamas leaders and activists. To stop the demonstration spilling out of the gates of the camp, the security forces blocked its main entrances, deploying armored vehicles and riot police nearby. Some Ikhwan officials participated in the demonstration and addressed the crowd before it dispersed.

After five days, the hunger strike was called off, in response to repeated pleas from a group of leading Jordanian personalities, who promised to intervene to bring the saga to an end. The Hamas prisoners were visited by an array of prominent figures, including lawyer Zuhayr Abu al-Raghib, and Dr. Ishaq al-Farhan, Abd al-Majid Dhunaybat, and Haytham Abu al-Raghib from the Jordanian Ikhwan, as well as Justice Minister Hamzah Haddad, representing the government.[25] A team of doctors visited the prisoners to express solidarity with them on behalf of the Jordanian Medical Association. They carried out medical examinations and prescribed treatment medicines for those who needed them.

Izzat al-Rishiq was finally apprehended on 7 November. The authorities had been watching many of his acquaintances, including two journalists, Samih al-Ma'aytah, who worked for the newspaper *Al-Arab al-Yawm*, and Mahmud al-Khatib, both of whom had formerly worked with al-Rishiq in Amman. Al-Ma'aytah asked al-Khatib to contact al-Rishiq to say he needed to see him urgently because he had an important message for him. Forty-five minutes after al-Rishiq and al-Khatib reached al-Ma'aytah's residence in Zarqa, east of Amman, GID agents supported by police raided the house and arrested all three.[26] They were held at the GID office in Zarqa, where al-Rishiq was severely tortured for six hours. The GID wanted to know the whereabouts of Muhammad Nazzal, but in fact al-Rishiq had no idea where Nazzal was.[27] He explained that each had his own safe house and that if they needed to meet they did so by leaving messages for each other with mutual acquaintances. The GID did not believe him. They took him to his previous safe house, a furnished apartment in Makkah Street, where they hoped to trap Nazzal, who of course never appeared. Two friends of al-Rishiq came to the flat the following day. They were beaten to make them divulge the whereabouts of Nazzal, but had no more idea where Nazzal was than did al-Rishiq. Al-Rishiq and his two companions were sent to al-Juwaydah prison, where they joined their other Hamas comrades. In desperation, the authorities intensified their search for Nazzal. GID agents in two cars monitored his house and a third car followed his wife wherever she went. Family members were repeatedly summoned to the GID headquarters in Amman to be interrogated about his whereabouts, but Nazzal continued to evade capture.

The government had made up its mind. Hamas's presence in Jordan was to be permanently terminated, and its leaders would have to choose whether to leave Jordan with Hamas or stay without it. As the crisis deepened, the Jordanian authorities once more sought the assistance of the Jordanian Ikhwan, hoping that they could convince the Hamas leaders to agree to leave peacefully. The intention was that their departure would appear to be the outcome of a voluntary initiative. This could have left the door open for the restoration of relations at some future date between Hamas and the Jordanian government. The Ikhwan, who were split over how to proceed, claimed their objective was an amicable resolution to the crisis.

On 11 November, Prime Minister Abd al-Ra'uf al-Rawabidah met an Ikhwan delegation comprising Abd al-Majid Dhunaybat, the leader of the Ikhwan, and Abd al-Latif Arabiyat, the secretary-general of the Islamic Action Front, together with Jamil Abu Bakr and Salim al-Falahat, members of the Ikhwan Executive Office.[28] This meeting signaled the government's failure to persuade the Hamas officials to renounce their right to remain in Jordan. Negotiations had to be conducted with the two Hamas Political Bureau members in Damascus, since those imprisoned in Jordan refused to engage in any talks while they lacked their freedom. The final attempt by the government to resolve the issue came in a message from GID Director Samih al-Battikhi, delivered to Khalid Mish'al and his fellow inmates by Abdullah al-Akaylah, a member of parliament in Jordan and a former senior Ikhwan official. Those imprisoned were offered the opportunity to continue to be Jordanian citizens and to be allowed to stay in the country provided they gave up all association with Hamas. Mish'al replied: "We do not relinquish our principles and we will never ever relinquish our movement."[29] The government now had to do something to end the crisis, which was beginning to cost Jordan dearly. Many Jordanians were unhappy at the treatment of the imprisoned Hamas leaders who were gaining the sympathy of more and more people every day.

On 20 November 1999, the Hamas detainees at al-Juwaydah were visited by their lawyer, Salih al-Armuti, accompanied by the chairman of the Jordanian Bar Association, Sayf al-Sharif. Al-Sharif said he had brought a message from Prime Minister Abd al-Ra'uf al-Rawabidah, requesting that they leave Jordan voluntarily. In exchange, a promise would be given that they would be able to visit Jordan every two or three months, after prior arrangement with the security authorities. They were also promised, should they accept the offer, not to be handcuffed while deported. Khalid Mish'al and Ibrahim Ghosheh both rejected this offer categorically. They said they would rather be dragged from the country in handcuffs than agree to leave voluntarily. Their lawyer left the prison to hold a press conference, where he declared that the government had already decided to deport the Hamas leaders, despite their wish not to leave. Prime Minister al-Rawabidah was angered by the lawyer's statement to the press, as the matter was supposed to be confidential. He told the press the government had made no such a decision. The prime minister spoke to the journalists with a leading figure of the Jordanian Ikhwan at his elbow, who also gave the press his assurance that the government had decided not to deport the Hamas leaders.

Less than 24 hours later, however, the Hamas leaders were put on a plane, against their will, and sent to Qatar. Having failed to find Muhammad Nazzal, the Jordanian authorities had apparently decided to leave him on the loose inside the country.

The Qatari Connection

The Jordanian authorities told the Qatari government, which had been involved in mediation efforts, that the Hamas leaders had decided to leave Jordan willingly, and that they themselves had chosen Qatar as their destination. Qatar sent a private jet, which landed at Amman's Marka airport, to fly the Hamas leaders to Doha. This is how the story then unfolded, as narrated by Ibrahim Ghosheh:

"Soon after we performed salat al-maghrib [sunset prayer] on 21 November 1999, the police came to our wing and took the three of us: myself, Mish'al, and al-Rishiq. They returned our valuables to us and took us away. Our companions stayed behind. We understood afterwards that following our departure they were freed and allowed to go home. Outside the prison, a different group of security men took over; they handcuffed us, placed black blindfolds on our eyes and pushed us into a prison van. We did not know where we were being driven. I joked that we were being shipped either to al-Jafr or to Yasir Arafat.[30] *About an hour into the drive, I said I could smell coffee and that I suspected we were going through Marka, which is famous for its coffee-roasting shops. A quarter of an hour later the van stopped and we could clearly hear the engines of helicopters and aircraft. They left us in the van while they unloaded whatever belongings we had. Then, they removed the blindfolds and we could see a Qatari private jet a few meters away from us. They told us to climb into the plane. We refused. Someone approached, saying he was from the royal court, and that we had no option but to go to Qatar. We said we did not want to go to Qatar. He said: "Nevermind; just get into the plane and discuss the matter inside." In the meantime, Sami Khatir arrived from Qafqafa prison. He had not been allowed to change out of the prison uniform and had no belongings with him. We sat in the plane waiting, and then the Qatari minister of state for foreign affairs appeared. He welcomed us saying: "Now, you will honor us by coming to our country which you should consider to be your own." Khalid Mish'al said to him: "But we do not want to leave Jordan for Qatar." The Qatari minister said: "Wait a minute!" and ordered the captain to switch off the engine. He called Jordanian Foreign Minister Abd al-Ilah al-Khatib, who was at the airport to*

bid him farewell. Mish'al told the Jordanian minister that we did not want to leave for Qatar. The minister replied: "But you did call the Qatari foreign minister, didn't you?" Mish'al said: "I called the Qatari foreign minister when we were in Tehran to ask him to mediate for our return to Jordan. This was all – we never asked to go to Qatar." In the end, the Jordanian minister said: "Here are your passports; you know you have to leave and you have no choice." Mish'al said: "Then we are being deported?" The minister said: "Interpret it how you wish." Mish'al turned to the Qatari minister and said to him: "Bear witness that we are being deported. There will be a trial one day and you'll be called to testify." The Qatari minister, who was shocked by what he had seen and heard said: "I shall definitely testify."[31]

When the Hamas leaders arrived in Qatar, they were treated as guests of honor. They were received warmly at all levels from the head of state, Amir of Qatar Sheikh Hamad, downward. They were given VIP treatment, and full freedom to do as they wished, including the freedom to leave and enter the country. Initially they were accommodated at the Sheraton Hotel, but were then moved to a compound of secure villas specially allocated to them.[32] In Amman, the Jordanian government continued to insist that the Hamas leaders had gone to Qatar at their own request in accordance with an agreement between Hamas and the Qatari authorities. Both Hamas and Qatar vehemently denied the Jordanian claim.

It may well be true that Qatar volunteered to play a part in resolving the crisis. It would not be too much to assume that the US might have asked Qatar to play such a part. However, there is no evidence to suggest that Qatar was involved in any conspiracy. The affair had become an embarrassment for the Jordanian regime, and for all those who had put pressure on it to get rid of Hamas, including the US. The result had been an outpouring of sympathy and support for Hamas in Jordan that had inevitably reflected badly on the Jordanian regime. King Abdullah admitted in private conversation with visitors that those who had been charged with terminating the Hamas presence in Jordan had done their job badly. A further indication of the king's anger was his decision to remove al-Battikhi from office less than a year later. Throughout the crisis, the king had remained aloof. Al-Battikhi, with his personal grudge against Hamas, had guided the entire operation.

The remark most frequently heard in Jordan at the time was that none of this would have happened had King Hussein still been alive. The late king was renowned for handling such sensitive matters with profound wisdom, fairness, and firmness. People found it hard to refrain from making comparisons between the fate of Hamas under Abdullah, and the treatment it received under his father. It was King Hussein who saved Khalid Mish'al's life when Mossad tried to kill him. King Hussein had also insisted on the release of Sheikh Yassin from Israeli detention. Finally, King Hussein had welcomed Musa Abu Marzuq back to Jordan when the Americans freed him from detention. King Abdullah's decision to leave matters in the hands of Samih al-Battikhi, who was later convicted and jailed for fraud and corruption, did much harm to the king's standing in his early days on the throne.

Al-Battikhi had used the government of Abd al-Ra'uf al-Rawabidah as a tool and as a cover to achieve his own ends. He had behaved in a manner that alienated even his closest associates. He evidently believed his powers were unlimited, and that none had the authority to question his actions. Above all, he insisted on removing Hamas from Jordan in the most humiliating manner, though it could have been done less ungraciously. Hamas's leaders knew of the enormous pressure exerted on Jordan from Israel, the Palestinian Authority, and the US. They acknowledged that their presence in Jordan, and the activities they had been allowed to conduct, were all based on a gentleman's agreement concluded between themselves and the Jordanian authorities in the time of the late King Hussein. Had the new monarch wished to end this arrangement, all he needed to do was to tell Hamas that the circumstances had changed, and that Jordan could no longer provide a safe haven for its leaders, with their media and political activities. It had been an unwise and unnecessary course of action to arrest the Hamas leaders and level preposterous charges against them, when all knew that their presence and activity in Jordan were perfectly legal and in accordance with a prior agreement. The Jordanians gravely miscalculated. They believed that the process of peacemaking between Israel and the PA was heading toward a breakthrough, and that Hamas would go into decline. They therefore imagined that they would find nothing to regret in bringing Hamas's operation in Jordan to an end.

In Doha, the Hamas Political Bureau members displayed from the outset their determination to fight for the right to return to Jordan. The Hamas group persuaded the Qataris, who had unwittingly played a minor role in their deportation, that they had a moral responsibility to facilitate their repatriation. The Qataris promised to spare no effort, but said they wanted to allow some time for calm to return. At the insistence of the deported Hamas leaders, however, Qatar soon resumed its mediation efforts. Foreign Minister Hamad bin Jassim conveyed messages on behalf of Hamas to the Jordanians. One such message was addressed to King Abdullah himself, reminding him that the deported individuals were Jordanian citizens, who had every right, according to the Jordanian constitution, to return to their country. The Jordanian authorities, on the other hand, wanted to lay down rules of communication. For example, they refused to recognize Khalid Mish'al as head of Hamas's Political Bureau if the issue under consideration was his return to Jordan as a Jordanian citizen. The position of the Hamas deportees was unequivocal. They insisted on a distinction being made between their absolute right as Jordanians to live in Jordan and enjoy the full rights of their Jordanian citizenship, and their wish to conduct Hamas's business inside Jordan. While the second issue was negotiable, the first was not, and they would not compromise on it.

A Jordanian delegation consisting of GID Director Samih al-Battikhi and Foreign Minister Abd al-Ilah al-Khatib visited Qatar for two days in mid-2000, a few months before al-Battikhi was removed from his job. Viewers watching Qatar TV on the day the delegation was received by the amir of Qatar could not help but conclude that al-Battikhi was in charge. In contravention of diplomatic protocol, he was seen delivering a letter from King Abdullah to the amir of Qatar. The purpose of the visit was primarily to request that the Qataris not ask Jordan to accept the return of the Hamas deportees. Al-Battikhi said to his Qatari hosts: "We do not want them; we were hoping that when they went to Tehran they would remain there. So, do not keep asking us to take them back." During the talks the delegation held with the amir of Qatar, al-Battikhi was handed a letter in reply to King Abdullah. He opened the letter while still in the amir's presence, read it, and said he did not agree with its contents. The amir of Qatar angrily told him the letter was not addressed to him and that he should not have opened it in the first place. Angered by the discourteous attitude of his Jordanian guest, the amir ended the meeting abruptly.

Later that year, Khalid Mish'al had an opportunity to meet the new Jordanian prime minister, Ali Abu al-Raghib, at the Organization of the Islamic Conference (OIC) summit in Doha in November 2000. Little had changed in Jordan's position. The new prime minister insisted that Mish'al and his colleagues had one of two options. First, if they agreed to renounce Hamas, they would be able to return to Jordan as Jordanian citizens. There, it would be open to them to join any political party, or to set up one of their own. If, however, they chose to stick to Hamas, they should return their Jordanian passports and accept limited two-year validity passports (of the type issued to Palestinians temporarily resident in Jordan). They would then be able to make limited visits to Jordan if they kept the security authorities informed. This was the arrangement enjoyed by the PFLP leader George Habash and the DFLP leader Nayif Hawatmah. Clearly, this encounter was unproductive.

The change of government in Jordan, however, together with the removal of Samih al-Battikhi from his post, and the second intifada, which started in September 2000, all paved the way for the rehabilitation of the one remaining Hamas Political Bureau member left in Jordan, Muhammad Nazzal. Here is how Nazzal reported the resolution of his problem:

I went into hiding on 30 August 1999 and remained underground until 27 December 2000. Throughout that period I continued to be wanted by the authorities, who did not cease to search for me until the second intifada began in September 2000. I believe that a number of factors then came into play. Firstly, the GID director was replaced by his deputy, Sa'd Khayr. It would have been very difficult for my problem to be resolved had Samih al-Battikhi still been in office. Secondly, a new government led by Prime Minister Ali Abu al-Raghib replaced that of Abd al-Ra'uf al-Rawabidah, who had largely contributed to the crisis. Thirdly, I had a friend inside the new cabinet. This was Faris al-Nabulsi, deputy prime minister and justice minister. Fourthly, the entire political climate had changed because of the intifada. A mutual friend contacted me to tell me of Faris al-Nabulsi's wish to find a solution to my problem. I said I would settle for anything, provided I did not lose my Jordanian nationality and I was not asked to resign my position in Hamas. After a series of communications I was informed that the problem had been resolved, and that all I needed to do before returning to normality was to meet with a GID official. I hesitated in the beginning lest this was a trap designed to apprehend me. Finally, I met the GID official, who assured me that I could return to normal life provided I did not engage in any media or political activity in Jordan on behalf of Hamas.

In the meantime, the Qataris continued to Jordan for a change of position, but to no avail. In March 2001, the Qatari foreign minister, who was attending the Arab Summit in Amman, told his Jordanian counterpart and the Jordanian prime minister that "the Hamas people insist on returning and if you do not solve the problem they will make their own way back."

The Jordanians seemed unconcerned. Having concluded that the Jordanian authorities were not serious about resolving the problem, Hamas's Political Bureau decided after thorough consideration to send two of its members, Ibrahim Ghosheh and Sami Khatir, back to Amman. The plan was to go in early June. It turned out, however, that Khatir could not travel because of family considerations and Ghosheh had to go alone. The Qatari government was informed that Ghosheh had purchased a one-way ticket to Amman and that their assistance would be appreciated. In turn, the Qatari authorities instructed the pilot of the Qatari passenger aircraft on which Ghosheh traveled not to bring him back to Doha under any circumstances. Qatar, already unhappy with the Jordanian attitude, was delighted to give Ghosheh a helping hand in his plane to return to Jordan.

The Ghosheh Affair

The Qatari aircraft carrying Ibrahim Ghosheh landed in Amman on Thursday afternoon, 14 June 2001. When he showed his passport, he was asked to wait. An officer approached him and asked him to follow. He was placed in a detention in a room in the airport immigration department.[33] A bed and a mattress were brought to what was in effect to be his prison cell for the next two weeks. Initially, the Jordanians wanted to put Ghosheh back on the Qatari plane and return him to Qatar. The captain refused to allow him on board, insisting that he had strict instructions from his government. The aircraft was then also detained, and was held for two weeks at Queen Alia International Airport.

Ghosheh was subjected to bizarre treatment. For a week, he was not allowed to change his clothes. His luggage was left where the baggage of arriving passengers waits for clearance. Ghosheh described the first day he spent in detention at the airport:

On the day of my arrival, my family had been waiting for me. They waited for five hours and then returned home. I requested permission to telephone them at home but this was denied. I was not allowed newspapers and there was no television set. I had a transistor radio but they took its batteries. My guards were GID agents and Preventive Security men. I slipped my mobile phone into my pocket and asked to go to the toilet. One of the guards followed me and insisted on keeping the toilet door open. He was barely two meters away from me. I flushed the toilet and called home. My daughter answered. I told her in a quiet voice that I was OK, and that they should not worry about me. I switched off the mobile, put it in my pocket and went out as if nothing had happened. That was my first communication. Then I made two more calls at dawn when the guards were sleepy. The door was open and one of them sat on a chair right in front of me but I spoke from underneath the blanket. I was glad I could reassure my family that I was well.[34]

To Ghosheh's surprise, the authorities claimed his Jordanian nationality had already been revoked. The Jordanian information minister Salih al-Qallab told journalists and concerned observers that Ghosheh had not been allowed in because he was no longer a Jordanian national. It transpired that soon after the deportation of the Hamas Political Bureau officials, the Jordanian government declared them all to have been stripped of their nationality and that the right of their families to Jordanian nationality had also been withdrawn. The authorities wanted Ghosheh to leave the country voluntarily, but he was adamant that Jordan was his home and no power on earth could force him out. A GID officer known under the alias of Abu Thamir conducted much of the interrogation. He was the same officer who had dealt with Ghosheh when he was arrested and detained at the GID headquarters in 1997. He came at midnight on the day of Ghosheh's arrival from Doha and then interrogated him every day for the first week or so. He would come at different times: sometimes the interrogation would start at midnight, sometimes just before dawn and sometimes at midday. Sleep deprivation was clearly the objective. He threatened Ghosheh that if he did not leave Jordan willingly, his nationality and the nationalities of his family members would be permanently revoked. Sometimes, he threatened to deport Ghosheh to the ends of the earth.

After a week, Abu Thamir showed signs of fatigue. Ghosheh was moved to another room and was allowed to have his belongings, but his mobile phone was discovered and confiscated. Abu Thamir came to see him on the afternoon of Wednesday, 20 June, to tell him to expect a telephone call from the Yemeni foreign minister. Ghosheh smelled treachery and decided not to accept any telephone calls. He had been in total isolation and did not know what was going on around him in the outside world. His assessment was that if he spoke to the Yemeni foreign minister and received an invitation from him to go to Yemen, it would look bad on his part to turn it down, since Hamas had a good relationship with Yemen. On the other hand, to accept the invitation would mean that his struggle had been in vain, and that he had chosen willingly to abandon his attempt to return home. The following day, Abu Thamir came with a more senior GID official, threatening once more that if Ghosheh did not agree to leave he would be forced onto a plane and deported to the most distant point on earth. They insisted that he could not enter Jordan because the decision to exclude him had come from the highest level of authority. He replied: "I have every right to be in my country. Let me in and if you have anything against me prosecute me in a court of law."

Throughout the period Ghosheh spent at Queen Alia Airport, the entire Arab world followed the course of his adventure with great interest. It was in the headlines every day and became virtually a daily soap opera. In the meantime, various Arab governments were actively seeking a resolution to the crisis, while the Arab League in Cairo announced that it was working with both Jordan and Qatar to find a solution. The Arab League secretary-general, Dr. Amr Musa, spoke of a proposal from Libya to fly Ghosheh out of Jordan. Meanwhile, in Gaza, Sheikh Yassin appealed to King Abdullah to let Ghosheh stay. The Jordanian authorities were adamant, however, that unless he renounced his links with Hamas he would never be allowed in. Hamas was once more gathering sympathy and support throughout the region and beyond. For the entire duration of the affair, Hamas's public relations arm worked tirelessly on behalf of its case and to keep alive public interest in the plight of those of its leaders who had been uprooted from their own country. All Ghosheh needed to do was remain steadfast, and that is what he did. For those who knew him this was not surprising. He is a very stubborn man: the more he is pressed, the more he endures.

On 28 June, exactly fourteen days after Ghosheh landed in Jordan, he was told he had a special visitor. He was taken back to the room where he had spent his first week in detention, where he found waiting for him his old colleague Muhammad Nazzal, whom he had not seen for two years. Nazzal recounts the background to this meeting:

Ten days after the detention of Ibrahim Ghosheh at the airport I was contacted by the same GID official with whom I negotiated the terms for ending my fugitive status and my coming out of hiding. He said he wanted to see me urgently. I had no idea what it was about. I went to the GID headquarters to meet him and discovered that the GID was desperate for help to end the confrontation with Ghosheh. They asked me: "How are we going to solve this problem?" I suggested they let him in. They said that it would be impossible to do this right away. It would undermine the prestige of the state, they explained. They then suggested that he might leave the country and then come back again. I said that it would be very difficult to convince the Hamas people that Jordan would eventually let him come back once he left. I asked them what guarantees would they give that they would let him in. They said they were not interested in creating a crisis with another Arab state. They explained that their relations with Qatar had already been strained because of this issue. I contacted the brethren in Qatar and conveyed to them the GID proposal but they did not accept the idea that he should leave and then come back, because they feared that if he left he might simply not be allowed back in. The GID officers asked us to propose a country and said they were ready to fly him there and back. I tried to persuade the brethren that, according to my own personal assessment, the Jordanians were serious and that it was not in their interest to create a new problem with another Arab state. I said I felt they were sincere in wanting to resolve the problem. In this way, I succeeded in convincing the brethren, and we agreed that it should be done through Yemen. The brothers suggested that Jordan should contact the Yemenis and if the Yemenis agreed then there would be no problem. But they said they wanted something in writing. I told them it was not customary to have a written agreement with the security agencies, but they insisted. I went every day to the GID to finalize the deal. To my surprise, the GID deputy director did not object to having a written agreement. He even asked me to dictate the text. I dictated the following: "The brothers in the Political Bureau have authorized me to inform the GID that we are prepared to allow brother Ibrahim Ghosheh to depart from Jordan, provided that he is allowed to return to Jordan on the condition that once in the country he will refrain from political and media activity." The senior GID officer signed on behalf of the GID and I signed my name on behalf of Hamas.[35]

The decision to conclude the problem in this way seemed to have been taken because the king, who had been on a visit to the United Kingdom, had given instructions that the affair must be resolved once and for all before his return. Some observers commented at the time that perhaps,

observing the situation from London, the king could see the damage being done to the image of Jordan by this affair.

Nazzal, who arrived at the airport in the company of the GID deputy
director, known as Abu Hashim, explained to Ibrahim Ghosheh that a deal
had been made between the movement and the GID that he was to go to
Yemen and then return. He showed him a copy of the written agreement
signed by both parties. When Ghosheh was reassured that this was the
decision of the Political Bureau he agreed, despite his initial qualms. Apparently, nothing could have given more pleasure to the GID official. He
had tried without success for two weeks to persuade Ghosheh to leave.
However, there was an unforeseen obstacle: Yemen backed down. The
Yemeni government was not happy that Jordan's foreign minister, Abd
al-Ilah al-Khatib, had asked the favor of his Yemeni counterpart, Abu
Bakr al-Qirabi. They insisted that King Abdullah should call President
Ali Abdullah Saleh and put the request to him personally. The Yemenis
were apprehensive that they might find themselves in the same position
as Qatar, as the unwilling host of a Hamas deportee. The GID officer
came back to Nazzal to tell him that they were in a real predicament
and did not know where else to send Ghosheh. Nazzal suggested Syria.
However, they decided to take him elsewhere. Nazzal had no knowledge
of what subsequently happened. Having waited for two hours to hear
from the officer to no avail, he was finally taken home. He called his Hamas colleagues in Doha and told them he did not know where Ghosheh
was heading. They contacted the Yemenis, who said they had made no
deal and knew nothing about the trip. The next 48 hours saw a war of
words between Hamas, which accused the GID of kidnapping Ghosheh,
and the Jordanian government, which scarcely knew what to say.[36] The
explanation began to emerge when the GID deputy director called Prime
Minister Abu al-Raghib and told him that he and Ghosheh were in Bangkok. The prime minister fumed with anger that he was the last to know,
but called Nazzal and assured him that no tricks were being played and
that their man would soon be on his way back to Amman.

This is how Ibrahim Ghosheh described what happened to him after
he parted with Nazzal:

I went to my room and left Nazzal with the GID official. Two hours later the
official came and asked me to get ready to leave. I boarded the plane thinking
I was being flown to Yemen. There were five of us altogether. I was seated in

143

the plane in between two guards, one to my left and another to my right, as if to prevent me fleeing! The captain announced that our destination was Bangkok. I was not alarmed because I knew it could have been Yemen or anywhere else. The reason we went to Bangkok was that the only Royal Jordanian flight to leave Amman that evening was for Bangkok. It was a long and rough ride with frequent turbulence. To make matters worse, we landed at Calcutta to drop some passengers. On arrival in Bangkok, we checked into the airport duty-free-zone hotel. Officially, we never entered Thailand. To prepare the way for my return, I was told to write a statement, after which the king would give his permission for me to fly back to Amman. I wrote a statement, which the GID deputy director faxed to his chief, Sa'd Khayr, in London, who had apparently been with the king during his visit to the United Kingdom. My statement did not satisfy them, and they produced an alternative text in which I seemed to be asking for pardon from the king and pledging to sever all ties with Hamas. I refused to sign what I considered a most humiliating statement. I told the GID official that he had my passport and my mobile phone, and that even if he were to desert me in the alleys of Bangkok I would never put my name to such a humiliating statement. Negotiations lasted six hours before we reached an agreement. Then they allowed me to make a phone call to my wife in Jordan to tell her that I was in Bangkok, that every thing was OK, and that soon I would be on my way back to Amman.[37]

At about midnight, the GID officers decided to leave Bangkok immediately. They had been alerted that the Thai authorities had been searching for them because of media reports that a senior Hamas official was stranded at the Bangkok airport. Escaping what might have been another embarrassing episode, they flew out on the first available plane to Kuala Lumpur. Arrangements were already made for them to take a Royal Jordanian flight from Kuala Lumpur to Amman, arriving in Jordan in the early hours of the morning of Saturday, 30 June 2001.

In an effort to save face, Jordanian Information Minister Salih al-Qallab announced that the king had pardoned Ibrahim Ghosheh, who, he asserted, had pledged in a letter to renounce all links with Hamas. He went out of his way to deny that there was any deal between the Jordanian authorities and Hamas, insisting that "we have no dialogue with Hamas." In fact Ghosheh wrote in the letter: "I shall freeze my political, media and organizational activities with Hamas," and never promised to renounce all links as al-Qallab claimed. This is why Khalid Mish'al found it necessary to tell the media and the public that Ghosheh would retain his role within Hamas under the deal reached with the government. He explained that the accord between Hamas and the Jordanian authorities "stipulates that Ibrahim Ghosheh halt all activity within Jordan in the name of Hamas, and not that he renounce his role and position within the movement."[38]

That was the end of the war of return between Jordan and Hamas, which found compensation for the loss of its position in Amman in the gains it made in a multitude of other capitals. Operationally speaking, Hamas leaders were able, from then on, to make use of Doha, Damascus, and Beirut. Jordan, on the other hand lost a very important asset: Hamas's good will. This was something the late King Hussein had valued highly, finding it extremely useful in his conduct of politics in the region. As events were later to prove, the Jordanian war on Hamas was a very costly miscalculation. Because of its attack on Hamas, Jordan no longer plays a significant role in the Palestinian question. For example, Jordan cannot match Egypt's achievements in the fields of mediation, the facilitation of talks, and negotiations among different Palestinian factions. Nor can it play the kind of role Turkey may play in the future, in terms of mediating between a Hamas-run PA and Israel.

Ibrahim Ghosheh remained in Jordan, keeping a low profile and abiding by the terms of the agreement by which he was eventually enabled to return to the country. However, the authorities imposed restrictions on his travel abroad. He was not allowed out of the country, not even for 'umra or hajj,[39] until December 2005, when he was allowed to travel to Sana'a in Yemen to attend the fourth conference of the trustees of the Quds Foundation, of which he is a trustee and a founding member.

Muhammad Nazzal, meanwhile, joined the rest of the Hamas Political Bureau members in Damascus. He visits Jordan frequently in accordance with an understanding he reached with the Jordanian authorities, who promised he would be allowed to come to the country by prior arrangement with them, provided that while in Jordan he does not engage in any political or media activities. The Jordanian authorities rescinded their earlier decision to strip the Jordanian members of the Political Bureau and their dependants of Jordanian nationality. The families of all the Hamas offcials continue to be free to travel in and out of Jordan as they please.

Meanwhile, relations between Hamas and the Jordanian Ikhwan finally reached an equilibrium whereby the two movements mutually agreed that they were no longer in any sense the same organization. They no longer even share the same objectives, as they had done until the mid-1990s. Those who desired a total separation between the two movements had their wish. It may be that the same outcome could have been achieved, however, in a manner that would have preserved a bridge between the two organizations. The Jordanian Ikhwan now regard Hamas as an organization illegal in Jordan. Hamas regrets that matters have ended this way, but appear to have no choice but to accept the situation until such a time as circumstances may change and relations between Hamas and the Jordanian regime can be restored. Despite all this, at the grassroots level, Hamas is still very popular in Jordan both within and without the ranks of the Ikhwan.

SEVEN

THE LIBERATION IDEOLOGY OF HAMAS

I want to proclaim loudly to the world that we are not fighting Jews because they are Jews! We are fighting them because they assaulted us, they killed us, they took our land and our homes; they attacked our children and our women; they scattered us. All we want is our rights. We don't want more.[1]

—Sheikh Ahmad Yassin

"This is What We Struggle for"

This is the title of a document written by Hamas's Political Bureau in the late 1990s. It was Hamas's response to a request by a European diplomatic mission in Amman for an explanation of Hamas's objectives, values, and ideals.[2] The document begins with the following statement: "The Islamic Resistance Movement (Hamas) is a Palestinian national liberation movement that struggles for the liberation of the Palestinian occupied lands and for the recognition of Palestinian legitimate rights."

The political language of this document is very different from the highly religious terms in which the Hamas Charter was framed. The Charter, in Arabic *Al-Mithaq* (the covenant), was Hamas's first attempt to produce a written document for others to learn what Hamas stood for. It was published on 18 August 1988, less than nine months after the foundation of the movement. Since then, however, it has hardly ever been quoted or even referred to by the Hamas leadership or its official spokesmen. Their language has become virtually indistinguishable from that of any freedom fighter in Latin America, South Africa, or East Asia. On 7 March 2004, the following statement was placed on the Izzadin al-Qassam internet site by the Hamas leader in Gaza, Dr. Abd al-Aziz al-Rantisi, just ten days before his assassination at the hands of the Israelis:

Hamas's strategy is underpinned by four principles:

1. Our homeland has been usurped in its entirety, but we cannot concede one inch of it.

2. There is an obvious imbalance of power in favor of the Zionist enemy.

3. We do not possess the armaments our enemy possesses, but we have a faith that generates a will that does not recognize defeat or retreat before our goals are accomplished. This is a faith that demands sacrifice for the sake of religion and homeland.

4. The Arab and Islamic umma is weak, feeble, and divided, and is therefore unable to support the people of Palestine. The international community is hostile to the hopes and aspirations of the Palestinian people and supports Zionist terrorism. Hamas's strategy therefore has two parallel goals:

— to resist occupation and confront Zionist aggression,

— to maintain the unity of the Palestinian people and safeguard the Palestinians from internal strife, which hinder resistance to the occupation.

The Hamas Charter has frequently been invoked by the movement's critics, as proof of either its inflexibility or its anti-Semitism. Until the late 1990s, this did not appear to concern anyone within the movement. Seemingly, the primary concern of the Hamas leadership was to address their own Arab and Muslim constituents inside and outside Palestine, paying little attention to the views of the rest of the world about the movement.

When it was drafted, the Charter was an honest representation of the ideological and political position of Hamas at that moment in time. Hamas had emerged from the Ikhwan (the Muslim Brotherhood), and the Charter was a reflection of how the Ikhwan perceived the conflict in Palestine and how they viewed the world. On the first page of the Hamas Charter, following a quotation from the Qur'an (Sura 3: 110–112), there is a quotation from Hassan al-Banna, who founded the Ikhwan in Egypt in 1928. Banna says: "Israel will be created and will continue to exist until Islam sweeps it away, just as it swept away what came before it."[3] While the Hamas leaders of today would not necessarily wish to revise phraseology of this kind, they are increasingly convinced that the Charter as a whole has been more of a hindrance than a help. Many would admit that insufficient thought went into the drafting and publication of the Charter. Once it had been drafted, Hamas institutions inside and outside Palestine were never adequately consulted over its content. According to Khalid Mish'al, the Charter was rushed out to meet what was perceived at the time as a pressing need to introduce the newly founded movement to the public. Mish'al does not view it as a true expression of the movement's overall vision, which "has been formulated over the years by inputs from the movement's different institutions." He sees the Charter as a historical document, which gives an insight into Hamas's original philosophy at the time of its establishment. However, it "should not be regarded as the fundamental ideological frame of reference from which the movement derives its positions, or on the basis of which it justifies its actions."[4] Ibrahim Ghosheh takes a similar view. According to him, "it goes without saying that the articles of the charter are not sacred; in other words they are subject to review and revision in a manner that does not contradict the main ideas with which the movement emerged and to which it continues to adhere."[5]

Such clarifications, or reservations, are quite recent. Until the beginning of the second intifada in September 2000, very little debate had taken place within Hamas on this issue, despite the fact that much of the criticism levelled against the movement has involved references to the Charter. It was as if Hamas had totally forgotten that it had issued a Charter, or as if its leaders were completely oblivious to the criticism that had hitherto been directed against it.[6] Only recently have certain Hamas leaders begun to voice their concern that it has perhaps taken them too long to recognize that "the text of the Charter does not reflect the thinking and understanding of the movement." They have only just started to admit that this may constitute "an obstacle, or a source of distortion, or a misunderstanding regarding what the movement stands for."[7]

Hamas has become increasingly visible in the world's media, and a very negative image has often been presented, mostly filtered through the views of Israel and its supporters. This has prompted the senior Political Bureau officials to seek advice on how to counter such negative publicity. Concern over this issue goes back to the mid-1990s, when the Political Bureau was still in Jordan and the movement was beginning to have some contacts with Western diplomats in Amman. However, it was in the aftermath of the events of 11 September 2001 that it took on a degree of urgency. Hamas began to feel that an image-building initiative was needed, in order to counter the efforts by certain hostile media and academic quarters to identify all Islamic movements and organizations with al-Qaeda. Israel in particular sought to capitalize on the American-led war on terror to further its campaign to convince the Western world of its continued strategic value as an ally, despite the end of the Cold War. Israel's contention was that no distinction existed between one strand of political Islam and another, and that Israel stood as a bulwark to protect the West.[8]

A series of consultations conducted in Beirut and Damascus from early 2003 until the end of 2005 reinforced the feeling of a number of senior Hamas Political Bureau officials that the time had come for the Charter to be rewritten. A process of consultation culminated in the commissioning of a draft for a new Charter. However, in the aftermath of the Palestinian legislative elections of 25 January 2006, in which Hamas won a majority, the project was put on hold until further notice, lest the new Charter be seen as a measure in response to outside pressure.

What's Wrong with the Hamas Charter?

The current Charter is written in a language that no longer appeals to well-educated Muslims. It may have been a major obstacle in the way of Hamas's efforts to win over pro-Palestinian secular Muslims and non-Muslims to its side. Its language and ideas typify the prevalent discourse of the Ikhwan at the time when the Charter was written, not only in Palestine but elsewhere in the world. The Ikhwan have moved on since then, but the Charter has remained unchanged. Today, the Charter gives the impression that its author wrote it for the benefit of his own immediate circle of devotees, rather than for the public as a whole. The author of the Charter is believed to have been Abd al-Fattah Dukhan, one of the seven founders of Hamas and a long-time leader of the Palestinian Ikhwan. He often acted as second-in-command to Sheikh Ahmad Yassin. At the time of Hamas's establishment and the publication of the Charter, he was the leader of the Ikhwan in Gaza, at a time when Sheikh Ahmad Yassin had not yet resumed his leadership responsibilities following his release from detention in the exchange of prisoners in May 1985.[9]

The Charter in fact reads more like an internal circular. It has been criticized from within Hamas itself for not having the correct tone for an official document, suitable for the introduction of the ideas of Hamas to the world. Not everyone in the movement at the time felt that the publication of a Charter was necessarily a good idea, though they may not have had any objection to its language or content. With hindsight it seems that the issue of the Hamas Charter formed part of the ongoing process of competition with the PLO. The PLO Charter was utterly secular, and therefore did not reflect the Islamic identity of the Palestinian people or their cause.

Many Hamas leaders now recognize that the fundamental and essential positions expressed in the Charter could be expressed in more universal language that could appeal to both Muslims and non-Muslims alike. Instead of justifying its statements in religious terms, which may mean little to those who do not share the same faith or the same vision, a new Charter should refer to the historical basis of the Palestinian cause. It should give a succinct account of the story of the Palestine conflict as it has unfolded. It should trace the roots of the problem to Europe in the 19th century, showing how the Palestinians have been the victims of the European plan conceived more than a century ago to resolve Europe's own Jewish problem. This was done at the expense of the Palestinians through the creation of a homeland for the "Jewish people" in Palestine. Such an argument would be more universally acceptable than the idea that Palestine is a *waqf* (endowment) "consecrated for future Muslim generations until Judgment Day."[10] As article 11 of the Charter itself explains, the lands conquered by the Muslims from the time of the second Caliph Omar onward were all assigned as *waqf* in order not to be distributed among the conquering troops. The same consideration applies equally to Iraq, Persia, Egypt, North Africa, and even Spain. The reference to this issue in the Charter was intended to condemn those who were willing to give away any part of Palestine to the Israelis as part of a peace agreement. This is the logic behind the passage: "It is not permissible to concede it or any part of it or to give it up or any part of it; that is not the right of any single Arab state or all the Arab states together nor any king or president or all the kings and presidents together nor any single organization or all the organizations together whether Palestinian or Arab. This is so because the land of Palestine is an Islamic *waqf* (endowment) property consecrated to the generations of Muslims up to the Day of Resurrection; and who can presume to speak for all Muslim generations to the Day of Resurrection?"[11] It is widely accepted today within Hamas that this is strictly a matter of Islamic jurisprudence, and that the Charter is not the best place in which to address it.

However, the biggest problem arising from the Charter lies in its treatment of the Jews. Part of the difficulty here is that of the language employed. The average Palestinian refers to Israelis as *yahud*, which is simply the Arabic word for Jews. Terms such as Zionist or Israeli figure mostly in the writings and conversations of an elite that has received secular education. They are not current in the vocabulary of the common man, and have until recently also been absent from Islamic discourse. When Arabic texts referring to the Israelis as *yahud* are translated into European languages, they may indeed sound anti-Semitic.

In his series of testimonies broadcast on Aljazeera between 17 April and 5 June 1999, Sheikh Yassin refers to the Israelis interchangeably at times as al-isra'iliyun (the Israelis) and at times as al-yahud (the Jews). In the second episode of the testimony, broadcast on 24 April 1999, he spoke as follows: "The Israelis usually deal with the Palestinian people individually and not collectively. Even inside the prisons, they would not agree to deal with the Palestinians except individually. However, we forced our will on them despite themselves and refused to deal with them except through a leadership elected by the Palestinian [prisoners] to face the Jews and resolve the problems with them." Most Palestinians and Arabs unconsciously use similar language. Leah Tsemel, an Israeli lawyer who has been defending Palestinians in Israeli courts for some 30 years, notes that her clients routinely describe soldiers or settlers as *al-yahud*, "the Jews." They complain for instance that "*al-yahud* [the Jews] took my ID card," or "*al-yahud* [the Jews] hit me," or "*al-yahud* [the Jews]" destroyed this or that. She expresses anxiety at the way Israel, in the minds of its Palestinian victims, becomes identified with all the Jews in the world and fears that, consequently all the Jews in the world may be seen as soldiers and settlers.

This problem is not confined to Palestine. The same phenomenon exists across the region, where Jews once lived in large numbers but from which, with a few exceptions, they are long departed. After the creation of the Israel State in Palestine in 1948, Jews living in various Arab countries were exhorted to come to the new Jewish entity, which, having expelled close to a million Palestinians, was in dire need of population.[12] Jews from Iraq, Yemen, and Morocco provided a source of cheap labor, doing work and performing functions the Ashkenazim (European Jews) were unwilling to do for themselves. The Ashkenazim presided over the Zionist colonial project in Palestine and set themselves up as first-class citizens of the newly founded Jewish state, in contrast to the Sephardic or Oriental (Mizrahi) Jews who came from the Arab countries.[13]

Until the beginning of the 20th century, Muslims, Christians, and Jews coexisted peacefully throughout the Muslim world. For many centuries, the Islamic empire, whose terrain extended over three continents, had provided a milieu of tolerance under a system that guaranteed protection for what are today referred to as minorities. Islam, whose values and principles governed the public and private conduct of Muslim individuals and communities, recognized Christians and Jews as legitimate communities within the Islamic State and accorded them inalienable rights. The adherents of both Christianity and Judaism participated on an equal footing with the Muslims in building the Arab-Islamic civilization on whose fruits the European Renaissance philosophers were nourished.

In contrast, in the European lands, the Jews suffered constant persecution. Many sought refuge in the Muslim lands, where they were welcomed and treated as people of the book in accordance with the Covenant of God and His Messenger. This Muslim perception of the Jews remained unchanged until the Zionist movement, which was born in Europe, began to recruit Jews in the Muslim lands for a project seen by the Muslims as an attack on their faith and homeland. The change in the Muslim attitude toward the Jews came as a reaction to the claims of the Zionist movement, which purported to represent the Jews and Judaism. Despite the secular origins of the Zionist project and the atheism of many of its founding fathers, the rationale of Zionism sought to justify the creation of the State of Israel in Palestine and the dispossession of the Palestinians in religious terms. The Zionist pioneers invoked scriptural justification for their actions, though few of them truly believed in religion or respected it. Their aim was to bestow religious legitimacy on their project and gain the support of the world's Jews, of whom many had initially opposed political Zionism.[14]

It is for this reason that the Hamas Charter characterizes the problem in Palestine as one of religious strife between the Jews and the Muslims. This idea continues to be dominant in many parts of the Muslim world today. The continued connection of Israel with the Jews, and the Jews with Israel, only reinforces the conviction of many Muslims that the conflict in the Middle East between the Palestinians and the Israelis is of a religious nature. Many Arabs and Muslims find it extremely difficult to believe in the existence of anti-Zionist Jews, who not only criticize Israel but in some instances refuse to recognize its legitimacy.[15]

Articles 17, 22, 28, and 32 of the Hamas Charter embody the accusation that the Jews are engaged in a conspiracy. The last of these articles goes as far as to refer to the Protocols of the Elders of Zion, a false document that purports to represent the plans of a supposed secret society of Jewish elders to conquer the world. What the author of the Charter wished to suggest was that there was a direct link between a supposed Jewish quest for global domination and the occupation of Palestine. Following a common tendency among Muslim writers of the time, the author of the Charter invoked the Qur'an and the Hadith (the sayings of the Prophet) to substantiate his claims. He seeks to show that there is a continuing Jewish conspiracy against Islam and the Muslims dating from the early days of Islam. Such selective readings and convenient interpretations of Islamic scripture are not uncommon in contemporary Muslim writings. In this case the Qur'an's chastisement of bad conduct and ill manners on the part of some of the Israelites of biblical times, or certain of the Jews during the time of the Prophet Muhammad, are taken out of their historical context. It is remarkable that, though the theory that the Jews are engaged in a conspiracy is in essence un-Islamic, it was widely espoused by Muslim intellectuals across the Arab world at least until the early 1990s. The pervasiveness of such thinking has been a symptom of decline and backwardness, which in turn have been instrumental in precipitating a profound sense of desperation and frustration.

Apart from its limited ability to explain, conspiracy theory tends to ascribe to human beings the powers of the Divine. Thanks to the efforts of thinkers such as Egypt's Abdelwahab Elmessiri, editor of the eight-volume Arabic *Encyclopedia of the Jews, Judaism, and Zionism*, the problem of Palestine is today seen by many Islamists, including leaders and members of Hamas, simply as the outcome of a colonial project. The conflict with Zionism should therefore be explained more in political, social, or economic terms than in terms of religion. There is a growing realization today that such explanations have more explanatory power and are more compatible with the Qur'anic paradigm of *tadafu'* (interaction or interplay).[16] Whereas the Qur'anic concept of *tadafu'* favors interpretations of events and situations in the world that offer motivation and hope, the theory that a conspiracy prevails leads to frustration and despair. In the first case, the only transcendental power in the world is that of God who empowers whom He so wishes and disempowers whom He so wishes.[17] One's actions may always be successful, if God wills. In the second case, little can be done to change the course of events, due to the assumption that a certain group of extremely powerful individuals, or community, has conspired to control the world and to seize all its resources. In this case, all contrary action will be in vain.

The only positive reference to the Jews in the Hamas Charter is seen in article 31, which states that "in the shade of Islam it is possible for the followers of the three religions, Islam, Christianity and Judaism to live in peace and security." It is anticipated that, while continuing to underline this historical fact, the new Hamas Charter will be cleansed of the ludicrous claim that there is a Jewish conspiracy. It will instead emphasize the racist nature of the Zionist project, explaining that many Jews are opposed to it. The idea that not every Jew is a Zionist is already widely accepted by the Islamists, who previously believed this was a myth invented by Palestinian secular nationalists. By shedding light on the roots of the conflict, a new Charter should appeal to the world's public opinion, attracting sympathy for the Palestinian victims rather than for their Israeli oppressors. To reach out to peoples and nations across the world, it will also need to adopt the conceptual framework of universal human rights. The new Hamas Charter is also expected to reassure the Jews that Hamas is not opposed to them because of their faith or race, and that it rejects the idea that the Middle East conflict is between Muslims and Jews, defined in terms of their religion. Nor is it between the faiths of Islam and Judaism. Sheikh Ahmad Yassin offered such a reassurance on a number of occasions before his assassination by the Israelis in 2004.[18] The new Charter will stress that Islam recognizes Judaism as a legitimate religion and accords its adherents respect and protection. The Charter must lay down as a basic principle that Jews and Muslims can live together today in peace and harmony, as did earlier Muslims and Jews for many centuries, once the legitimate rights of the Palestinians are recognized and restored. This has been said repeatedly by Hamas leaders since the early 1990s.

Khalid Mish'al told a Canadian TV journalist that the liberation of Palestine "does not mean that either the Palestinian people, or we in Hamas, want to kill the Jews or want to throw them into the sea as Israel claims." He expressed his determination to continue the struggle to liberate Palestine and regain the rights of the Palestinians, but denied categorically that there was a war against the Jews. "No, we do not fight the Jews because they are Jews. We fight them because they stole our land and displaced our people; they carried out an aggression. We resist this Zionist project which is hostile." As for those Jews who do not fight the Palestinians, he said: "I have no problem with them, just as I have no problem with peaceful Christians or peaceful Muslims." He went on to explain that "if a Muslim were to attack me and steal my land, I have every right to fight back. This applies to all others irrespective of their race, identity or religion. This is our philosophy."[19]

The Idea of Hudna (Truce)

One thing that will remain unchanged in a new Hamas Charter is the movement's opposition to the State of Israel. If Hamas remains loyal to its founding principles, it will not recognize Israel's right to exist. Born out of the intifada (uprising) of 1987, Hamas declared that it had emerged "in order to liberate the whole of Palestine, all of it."[20] The movement came into existence partly in response to the oppressive treatment suffered by the Palestinians under Israeli occupation in the West Bank and Gaza, and partly because many felt strongly that Fatah, while carrying the banner of the Palestinian national liberation movement, had faltered. Like the membership of Fatah before it, most of Hamas's members and supporters had been refugees or children of refugees whose original homes were not the appalling camps in which they were born or where they grew up. They had previously lived on the other side of the so-called Green Line in the lands now colonized by Jewish immigrants who have come from Europe and elsewhere in the world. Like millions of Palestinians inside Palestine and in the diaspora, the founders of Hamas felt betrayed when the leadership of Fatah, which controlled the PLO, decided to give away the right of return of the Palestinians to their homes.

It is highly unlikely, therefore, that Hamas will ever recognize the legitimacy of the state of Israel or its right to exist. The movement regards Israel as nothing but a colonial enclave planted in the heart of the Muslim world, whose effect is to obstruct the revival of the umma, the global Muslim community, and to perpetuate Western hegemony in the region. Another consideration is that Palestine is an Islamic land that has been invaded and occupied by a foreign power. It would contravene the principles of Hamas's Islamic faith to recognize the legitimacy of the foreign occupation of any Muslim land. This applies all the more to the land that is the site of the first *qibla* of the Muslims (the spot toward which Muslim worshippers face during prayer), and the third most important mosque on earth.

This position is not exclusive to Hamas. Muslim scholars, with a few exceptions, have never ceased to express their absolute opposition to any recognition of the legitimacy of the creation of a Jewish state in Palestine. Over the past century Muslim scholars and jurists have issued numerous fatwas, or religious edicts, declaring null and void any agreement that legitimized the occupation of any part of Palestine. The first collective fatwa on this issue predates the creation of the State of Israel in Palestine. On 26 January 1935, more than 200 Islamic scholars came to Jerusalem from around Palestine to issue a fatwa prohibiting the forfeiture of any part of Palestine to the Zionists. Similar conferences were held and fatwas issued at various junctures in the history of the Middle East conflict. During the Nassirist era (1952–1970) in Egypt, the prestigious al-Azhar Islamic institution in Cairo prohibited any recognition of the State of Israel or any initiative to make peace with it. Sheikh Yusuf al-Qaradawi, one of the most authoritative scholars of contemporary times, frequently reiterated this position, which was unanimously adopted by more than 300 Islamic scholars from around the Muslim world during a meeting of the Islamic Jurisprudential Council in Kuwait in the mid-1990s. He explained that the fatwa that prohibited the recognition of Israel was based on the consideration that "Palestine is an Islamic land that cannot be forfeited voluntarily." He added that the same fatwa was re-issued at a later Islamic Jurisprudence conference in Bahrain.[21]

However, this doctrinal consideration does not deny the right of the Jews to live in Palestine, provided their presence there is not the outcome of invasion or military occupation. Nor does it prevent Muslims, including the Hamas movement, from negotiating a cease-fire agreement with the Israeli State in order to put an end to the bloodshed and to the suffering on both sides for as long as can be agreed on. The idea of a *hudna* (truce) with Israel originated in the early 1990s. Reference was made to it by the Amman-based head of Hamas Political Bureau, Musa Abu Marzuq, in a statement published by the Amman weekly *Al-Sabeel*, the organ of the Jordanian Islamic Movement, in February 1994. At about the same time, the founder of Hamas, Sheikh Ahmad Yassin, speaking from his prison cell, made the first similar reference to the idea of a *hudna*, when he proposed such a truce as an interim solution to the conflict between the Palestinians and the Israelis. Both Abu Marzuq and Sheikh Yassin repeated the offer on several occasions, but failed to interest the Israelis. Recently, Hamas spokesmen have made frequent reference to the idea of *hudna*.

Hudna is recognized in Islamic jurisprudence as a legitimate and binding contract whose objective is to bring about a cessation of fighting with an enemy for an agreed period of time. The truce may be short or long depending on mutual needs or interests.[22] Such a truce would be different from the Oslo peace accords, under which the PLO recognized the State of Israel and its right to exist. The difference is that under the terms of *hudna* the issue of recognition would not arise. This is because Hamas cannot, as a matter of principle, accept that land seized by Israel from the Palestinians has become Israel's. Hamas has no authority to renounce the right of the Palestinians to return to the lands and the homes from which they were forced out in 1948 or at any later time. It can, however, say that under the present circumstances the best it can do is regain some of the land lost, and secure the release of prisoners, in exchange for a cessation of hostilities.

In their justification of *hudna*, Hamas leaders look to the example of what happened between the Muslims and the Crusaders in the last decade of the 12th century. The conflict between the two sides in and around Palestine lasted for nearly 200 years. Of particular interest to Hamas in this regard is the Ramleh treaty concluded by Salah al-Din al-Ayyubi (Saladin) with Richard the Lionheart on 1 September 1192. The truce, which marked the end of the Third Crusade, lasted for a period of three years and three months. During this period, the Crusaders maintained control of the coast from Jaffa to Acre and were allowed to visit Jerusalem and to conduct commerce with the Muslims. In addition, reference is also frequently made to the first *hudna* ever in the history of Islam. Known as al-Hudaybiyah, the name of the location on the outskirts of Mecca where it was concluded, this agreement saw the suspension of hostilities between the Muslim community under the Prophet's leadership and the Meccan tribe of Quraysh. The duration of the *hudna* agreed to by both sides was ten years. However, it came to an end less than two years later when Quraysh breached it with the unlawful killing of some members of the tribe of Khuza'ah, which was allied to the Muslim side. Once *hudna* is concluded, it is considered sacred, and the fulfillment of its obligations becomes a religious duty. As long as the other party observes it, the Muslim side must not breach it; to do so is considered a grave sin. As in the case of other international treaties, a *hudna* is renewable by mutual agreement at the expiration of its term.

The general and long-term *hudna* proposed by Hamas stipulates as a first condition an Israeli withdrawal to the borders of 4 June 1967, which means the return of all the land occupied by the Israelis as a result of the Six-Day War, including East Jerusalem.[23] This would entail the removal of all Jewish settlers from those areas.[24] In addition, Israel would have to release all Palestinians held in its prisons and detention camps. It is highly unlikely that Hamas would settle for anything less in exchange for a long-term truce that could last for a quarter of a century or longer.

The Suicide Bomb

Hudna was Sheikh Ahmad Yassin's solution to the crisis created by Hamas's suicide bomb campaign. In April 1994, Israeli army and intelligence officers visited Sheikh Ahmad Yassin in his prison cell in the hope of obtaining from him a statement that might dissuade Hamas's military wing from carrying out more suicide or "martyrdom" operations. Hamas had launched a series of devastating suicide bomb attacks in April 1994 in retaliation for the massacre perpetrated on 25 February 1994 in al-Haram al-Ibrahimi Mosque in Hebron by an American-born Jewish settler, Baruch Goldstein. Goldstein is believed to have secured the assistance of Israeli troops to gain entry to the mosque, where he fired on the worshippers and threw hand grenades at them as they kneeled during the dawn prayers, killing 29 and wounding scores of others.

The series of revenge acts began at noon on 6 April 1994, when Ra'id Abdullah Zakarnah, an Izzadin al-Qassam Brigades member, drove a booby-trapped vehicle with an Israeli license plate into Afula bus station and blew it up, killing nine Israelis and injuring more than 150. A statement issued soon afterward by Hamas's military wing, the Izzadin al-Qassam Brigades, claimed responsibility for the bombing and warned the Israelis to evacuate their settlements in the West Bank and Gaza. In a clear reference to Goldstein's actions inside the mosque, Hamas vowed to make the Israelis pay for the pain and harassment Jewish settlers inflict on the Palestinians under occupation.[25] On 31 April 1994, Ammar Amarnah, another member of the Izzadin al-Qassam Brigades, carried out the second attack. The target this time was an Israeli Egad bus, at al-Khadirah (Hadera) to the northwest of Tulkarm. Amarnah blew himself up on the bus killing five Israelis and wounding more than thirty. More operations were carried out that year and many more in succeeding years. They were for the most part in response to attacks on Palestinian civilians by Israeli troops or Jewish settlers. Sheikh Ahmad Yassin told his Israeli prison visitors that if they wanted to see an end to these attacks they could make a deal, which could be either limited or comprehensive. In its limited format the *hudna* would at least spare civilians on both sides. In its more comprehensive format it would entail an end to hostilities of all kinds between the two sides. There is no evidence to suggest that the Israelis have ever taken the offer of *hudna* seriously.

Resorted to out of utter desperation, suicide missions — "martyrdom operations" — were controversial when they were first launched. Many Palestinians were initially shocked by the suicide bomb tactic. Some argued against it from a purely pragmatic point of view, arguing that it was so shocking that it would harm the Palestinian cause. The operations were also opposed on the ground that they were, by their very nature, indiscriminate and resulted in killing innocent civilians, something the critics believed could not be justified or legitimized under any circumstance. The Fatah-led Palestinian Authority opposed the operations primarily on the grounds of its commitment to its own version of the peace process and the potential damage such operations could cause to it.

Hamas spokesmen maintained that the suicide bomb was the only means available to the Palestinians to deter those who might emulate Baruch Goldstein from launching further attacks on the defenseless Palestinian population. Over time, an increasing number of Palestinians accepted that the suicide bomb was necessary to offset the balance of power, which evidently favors the Israelis, who have acquired highly advanced military technology from the US and Europe. On the whole, Palestinians have generally approved of and admired the heroism and altruism of the men and women who have volunteered their bodies and souls to go on sacrificial missions on behalf of the cause of Palestine. The more the Palestinians have felt vulnerable, the more they have supported martyrdom operations and even demanded more. It did not take much to convince those who had qualms that nothing else seemed to be effective as a means of self-defense or deterrence. Nevertheless, Palestinian public support for martyrdom operations has varied. Polls conducted at different times have given different results, but rarely has support for these operations dropped below fifty percent. In a poll conducted in the Gaza Strip by the Norwegian organization Fafo in the first week of September 2005, 61 percent of those questioned agreed with the statement: "Suicide bombings against Israeli civilians are necessary to get Israel to make political concessions." Fafo also conducted a face-to-face survey with 875 respondents on Palestinian views of the Israeli withdrawal from the occupied Gaza strip.[26] The *Jerusalem Post* reported on 16 October 2003 that a poll showed that 75 percent of Palestinians supported the suicide bombing of the Maxim restaurant in Haifa on 4 October 2003. The opinion poll was conducted by the Palestinian Center for Policy and Survey Research (PSR) in Ramallah.[27] An earlier poll conducted by the Palestinian Authority's State Information Service (SIS) between 11 and 13 June 2002 in both the West Bank and the Gaza Strip revealed that 81 percent of the sample polled objected to the PA's designation of martyrdom operations as terrorist acts. Fifty-two percent of them said the PA resorted to labeling these operations as terrorist actions because of international pressure. The total number of those polled was 1,137, aged 18 years and above, 456 of them from the Gaza Strip and 681 from the West Bank. Incidentally, the poll also revealed that 86 percent of the sample "supported military attacks against Israeli occupation troops and Jewish settlers inside the Palestinian territories." Sixty-nine percent believed that the objective of carrying out martyrdom operations inside Israeli towns was to end the occupation, while 13.4 percent believed the objective was to undermine the peace process. Finally, 11.3 percent said the operations were intended to weaken the Palestinian Authority and embarrass it before the international community.[28]

Until it was employed in Palestine, the notion of the suicide bomb was seen as alien to the Sunni community within Islam. It had been more commonly associated with Shi'ism: the Iranians are believed to have been the first Muslims to employ it. They did so with some success in the war with Iraq throughout the 1980s. Hundreds of Iranian young men were sent on martyrdom missions along the borders between the two countries, to deter the Iraqi troops, who were well-equipped and heavily armed, thanks to Western and Arab support. The tactic served the Iranians well, since their Iraqi counterparts, many of whom had not been convinced of the legitimacy of the war with Iraq's neighbor launched by their government, were not prepared to make similar sacrifices.

The tactic then moved to Lebanon in the aftermath of the Israeli invasion in 1982. The first martyrdom operation within Lebanon took place on 11 November 1982, when a young Shi'a, Ahmad Qasir, identified as a member of the Islamic Resistance, drove his car into the headquarters of the Israeli military governor in Tyre, detonating its 440 pounds of explosives and killing 74 Israelis. From then on, the suicide bomb became a routine tactic employed by the Lebanese resistance against Israeli occupation troops. The most memorable of all suicide bombings in Lebanon were the two simultaneous attacks carried out on 23 October 1983 against the US Battalion Landing Team headquarters and the base occupied by the French Paras, which were situated just 3.7 miles apart in Beirut. The two suicide bombers, both of whom died in the attack, were named as Abu Mazen, 26, and Abu Sij'an, 24. A previously unknown group called the Free Islamic Revolutionary Movement (FIRM) claimed responsibility for the two attacks, which together killed 241 American and 58 French soldiers. FIRM was apparently made up of Lebanese Shi'a Muslims associated with the Amal militia. Hezbollah had not yet emerged, but FIRM may have been its precursor. Lebanon also produced the first female suicide bomber in the Arab world: her name was Sana'

Mhaidli. Her car bombing of an Israeli military convoy on 9 April 1985 was claimed by the secular Syrian Nationalist Party. The Lebanese Hezbollah, founded with Iranian backing as a Shi'ite Muslim response to the Israeli occupation of South Lebanon, inherited the task of resistance and the tactic of the suicide bomb. It continued to employ the technique until Israel withdraw unilaterally from South Lebanon in May 2000, having concluded it could no longer bear the human cost of its military presence in part of Lebanon, in which more than 1,000 Israeli soldiers had died.

Suicide bombing is far from being a uniquely Muslim phenomenon. Elsewhere in the world, the Sri Lankan Tamil Tigers, who struggle for an independent Tamil state, began to carry out suicide bombings in 1987. It is estimated that they have since perpetrated over 200 such attacks. The Tamil suicide bomb attacks were employed primarily to assassinate politicians opposed to their cause. In 1991, they assassinated former Indian Prime Minister Rajiv Gandhi, and in 1993, they assassinated President Ranasinghe Premadasa of Sri Lanka. In 1999, the Tigers attempted to assassinate Sri Lankan President Chandrika Kumaratunga using a female suicide bomber.

Until the outbreak of the second intifada, Islamic groups in Lebanon and Palestine did not deem it appropriate to use female suicide bombers. Hamas was reluctant to recruit female bombers but removed the ban under pressure from its female members, some of whom threatened to act on their own initiative or in association with other factions. The first female bomber in Palestine was Wafa Idris, aged 26, who blew herself up in Yaffa Street in Jerusalem on 28 January 2001. She was the first of ten other female "martyrs." The last of these was Zaynab Ali, who blew herself up on 22 September 2004. The campaign of female suicide bombings was launched by Fatah's al-Aqsa Martyrs' Brigades, which was soon joined by the Palestinian Islamic Jihad and Hamas.

It is very likely that Hamas was persuaded to use suicide bombers when it became clear that the tactic was delivering results in Lebanon. It could not have been a coincidence that the first martyrdom operation was carried out in Palestine in the year after the return of the Hamas and Islamic Jihad deportees from South Lebanon, where for a year they had ample time to listen and learn from their Lebanese hosts. This brought pressure to bear on Hamas's political leaders who, while defending the tactic, were keen not to be directly associated with planning the operations or authorizing them. They delegated this task to the Izzadin al-Qassam Brigades. Hamas spokesmen were at pains to explain the distinction between the military and political wings of the movement. They explained that the latter also ran educational, relief, and media institutions that had to be protected from Israeli reprisals or from punitive measures by the international community. The theory was that the political leadership of Hamas laid down the general policy of the movement, whereas the military wing was an autonomous body that functioned independently of the political leadership, but in accordance with the general lines the political leadership laid down.[29] The Israelis were never convinced by this, and nor were the Americans or the Europeans. By 2003, Hamas and many of the organizations identified as having been associated with it, directly or indirectly, were banned and put on the Western lists of terrorist organizations. The political leaders of Hamas were targeted for assassination by the Israeli army or by Mossad. Some escaped but many died.

Suicide Bombs: Strategy or Desperation?

There has been much debate over whether the tactic of suicide bombing arises from the dire economic conditions suffered by the Palestinians, or if it is simply part of a strategy aimed at the achievement of particular political objectives. It would be wrong to suggest that either explanation necessarily excludes the other. Many visitors to the occupied territories have privately or publicly expressed a degree of understanding as to why the Palestinians resort to these operations. However, the majority of "martyrs" do not come from poor or desperate backgrounds, while many of them are well educated and of good standing in the community. It is true that in general the condition of despair and frustration contributes to the motivation. But it is simply wrong to say that such operations are a reaction to the grave economic crisis caused by occupation, though they are occasionally presented as such. They have a strategic purpose, and are seen as the only means of pressuring the Israelis, both the government and individuals, to recognize the rights of the Palestinians and eventually to agree to a cease-fire deal that would at least spare the civilians in future.

Hamas is explicit in its objectives. In the document entitled "This is What We Struggle for," cited above, the movement declares that martyrdom operations "are in principle directed against military targets." It explains that "targeting civilians is considered an aberration from Hamas's fundamental position of hitting only military targets. They represent an exception necessitated by the Israeli insistence on targeting Palestinian civilians and by Israel's refusal to agree to an understanding prohibiting the killing of civilians on both sides, comparable to the one reached between Israel and Hezbollah in southern Lebanon." This refers to the agreement concluded between Hezbollah and Israel on 26 April 1996 in the aftermath of the Qana massacre perpetrated by the Israeli army on 18 April 1996. Sheikh Ahmad Yassin has repeatedly offered the Israelis a truce. He is quoted in this same document as saying: "Hamas does not endorse the killing of civilians, but that is sometimes the only option it has if it is to respond to the murdering of Palestinian civilians and the cold-blooded assassination of Palestinian activists."

In an interview recorded for a Canadian TV production company, Khalid Mish'al summed up his view on the martyrdom operations as follows:

Martyrdom operations are acts of legitimate self-defense forced on us because the battle between us and Israel is not between equal sides and because the Israeli occupation has not left our land and no one has done us justice. We do know that, as you have said, many sympathizers [with the Palestinians] around the world do not understand the issue of the martyrdom operations which may prompt them to reconsider their sympathy. However, we ask, "what is the alternative?" There is no alternative. Had the Palestinian people found the alternative they would have done without the resistance and without the martyrdom operations. They have been forced to resort to them. Nevertheless, we took the initiative more than ten years ago to propose sparing civilians on both sides of the conflict. We said we were prepared to stop the martyrdom operations, provided Israel also stops killing Palestinian civilians including women, children and the elderly and stops destroying homes. Should Israel stop, we would be ready to stop. But Israel refused. Israel wants the Palestinian people to watch the aggression and the occupation but do nothing and refrain from self-defense. In the meantime, it wants to maintain the right to continue aggression, occupation and murder the way it wants. Which law in the world would permit the continuation of this condition whereby Israel is free to commit aggression, occupation and assassination while the Palestinians are denied the right to self-defense? If the world wishes to stop the bloodshed inside occupied Palestine, it should address both sides saying, "Israel must stop the aggression and the Palestinians must stop their military operations." The world should force Israel to withdraw from our occupied land, serve justice to our people and give them back their rights. When they do that then we shall not be compelled to exercise martyrdom operations or resistance operations. Do not demand the Palestinians to give up their right to self-defense while Israeli is continuing its aggression and murder and continuing the occupation of their land and holy shrines." [30]

Tahdi'ah

Hamas only resorted to the suicide bomb in the hope of forcing Israel to agree to spare the civilians on both sides, or, still better, to negotiate a long-term ceasefire agreement. Following his release from detention and his return to Gaza in October 1997, Sheikh Ahmad Yassin offered to suspend Hamas martyrdom operations if the Israelis were ready, as he put it, "to stop their attacks on [Palestinian] civilians, end land confiscation and house demolitions, and release the prisoners and detainees." This is not quite the same as the long-term truce in which he said his movement was ready to engage, provided Israel agree to withdraw from the West Bank and Gaza and dismantled its Jewish settlements. [31] The offer of truce was reiterated in October 1999 by the Izzadin al-Qassam Brigades, who said they were ready to halt their attacks on Israeli civilians "provided Israel stops its settlement activities and land confiscation and provided Israeli troops and Jewish settlers stop attacking Palestinian civilians." [32]

There were at least three occasions on which a "temporary *hudna*," usually referred to as a *tahdi'ah* (calming), was unilaterally declared by Hamas and other Palestinian factions. The most recent *tahdi'ah*, which Hamas continued to abide by at least until 9 June 2006, was agreed upon during the Cairo talks of March 2005; it was supposed to last until the end of 2005 but went well beyond that. The first *tahdi'ah*, however, was in 2002, and was brokered by European Union emissary Alastair Crooke. This *tahdi'ah* was shattered several weeks later, when the Israelis assassinated Hamas leader Salah Shihadah on 22 July 2002. On 29 June 2003, Hamas and Islamic Jihad declared a unilateral truce. The decision to observe this *tahdi'ah* was announced by Hamas leader Abd al-Aziz al-Rantisi, who explained that it was a gesture to give a chance to the newly elected Palestinian Prime Minister Mahmud Abbas to negotiate with the Israelis. This second *tahdi'ah* came to an end seven weeks later, when Israel assassinated the Hamas leader Isma'il Abu Shanab on 21 August 2003. Israel claimed that the assassination was in retaliation for the bombing of a Jerusalem bus that left 21 Israelis dead and more than 100 wounded.

In fact, the Israelis never recognized or accepted the unilateral truces declared by the Islamic factions in Palestine, continuing to pursue their strategy of eliminating whomsoever they considered a potential threat to their security. Throughout the month of July 2003, a number of Palestinians were assassinated in Nablus and Hebron. On 19 August 2003, an attack in Jerusalem was carried out by Ra'id Misk, a native of Hebron, in retaliation for the assassination of some of his fellow Hamas members in Hebron by Israeli army special units after the declaration of the truce. It transpired later that Hamas members in Hebron were ordered to observe the truce despite the Israeli provocations. However, they could not stand by while their colleagues were being hunted down, one after the other. The Israeli campaign of targeted assassinations in the Hebron area began before Hamas declared its unilateral truce and included the murder of a local Hamas leader, Sheikh Abdullah al-Qawasimi, on 22 June 2003.

Israel's refusal to reciprocate led many Palestinians to lose confidence in the usefulness of declaring a unilateral truce. The sense of frustration was heightened when the European Union decided in August 2003 to proscribe Hamas and place it on its list of terrorist organizations. On 6 September 2003, emboldened by the EU decision, Israel made its first attempt to assassinate Sheikh Ahmad Yassin. An Israeli fighter jet dropped a 500-pound bomb on a residential building in Gaza City where Sheikh Yassin was paying a visit, in the company of a number of Hamas figures including Isma'il Haniyah, who in 2006 became prime minister. Fifteen Palestinians were wounded, and Sheikh Yassin was lucky enough to escape with scratches. In a statement given to journalist Graham Usher following this failed assassination attempt, Sheikh Yassin said: "We gave the Israeli enemy a *hudna* for 50 days, but the Israelis did not commit to it. They continued with their aggression, killings and crimes and erected this separation wall that they continue to build. Their settlements are still stealing our land. There are house demolitions and destruction all over the West Bank and Gaza. Just yesterday in Gaza they demolished three towers under the pretext that they were built close to a settlement. Tell me, where are the families living in those towers to go? So it is not a question of what Hamas thinks or what Fatah thinks. It is a question of the Palestinian national interest: does this lie in resistance or in the declaration of a *hudna*?"[33]

The Israelis also attempted to assassinate Dr. Mahmud al-Zahhar with an air strike on his family home that leveled it to the ground. Dr. al-Zahhar escaped with injuries but lost his eldest son in the attack, which left his wife permanently paralyzed and his daughter seriously wounded. At a rally held in November that year, Sheikh Yassin declared that the movement found it futile to observe a cease-fire unilaterally. He said, "We declared a truce in the past, but it failed because Israel did not want peace or security for the Palestinian people." Addressing the same rally, Hamas leader al-Zahhar urged the Palestinians to resume armed resistance.[34]

In the aftermath of the 11 September 2001 attacks on Washington and New York, the controversy over suicide bombing intensified. The ongoing debate in Islamic jurisprudential and political circles about martyrdom operations will be discussed in the following chapter.

What Comes After Hudna?

Hamas is silent about what happens when a notional long-term *hudna* signed with the Israelis comes to its appointed end. While Hamas's leaders have left open the length of the term of the proposed *hudna*, regarding this as a subject for negotiation with the Israelis once they have accepted the principle, their general philosophy is that the future should be left for future generations. It is usually assumed that a long-term *hudna* will probably last for a quarter of a century or more. That is viewed as too long a time for anyone now to predict what may happen afterward. There will always be the possibility that the *hudna* will come to a premature end because of a breach. If that were to occur, it would be highly unlikely that the breach would come from the Hamas side. This is for the simple reason that it is a religious obligation on the Islamic side to honor such an agreement to the end, once made, unless it is violated by the other party. Should the *hudna* last till the prescribed date, one scenario is that those in charge then will simply negotiate a renewal.

Another scenario prevalent within the thinking of some Hamas intellectuals is that the world situation will change so much that Israel, as a Zionist
entity, may not wish, or may not have the ability, to continue to exist. In
principle, there is no reason why Muslims, Christians, and Jews could not
live together in the region in future as they lived together before for many
centuries. What Islamists usually have in mind here is an Islamic state,
a caliphate, which it is envisaged would encompass much of the Middle
East. This would reverse the fragmentation that the region underwent as
the result of 19th-century colonialism, and of the Sykes–Picot agreement
of 1916. The entities thus created became separate territorial states in the
aftermath of the collapse of the Ottoman order in the second decade of
the 20th century. While the existence of Israel as an exclusive state for
the Jews in Palestine is something an Islamic movement such as Hamas
could never accept as legitimate, the Jews could easily be accommodated
as legitimate citizens of a multifaith and multiracial state governed by
Islam. The post-Israel scenario, which has become a subject for debate
within Hamas, is one that envisages a Palestine, or a wider united Middle
East, with a Jewish population but no political Zionism. This is a vision
inspired by the South African model of reconciliation that ended apartheid
but allowed all the country's communities to continue to live together.
In Hamas's thinking, Zionism is usually equated with apartheid, and its
removal is seen as the way forward if Muslims, Christians, and Jews are
ever to coexist in peace in the region. It would be impossible for such a
scenario to translate into reality without a long-term *hudna*, which for the
lifetime of an entire generation would offer communities and peoples in
the region the opportunity to restore normality to their lives.

Those who are skeptical about the concept of *hudna* may argue that
in reality it signifies nothing but a prelude to the process of destroying
Israel entirely. However, without a *hudna*, the Palestinians will continue
to struggle for the freedom of Palestine until their right to return to their
homes is restored, pursuing that end using whatever means are at their
disposal, however violent. The advantage of the *hudna* is that it brings
to an end the bloodshed and the suffering because of the commitment to
maintain it for a specific time. There will be a breathing space, in which
each side can dream its dreams of how the future may look, while keeping
the door open to all options. Under normal circumstances, the best
option is always that which involves least cost.

EIGHT

JIHAD AND MARTYRDOM

*When the Muslim explodes himself in the midst of combat-
ant enemies, he only performs an act of self-defense; it is martyrdom because the recompense for an injury is an injury equal thereto.
What Israel is doing inside the Palestinian territories would only
drive any Muslim to seek revenge and act in self-defense.*[1]

—Sheikh Sayyid Tantawi

HAMAS IS BELIEVED TO HAVE BEEN THE FIRST SUNNI MUSLIM GROUP TO employ the strategy of suicide bombing, which stirred up an intense debate within Sunni circles. With no single Sunni Muslim authority empowered to issue a decisive fatwa on the matter, and with the spread of the strategy, the controversy is far from over.

The first and most critical question is whether the act is suicide or sacrifice. The second issue relates to the problem of the indiscriminate consequences of suicide bombing, and the inevitability that it may, despite all precautions, result in the deaths of innocent civilians, and particularly of children. The third problem concerns the consequences of the strategy for the lives of the community in whose defense such operations are carried out. Because the Israelis have both the means and the will to respond with air attacks, incursions, and every form of collective punishment, the utility of suicide bombing as a means of deterrence or a weapon of retaliation has been a central point of contention. However, Palestinian factions that employed the tactic in the years leading up to Ariel Sharon's decision to implement his plan for a unilateral withdrawal from Gaza believe they should be credited for forcing the Israelis to withdraw.

Opponents disagree and attribute the Israeli decision to other factors, including Israel's concern about the growth of the Palestinian population in areas under its control and its plan to annex much of the land in the West Bank where large Jewish settlements exist. Meanwhile, both the supporters of martyrdom operations and their opponents justify their positions, which in essence are entirely political, on the basis of contentions drawn from Islamic sources and Islamic historical precedent.

Life and Death

Islam teaches that none but the Creator Himself has the right to take the life of any human being. One of the five essentials that the Islamic Shari'ah is said to seek to protect is human life itself.[2] Having recounted the story of the murder of Adam's son Abel by his brother Cain, the Qur'an concludes, "On that account, we have ordained for the children of Israel that if anyone slay a person, unless it be in retribution for murder or spreading mischief in the land, it would be as if he slew the whole people. And if anyone saved a life, it would be as if he saved the life of the whole people" (Surat al-Ma'idah 5:32). The Qur'an also says: "Take not life which Allah made sacred otherwise than in the course of justice" (Surat al-An'am 6:151).

It is therefore only in the course of justice that there is authority for life to be taken. In such circumstances, the taking of life is intended to save life. "In the Law of Equity [capital punishment for murderers] there is [the saving of] Life for you, O ye men of understanding; that ye may show piety" (Surat al-Buqarah 2:179). The Shari'a goes into much detail in defining the conditions where taking life is permissible, whether in war or in peace. To prevent abuse, the Islamic criminal law takes every precaution, in order to minimize the need for capital punishment, and to ensure that justice is served.[3]

War in Islam is considered a necessary evil. This can clearly be inferred from the Qur'an itself. "And Allah turned back the Unbelievers for [all] their fury: no advantage did they gain. And Allah has spared the Believers the need to fight. And Allah is full of Strength, Able to enforce His Will" (Surat al-Ahzab 33:25). It is from this verse that Sheikh Yusuf al-Qaradawi, a renowned Egyptian scholar identified with the Muslim Brotherhood, who is resident in Qatar, concludes that war in Islam is a necessity, but should be resorted to only when the necessity is extreme. "The rule in Islam is to make peace and to promote it." In Islam, he explains, if hostility could be assuaged and crisis resolved without the need to engage in battle, that would be best. "The Qur'an describes a situation where God spares the believers the necessity of fighting, as if fighting is a negative thing rather than a positive thing."[4]

There are two words in the Islamic lexicon associated with fighting. *Qital*, which derives from the Arabic triliteral root of the verb *qatala*, means to kill or to slay. The word *qital*, and all its derivatives, which relate to the concept of combat, feature in the chapters of the Qur'an that were revealed in Medina, following the creation of the Islamic state that came after the migration of the Prophet and his earliest followers from their homes in Mecca. The word jihad, which derives from the triliteral root of the verb *jahada*, features in the chapters of the Qur'an revealed during the Meccan period, which lasted thirteen years. The verb *jahada* may mean to endeavor, strive, labor, or take pains. It may also mean to overwork, overtax, fatigue or exhaust, strain, exert, tire, wear out or give trouble, concentrate on, or put one's mind to something. It has also been used with a similar meaning to *qatala*, to fight or combat.

Jihad

The earliest appearance of the word *jahada* or jihad in the revelation of the Qur'an was associated with the struggle of the nascent Muslim community against oppression. Jihad was a struggle for the freedom for the community to worship according to their monotheistic faith and for the right to invite others to embrace it. When Islam was first preached to the Arab community in Mecca, the city's elders perceived it as a rebellion aimed at changing the political status quo. Those in power felt threatened by Muhammad's call to the people to re-examine their inherited beliefs and values. What was especially threatening was his powerful critique of the way of life of his fellow citizens, which the Qur'an described as sinful and misguided.

The revelations of the Qur'an, recounted by those few who dared follow the Prophet despite the intimidation to which they were subjected, poured scorn on idolatry and chastized the Arabs for claiming that their Gods had given them authority to commit what Islam regarded as heinous crimes and sinful acts. The challenge to those in authority was serious. The Prophet of the new creed claimed to be the rightful inheritor of Abraham, the ancestral father of the Arabs and the Israelites, and presented himself as the confirmation of all the messages and prophets that preceded him. He appealed to the weak and the oppressed, to the poor and the destitute, and to all those discriminated against by the Arabs. During the first thirteen years of his mission, from around 610 to 622, the Prophet refrained from challenging the Arab polytheists, apart from engaging them in debate and reciting the Qur'an to them. He attracted to himself the oppressed members of the community, who saw in his message a promise of emancipation, and of deliverance from servitude. His challenge to the mighty and powerful was: "allow me the freedom to speak and the people the freedom to choose."

The principal tribe in Mecca, into which Prophet Muhammad was born in around 570, was that of the Quraysh. The elders of the tribe were determined not to allow him to strip them of their prestige or deprive them of their authority by turning the young men of the tribe, and their women, slaves, and servants, against them. They orchestrated a campaign to denigrate him, claiming he was a charlatan, a magician, a poet, and a fortune teller. People were warned to stay away from him, in case they should come under the influence of his spell. When these tactics failed to work, the Prophet Muhammad's opponents used force against him and his followers. Those among them who were weak and could call on no strong tribal support were persecuted. They were tortured, and some lost their lives. At one point, the entire community of monotheists was banished into a barren valley. Trade with them was forbidden for three years and the Arabs in and around Mecca were ordered to boycott them. When that too failed to curb the growth of the Prophet Muhammad's following, the elders sought to negotiate a compromise with him. They offered to recognize his God provided he recognized their idols. Their suggestion was that all the supposed deities, both his and theirs, should be worshipped.

The Prophet was instructed by the Qur'an not to heed the call for any such compromise: "Say: O you *kafirun* [those who are thankless or reject faith], I worship not that which you worship, nor will you worship that which I worship. And I will not worship that which you have been wont to worship, nor will you worship that which I worship. To you be your Way, and to me mine" (Surat al-Kafirun 109:1–6). Instead he was instructed by the Qur'an to perform *jihadan kabiran* (a most strenuous struggle) against them (Surat al-Firqan 25:52). This verse from the Sura al-Furqan was revealed in Mecca, and forms part of the Qur'an's response to the constant endeavor by the polytheists of Mecca to dissuade the Prophet from preaching monotheism. In chronological terms, this verse is believed to be the first Qur'anic reference to jihad. Similar to this is the following reference to jihad in the Sura al-Hajj: "And strive hard in Allah's Cause as you ought to strive [with sincerity and with all your efforts]. He has chosen you [to convey His Message to mankind] and has not laid upon you in religion any hardship: it is the religion of your father Abraham" (Sura 22:78).

Jihad at the time involved no *qital* (fighting or combat): it was an entirely nonviolent form of struggle. In fact, throughout the Meccan period, thirteen years out of a total of twenty-three years of Muhammad's Prophethood, the Muslims were forbidden to use force. The prohibition was not self-imposed but in accordance with divine commandment. Not even when they suffered persecution or were tortured were they allowed to respond with violence. They were told to be patient, show self-restraint, and withhold their hands.[5]

Observance of patience and self-restraint was hailed as a noble act, a jihad, for which God promised the highest of rewards in the Hereafter. Consider for instance the reference to jihad in the last verse of Sura al-'Ankabut: "And those who perform jihad [strive] in Our Cause. We will certainly guide them to Our Paths: for verily Allah is with those who do right." It would not be possible to interpret this verse correctly without taking into consideration the first few verses of the same chapter. Verses 1–6 unequivocally associate jihad with self-restraint and abstention from the use of violence in response to persecution: "Do people think that they will be left alone because they say: 'We believe,' and will not be tested. And We indeed tested those who were before them. And Allah will certainly make [it] known [the truth of] those who are true, and will certainly make [it] known [the falsehood of] those who are liars. Or do they think, those who do evil deeds, that they can outstrip Us? Evil is that [which] they judge. Whoever hopes for the Meeting with Allah, then Allah's Term is surely coming, and He is the All-Hearer, the All-Knower.

And whosoever strives, he strives only for himself. Verily, Allah stands not in need of any of His creation" (Surat al-'Ankabut 29:1–6).

Despite the clarity of the nature of the original concept of jihad, an English language dictionary can scarcely be found that does not suggest "holy war" as its meaning. According to the Merriam-Webster Dictionary, for instance, jihad is "a holy war waged on behalf of Islam as a religious duty." The dictionary provides two other meanings: "a personal struggle in devotion to Islam especially involving spiritual discipline"; and "a crusade for a principle or belief." However, there is nothing whatsoever in the Islamic sources that describes war as holy. The rendering of the word jihad into "holy war" has more to do with the history of Christianity in Europe than with the teachings or the history of Islam. The term "holy war" is a European Christian invention dating back to around 1096 CE, when Rome began to preach a "Holy Crusade" "to free the Holy City of Jerusalem from the clutches of heretics and infidels."[6]

Qital

The ban on fighting was lifted a few years after the *hijra*, the migration in 622 of the Prophet and his followers from Mecca to Medina in search of a safe haven. The Muslim community of Medina endowed itself with a political structure by virtue of a constitution known as the Medina Document. Only when this community needed to defend itself against external threats was permission given to use force and engage the enemies in battle. "Permission to fight [against disbelievers] is given to those [believers] who are fought against, because they have been wronged; and surely, Allah is able to give them victory. Those who have been expelled from their homes unjustly only because they said: 'Our Lord is Allah.' For had it not been that Allah checks one set of people by means of another, monasteries, churches, synagogues, and mosques, wherein the Name of Allah is mentioned much, would surely have been pulled down. Verily Allah will help those who help His [Cause]. Truly Allah is All-Strong, All-Mighty" (Surat al-Hajj 22:39–40).

Nevertheless, the license to fight is not unrestricted. Only when attacked, or when they perceive the threat of imminent attack, are Muslims allowed to take to arms. "And fight in way of Allah those who fight you, but transgress not the limits. Truly, Allah likes not the transgressors"

(Surat al-Baraqah 2:190). Once engaged in battle, Muslim troops are supposed to abide by a strict code of conduct. The terms of this code are stated clearly in the hadith (the sayings and tradition of the Prophet) and are elucidated in the books of *fiqh* (Islamic jurisprudence). It is reported that the Caliph Abu Bakr said in a farewell sermon to Muslim troops heading for battle with the Byzantines: "I recommend to you that you fear Allah and obey Him. When you engage the enemies do not loot, do not mutilate the dead, do not commit treachery, do not behave in a cowardly way, do not kill children, the elderly or women, do not burn trees or damage crops, and do not kill an animal unless lawfully acquired for food. You will come across men confined to hermitages in which they claim to have dedicated their lives to worshipping God: leave them alone. When you engage the pagan infidels, invite them to choose between two things. Invite them to embrace Islam. If they do not wish to do so, invite them to pay the *jizyah* [a tax paid by non-Muslims who reside in a land conquered by force]. If they agree to either, accept it from them and stop fighting. But if they reject both, then fight them."[7]

In Islamic literature on hadith and *fiqh*, when jihad is mentioned without further designation, it usually refers to *qital*. In this case it includes, in addition to carrying arms and fighting the enemies in the battlefield, the contribution of money or effort to the cause for which *qital* is undertaken: "O you who believe! Shall I lead you to a bargain that will save you from a grievous Chastisement? That you believe in Allah and His Messenger, and that you perform jihad [strive your utmost] in the Cause of Allah, with your wealth and your persons: that will be best for you if you only knew" (Surat al-Saff 61:10–11). Great risk is involved in jihad. However, Islam enjoins its followers to take that risk in anticipation of a great reward in the life after death. "Allah has purchased of the believers their persons and their wealth; for theirs in return is the Garden [of Paradise]: They fight in His Cause, and slay and are slain: a promise binding on Him in Truth, through the Torah, the Gospel, and the Qur'an. And who is more faithful to his Covenant than Allah? Then rejoice in the bargain which you have concluded: that is the achievement supreme" (Surat al-Tawbah 9:111).

Belief in the Day of Resurrection, in the inevitability of being brought to account and of being questioned and then rewarded or punished for one's deeds in this life, is one of the basic tenets of the Islamic faith.

To the faithful, this life is a temporary abode, a passageway toward the permanent abode, an eternal life in the Hereafter. Therefore, a believer has a mission in this life, namely to worship the One and Only God and submit oneself to no authority but His. Submission to the One and Only God entails freeing oneself from all other deities.

Resisting oppression and striving for a just world is an integral part of a believer's mission in life. According to the Tunisian Islamic thinker Rachid Ghannouchi, one of the basic features of the Islamic faith is that it generates within the believer a passion for freedom. The Algerian thinker Malik Bennabi had earlier asserted that the Islamic faith accomplishes two objectives: first, it liberates man from servitude and renders him impossible to enslave; and secondly, it prohibits him from enslaving others.[8] Many contemporary Islamic scholars and thinkers agree, explaining that this is precisely what the modern idea of "jihad" is about. For this reason it is not only on the battlefield that a believer is expected to perform jihad, which may be seen as the constant endeavor to struggle against all forms of political or economic tyranny whether domestic or foreign.

Martyrdom

Despite its sanctity in Islam, life can be sacrificed for the sake of ending oppression. Both the Qur'an and the hadith exhort Muslims to resist oppression and struggle against it by means of *al-amr bi-l-ma'ruf wa al-nahy 'an al-munkar* (enjoining the good and forbidding the evil). There is a hadith that instructs Muslims to deter evil with the hand, or with the tongue if that is all they can afford, or with the heart if they lack the power to do more. Muslim scholars, both past and present, have identified three levels of resistance or struggle. The minimum level is a psychological process whereby a Muslim prepares himself or herself to ascend to the next highest level by means of boycotting evil and detesting it. The higher level of resistance entails the condemnation of evil by way of various nonviolent means, such as speaking out against it, writing or demonstrating, or mobilizing public opinion to identify that which is wrong and endeavor to change it. The highest level of all is resistance by whatever force may be available.

What really matters is that oppression should never be given a chance to establish itself in society. A Muslim is supposed to be a conscientious

individual responding with appropriate action to whatever injustice may
be perpetrated in society, provided the chosen action does not produce a
greater evil than the one it is directed against. A Muslim is thus a force for
positive change, a citizen whose faith reinforces within him or her a sense
of responsibility to combat oppression. It is natural that a Muslim may
lose his or her life struggling against oppression, and for this he or she
is promised a great reward in the life after death. In other words effort
made is not wasted, and sacrifice is not in vain.

The Prophet Muhammad is quoted as saying: "The noblest of jihad is
speaking out against an unjust ruler in his very presence." He also said:
"Hamza [the Prophet's uncle and one of the earlier martyrs in Islam] is
the master of martyrs, and so is a person who stands up to an unjust ruler
enjoining him and forbidding him, and gets killed for it." It would only
be right to draw from this Prophetic tradition that martyrdom, by Islamic
criteria, is not failure. A martyr is not one who loses, but a hopeful human being who offers his or her life for what is perceived as more valuable and, at the same time, eternal. For this reason, martyrs are elevated
to the highest of all ranks. Muslims pray regularly for the attainment of
such status. A Muslim recites at least seventeen times a day in his *salat*
(prayer): "Show us the straight way, the way of those on whom you have
bestowed your Grace" (Sura 1:6–7). Those on whom God has bestowed
his grace belong to one of the categories listed in another Qur'anic verse,
which says: "Those who obey Allah and the Messenger are in the company of those on whom is the Grace of Allah: the Prophets, the sincere
[lovers of truth], the martyrs, and the righteous [who do good]. How
beautiful is their Company" (Sura 4:69).

By choosing to offer his or her life in the Cause of God, a believer
who is a would-be martyr enters into a transaction with his Lord, Allah.
Such a covenant is mentioned at least twice in the Qur'an and is referred
to in a number of hadith.[9] Martyrdom, the idea of sacrificing one's life
for a noble cause, is an Islamic concept. It is one of only two acceptable
outcomes of fighting in the cause of Allah: the other is victory. It would
seem, therefore, that from an Islamic perspective, life is not the most
precious thing, since it is highly commendable to give it up for what is
more precious: the freeing of one's self or one's community from the
shackles of servitude.

Martyrdom in the modern world is less simple than it may have been in the past. In historic times, Muslims went to war in a jihad to achieve either victory or martyrdom. A martyr was one who lost his life because of wounds inflicted on him by the enemy. Of course, it was uncertain which of the two wishes would be granted. Today, many of those who undertake jihad are virtually certain that martyrdom will be their fate. Those who fight are aware that victory is likely to be beyond their grasp, against a powerful enemy. Meanwhile, he who goes into the battle strapped round with dynamite will predetermine his fate when he detonates his explosives. Rather than be killed by the enemy he chooses to kill the enemy by killing himself. The wars such martyrs fight are not conventional ones. They know they cannot inflict damage on their enemy without destroying themselves as well as their adversaries.

Muslims did not invent suicide bombings, which those who advocate them describe as "martyrdom operations." Today, however, the strategy is identified with them and with their religion. In fact, Arab secular leftists carried out the first suicide missions in the Middle East. These operations mainly took the form of daring attacks from which the attacker had virtually no chance of escaping alive. The attack by members of the Japanese Red Army in 1972 at Lod Airport in Israel is regarded as one of the first such attacks in the Middle East. However, it was the Lebanese Hezbollah, which was founded in response to the Israeli invasion of Lebanon in 1982, who refined the strategy in the 1980s, as discussed in the previous chapter.

Sacrifice or Suicide?

The defenders of suicide bombing deem it an act of sacrifice, while those who oppose it see it as mere suicide. Those who speak in its favor regard the perpetrator as a martyr, a person who offers himself (or herself) for the sake of a noble cause, who earns the greatest of rewards and is designated to the highest ranks in Paradise. From this perspective, not only is the act permissible but is also highly commendable and appreciated. Those who defend that tactic believe it would not be right to designate the protagonist as having properly committed suicide, because suicide is strictly forbidden in Islam. The perpetrators do not resort to killing themselves out of desperation, they argue, otherwise their action would be a major sin. What they do should be seen as a sacrificial act.

Those who oppose suicide bombings on religious grounds, however, assume that their perpetrators are desperate individuals, who prefer to die than to live, having lost hope or patience. Such persons argue that what these individuals commit is nothing more than suicide, because of their knowledge that their course of action will lead inevitably to their death. Thus, they conclude that the suicide bomber is a sinner destined for the Fire of Hell.

Certainly, the Qur'an is unequivocal about the prohibition of suicide: "O ye who believe! Eat not up your property among yourselves in vanities: but let there be amongst you traffic and trade by mutual good-will: nor kill [or destroy] yourselves: for verily Allah hath been to you Most Merciful! If any do that in rancour and injustice, soon shall We cast them into the fire: and easy it is for Allah" (Surat al-Nisa' 4:29–30). Al-Bukhari reported that Prophet Muhammad said: "There was once a man before you who suffered a wound; he could not bear the pain, so he took a knife and bled himself to death. The Almighty Allah said: 'my servant has taken his own life; therefore I shall deny him admission to Paradise.'" The Prophet is also reported to have said: "Whoever kills himself with an iron instrument will carry it forever in hell. Whoever takes poison and kills himself will forever sip the poison in hell. Whoever jumps off a mountain and kills himself will fall forever down into the depths of hell."

In fact, only a fine line separates suicide from sacrifice. Which is which is determined by the intention of the actor. In contrast to suicide, the sacrifice of one's life for a noble cause is something Islam enjoins and for which it promises the highest of rewards. A person who turns himself or herself into a bomb to thwart or frustrate the enemy is therefore seen as a hero who makes the greatest of sacrifices for the sake of his faith, country, or umma.

Few Muslim scholars, if any, inside Palestine today subscribe to the opinion that self-immolation of this kind is an act of suicide. Sheikh Ikrima Sabri, the mufti of Jerusalem and the official mufti of the Palestinian Authority, has designated martyrdom operations as a noble act of sacrifice for the sake of God. He also harshly criticizes those scholars, mainly from Egypt and Saudi Arabia, who have denounced martyrdom operations as suicide, accusing them of ignorance, due to having failed to understand the context in which these operations take place inside Palestine. The Palestinian Chief Justice Sheikh Taysir al-Tamimi takes a similar view.

Defenders of martyrdom operations argue that the Islamic code of war applies only in conventional warfare, and refuse to accept that it should apply in the case of Palestine, where the situation is far from conventional. Palestine, in such a view, is an exception. The unarmed and defenseless people of Palestine have been invaded and oppressed by a power that is heavily armed with the most modern weapons, which enable them to kill, maim, and destroy while well out of the reach of retaliation on the part of their victims. From this viewpoint, whatever the Palestinians do to defend themselves and deter their oppressors is legitimate. It is often argued that only when the Palestinians have access to the sort of weapons possessed by the Israelis will it be illegitimate for them to resort to unconventional means of self-defense.

However, the attitude of scholars and religious institutions outside Palestine toward martyrdom operations has been varied. The divisions seem to be prompted by political rather than jurisprudential considerations. In principle, no one denies the existence of the concept of self-sacrifice since it is explicitly defined in the Qur'an and the hadith. However, a number of establishment scholars, representing government-controlled religious institutions in Saudi Arabia and Egypt, have argued that martyrdom operations are illegitimate. Some of these deem such actions to be acts of suicide because of the certainty of death. Others oppose them because they violate the Islamic code of war, through the indiscriminate killing of innocent civilians, including children.

One of the most outspoken of the scholars who oppose martyrdom operations has been the mufti of Saudi Arabia, Sheikh Abd al-Aziz al-Sheikh, who is appointed by a royal decree. He has deemed such operations illegitimate. He has said he does not regard them to be a legitimate part of jihad and has expressed concern that they might amount to suicide. Several scholars in Saudi Arabia have issued statements or fatwas in opposition to his position. Critics of the mufti discount his fatwa on this issue, suspecting that he issued it only in response to a request from the Saudi government, which has come under pressure from its ally, the United States, to obtain such a religious edict from its most senior scholar.

On the other hand, Sheikh Hamud bin Uqlaa al-Shu'aybi has been one of several leading independent scholars in Saudi Arabia to defend martyrdom operations. The sheikh, who commands a considerable following inside as well as outside the kingdom, has ruled them as legitimate martyrdom operations carried out by Muslims in Palestine, Chechnya, and other Muslim countries that struggle against invading enemies. He has gone further, saying these operations are part of the jihad in the Way of Allah and are some of the most effective means of jihad against the Muslims' enemies. He concluded his fatwa with an explanation of the difference between suicide and martyrdom: "A person who commits suicide kills himself out of desperation, impatience or loss of hope, in an act that does not please Allah. However, a *mujahid* [struggler] who carries out a martyrdom operation acts while in a state of happiness and longing for Paradise. His objective is to inflict harm on the enemy. Therefore, equating a person who offers himself in martyrdom with one who commits suicide is an error."

In Egypt, there is also disagreement. Another outspoken critic of martyrdom operations has been the grand sheikh of al-Azhar, Sheikh Muhammad Sayyid Tantawi, who is appointed by the President of Egypt and reports to him directly. Whereas the mufti's office in Saudi Arabia has at least been consistent in its position, Sheikh Tantawi has contradicted himself on a number of occasions. He appears to reflect the political mood inside Egypt each time he speaks. His initial fatwa expressed outright prohibition, arguing that martyrdom operations were illegitimate because of the innocent people they kill. He did not appear to object to the use of such operations against military personnel. Then he came out in full support of martyrdom operations, considering those who carry them out to be martyrs of the highest degree. In 2003, however, speaking at a conference on terrorism in Kuala Lumpur, he reverted to his original position of outright condemnation.

Meanwhile, Sheikh Yusuf al-Qaradawi issued a fatwa discriminating between martyrdom and suicide. "Martyrdom operations are of the greatest types of jihad in the cause of Allah whereby a person sacrifices his soul in the cause of Allah in full compliance with the Qur'anic verse 'Among the people there are those who trade themselves in pursuit of the Pleasure of Allah.' A person who commits suicide does so out of desperation because of some kind of failure: he is one who seeks to rid himself his life. In contrast, to give oneself to martyrdom is an act of heroism, and an act deemed by the majority of Muslim scholars to be the greatest form of jihad."[10]

Like al-Shu'aybi and al-Qaradawi, most independent scholars have opted to regard suicide bombings inside Palestine as martyrdom operations, which are identified with the noblest level of jihad. Scholars in Jordan, Lebanon, Saudi Arabia, Egypt, Iran, Pakistan, Malaysia, and Indonesia have also been quoted in confirmation of the legitimacy of the strategy of suicide bombing in Palestine. A number of reasons are in general given for supporting martyrdom operations against Israeli targets. These include the following:

- The operations are not suicide because they involve sacrifice of the highest kind for the noblest of causes.
- Israel is a military outpost in which none count as civilians who should be spared, except the children. All men and women in Israel serve in the army. So long as attackers take every precaution to avoid children, all other targets in Israel are legitimate. If children are inadvertently hit, this is because it is unavoidable.
- The Palestinians have been given no other choice, since their enemy is heavily armed while they lack even the basic means of self-defense. As long as this situation continues, the Palestinians are not culpable for engaging in such attacks. Therefore, the Palestinians are exempt from the Islamic code of war.
- If the Israelis wish such operations to end, they should accept the offers of truce made to them repeatedly by Hamas and other Palestinian factions. However, to expect the Palestinians to unilaterally stop all resistance in the hope that the Israelis will stop attacking them is unfair and unacceptable.

Further Controversy

Suicide or "martyrdom" operations are by no means restricted to Palestine but are also carried out by Muslims elsewhere in the world. The debate over martyrdom has intensified, with divisions growing wider than ever. Few scholars are willing to endorse all suicide bombings as martyrdom operations no matter where or when they may be carried out. It is noteworthy that a number of prominent scholars who support "martyrdom" operations in Palestine were unequivocal in condemning the 11 September attacks in New York. These scholars have also condemned the later bombings in Bali, in Riyadh, in Rabat, in Istanbul, in Madrid, and in London, as well as bombings that target civilians in various parts of Iraq or Afghanistan. They judge these bombings as acts of criminality and not as acts of lawful jihad.

In July 2004, Sheikh Yusuf al-Qaradawi, who leads the group of scholars who take this view, was invited by the mayor of London, Ken Livingstone, to convene the annual meeting of the European Council for Fatwa and Research at the headquarters of the Greater London Authority. This initiative was meant as a gesture of benevolence on the part of the mayor toward the Muslims of London, who constitute about ten percent of the city's population. Sheikh al-Qaradawi took the opportunity to invite hundreds of scholars from around the Muslim world to come to London during his visit to inaugurate the International Union of Muslim Scholars, a project on which he and many of his invitees had been working.

Pro-Israel groups in the United Kingdom condemned the presence of Sheikh al-Qaradawi in London, accusing him of supporting terrorism. The British Labor Member of Parliament Louise Ellman and the Jewish Board of Deputies led the campaign to have the sheikh deported, having failed to prevent his visit in the first place. The controversy about Sheikh al-Qaradawi's visit attracted the attention of the media. The right-wing press focused its attention on the sheikh's position on suicide attacks. Pressed to clarify his position, the sheikh insisted that Palestine was a special case where "martyrdom operations are legitimate because the Palestinians have no other effective means of self-defense." Questioned about suicide bombings in Iraq, al-Qaradawi explained that he supported the right of the Iraqi people to resist the US-led invasion of Iraq and to fight to liberate their country from foreign occupation. However, he did not believe that the use of suicide bombings was justified, because the Iraqis, unlike the Palestinians, had an abundance of resources with which to resist foreign occupation and were not obliged to employ martyrdom operations, which he described as the weapon of last resort.

When four Muslim men carried out a suicide bombing in London on 7 July 2005, Sheikh al-Qaradawi condemned the attack, both in his individual capacity and in the name of the International Union of Muslim Scholars. He refused to equate it with what he insisted were legitimate martyrdom operations in Palestine. He said at the time that unlike the Palestinians, whose land is occupied and who suffer because of Israeli occupation day and night, these young men had no justification whatsoever to attack Londoners as they did.

It should be said, however, that there are a few influential scholars, especially in Saudi Arabia, who consider the perpetrators of all suicide bombings as martyrs, and their actions to be legitimate. The disagreement in this case is not over the question of whether the act itself is suicide or martyrdom but rather over which targets are legitimate and which are illegitimate.

Palestinian organizations that use martyrdom operations maintain that they never target children. They insist that they target primarily army personnel, and that any attacks on civilians are either unintended or inevitable, as long as Israel continues to target Palestinian civilians. Additionally, they argue that Israel is a military state where every man and woman, apart from the ultra-Orthodox Jews, serves in the army. They explain that they target buses because soldiers travel in them. When they target bars and nightclubs, it is because these are meeting places for off-duty service men and women who earlier in the day would be actively engaged in military operations in the occupied territories.

Palestinians have reached a broad consensus regarding the military nature of Israeli society. For many Palestinians it remains the means, rather than the target, which has become the subject of theological and jurisprudential investigation. The nature of the operation has been the central issue in the assessment of the legitimacy or illegitimacy of the suicide bomb or martyrdom operation. As always, in the case of the issue of a fatwa on any issue, the difficulty emanates from the fact that in Sunni Islam there is no single or undisputed authority to which reference can be made. Furthermore, it is commonplace in such turbulent times as ours today for politics to have a great bearing on the opinion of the religious scholars.

NINE

HAMAS, THE PLO, AND THE PALESTINIAN AUTHORITY

The PLO met Hamas in the beginning with total disregard, then it tried to cast doubt on its authenticity, then it endeavored to belittle it and refused to recognize it, then it went into a stage of open confrontation followed by an attempt to contain it.[1]

—Khalid Mish'al

THE LATE YASIR ARAFAT AND HIS COLLEAGUES IN FATAH, THE PRINCIPAL faction within the Palestine Liberation Organization, struggled hard until they won recognition both from the Arabs and from the world at large that the PLO was "the sole legitimate representative of the Palestinian People."[2] They never gained complete recognition, however, because many of the Palestinians themselves never recognized the PLO. The Palestinian Islamists in particular, led by the Ikhwan and then by Hamas, refused to accept the PLO's claim, insisting that because the PLO was not elected by the people it had no mandate to monopolize the representation of the Palestinians.

The decision by the 1974 Arab Summit Conference to bestow such a role on the PLO was perceived by some Palestinians as a somewhat negative step, in the sense that it appeared to divest the non-Palestinian Arabs of their responsibility for the liberation of Palestine. In other words, the move officially demoted the conflict with the Zionist project from a pan-Arab concern to a localized Palestinian issue, the sole responsibility for which lay in the hands of the Palestinians. This meant that whatever the PLO agreed to accept would be accepted by the rest of the Arab world.

It should in addition be borne in mind that the PLO, which was created by the Arab League, has never been free from the intervention and manipulation of various Arab governments, and above all that of Egypt.

Egypt, whose aim was to be absolved completely from any obligations toward the Palestinian revolution while retaining its influence over it, was instrumental in securing an Arab consensus on the issue. In the aftermath of the 1973 war with Israel, Egypt's principal objective was to negotiate a peace treaty to end its own conflict with Israel once and for all. It would not be far-fetched to conjecture that the Egyptians may also have played a role in devising the ten-point plan proposed by the PLO leadership around the same time. According to this plan, which was adopted officially by the PLO some six years later, armed struggle was declared to be one route toward the liberation of Palestine, but not the only one. The PLO would therefore be open to accepting a negotiated settlement with the Israelis, with the objective of the immediate establishment of a Palestinian state on any part of Palestine that became available. As early as the mid-1970s, many Fatah members were already concerned that the ten-point plan was the beginning of the derailment of their national liberation project.[3] However, PLO loyalists insisted that it implied no more than the recognition of the necessity of a gradual approach to the project of liberation without conceding any of the fundamental rights of the Palestinian people.

Throughout the 1970s and the 1980s, the PLO suffered a series of setbacks, first in Jordan and then in Lebanon. Critics from within the organization maintain that most of these setbacks were self-inflicted. The PLO leadership became indistinguishable from the other Arab authoritarian regimes of the region. In the absence of transparency and any meaningful measure of accountability, and as corruption spread throughout its hierarchy, internal feuds and splits became inevitable.[4] Neverthelesss, for much of those two decades, the Islamists did nothing to compete with the PLO's endeavors to implement its role of representing the Palestinians in the international arena. The efforts of the Islamists were focused instead on social reform, which included penetrating social strata that had until the early 1970s been the prerogative of the secular nationalist movement. The gains made by the Islamists in the universities and in the trade unions sometimes aroused tension between the two sides. However, it was not until the intifada gave birth to the Hamas movement that the PLO leadership felt its authority was being seriously threatened. Hamas was perceived as the Ikhwan's bid to supplant the PLO as the sole legitimate representative. Indeed, Hamas's own rhetoric presented it in this light. Its literature, from the first communiqué to the Charter, implicitly or explicitly accused the PLO leadership of abandoning its responsibilities and of compromising the cause.

Initially, Yasir Arafat requested that the leadership of the Egyptian Ikhwan persuade their Palestinian brethren to step back. He argued that a parallel movement to the PLO would only harm the struggle and benefit the enemy. When he met the Ikhwan's al-Murshid al-'Amm (general guide or chairman) in Cairo, Arafat appealed to him to persuade the Palestinian Islamists to join Fatah, which, according to Arafat's protestations, was in any case born out of the womb of the Ikhwan. In private, however, he poured scorn on the Palestinian Islamists. In a speech Arafat made at a meeting of Fatah supporters in Yemen soon after the emergence of Hamas, which was recorded without his knowledge, he described its members as ants who should cower in their holes lest he and his forces crushed them.[5]

Arafat invited Hamas to become part of the PLO. In April 1990, in his capacity as Hamas's spokesman, Ibrahim Ghosheh visited Sheikh Abd al-Hamid al-Sa'ih, speaker of the Palestine National Council (PNC), in his office in Amman, and presented him with a memorandum entitled "Our Vision of the Palestine National Council." In this document, Hamas expressed its readiness to join the PNC, provided the members of the PNC were chosen through election. If an election was not feasible in practice, Hamas proposed that it should be allocated no less than 40 percent of the PNC seats, since 40 percent of the Palestinian people were Hamas supporters. The atmosphere at the meeting was cordial, and al-Sa'ih promised to give Hamas a response. Initially, the PLO offered Hamas eighteen seats, which at the time amounted to no more than four percent of the total number of PNC seats, all of which were filled by appointment.[6] Hamas refused the offer. Yasir Arafat, who was in overall authority of the allocation of the PNC's seats and the appointment of its members, increased the number offered to Hamas to 24. This too, however, fell far short of what Hamas had in mind.[7]

In the early 1990s, despite the tense relations between the two sides, Hamas representatives met Yasir Arafat on a number of occasions to resolve pressing issues. One of these meetings took place in Yemen, where the subject discussed was the situation inside Israeli prisons and the resolution of the occasional disputes that broke out among Hamas and Fatah prisoners. Another meeting took place in the aftermath of Israel's mass deportation to South Lebanon of Hamas and Islamic Jihad activists. A Hamas delegation headed by Musa Abu Marzuq, including Ibrahim Ghosheh, Imad al-Alami, and Muhammad Nazzal, travelled to Tunis to discuss the diplomatic efforts to resolve the crisis and secure the return of the deportees with Yasir Arafat.

From Containment to Confrontation

Rendezvous such as these were usually set up through the good offices of intermediaries. One such meeting, seen as particularly significant at the time, was arranged in Khartoum through the good offices of Sudanese Islamic leader Hassan al-Turabi in January 1993. The Hamas delegation was again headed by Musa Abu Marzuq and consisted of Ibrahim Ghosheh, Muhammad Siyam, and Muhammad Nazzal. The PLO delegation was headed by Yasir Arafat and included PNC Speaker Salim al-Za'nun, Nasr Yusuf, Muhammad Dahlan, and Abu Ali Shahin. There were indications at this meeting that the tension between the two sides might be eased. Relations soon deteriorated once more, however, when it was announced that Israel and the PLO had reached a settlement after the secret negotiations in Oslo. Hamas condemned the signature of the Declaration of Principles on the White House lawn on 13 September 1993 as an act of betrayal of fundamental Palestinian rights.

As Yasir Arafat began to prepare to return to Gaza in 1994 under the terms of the Oslo Accords, he was apprehensive about what kind of reception might await him. Conscious of the popularity of Hamas inside the Gaza Strip and the extent of its authority there, he was concerned that Hamas might in some way disrupt his arrival. He appealed through mediators to the leadership of Hamas to allow him to return peacefully. This was in fact unnecessary, as Hamas actually had no objection to Arafat's return to the homeland, and did not intend to cause trouble. On the contrary, when the newly formed Palestinian security force had arrived from Jordan earlier in the year to deploy in the Gaza Strip and Jericho, Hamas had welcomed them and provided them with food and shelter. It would not have served Hamas's interest to be seen to object to the return of any Palestinian or to the replacement of Israeli occupation troops by a Palestinian force.

One of the main tasks of the Palestinian Authority that was established under the terms of the Oslo Accords was to curb and disarm the Palestinian factions and halt all hostilities against the Israelis. This task was by no means easy to accomplish. Testing the waters, the PA's security forces intervened to disperse the crowds as they left the Filastin Mosque in Gaza on 18 November 1994. The crowds were peacefully protesting against the continuation of the occupation despite the peace agreement with Israel. Fourteen pro-Hamas worshippers were shot dead and several others wounded. There was an outburst of popular fury and a crowd marched to the Palestinian Authority headquarters, tearing down the fence in a bid to ransack the building. Appeals by Hamas to the public to calm down and go home eventually ended the crisis. Hamas's leadership said that public anger should be directed against the Israeli occupation authorities in the form of further resistance rather than against the Palestinian police force. Hamas won additional respect and authority by maintaining a policy of forbidding armed clashes between Palestinians.

The PA leadership in Gaza experienced problems in communicating with Hamas. Many of the movement's leaders in the territories were still in detention in Israeli prisons. In addition, decision-making power in Hamas had already been transferred from inside the territories to outside after the massive Israeli crackdown on the movement in 1989. This meant that the final say on policy matters and strategic issues lay in the hands of the Jordan-based Political Bureau headed by Musa Abu Marzuq. In April 1995, Yasir Arafat sent Abd al-Razaq al-Yahya to Amman to meet the Hamas leadership and ask them to order an end to all forms of violence in the whole of Palestine so as to give his efforts to make peace a chance of success. When neither threats nor inducements gained any acceptance for his proposal, Arafat turned to the local Hamas leaders in the Gaza Strip. In particular he wanted to persuade Hamas to take part in the Palestinian Legislative Council (PLC) elections that had been set for 20 January 1996. At his insistence, the Hamas leadership in the Gaza Strip and West Bank agreed to consider participating, provided they were allowed first to consult the other branches of the movement.

In December 1995, the PA persuaded the Israelis to allow an inside Hamas delegation to leave Palestine to travel to Khartoum, the capital of Sudan, to meet with a group of outside Hamas leaders, and then to hold talks with the Palestinian Authority in Cairo. The delegation consisted of Jamil Hamami, Jamal Salim, Abd al-Khaliq al-Natshah, and Hassan Yusuf, from the West Bank, and Abd al-Fattah Dukhan, Sayyid Abu Musamih, Mahmud al-Zahhar, and Muhammad Hasan Sham'ah, from the Gaza Strip. The outside delegation consisted of Khalid Mish'al — who had just been elected head of the Political Bureau — Muhammad Nazzal, Imad al-Alami, Osama Hamdan, and Ibrahim Ghosheh. Since the movement's formation eight years earlier, this was the first top-level Hamas leadership meeting to have taken place between those inside and those outside. Some of the key players were missing because they were in detention. These included Sheikh Ahmad Yassin and Abd al-Aziz al-Rantisi in Israel, and Musa Abu Marzuq in the United States. The most pressing issues on the agenda were armed resistance and the forthcoming elections. The Palestinian Authority wanted an end to the first, and Hamas's participation in the second. Both the Palestinian Authority and Israel hoped that when the Hamas delegation from Gaza and West Bank met their outside colleagues, they might persuade the outside leaders to call a halt to Hamas's military activity and to participate in the political process.

The Khartoum meeting was a golden opportunity for Hamas's senior leadership to exchange opinions and to debate policy and strategy issues in a relaxed and free environment. At times, discussions were heated. Some of the delegates from inside Palestine had been strong proponents of both a halt to military activity and participation in the election. They had become convinced that the peace process would bring a solution to their existing problems if given a chance, but that an end to all violence and cooperation with the Palestinian Authority were required before such a chance could exist. Over four days and four nights of discussion, the delegates reached agreement on two important conclusions, not unanimously but with a comfortable majority. The first of these was that resistance was crucial and should never be abandoned, whether at the behest of Arafat or of anyone else. The decision whether to intensify, moderate, or qualify the level of resistance should remain the prerogative of the movement, which would assess the situation and take appropriate action. Secondly, they agreed not to participate in the PLC elections. This decision was taken for a number of reasons, including the consideration that the elections "were a product of the Oslo Agreement which in turn is a Zionist project." The opponents of participation argued at the time that, according to the Oslo Accords, the Israelis retained the final say on what fell within the remit of the PLC. Several of those who supported the suspension of the resistance and participation in the election switched sides during the debate, but others remained unconvinced. All accepted that the meeting had been conducted in a fully democratic manner.[8]

Apart from Ibrahim Ghosheh, who returned to Amman, the Hamas leaders then went on to Cairo, where they held several days of talks with a delegation from the PA. The PA team was headed by Palestine National Council Chairman Salim al-Za'nun, and included some of the most anti-Hamas figures from within Fatah, such as Abu Ali Shahin, Al-Tayyib Abd al-Rahim, Hasan Usfur, Frayh Abu Maddayn, and Nabil Amr. These Fatah diehards had never viewed Hamas with anything but contempt, so it was highly unpropitious that they were the representatives chosen by the PA to negotiate with the Hamas team. The meeting was fruitless, possibly for this reason. Though the talks concluded with a bland, politically correct statement, they actually achieved very little.

Throughout, the talks were marred with recriminations over all sorts of issues. The past two years in particular had seen the emergence of profound ill-feeling between the two sides. Within Hamas, some were convinced that Fatah had made peace with Israel primarily in order to undermine Hamas. Their view was that Fatah wished to appropriate the gains made by the intifada by conspiring with the US and Israel to abort the project of Islamic resistance against Zionism. Inside Fatah, on the other hand, some believed, or affected to believe, that Hamas was a conspiracy fomented by Israel and directed against their own movement.

An issue raised at the start of the talks that further muddied the waters was the question of who had initiated the intifada in December 1987. When some Fatah delegates insinuated that Hamas had played no role in the popular uprising, Hamas delegate Abd al-Fattah Dukhan protested.

He declared that he had been the chairman of the Ikhwan Executive Office that had met soon after the traffic incident in which a number of Palestinians died, and had decided to mobilize the public to respond to the outrage. This did not, he said, "annul the role of the brothers in Fatah and the other factions or belittle the popular spirit that fed the intifada." It simply meant, however, that whatever happened on the morning that followed the day of the traffic incident was not simply a spontaneous reaction but the outcome of preparation and deliberate escalation.[9]

Yasir Arafat passed through Cairo while the meeting was taking place, and had been intended to meet with the two delegations. When he was informed, however, that Hamas had not changed its position on the use of armed resistance against Israel and participation in the forthcoming elections, he decided it would be better not to join the talks.[10] There was little further the PA could do to persuade Hamas to join the political process or renounce violence. Hamas leaders feared that their participation in the elections would have bestowed legitimacy on the Oslo process, to which they were fundamentally opposed. Equally, they were unable to promise to end the use of force against Israeli troops or settlers while the occupation continued and Israel detained thousands of Palestinian activists.

The failure of the PA to bring Hamas on board through negotiation, however, did not deter it from pursuing different means of persuasion. In its 1996 Annual Report, covering the period from 1 January 1995 to 31 December 1995, Amnesty International noted that the PA's security forces detained more than 1,000 Palestinians on political grounds. More than 40 of these detainees were brought to trial before a newly established State Security Court that did not meet international standards for a fair trial. Some were sentenced to up to 25 years of imprisonment. The Amnesty International report accused the PA of torturing detainees, five of whom died in custody. The State Security Court was set up in February 1995 following a decree issued by Yasir Arafat. Trials were held in secret, often in the middle of the night, and were thus nicknamed midnight trials. They were presided over by military judges, and military prosecutors presented the cases. The court even appointed the defense lawyers, who usually worked for the security forces. Relatives were informed of charges and trials only after hearings had taken place.[11] Despite denunciations by Amnesty International and other leading human rights organizations of these proceedings as "grossly unfair and violating the minimum standards of international law," the *New York Times* reported on 4 May 1995 that "Israeli and American officials have welcomed the hearings." The newspaper added that the so-called midnight trials would remain a necessity as long as the Palestinian Authority needed to clamp down on "extremists whose acts of terror threatened the peace process."

Fifty days after Israel's assassination of the Hamas military commander Yahya Ayyash on 5 January 1996, the movement's military wing launched a campaign of martyrdom operations in retaliation. Some fifty Israelis were killed and many more wounded in the first three operations, which were carried out in Jerusalem and Ashkelon between 25 February and 3 March 1996. The Palestinian Authority responded with a campaign against Hamas that intensified following the US-sponsored anti-terrorism summit conference at Sharm al-Sheikh on 13 March 1996. This included the detention of more than 1,000 Hamas members and supporters and the closure of a number of social welfare organizations run by the movement. In the months that followed, at least two dozen Palestinians lost their lives under torture while being interrogated in Palestinian Authority prisons, according to a 1998 report by Amnesty International.

Tension between Hamas and the PA reached a peak when a number of Hamas military commanders became the victims of targeted assassinations. Hamas accused the PA intelligence services of collusion in the assassination of Muhyiddin al-Sharif on 29 March 1998 and of the two brothers Imad and Adil Awadallah on 10 September 1998. One of the Awadallah brothers had been released from detention by the PA in mysterious circumstances. At different times and for varying periods, the PA also arrested and detained a number of senior Hamas leaders. In the Gaza Strip these included figures such as Abd al-Aziz al-Rantisi, Sayyid Abu Musamih, Mahmud al-Zahhar, Ibrahim al-Maqadmah, Muhammad Taha, and Ahmad Nimr Hamdan. Those whom the PA security forces detained in the West Bank included Jamal Salim, Jamal Mansur, Yusuf al-Sarkaji, Mahmud Muslih, and Muhammad Jamal al-Natshah.[12]

The crackdown by the PA prompted the founder of Hamas, Sheikh Ahmad Yassin, who had recently been released from Israeli detention, to tell Yasir Arafat to stop harassing Hamas and instead to stand up to Israel and the US.[13] He reaffirmed his belief that Israel and the US were behind the campaign against Hamas. Challenging the PA to put those it arrested properly on trial "if they have broken the law," he denounced the closing down of Hamas-run humanitarian institutions, saying this was something to which not even the Israelis had stooped. Sheikh Yassin blamed the situation in its entirety on the peace agreement between Israel and the PA, which he said was flawed from the outset and should be abandoned. He mocked the Israelis for asking the PA to do on their behalf what they had been unable to achieve themselves when they were in direct control of the Gaza Strip.

In a bid to lure Sheikh Yassin to lead Hamas in the direction of working with the PA rather than against it, Yasir Arafat avoided direct confrontation with the sheikh, though he sometimes spoke very critically about him. Instead, Arafat sought to turn the tables on the Hamas leadership in Amman blaming it for the lack of progress toward peace with Israel. He criticized Hamas for carrying out "suicide bomb attacks, which have been aimed at civilians," insisting that they had given Israel an excuse for not handing over more land to the Palestinians. Renewing his commitment to carrying out his side of the Oslo peace accords, Arafat pledged that his forces would continue working to prevent fresh attacks by Hamas.[14]

About a year later, Yasir Arafat invited Sheikh Yassin to come as an observer to the meetings of the PLO Central Council, which convened in Gaza in late April 1999 to debate the proposed unilateral declaration of independence of the Palestinian state, due to be made on 4 May. The Sheikh accepted the invitation despite objections from the Hamas Political Bureau in Jordan, which saw Arafat's move as another ploy to split the movement. The Political Bureau issued a statement saying that Sheikh Yassin's initiative had been personal and did not represent the official position of the movement. This prompted the sheikh to withdraw from the PLO meetings and to confirm that his attendance had indeed been on a personal basis, and had been intended only to give him an opportunity to voice his objections to the Oslo Accords and to demand their repeal. When asked later about his decision to take part he said:

We went to the Central Council to explain our point of view on this important issue of the declaration of the state. We could have sent a letter or held a news conference, but I preferred to state our position publicly in front of the whole

*Palestinian people so that they would know that we were not sparing any effort
in our fight for their interests. I stated publicly that the Oslo Accords to which
the Palestinian Authority has committed itself, and all other agreements that
followed, were unfair and have proved to be a failure because the enemy does
not believe in peace. The enemy wants to steal everything. It has the power to
do so and we don't have the power to resist. The Palestinian people have lost all
their options in fighting the enemy. Nowhere in the world do resistance movements surrender their arms until they have gained their rights, and by retaining
their arms they maintain their freedom of action. But we gave up our arms at
the beginning of the road and then sat waiting for handouts and rewards from
the enemy. This means that we have lost the first round. Therefore, I have asked
our brothers in the Palestinian Authority to get rid of Oslo and all that is related
to it because it is the reason for all the suffering we are facing right now. ... We
always make our decisions in Hamas on the basis of discussion. We tried to contact our brothers abroad about our taking part in the meeting but we received
the invitation to attend two days before the meeting. It was difficult to get in
touch with them.*

He insisted that there were no differences within Hamas between the
inside and the outside, but only a lack of proper channels of communication. He added that, as he had taken part in the meeting only as an
observer and not as a participant, Hamas had not participated in any PLO
decision making. He had been present only in order to make a public
declaration of his position.[15]

The significance of this incident was that it illustrated clearly that, at
least up to that time, the Hamas Political Bureau in Jordan and the local
leadership in the Gaza Strip had failed to reach agreement on the issue
of who was in charge. It is conceivable that Sheikh Yassin, and perhaps
other members of the leadership in Gaza, neither saw the need nor felt
obliged to consult the Political Bureau in Jordan, though the Political
Bureau had been meant since 1989 to be Hamas's senior decision-making body. It seems probable that Sheikh Yassin's attendance at a meeting
of the PLO Central Council was seen as only a minor issue by the Hamas leadership in Gaza, though it actually represented a radical shift in
policy. For many in Hamas, it was a step too close to the recognition of
the PLO as the sole legitimate representative of the Palestinian people.
Sheikh Yassin's eventual compliance with the Hamas leadership's deci-

sion on this matter represented a final ruling as to who was in charge of the movement.

The Second Intifada

When Ehud Barak was elected Prime Minister of Israel on 17 May 1999, the Palestinian Authority breathed a sigh of relief. Optimism replaced the gloomy atmosphere that had prevailed for much of the time since May 1996, during which Binyamin Netanyahu had headed the Israeli government. Barak came to power determined to end the conflict with the Arabs on all fronts. He said he wanted to negotiate a settlement with Syria, and in March 2000 he persuaded US President Clinton to convene a summit meeting in Geneva with Syria's President Hafiz al-Assad. In May 2000, he ordered the withdrawal of Israeli troops from South Lebanon. He also sought a comprehensive deal with the Palestinian Authority that would resolve once and for all the outstanding permanent status issues including the frontiers, the refugees, the settlements, and Jerusalem.

The Geneva summit failed miserably, however, and Israel's withdrawal from Lebanon was implemented unilaterally and in haste, prompting the Lebanese, as well as the Palestinians and the Arabs and the Muslims across the region and around the world to celebrate Israel's humiliating defeat at the hands of Hezbollah. On the Palestinian track, Barak persuaded President Clinton to convene another summit conference to negotiate the end of the conflict with the Palestinians. Yasir Arafat was hesitant: he feared that the summit was unlikely to produce much, as Barak had failed since his election to implement previous agreements between the Israelis and the Palestinians. Barak had been supposed to release 350 Palestinian prisoners and hand over three villages in the Jerusalem area to the PA. Instead, he had actually authorized the expansion of some of the Jewish settlements around Jerusalem. Arafat was easily persuaded to attend, however. Hosted by Clinton and attended by Barak and Arafat, the summit convened at Camp David on 11 July and ended on 25 July 2000 without agreement.[16]

The failure of the Camp David summit was greeted with relief in the West Bank and Gaza. It had been feared that its success might involve major concessions that would compromise Palestinian rights. On 27 July

2000, Yasir Arafat received a hero's welcome on his return. In the eyes of many hitherto disillusioned Palestinians, he had once more beome a patriotic leader, who had refused to surrender to pressure. On the other hand, the Israelis, the Americans, and even some members of his own negotiating team regarded the lack of success at Camp David as a failure on Yasir Arafat's part.[17] Arafat's refusal to concede on the two issues that mattered most to the Palestinians, the status of Jerusalem and the right of return, had two unexpected outcomes. On the one hand, it paved the way for a genuine rapprochement between Arafat and Hamas. Soon, Arafat too was to become a victim of the punitive measures adopted by Israel with the tacit approval of the new administration of US President George W. Bush. On the other hand, it created a rift within the ranks of Arafat's closest aides, turning some of them against him.

On 28 September 2000, Ariel Sharon's uninvited intrusion into al-Haram al-Sharif, Islam's third holiest place on earth, under the protection of 1,000 members of Israeli security forces, ignited the second intifada and united the Palestinians as never before. On Sunday, 8 October 2000, a meeting of all the factions within the PLO, chaired by Yasir Arafat, was held in Gaza to discuss the latest situation in the West Bank and the Gaza Strip. This meeting was the first of its kind to include an official representative of Hamas, which up to then had boycotted meetings with the PA. The meeting was of sufficient significance to attract wide comment from observers inside and outside Israel. The Israeli newspaper *Ma'ariv* described the Gaza meeting as "a rare demonstration of national unity" among the Palestinians.[18] The report quoted an unnamed security source that said it was "concerned that the recent moves in the domestic Palestinian political scene will be 'a catalyst that will encourage Hamas and the Islamic Jihad to resume the wave of terrorist attacks in Israel.'" The newspaper went on to say that security sources explained that the embrace accorded by Arafat to "the terrorist organizations" could be "construed by them as a 'turning of a blind eye' by the PLO chairman and as a 'green light' to resume their murderous activity." Ismail Abu Shanab, the Hamas Political Bureau member in Gaza, represented Hamas at the Gaza talks. In a statement to Quds Press afterward, he said that the meeting had been the first in a series to "find formulae to confront the Israeli occupation." He added that in the meeting he called for reconciliation in internal relations between Palestinians.[19]

Less than a week later, Palestinian militants held in PA jails in Gaza and the West Bank were freed by public demand, after Israel launched a bombardment of the West Bank and Gaza Strip for the first time since the start of the second intifada. It seems conceivable that this may have been prompted by Arafat's inter-factional meeting and the prisoner release. Many of those released were members of Hamas, which led the Israeli Prime Minister Ehud Barak to threaten that he would hold the PA responsible for any attacks carried out on Israeli targets following the release of the Hamas activists. The PA said that prison guards had acted on their own initiative in releasing the militants, because they feared for the prisoners' safety. Isma'il Haniyah, speaking for Hamas, was quoted by the Associated Press news agency as saying that the 350 prisoners were freed because the PA could not protect them in prison. The Israelis were not convinced. The Israelis themselves had failed to comply with many of the commitments required by the interim peace accords. They nevertheless insisted that the primary responsibility of the Palestinian security forces under the accords was "to look out for Israel's security interests and prevent Islamic militants from carrying out terror attacks against Israeli targets." Danny Yatom, then an adviser to Barak, accused Arafat of reneging on his commitment to fight terrorism and said: "The Palestinian Authority has committed to fight terror and the terror infrastructure, not just before us but before the CIA and the Americans."[20]

A subsequent attempt to reopen the peace negotiations failed. A summit between Arafat and Barak that took place from 21 to 27 January 2001 at the Egyptian tourist resort of Taba came too late. Clinton had just left office, Barak was uncertain of success in the upcoming Israeli elections, and Arafat would not put his name to a deal with the Israelis without the involvement of the United States. He believed that unless the Americans gave a guarantee, no deal was worth the paper it was written on.

Ariel Sharon, who was elected prime minister of Israel on 6 February 2001, had never liked Yasir Arafat. He had said he could never imagine himself shaking Arafat's hand, let alone embracing him. He convinced President George W. Bush's new administration that Arafat was not a man of peace, and that he was implicated in attacks on Israel. Despite accusations that he had ignored his commitment to rein in such groups as Hamas and Islamic Jihad, Yasir Arafat continued to insist that he had made a genuine effort to maintain control of the Palestinian factions. He was in a dilemma. He needed to maintain his credibility in his own people's eyes by showing them that he stood shoulder to shoulder with them if they were attacked by Israel. At the same, those who wanted rid of him accused him of complicity in terrorism. Inevitably, this soured his relations with Hamas. On one occasion, he ordered his security forces to arrest two Hamas activists, Abdullah and Bilal Barghouti, for their alleged role in a suicide bombing in Jerusalem on 9 August 2001. Around 20 Israelis were killed in this "martyrdom operation," carried out by 23-year-old Izzaddin Shuhayl al-Masri. It was carried out, Hamas claimed, in retaliation, for the targeted assassination on 31 July 2001 of two Hamas top leaders in Nablus, Jamal Mansur and Jamal Salim. Four other Hamas employees and two children were also killed when an Israeli plane fired a rocket at the Hamas media office where the men were meeting. Hamas, which gauged that the mood in the street was at the time highly support-ive of its retaliatory attacks, responded angrily to the detentions and said that such arrests should have ended when the intifada began.[21]

On 23 November 2001, Israel assassinated a senior Hamas military commander, Mahmud Abu Hannud, and two of his comrades, Ma'mun and Ayman Hashaykah. In retaliation, Hamas carried out a series of bombings on 1 and 2 December 2001, killing more than 25 Israelis and wounding close to 200.[22] Yasir Arafat immediately ordered a crackdown on Hamas. His security forces arrested close to 200 Hamas members. An attempt to put Sheikh Yassin under house arrest prompted running gun battles between Hamas supporters and the Palestinian Authority police. One Hamas supporter was killed but eventually Hamas fighters seized control of the street where Sheikh Yassin lived, driving out the Palestinian Authority's security forces. This was a measure of Hamas's popularity in the Strip. When the news spread of the attempted house arrest of the sheikh, furious crowds descended upon the area and vowed to defend the sheikh "with their blood and souls," in the words of the Arabic slogan.

On 19 December, a similar incident occurred when Palestinian securi-ty forces went to the home of senior Hamas leader Abd al-Aziz al-Rantisi, seeking to detain him. Clashes erupted when Hamas supporters inter-vened to prevent his arrest. A gun battle between Hamas supporters and the Palestinian police resulted in the deaths of six people. Meanwhile, the PA arrested 15 members of its own security forces and closed 33 Hamas offices.[23] The Palestinian Authority found itself on the defensive every time it cracked down on Hamas, since most of Hamas's attacks on Israel were reactions to targeted killings of Hamas leaders by the Israelis.

For the Israeli authorities, nothing the PA did was satisfactory. It seemed as if Ariel Sharon was waiting for some event to justify a terminal blow to Yasir Arafat. In early January 2002, while Arafat was receiving the American envoy General Zinni at his compound in Ramallah, the Israelis said they had intercepted a ship called "Karine A," which was loaded with weapons allegedly ordered by Yasir Arafat and destined for the Gaza Strip. The arms shipment provided the Israelis with the pretext for ending all ties with the PA until a new leader, with whom they could do business, was appointed. In due course, they decided to try and get rid of Arafat themselves. Arafat's fate was sealed on 24 June 2002, when, after a visit to the White House by Ariel Sharon, President George W. Bush said the Palestinians needed to find another leader. The president had committed himself entirely to supporting Sharon's position. In its pursuit of a negotiated settlement with the Palestinians, the American administration and the Israeli government chose to ignore an important fact: no leader can negotiate peace on behalf of his people if his credibility has been destroyed.

Finding an alternative to Arafat was a problem. He never appointed a deputy, and no one within the Fatah organization seemed able to emulate the historic and revolutionary legitimacy or the popularity enjoyed by "the old man" (al-Ikhtiyar), as the Palestinians called him. The plan to create the position of a prime minister within the Palestinian Authority in order to divest Arafat of some of the authority he held was a first step toward a solution of the problem. This condition was stipulated by the Americans before they went ahead with their plan for a "road map" for peace. The idea of a "road map" came initially from Jordan's King Abdullah on 1 August 2002 during a visit to President Bush in Washington. The king told Bush that the Arabs needed an American initiative to resolve the Palestinian–Israeli conflict if Arab leaders were to be able to back the United States in its "war on terror." Yasir Arafat was told of the American condition that he should delegate some of his power to a prime minister and had no choice but to accept it. He therefore appointed Mahmud Abbas as Palestine's first prime minister in March 2003.

By the end of April 2003, and as the US-led invasion of Iraq was nearing completion, a document entitled "A Performance-Based Road Map to a Permanent Two-State Solution to the Israeli-Palestinian Conflict" had been drawn up. Responsibility for it was taken by the so-called Quartet: the United States, Russia, the United Nations, and the European Union. President Bush announced on 1 May 2003 that his mission in Iraq had been accomplished, and dispatched his Secretary of State Colin Powell to propose the road map plan to both the Palestinians and the Israelis. In his capacity as the Palestinian prime minister, Mahmud Abbas immediately accepted the plan. The Israelis considered it for some time, only to come up with an amended version. Both Arafat and Hamas saw the road map as directly targeted at them. Both must have breathed a sigh of relief to see the Israelis kill it in its infancy by accepting it only in their own modified version, which was intended to meet their special security needs.[24]

From the day Arafat's old friend and comrade in arms, Mahmud Abbas, was named prime minister the two men became rivals. Abbas felt he could not do much unless he had real power in his hands, but real power was not readily available. He attempted to consolidate his position by surrounding himself with a group of Arafat's detractors, who happened to be favored by both Israel and the US, but this did him little good. He called for the unification of the three main Palestinian security bodies under the command of the interior minister, who would report to him alone, but Arafat would not agree. Eventually Mahmud Abbas fell from grace when the public became disenchanted with his repeated condemnations of what he called "the militarized intifada." Like many Palestinians, Hamas disliked his insistence that the Palestinians should renounce violence at a time when the Israelis were continuing their punitive measures against the entire Palestinian population. In Mahmud Abbas's dispute with Yasir Arafat, it was with Arafat that Hamas sided. If Abbas had been able to acquire more power, he would have curbed Hamas and other resistance groups. The conciliatory language adopted by Abbas toward the Israelis earned him little sympathy from the general public, as he appeared more sympathetic to Israel's interests than to Palestinian concerns. The last straw for his tenure in the position of prime minister came during the Aqaba summit in Jordan on 4 June 2003. His speech at the televised ceremony, in which he made a strong commitment to ending what he called Palestinian violence, cost him popular sympathy and expedited his downfall. The overt support he had enjoyed from Israel and the United States also did enormous harm to his reputation, making him seem like a puppet for the Americans, installed by them to undermine Arafat.

Under siege by the Israelis and conspired against by some of his closest associates within Fatah and the Palestinian Authority, Arafat may well have begun at times to feel closer to Hamas. Khalid Mish'al called him frequently from Damascus to express his support and solidarity.[25] Such warmth in relations might not have appealed to those within Fatah who saw Hamas as the real enemy. Many were trying hard to convince Arafat that the way out of his predicament lay in taking action against Hamas, rather than in forging friendships with its leaders. Arafat had already decided that no crackdown on Hamas would work. The Palestinian mood did not favor making any concessions to Israel before guarantees were received that something substantive would be offered in return. At the same time, nothing seemed to be sufficient for the Israelis. Unilateral truces had been offered to Israel at least twice. In exchange, the Israelis continued to impose collective punishment on the Palestinians and to carry out targeted assassinations on their leaders, thus fueling Palestinian anger and consolidating their defiance. Israel was particularly harsh on Hamas, which had carried out a series of some of the most devastating suicide bombings inside Israel in response to Israeli targeted assassinations of several of its political leaders and military commanders. Arafat saw clearly that Hamas was growing stronger, despite Israel's crackdown and the assassination of the movement's top leaders.[26] Any further punishment inflicted on Hamas by the Palestinian Authority, such as had been tried before, would only be likely further to erode Arafat's authority and benefit Hamas. Having observed Mahmud Abbas's miscalculation at Aqaba, in his efforts to prove to the Israelis and the Americans that he was worthy of their confidence as a leader capable of delivering peace, Yasir Arafat was very anxious not to lose whatever remained of his own credibility. He preferred to die under siege rather than go down in history as a traitor.

The Israelis and the Americans may live to regret the shabby way they repaid Yasir Arafat for the way he had extended his hand to them in peace. Arafat eventually realized, somewhat belatedly, some might argue, that what Israel was looking for in him was not so much a partner as a collaborator. What Israel wanted was an interlocutor who would comply with whatever Israel dictated, even if that meant turning against his own people. In this case, the Palestinians would naturally have seen Arafat as a traitor, and not as a nationalist or a revolutionary as he wished to be remembered.

On 18 December 2003, Ariel Sharon opened a new phase of the peace process with the Palestinians when he announced his unilateral plan of disengagement. He declared to the Palestinians: "It is not in our interest to govern you. We will not remain in all the places where we are today." He told them that he would give them back the Gaza Strip and that he would order the evacuation of all Jewish settlements there. But he explained that as part of the disengagement plan, Israel would "strengthen its control over other areas of Greater Israel," which would become an integral part of the State of Israel in any future agreement.[27] A number of factors might have prompted Sharon to opt for his unilateral disengagement plan. Firstly, Gaza had become too costly for Israel. Some of Sharon's acquaintances have said they heard this directly from him.[28] The view that Palestinian resistance was what prompted Sharon to consider withdrawing from Gaza is by no means exclusive to the Palestinians. Many Israelis also interpret it this way. *Haaretz*'s Danny Rubinstein, for example, wrote that Sharon, who never once mentioned or alluded to the need to withdraw from Gaza before, needed suicide bombers, rockets, and mortars to persuade him.[29] Secondly, many Israelis worried increasingly about the threat posed to Israel's exclusive Jewish identity by the continued growth of the Palestinian population. A total separation between the two sides seemed the best solution in light of the rapidly changing demographics. Thirdly, Sharon did not mind making a small sacrifice in order to win American support for his plan to annex permanently the major Jewish settlements on the West Bank, a substantial gain for Israel.

On 14 April 2004, President George W. Bush, who was entertaining Ariel Sharon at the White House, endorsed a change in Israel's frontiers. In his speech, he said: "In the light of new realities on the ground, including the already existing major Israeli population centers, it is unrealistic to expect that the outcome of final status negotiations will be a full and complete return to the armistice line of 1949." The President went on to stress that it was neither realistic nor practical for the Palestinian refugees to return to Israel: they should return to the Palestinian state that would be created alongside it.[30] The President's statement signaled full American approval of Sharon's unilateral disengagement plan, a further blow to the road map, and backing for his ongoing campaign against Hamas and other Palestinian resistance groups inside the Gaza Strip.

On 22 March 2004, Sheikh Ahmad Yassin, the founder of Hamas and its leader in the Gaza Strip, was assassinated on the orders of Ariel Sharon. Sharon later authorized the assassination of Sheikh Yassin's successor, Dr. Abd al-Aziz al-Rantisi, on 17 April. The Israeli prime minister wanted to be sure that when he withdrew from Gaza later in a year's time Hamas did not take over.

Nevertheless, many of the measures Israel took from the time Sharon was elected until Arafat's death on 11 November 2004 actually had the effect of undermining the PA.[31] Rather than weakening Hamas, these measures contributed to deepening the crisis within the Fatah movement, the PA's backbone and Israel's Palestinian peace partner, damaging Fatah beyond repair. Fatah had lost some of its best field commanders either through liquidation, as in the example of Ra'id Karmi, or through detention, as in the case of Marwan Barghouti.[32] Now many of Fatah's prominent figures had become discredited, and their loyalty to the Palestinian cause had been called into question. In addition, Fatah the movement had been afflicted with a plague of rampant corruption and wracked by corrosive rivalries that sickened many Palestinians, including some of Fatah's own members.

The Israelis began the process of withdrawing from the Gaza Strip on 15 August 2005, and by 12 September 2005 their 38 years of occupation of this part of Palestine was officially ended. The Palestinians of Gaza, led by Hamas, celebrated the liberation of the Strip, attributing it primarily to the defeat of Israel's superior military machine. Certain Palestinian Authority officials affiliated with Fatah saw no cause for celebration. They warned that Sharon's disengagement plan would in the end cost the Palestinians more land in the West Bank, since the intention was to expand the Jewish settlements there preparatory to annexing them permanently. Some of these officials may have also been concerned that Israel's withdrawal from Gaza would end up strengthening Hamas, just when Fatah itself had been left weaker than ever before.

Indeed, from Israel's unconditional and unilateral withdrawal from Lebanon to its unconditional and unilateral withdrawal from Gaza, it was Hamas that reaped the benefits and emerged victorious despite the losses. The failure of peace negotiations, whether the Oslo Accords, the road map, or Sharon's disengagement policy, seemed in the eyes of many Palestinians to vindicate Hamas's approach.

TEN

Hamas in Government

We did not take part in the 1996 legislative elections because they emanated from Oslo; that is, from a political program that we reject and oppose. As for our stance toward any future elections, that will be decided at the time.[1]

—Khalid Mish'al

HAVING DEPARTED FROM THE PALESTINIAN POLITICAL SCENE FOLLOWING his resignation as prime minister in September 2003, Mahmud Abbas was rushed back to Ramallah by his Fatah associates in October 2004, just before Yasir Arafat was airlifted on 29 October to Paris, where he died on 11 November. The members of Fatah's inner circle were anxious to keep the rapidly developing situation under their control. Some in fact may have been secretly relieved that Arafat, whom many had increasingly regarded as an obstacle, had left the scene for good. Most thought that only Mahmud Abbas could persuade all the tendencies within Fatah to rally behind him. He was in any case one of the very few remaining founding members of Fatah. He succeeded Yasir Arafat as chairman of the PLO Executive Committee on 11 November 2004, the day of Arafat's demise. His colleagues wanted him to be Fatah's sole candidate for the presidential elections that were constitutionally due no later than the sixty-first day following Arafat's death. Obviously, he was the favored candidate of Israel, the United States, and Europe.

A younger generation within Fatah wanted to nominate Marwan Barghouti, a hero of the second intifada who had been jailed for life by Israel. Great pressure was brought to bear on Barghouti, with a combination of threats and blandishments, to persuade him not to make difficulties for Fatah by standing against Abbas in the election. Initially Barghouti might have had more support within Fatah than Abbas. But Israel insisted Barghouti would never be released from prison, even if he were to be elected to the presidency. Additionally, many within Fatah began to express their concern over the potential threat of a split within Fatah that would only serve to strengthen the position of its rival, Hamas. These concerns persuaded the feuding tribes of Fatah to suspend their factional conflict and rally behind one man. Marwan Barghouti agreed to withdraw his nomination after successive Fatah visitors to his prison cell convinced him that Fatah could lose American and European political and financial support should anyone other than Abbas win the election.

Hesitant Democracy

On 9 January 2005, nearly two months after the death of Yasir Arafat in a Paris hospital, the Palestinians were summoned to the polls to elect a new president. The only candidate with a realistic chance of winning was Mahmud Abbas, and therefore his victory did not come as a surprise.[2] Hamas took the view that the election was Fatah's affair and decided to stay away. A number of other Palestinian factions, who had concluded that the exercise was futile, also joined the boycott.

From the day Mahmud Abbas took office on 15 January 2005, he pledged himself to the cause of political reform and promised to fight corruption. There was much to do to put Fatah's own house in order. There was also a pressing need for Fatah to open a dialogue with the other Palestinian factions, and especially with Hamas, which had been deliberating within its own ranks inside and outside Palestine as to what its strategy in the post-Arafat era should be. One priority was to decide whether to participate in the legislative elections Mahmud Abbas promised to conduct on 17 July 2005. Hamas had already taken part in other forms of elections such as student unions, trade associations, and the first municipal elections to be held in the territories since 1967.

The Palestinian Authority had decided to hold municipal elections in three stages that would take a year to complete. The first round of the first stage took place on 23 December 2004 in Jericho and 25 villages across the West Bank. Fatah won the majority of seats in 17 municipal councils (with 135 seats in total) while Hamas won the majority of the seats in nine councils (with 75 seats in total). The PFLP came in third place. What excited Hamas and alarmed Fatah was the result of the second round of these municipal elections, held in Gaza on 27 January 2005. Here Hamas won control of seven out of ten municipal councils (with 78 out of 118 seats). Fatah won 30 seats and the PFLP just one seat, while nine seats went to independent candidates.

Clearly, these results encouraged Hamas members in the Gaza Strip, who became highly enthusiastic about participating in the forthcoming legislative elections. They felt confident that they could win a comfortable majority. In contrast, Hamas members in the West Bank were less keen on the idea, and the Hamas branch in Hebron was very unenthusiastic. Hamas members inside the prisons expressed mixed feelings, while Hamas members abroad were cautiously supportive of participation. The outcome of all the consultations was submitted to Hamas's highest authority, the Istishari Council, which made the final decision that Hamas should seize the opportunity offered by the election and should participate fully in it.

Izzat al-Rishiq, a member of the Hamas Political Bureau and the head of its election committee, gave this explanation of Hamas's decision to participate in the elections:

The decision by the Islamic Resistance Movement [Hamas] to participate in the legislative elections was reached after extensive deliberations and thorough consultations. All of the movement's leading institutions and organs inside and outside Palestine were consulted, including the movement's captives inside the prisons of the Zionist occupation. It was agreed that our participation should in no way prejudice our commitment to safeguard our people's legitimate rights and to protect the program of resistance as a strategic option until the occupation comes to an end. The decision was in some respects a response to the popular sentiment and in fulfillment of our people's desire to see all Palestinian factions participate in the political process. It also took into account the outcome of the movement's assessment of the radical changes which have taken place inside Palestine thanks to the resistance, the intifada and the sacrifices our people have made over the past years. The process of consultation concluded that the Oslo era was at an end, and therefore the legislative elections, which were supposed to take place in July 2005 but were postponed to January 2006, were likely to be free from manipulation or constraints. It was these constraints and the monopoly over the political process that discouraged us from taking part in the 1996 elections. Our boycott at that time was not ideological. It had nothing to do with whether participation was halal [permissible] or haram [forbidden]: it was based only on our own assessment of what was in the interest of our cause and our people and what was not. We knew the Oslo Accords were doomed and that it was only a matter of time before the peace process between the Palestinian Authority and Israel reached a dead end and collapsed. We decided to stay away because we did not wish to support the unjust settlement in any way. Our participation at that time would have bestowed legitimacy on what was in our opinion illegitimate.[3]

Hamas's position on democracy and power-sharing in a non-Islamic regime is no different from that of mainstream Islamic groups. Hamas subscribes to the principle universally espoused by the Ikhwan, which accepts that democracy is compatible with Islam. As explained by Izzat al-Rishiq, the movement's decision to boycott the January 1996 presidential and legislative elections and the January 2005 presidential elections was not ideological, but arose from the conviction that the elections were conducted in circumstances that did not guarantee fair play. Several factors contributed to boosting Hamas's confidence that political circumstances were now more favorable. Among these were the utter failure of the peace process, the disappearance of Yasir Arafat from the political scene, and Israel's unilateral decision to end its occupation of the Gaza Strip. Other factors were the belief prevalent among the Palestinians that resistance by Hamas and other factions had forced the Israelis out of Gaza, and the disarray within the Fatah movement. Finally, there was the disillusionment of the public with the Palestinian Authority, which had arisen because of the prevalence of corruption and the PA's failure to carry the peace process through to a conclusion. On 12 March 2005, a Hamas spokesman announced that the movement had taken the decision to participate in the election.

The Cairo Talks

The plan to hold talks in Cairo was announced as the Palestinian Authority continued its efforts to conduct a dialogue with the main Palestinian factions. The Egyptian government had mediated between Fatah and Hamas in the past and had already brokered several meetings in Cairo. Between 15 and 17 March 2005, Egypt invited representatives of the different Palestinian factions to a meeting to be co-chaired by Omar Suleiman, the head of Egyptian intelligence, and the Palestinian President Mahmud Abbas. The meeting was attended by representatives from twelve Palestinian factions and produced the six-point "Cairo Declaration." This reaffirmed the basic principles to which the Palestinians adhered, including the right of the Palestinian people to resist the Israeli occupation and the right of the refugees to return to their homes and property. The declaration agreed to extend the period of non-belligerence (*tahdi'ah*), providing Israel consented to halt all forms of aggression against the Palestinian land and people. It also provided for basic political reform within the PLO to pave the way for both Hamas and Islamic Jihad to join it.

The Cairo meeting was a major boost for Hamas and Islamic Jihad. By endorsing its concluding declaration, both Egypt and the PA recognized the legitimacy of resistance. They also accepted the necessity of reform within the PLO as a precursor to the expansion of its membership to become truly representative of the Palestinian people. Egypt and the PA wanted an extension of the unilateral truce that had been intermittently implemented on the Palestinian side since 2002. Israel and the United States needed the continuation of the truce in order to enable Sharon to proceed with the withdrawal of troops and settlers from the Gaza Strip as the first phase of his disengagement plan. Hamas was well aware of this fact, but calculated that it also stood to gain much from the deal. The Hamas leadership was conscious that the majority of the Palestinians in the Gaza and the West Bank favored an extension of the period of calm. Undeniably, the Palestinians in the occupied territories had been exhausted by Israel's collective punitive measures.

Of paramount importance, however, as was emphasized by Khalid Mish'al, who headed the Hamas delegation to the Cairo talks, was the political and administrative reform of the Palestinian Authority and the PLO that had been agreed upon. As Khalid Mish'al explained to a round-table discussion organized at the offices of the Egyptian newspaper *Al-Ahram*, the PLO had existed in three forms. The first was that originally established in 1964. The second came into being in 1968, when the powerful Fatah faction came to dominate the organization. The time had now come for a third PLO, in which Fatah's long monopoly of the organization would be ended.[4] If a third PLO were to be restructured to reflect the affinities and the affiliations of the Palestinian people inside as well as outside Palestine, Hamas would most likely be the biggest beneficiary. Mish'al saw the Cairo agreement as the beginning of a process that might enable Hamas to take an active part in ending Fatah's monopoly on decision making within the PLO, and the widespread corruption within the Palestinian Authority. The extension of the period of calm until the end of 2005 was also seen as an opportunity to consolidate as many of Hamas's gains as possible at both the local and the international level.[5]

Tension between Hamas and Fatah resurfaced with the second stage of the municipal elections. On 5 May 2005, Palestinians were called upon to cast their ballots in the local elections in 76 villages in the West Bank and 8 villages in the Gaza Strip. The 906 seats were contested by 2,500 candidates. Fatah came first, winning 50 municipal councils. Hamas came second with 28 councils, the PFLP won one council and four councils went to a coalition of secular groups. While Fatah did very well in the rural areas, Hamas won the major urban centers. Hamas won most of the seats in Rafah, Beit Lahia, and al-Buraij, prompting Fatah to query the results and call for the election to be held again in these three key municipalities. On 21 May 2005, a Palestinian court ruled in favor of a re-run of the elections in the three areas. Hamas agreed, provided an understanding was first reached on the rules governing the process, and that a guarantee was given that this time the results would be respected whoever was the winner. The two sides failed to reach an agreement on the ground rules, but Fatah announced it intended in any case to proceed to hold new elections. In response, Hamas announced on 30 May that it would boycott the repeated elections if they were held with no prior agreement on the parameters. Hamas insisted on a postponement, while Fatah insisted on going ahead. Influential Fatah officials within the PA had been extremely concerned that the elections would end the monopoly Fatah had enjoyed for many years, if they followed the pattern of the local elections already held. The plan to conduct a repeat of the election collapsed when Hamas threatened to ask the electorate to stage a boycott. Fatah then agreed to a postponement.

On 4 June 2005, President Abbas issued a decree postponing until further notice the legislative elections that were supposed to be held in July. Hamas and several other Palestinian factions objected to the decision, declaring that it showed a lack of commitment on the part of the Palestinian Authority to what had been agreed during the Cairo talks. The postponement was not unexpected; rumors to that effect had already been circulating. According to the London *Al-Hayat* daily newspaper, several Fatah leaders in the Gaza Strip advocated the postponement of the legislative elections out of concern that Fatah might not do well. Some of them took the view that holding the elections as scheduled prior to the planned Israeli withdrawal from Gaza was likely to improve the position of Hamas. The Hamas leadership would be able to make use of the election campaign to claim the credit for forcing the Israelis out of the Gaza Strip.[6] One of the reasons given for the decision to postpone the election was a dispute over reform of the election law.[7] In fact, disagreement within Fatah over the list of candidates standing in Fatah's name was believed to be one of the main reasons for the delay. President Abbas attempted to resolve the problem by ordering an internal poll to determine which candidates were favored by Fatah's grassroots membership, but this only intensified the dispute and deepened the divisions within Fatah.

Alarmed by Hamas's success in the municipal elections, the Israeli government was also apprehensive. Prime Minister Ariel Sharon and other members of his cabinet had issued warnings that a Hamas win in the legislative elections would leave them with no option but to call off their planned withdrawal from the Gaza Strip. They were strongly opposed to the idea that Hamas might inherit power after their departure. Soon after his meeting with Mahmud Abbas in Washington on 26 May 2005, US President George W. Bush declared that Hamas was a terrorist organization that should not be allowed to take part in the elections. If it were to win, he added, its victory should not be recognized. Both the Israelis and the Americans were apprehensive that Hamas might in fact win, which could mean they might have to deal directly with its officials. The member states of the European Union, which had put Hamas on its own list of terrorist organizations in 2003 at the behest of the US and Israel, had similar concerns.

The major international actors found themselves in a real dilemma. While keen to maintain an active role in the quest for a settlement in the Middle East, they did not wish to be seen to be reneging on their commitment not to deal with what were regarded as terrorist organizations, or their members. On 8 June 2005, Britain's Foreign Secretary Jack Straw provided an illustration of the predicament when, just before his departure from London on a visit to Jerusalem, he admitted to the press that British diplomats had already held talks with Hamas officials. In March 2005, British officials had met Ahmad al-Kurd, the mayor of Deir al-Balah, in the Gaza Strip, and in May 2005 they met Hashem al-Masri, the acting mayor of the West Bank town of Qalqilya. Both these men were senior members of Hamas. While Hamas did not recognize Israel's right to exist, the acting Mayor of Qalqilya had no other option than to deal with Israeli officials in matters pertaining to the daily needs of the municipality, which shared resources and services with its Jewish neighbors. Nevertheless, the British seemed profoundly embarrassed by the admission of these contacts with Hamas. At the Israeli foreign ministry in Jerusalem, Straw sought to assuage the anxiety of his Israeli counterpart Silvan Shalom that the meetings between British officials and Hamas could signal a shift from the British and EU position that the group was a terrorist organization. Straw went as far as to claim that he had been personally responsible for the introduction of legislation placing Hamas and the Palestinian Islamic Jihad on the list of proscribed organizations. He said Britain had been at the forefront in seeking EU sanctions against those groups. Shalom responded by stressing that Israel wanted Hamas to stay on the EU's list of terrorist organizations.

Hamas officials admit in private that one of the motivations for its decision to play a part in the democratic process was to oblige the international community to abandon its boycott of Hamas. They calculated that their officials, once elected, would have to be recognized internationally as the legitimate representatives of at least some parts of the Palestinian community in the West Bank and the Gaza Strip. Eventually, they conjectured, Hamas could conceivably achieve its removal from the international lists of terrorist organizations, simply because nations would have no option but to deal with it directly.

On 18 June 2005, with no date yet set for the legislative elections, the Palestinian Legislative council convened to endorse various amendments to the electoral law. These amendments included an increase in the number of the council's seats from 88 to 132 and the introduction of a degree of proportional representation through a parallel voting system. According to the new system, each voter had two types of vote at his disposal. One of these was for choosing representatives from one of the national party lists. Each voter had one such vote, and half the total number of seats in the PLC, 66 in all, would be distributed in proportion to the number of votes cast for the party lists. It was stipulated that no list that received less than 2 percent of the total number of votes cast could receive any seats. The new law laid down that each list should include at least one woman in the first three names, at least one woman in the next four names, and at least one woman in the five names that followed. The second type of vote was for representatives for the voter's own multi-member local constituency. Each voter would have as many votes to cast for individual candidates as there were seats in his or her constituency. Those who won the most votes in the constituency, up to the number of seats set for that particular constituency, would be allocated seats in the PLC. In all, these seats would also total 66. To set a minimum quota for Christian representation in the PLC, a total of six seats were allotted to Christian candidates in various constituencies across Palestine.[8] President Abbas and the PLO Executive Committee had wanted to allocate all 132 seats on the basis of proportional representation, but this was not the solution favored by the Fatah-dominated PLC. Hamas showed no preference. It was confident that whatever electoral system method or combination of systems were adopted it would do well.

On 20 August 2005, following a series of discussions between the leaderships of Fatah and Hamas in the Gaza Strip on a new date for the legislative elections, President Mahmud Abbas announced that the elections would be held on 25 January 2006. However, as the election date approached, Fatah officials became increasingly nervous. Disputes within Fatah had not abated, and meanwhile Hamas seemed the party best prepared. On 21 December 2005, the Israelis announced that they would not allow voting in East Jerusalem. Rumors circulated that this was a plot concocted by Fatah and Israel in order to get the elections postponed for a further period or to have them canceled altogether. Israel did not conceal its real motivation. This actually had nothing to do with sovereignty over East Jerusalem, whose Palestinian residents had been were allowed to vote in previous Palestinian elections despite the Israeli assertion of sovereignty. The Israeli government was concerned simply because it was becoming increasingly clear that if the elections went ahead with the participation of Hamas, the movement would do well and perhaps even emerge as the victor. The rumor of a conspiracy intensified when the response of the Palestinian Authority to Israel's ruling was that the election would not be held if the voters of East Jerusalem were not allowed to participate. Few people failed to see this move more as a pretext to postpone an election that Hamas might win than as a debate over principle. Hamas insisted that the elections be held as scheduled regardless of

Israel's decision over the participation of the Jerusalemites. The Israelis soon recanted, announcing on 10 January 2006 that a limited number of Palestinians in East Jerusalem would be able to cast votes at post offices, as they had done in 1996, while other Jerusalemites would be obliged to go to PA-controlled areas to vote. Despite stating that Palestinian candidates would also be allowed to campaign in East Jerusalem as long as they registered with Israeli police, a police spokesman warned that no Hamas supporter would receive permission. During the campaign, the Israeli police closed at least three Hamas election offices in East Jerusalem.

The elections were eventually held in a highly charged climate. International observers were anxious. Fatah leaders dreaded the worst: up to the last minute, they did their best to reassure the public that they deserved to remain in charge. On 24 January 2006, Donald Macintyre assessed the situation in the British newspaper the *Independent*. Under the title "Fatah Invokes Memory of Arafat as Campaign Closes," he wrote: "Fatah leaders invoked the memory of Yassir Arafat, apologised for mistakes, and reminded voters that the mainstream Palestinian movement had resisted Israel long before Hamas." In his dispatch, from Khan Yunis in the Gaza Strip, Macintyre described what he said was Fatah's "frenetic last day of election campaigning."[9]

The Earthquake

Observers around the world knew Hamas was likely to do well in the elections. Few, however, expected it to do as well as it did. Pre-election opinion polls insisted to the end that Fatah was likely to come first, followed by Hamas, which might constitute the largest opposition bloc inside the Legislative Council. In one of these polls, conducted by the US-funded Palestinian Center for Policy and Survey Research in early December 2005, Fatah was said to enjoy 50 percent of public support, with Hamas second at 32 percent. A second poll conducted by the same Center in the period 29 to 31 December 2005 claimed that Fatah was likely to win 43 percent of the vote, while Hamas's "Change and Reform" list would achieve 25 percent. A poll by Palestinian Public Opinion Polls, conducted on 5 and 6 January 2006, seemed to narrow the gap between the two rivals; Fatah was expected to win 39.3 percent with Hamas's "Change and Reform" list at 31.3 percent. The Independent Palestine list was assessed at 10.4 percent, the Martyr Abu Ali Mustafa list at 6.8 percent, and the Third Way list at 5.5 percent. On election day, exit polls were reported to indicate that Fatah was winning more seats than Hamas. A poll conducted by the Palestinian Center for Policy and Survey Research estimated that Fatah had won 42 percent of the national vote and Hamas 35 percent. A Birzeit University poll claimed that Fatah won 46.4 percent of the vote and Hamas 39.5 percent. Birzeit's tentative prediction of the distribution of seats anticipated that Fatah would win 63 seats and Hamas 58.[10] Foreign observers were also guarded over the predictions of Hamas's likely performance. On the eve of the election, Hussein Agha and Robert Malley made their assessment in the British newspaper the *Guardian*: "There is more uncertainty than clarity surrounding tomorrow's Palestinian elections, though this much is plain: Hamas, the Islamist movement designated a terrorist organization by the US and Europe and considered a mortal enemy by Israel, will be joining the legislature. Riding an unprecedented wave of popularity and having exceeded expectations in recent municipal elections, it is on course to capture a sizeable portion of votes and, who knows, a seat at the cabinet table."[11]

The official results proved the pollsters completely wrong: Hamas won 74 seats and Fatah 45. Even before the count was over, in the early hours of the day after the election, Hamas and Fatah officials made a joint statement that Hamas was expected to win a majority. Isma'il Haniya, head of the Change and Reform list, declared that "Hamas has won more than 70 seats in Gaza and the West Bank." The Hamas spokesman and candidate Mushir al-Masri said he expected Hamas to win 77 seats. Conceding defeat later in the morning, Fatah's Prime Minister Ahmad Quri' resigned, along with his cabinet, saying, "it now falls to Hamas to form a government." For the first few days, the media quoted experts who said Hamas's victory was a surprise even to Hamas itself. Many observers had expected Hamas to win enough seats to become the main opposition to Fatah within the new Legislative Council, perhaps even becoming a partner in the government. However, the result did not surprise some who had been following developments in Palestine closely.[12] In a dispatch from Khan Yunis in the Gaza Strip, Chris McGreal wrote in the *Guardian* that "corruption and incompetence in Yasir Arafat's faction are helping Hamas win support in run-up to Palestinian election."[13]

On election day, the international media seemed more certain of their prediction. Chris McGreal reported that "the armed Islamist group Hamas is expected to break the ruling Fatah movement's 40-year domination of the Palestinian cause in bitterly contested parliamentary elections today."[14] Meanwhile, Donald Macintyre reported in the *Independent* from Gaza City: "More than a million residents of the West Bank, Gaza and East Jerusalem are expected to vote today in elections that will see Hamas end Fatah's monopoly of control over the Palestinian Authority."[15]

The claim that the result surprised Hamas as much it surprised others was repeatedly denied by Hamas officials. They maintained that the movement expected to win but that there was no agreement on the margin. There were two schools of thought within the movement. Those who had worked closely with the election campaign committees had predicted Hamas would win between 70 and 75 seats. They based their predictions on the feedback from their own election workers, who had been gauging grassroots opinion. Campaigners for Hamas visited households and associations and spoke to family elders, tribal chiefs, and professional association leaders regularly throughout the campaign and on election day. Other Hamas officials, however, were more cautious, guessing Hamas was set to win close to fifty percent of the seats but not more.[16]

The explanation for the result most commonly put forward was the assumption that the electorate voted for Hamas to punish Fatah. In reality, only a fraction of the votes cast was made up of protest votes. In Palestinian elections conducted over the past decade, whether among students on campus, in ballots within trade unions, or more recently at the municipal level, Hamas invariably gained at least 40 percent of the total votes. The figures for the 25 January 2006 legislative elections indicate that only a small proportion of those who voted for Hamas seem to have done so to punish Fatah. Proportional list voting showed that 44.45 percent voted for Hamas, not much more than the 40 percent that seemed to be Hamas's usual score, while 41.43 percent voted for Fatah. Hamas's popularity had been built up over a much longer period than many electoral experts acknowledged.

In hindsight, Hamas's massive victory has been attributed to a number of factors. Some Hamas voters were already convinced Hamas supporters, while others made up their minds much closer to the day of polling. Some who chose to vote for Hamas gave more than one reason for having decided to vote for the movement. The primary reason for casting a vote in favor of Hamas was Hamas's fidelity to the Palestinian dream. Most Palestinians, including those who have at various stages expressed their readiness to settle for less, cannot help but dream of seeing Palestine, all of it, completely free. They imagine the day when millions of Palestinian refugees will return to the towns and villages from which they were driven when Israel was created in 1948. Hamas, which believes that the State of Israel is an illegitimate political entity that will one day disappear, just as the 11th-century Crusader kingdoms in Palestine and Syria disappeared, keeps the dream alive. The 1988 Fatah-dominated PLO's decision to recognize Israel's right to exist in exchange for being recognized as the sole legitimate representative of the Palestinian people was the turning point for many Palestinians. From then on Hamas, which had been in existence for no more than a year, began to be perceived by an increasing number of Palestinians as the alternative to Fatah, which, they believed, had lost its way.

The second reason for preferring Hamas relates to the record of the Muslim Brotherhood, and thus of Hamas as its successor, as a provider of services to the population. Many Palestinians would scarcely be able to manage without the social, educational, and medical services provided by the United Nations and an army of NGOs, the most efficient of which have been the ones set up and run by Hamas. As Israel collectively punished the Palestinians, destroying the infrastructure of their society and its organization, it unwittingly provided Hamas with the greatest of opportunities. Many Palestinians compared the rampant corruption that had spread throughout the Palestinian Authority and among the rank and file of Fatah with the clean hands of Hamas's officials. The Palestinian people could not help but admire the decency, honesty, and transparency with which Hamas conducted its affairs and provided its services to the public. Hamas officials channeled millions of dollars worth of aid to those in need every year, but continued to live as they had always done. They lived like ordinary Palestinians and many had their homes inside the refugee camps. They were part of the people, close to their minds and hearts. Sheikh Yassin passed his whole life in a refugee camp, with a standard of living scarcely different from that of his neighbors. His way of life offered a stark contrast to the leaders of Fatah, many of whom had made fortunes and built empires in the margins of the peace process with the Israelis.

The third reason for Hamas's electoral success was its Islamic ideology, which, unlike Fatah's secular nationalism, was in sympathy with the powerful inclination toward Islam within Palestinian society. Since the early 1970s, Palestine has seen a massive Islamic revival that was in part a reaction to the failure of secular Arab nationalism, which Palestinians blamed for the loss of the remainder of Palestine to the Israelis in 1967. As an increasingly religious community, the Palestinians came more to identify with the moral code espoused by Hamas than with the more liberal agenda of the leaders of Fatah. Even some previously diehard members of Fatah itself, who had in recent years become more religious, began to find themselves closer to Hamas than to Fatah.

The fourth reason concerned the failure of the peace process. Rather than deliver the Palestinians from their misery, the apparently endless process seemed only to have aggravated their suffering. Hamas had predicted all along that Israel would not fulfill its bargain, and that it was using peacemaking in order to expropriate more land. The Hamas view was that only jihad would force the occupation to come to an end. Israel proved Hamas right when it turned against its own partners in the peace process, destroying the Palestinian Authority's institutions and literally besieging Yasir Arafat, whom many Palestinians believe eventually met his death by poisoning. Israel's unilateral withdrawal from Gaza served only further to vindicate Hamas, which claimed that it was its efforts that had Sharon unconditionally to withdraw the settlers and troops.

Israel's Self-Inflicted Predicament

The Hamas victory may also be seen as the response of the Palestinians to Israel's unilateralism. Israel's policy has been to proceed toward the establishment of a permanent status of some kind while neither negotiating nor coming to any arrangement with the Palestinians. Many observers have warned the Israelis that this policy is only likely to exacerbate their predicament rather than resolve it. Nevertheless, the Israeli withdrawal from the Gaza Strip was not the result of a peace deal, nor was it part of an agreement. It was a unilateral decision predicated on the assumption that withdrawal would rid Israel of a chronic problem. Consequently, neither the Palestinian Authority nor any of the Palestinian factions active inside the Gaza Strip could be held responsible for keeping the peace along the borders with Israel in the aftermath of the withdrawal from Gaza of the Israeli troops and settlers.

For the Palestinians, the withdrawal did not end the conflict. After all, the majority of the inhabitants of the Gaza Strip were refugees, whose struggle had been directed from as long ago as the early 1950s at securing their right to return to their homes in the land from which they were forced out in 1948. A further reason the conflict did not end was that although Israel withdrew both troops and settlers, it nonetheless continued to maintain a tight grip on the borders of the Gaza Strip, controlling the movement of persons and goods into and out of it. Palestinian farmers in particular were at Israel's mercy, as they were unable to export their produce or import any goods or equipment without Israeli permission. The restrictions also covered medical supplies, educational materials, fuel, and all sorts of other essential commodities. The entire Palestinian population of the Gaza Strip, nearly 1.2 million people, became prisoners.

In addition, Israel did not halt its efforts to eliminate those inside Gaza whom it regards as its enemies, in their houses and offices and as they moved across Gaza on foot or in vehicles. These attacks were facilitated by Israeli reconnaissance aircraft and executed by the Israeli assault aircraft and Apache helicopters that control the skies over the Gaza Strip, instilling horror in the hearts of its residents. Israel also continued to operate inside the Gaza Strip by proxy. It had the services of hundreds of collaborators, who assisted it by informing on fellow Palestinians and hunting down activists who were deemed to be a potential threat. Some of the collaborators working for Israel were senior members of the Palestinian security agencies set up in the 1990s as part of the peace process between Israel and the PLO. In the months leading up to the legislative elections won by Hamas, some of these individuals were encouraged to use their powers and utilize the resources at their disposal to stir up internal strife among the Palestinians. The tactic ended by harming Fatah, because those perceived by the population as fomenting sedition were or had been members of Fatah, and were often known to be corrupt as well as traitors.

Another crucial issue was that Israeli unilateralism was so far confined to the Gaza Strip. Israel's occupation of the West Bank continued and so did the provocation and persecution of its Palestinian population. Targeted assassinations and the detention of Palestinian activists in the West Bank did not abate. However, the Israelis liked to believe that the Gaza Strip and the West Bank were two separate entities and that the people living in one had nothing to do with, or had little sympathy for, those living in the other. In reality, the Palestinians in the supposedly liberated Gaza Strip could not ignore the worsening situation in the West Bank's towns and villages. Palestinian factions whose members in the West Bank were being hunted down by Israel had no option but to respond to the calls for revenge, which was sometimes easier to take in Gaza than in the West Bank. Of all the factions, only Hamas had been observing a unilateral truce at the time and continued it despite Israeli provocations.

Finally, there was also a further bleeding wound that the Israelis insisted on keeping open despite their withdrawal from the Gaza Strip. Israel continued to hold more than 10,000 Palestinian prisoners, including hundreds of women and children, in a number of detention camps across the country. Some of these prisoners were from the West Bank but a great many were from the Gaza Strip itself. It was extremely naïve on the part of the Israeli leadership to suppose that a unilateral withdrawal from Gaza without the return of these thousands of detainees to their loved ones would inspire gratitude in the Palestinians. The continued detention of such a large number of Palestinians simply meant that the conflict was far from over. This is exactly the mistake the Israelis have also made in the case of Lebanon, where not only is land held by Israeli troops but also there are Lebanese detainees in Israeli custody.

There may be more than one explanation for Israel's attitude toward the detainees. One suggestion is that the Israelis regard detainees as an important asset because they constitute an essential source of information about present and future situations. Information is not difficult to obtain from them: Israel is the only United Nations member state whose legal system condones the subjection of detainees to physical pressure, or torture, in order to extract confessions and obtain information. Deterrence may be another aim. If so, however, it has failed miserably. Keeping people in detention for long periods has proved to produce the opposite effect. Their families and the organizations to which they belong derive from their fortitude the inspiration that enables them to continue the struggle and to mount more resistance against Israel.

After Fatah, the Flood

The political tremor caused by Hamas's victory in the elections had a devastating effect on the losers. The leaders of Fatah could not conceal their bitterness. While the Hamas spokesman and elected legislator Mushir al-Masri called for what he described as a political partnership with Fatah, a prominent Fatah figure, Jibril al-Rajub, rejected the idea of a coalition and called on Fatah to form what he described as a "responsible opposition."

Soon after the election results were confirmed, Khalid Mish'al sought to reassure the Palestinians and the other Arabs that they had nothing to fear from Hamas's election victory. He pledged that a Hamas government, once formed, would dedicate itself to serving the Palestinian people to the best of its ability. On 28 January 2006, in a press conference held in Damascus, his first ever in the city,[17] he declared his movement's commitment to a partnership with Fatah and all the other Palestinian factions in forming the new government. He stressed the need to agree with all Palestinian organizations on a unified political agenda, in the face of US and EU threats to cut off aid to a Palestinian Authority led by Hamas. In his statement, intending to reassure all those concerned both within Palestine and in the region, he emphasized that Hamas would not adopt an authoritarian approach in government. He said Hamas would not dismiss people from their jobs, and that it would approach the current political situation in Palestine, including what had resulted from the Oslo process, in a spirit of what he called "extreme realism." He also said Hamas would respect the commitments of its predecessor as long as this did not conflict with the best interests of the Palestinian people. He expressed enthusiasm for the idea of integrating all the military organizations, including Hamas's Izzadin al-Qassam Brigades, into a unified army like those possessed by other countries. However, nothing Mish'al could have said would have assuaged the fears of his Fatah rivals, who had never imagined the day would come when they were no longer in charge of the affairs of the Palestinian people.

Mish'al's remarks were not sufficient to pacify the worldwide alarm that followed Hamas's victory, which came as a particularly unpleasant surprise for the United States, Israel's ally. There were conflicting reports over the reactions of President Bush's close circle of advisers in the White

House. Some, it was said, had voiced doubts over the wisdom of "pressing ahead with a crash course in democracy for the Middle East." US Secretary of State Condoleezza Rice was said to be reviewing where her officials had gone wrong in their assessments and analyses before the election. Some US officials said they had not expected Hamas to win, while others claimed they had expected it. The Bush administration said there would be no recognition, no dialogue, and no financial aid for a Hamas-led Palestinian Authority until Hamas complied with three conditions. First, Hamas had to recognize Israel; then it had to renounce violence and disarm; and finally it had to accept all previous Palestinian–Israeli agreements.[18] That Hamas was democratically elected, and that the majority of the Palestinians identified with its political agenda, appeared to be of no concern.

Immediately after its election victory, Hamas announced the extension of its unilateral truce. Hamas's leaders were hoping that the new Israeli leadership would choose to reciprocate and perhaps negotiate a long-term arrangement. Additionally, having demonstrated to the Palestinian people its unswerving loyalty to the cause of resisting Israeli occupation, Hamas hoped to be given the chance to provide a model of good governance. Some of Hamas's leaders in the West Bank and Gaza, as well as some members of the Damascus-based Political Bureau, were optimistic. Their view was that since the movement had been democratically elected to run the Palestinian Authority, it might perhaps be given a chance to prove its credentials and implement its manifesto promise of "Change and Reform."

To Hamas, the three conditions set by the United States seemed to be nothing but a face-saving maneuver to justify its already formulated intention to refuse any relationship with Hamas. The United States was well aware that Hamas would not agree to any of the conditions while Palestinian land was still occupied. Hamas believed the problem lay with Israel, and not with the Palestinians. Hamas's leaders argued that if the Americans truly wished to see peace prevail in the region they should put pressure on Israel to end its occupation, rather than on the Palestinians, who are the victims and not the oppressors. The Americans, for their part, may have felt rueful that they had been among those who insisted loudest on holding elections as the means of effecting political reform in the territories. They should have been aware that Fatah, their favorite, was in bad shape and stood only an extremely slim chance of winning.

When Hamas showed no signs of yielding, the United States, Israel, and the European Union took joint action to oblige it either to change, or, failing that, to face total exclusion from the political arena. Various tactics were employed to bring about one or other of these two outcomes. Countries round the world were exhorted to withhold recognition from Hamas and to refuse to deal with it. This tactic met with limited success. It certainly failed with most Arab and Islamic countries, which invited Hamas officials for visits and expressed their willingness to give political and financial help. Turkey, which is a member of NATO, annoyed both Israel and the US by inviting a high-level top Hamas delegation to Ankara. Pressure was put on Turkey, however, to downgrade the visit by not inviting the delegation to meet the prime minister. Nonetheless, the Turks promised to give what help they could, and offered to mediate between Israel and Hamas.[19]

A major blow to the US-led campaign against Hamas was an invitation to the movement issued by the Russian leadership to visit Moscow for talks.[20] Despite insisting in public that their intention was to persuade Hamas to change its position, in the private meetings the Russians held with the Hamas delegation they said very little, if anything, along these lines. The Russians saw in Hamas's victory an opportunity for them to regain a foothold in the Middle East, after having lost virtually all their influence following the collapse of the Soviet Union. The official visit in early March was preceded by a number of contacts between the two sides as well as by an informal visit by a Hamas team to Moscow immediately after the elections.

Encouraged by the Turkish and Russian gestures, the South African government also expressed a desire to invite Hamas to visit Pretoria for talks. For more than a year, the South Africans had indicated that they were keen to extend an invitation to Hamas's senior leadership. They constantly deferred the date, however, for political reasons, which may have been the result of pressure from the United States and Israel. After the election, the visit was on the point of taking place, but Mahmud Abbas intervened to persuade his "old comrades" in the South African leadership that the time was not propitious. In addition to Turkey and Russia, however, Hamas Political Bureau members visited and held talks with the leaders of Iran, Syria, Saudi Arabia, Qatar, Kuwait, Bahrain, the UAE, Yemen, Sudan, Oman, Algeria, and Libya. Malaysia extended an invitation but the visit was put on hold when Mahmud Abbas put the Malaysian government in a diplomatic dilemma by expressing a desire to visit Malaysia first.

The outgoing Fatah-dominated Palestinian Legislative Council was determined to undermine the victorious Hamas movement. Many of the Fatah members had not been re-elected, and morally speaking, exercised no mandate after the election. Nevertheless, on Monday, 13 February, just days before Hamas took control of the legislature, the outgoing Fatah members of the PLC held what they called a farewell session, at which they granted Mahmud Abbas sweeping new powers. As president, Abbas was given the authority to appoint a new constitutional court to serve as the final arbiter in disputes between himself and the government, which, as all were aware, would be formed by Hamas. The constitutional court, which would consist of nine judges, would be empowered to resolve any dispute between Abbas and the incoming Hamas government or the Hamas-dominated parliament. The court would also have the power to veto legislation deemed to violate the Palestinian basic law, the forerunner to the Palestinian constitution. Legal experts warned at the time that the new legislation would allow Abbas to annul any law approved by the new parliament on the pretext of its being unconstitutional. The outgoing legislators also appointed Fatah loyalists to four key posts, including the head of the government anti-corruption commission, with the clear objective of obstructing the fulfillment of Hamas's election pledge to end the years of nepotism, graft, and Fatah mismanagement. The other three positions were Palestinian Authority's head of personnel, the chief administrator of the parliament, and the director of the government's salaries and pension fund. Hamas described these actions as "illegitimate" and the procedure as "a bloodless coup," vowing to overturn them. At its first session on Monday, 6 March, the new Palestinian Legislative Council, with its comfortable two-thirds majority of Hamas members, repealed Fatah's last-minute legislation, prompting the Fatah members to walk out and boycott the rest of the session.

In another bid to weaken Hamas, Mahmud Abbas brought pressure to bear on members of Fatah's leadership not to join the government, which Hamas had hoped would be a government of national unity. Some leading members of Fatah had favored the formation of a national unity government led by Hamas. However, it was widely reported that Fatah legislators were cajoled and threatened by their leadership not to join any such administration. They were promised that they would continue to receive payments through the president's office so that they would not be affected by sanctions. Meanwhile, they were also warned that should they join a Hamas national unity government without a prior change in Hamas's attitude towards Israel, they would be punished and could risk being placed on lists of terrorist suspects. It transpired later that by the time Fatah began to discuss the formation of the government with Hamas, Fatah's Revolutionary Council, a key decision-making body within the Fatah organization, had already decided to boycott the government. Fatah was determined to thwart Hamas where possible, and to cause the Hamas government to fail.[21]

At the same time, ironically, Fatah negotiators continued to insist that Hamas accept the three conditions laid down by the US if they wished Fatah members to consider joining its cabinet. However, Fatah spokesmen such as Sa'ib Urayqat, Jibril al-Rajub, and Muhammad Dahlan had already indicated that Fatah would rather be part of the opposition. Fatah wished in this way to give itself a respite and a chance to rebuild its structure and purge its procedures of corruption, leaving Hamas to its own devices to see how it would succeed in running the Palestinian Authority. By the time Hamas had approached the other factions to discuss the possibility of forming a national unity government, the official position of Fatah had changed. It now laid down two conditions that Hamas must meet. These were, first, to recognize Israel's right to exist, and second, to recognize the PLO's claim to be the "sole legitimate representative of the Palestinian people." Neither condition was acceptable to Hamas, which proceeded to form a government on its own. This took office on 29 March 2006.

Having failed to persuade Hamas to agree to the formation of a national unity government, as desired by the international community, President Abbas issued a number of presidential decrees stripping the newly formed Hamas cabinet of control of much of the government's institutional base. In effect, he stood on its head the principle of the delegation of authority he had himself struggled to implement when he was prime minister under Yasir Arafat. He claimed exclusive presidential authority over the police force, the various media outlets such as TV, radio, and the WAFA news agency, the Property Sale and Registration Department, and control over the crossing points between Israel and the Palestinian territories. Even the department in charge of hajj and 'umra (the pilgrimage to Mecca) within the Ministry of Islamic Affairs was attached to his own office. In a direct blow to the new government's reform plans, he appointed Rashid Abu Shbak in charge of internal security, a position supposed to be under the control of the Interior Ministry. At the same time, to reinforce his control over the already much-weakened ministries, he appointed nine undersecretaries, none of them technocrats and all of them Fatah members who were loyal to him and reported to him alone. Thus, the Hamas-led government had no police force at its disposal, no government-controlled media, little control over land sales and registration, and no authority whatsoever over the frontier crossings. The US assistant secretary of state for Near Eastern affairs was reported to have suggested to Mahmud Abbas that he should appoint Salam Fayyad, a former finance minister, as a finance director within his own office with the responsibility for the management of incoming funds.

With the full support and financial backing of the international community, led by the United States, Mahmud Abbas contrived to establish a parallel government whose policies were diametrically opposed to those of the elected government and whose powers had the effect of rendering the legitimate government powerless. By the end of May 2006, Abbas had embarked on the process of setting up a 10,000-strong presidential guard, whose training and armament was secured thanks to the funding and cooperation of the US, Israel, and Jordan. With no intention of giving way, Hamas's interior minister held a public rally in one of Gaza's largest mosques, where he told community leaders that he needed their support if he was to be able to provide security. Armed criminals had been terrorizing the population, looting and killing, while the police force under the command of Mahmud Abbas stood by and did nothing. With public approval, Interior Minister Sa'id Siyam announced the formation of a special Interior Ministry task force to keep the peace and maintain law and order. It was anticipated that this measure would attract Fatah's condemnation and might perhaps be used as a pretext to stage an armed clash. Mahmud Abbas threatened to veto the Hamas measure, and actually issued a presidential decree declaring it to be null and void, but failed to frustrate Hamas's intentions.

The most painful measure taken against Hamas has so far been the economic sanctions imposed by the international community. The Hamas-led government inherited from its Fatah-controlled predecessor a huge bureaucracy with more than 160,000 employees, including the many thousands of policemen recruited to keep order in accordance with the commitment given by the Palestinian Authority to maintain peace with Israel. It also inherited an empty treasury and a huge debt incurred by the previous government. Local banks could no longer afford to lend funds to the government because the outgoing Fatah government had reached the upper limit of borrowing the banks were able to permit. A freeze on aid from the US and the EU would not alone have caused that much pain. In fact, Hamas might have been able to manage without funding from the West. Funds promised by the Arabs and Muslims, as well as by the Russians and other friends of Palestine, would have sufficed. The real problem was that there was virtually no means of delivering money to the government; all channels had been blocked. The United States and Israel used all the resources at their disposal in order to prevent any money from getting through. The US government threatened to take measures against banks that transferred funds to the Hamas-led government, even threatening to include them in lists of terrorist supporters. It soon became clear that the real intention was to provoke Palestinian Authority employees and members of the various police forces, who were mainly Fatah supporters, to turn against the new Palestinian Authority for failing to pay their salaries. These employees and their families were being punished in order to encourage them to rebel against the Hamas-led government, which they were supposed to perceive as culpable for their plight.

Peaceful protests soon escalated into acts of sabotage directed against government buildings. It did not take long for the protests to develop into armed clashes. Agents provocateurs made a number of attempts to bring about armed conflict between Hamas and Fatah. Thanks to the moderating influence of the traditional structures of Palestinian society, the potential for civil war between Palestinians has always been slight. However, the possibility of armed conflict between Fatah and Hamas could not be ruled out entirely; certain elements were sufficiently determined to put an end to the Hamas era that they might not even shrink from precipitating a bloodbath. Large-scale business interests depended on the peace process with Israel. Those who have squeezed personal profits out of the billions of dollars of aid that came from overseas to the previous Palestinian Authority fear for the loss of some or all of the sources of their wealth should a Hamas government become well established. Hamas has promised to install an independent judiciary and to implement a strict system of accountability. The problem is not confined to former revolutionaries whom the peace process has transformed into millionaires or multi-millionaires. These Palestinian profiteers also have partners in neighboring Arab countries who have shared the spoils of peace with them. However, as economic sanctions seemed to be becoming less likely to be able to break the Hamas-led government, its rivals have looked more likely to resort to violence to bring Hamas down.

For months, the siege failed to break the resolve of Hamas's supporters, who have soldiered on in the face of adversity. Rather than cause public opinion to swing against Hamas, the sanctions have only served to consolidate its position. Palestinian society may have become further polarized, but this has certainly not been to the detriment of Hamas. According to a poll conducted by the Almustaqbal (Future) Research Center between 1 May and 4 May 2006, 84.6 percent of the Palestinians in the Gaza Strip oppose the idea that the Hamas-led government should bow to the demands of the United States, the European Union, and Israel. Only 10.6 percent said they were in favor. Nearly 60 percent of those polled expected the government to withstand the pressure of the sanctions for as long as they might last, while only 12 percent said they did not expect it to withstand the pressure for more than six months.[22]

Jordan Revisited

Much of the funding raised in Arab and Muslim capitals for the Palestinian Authority under Hamas is on deposit in banks in the Jordanian capital Amman. The Hamas leadership has been suspicious that the Jordanian authorities may be collusion with the US to impose a strict regime of sanctions on the Palestinians in the hope of forcing a change in Hamas's attitude. The financial crisis has revived suspicions that the Jordanians have been directly involved in what Hamas officials perceive as a global conspiracy against their movement.

Soon after Hamas's election victory, Jordanian government officials contacted Muhammad Nazzal, the Hamas Political Bureau member based in Damascus to ask for a meeting with him in Amman. The Jordanians appeared eager to turn over a new leaf in their relations with Hamas, and their official invitation to senior Hamas officials to visit the Hashemite Kingdom for talks was meant as a demonstration of their good intentions. On 16 February 2006 Jordan's Prime Minister Ma'ruf al-Bakhit told parliament in Amman that Jordan would welcome a visit by the leaders of Hamas. Al-Bakhit's remarks were taken at the time to indicate a change in the position so far firmly maintained by the Jordanian government. Jordan had hitherto refused to deal with Hamas officials who lived outside the Palestinian territories, because of what were referred to as "existing legal obstacles." At this juncture, however, a resumption of relations with Jordan was something Hamas earnestly desired. For geographical and demographic reasons, no country in the region is closer to the Palestinians than Jordan. However, the Hamas visit to Jordan never materialized because the Jordanians had second thoughts about whom to invite. Initially no strings were attached to the invitation, but then the Jordanian authorities decided they did not want the Hamas delegation to include anyone with a Jordanian passport. This was clearly a reference to Khalid Mish'al and his colleagues who had been forced out of Jordan in 1999. The Jordanians said they would prefer a delegation from Gaza, but Hamas refused to be dictated to.

In April 2006, renewed hopes were raised of an imminent rapprochement between Jordan and Hamas when the Jordanians extended an invitation to the Palestinian Authority Foreign Minister Mahmud al-Zahhar, who had been making a tour of a number of Arab and Islamic countries. However, less than 24 hours before the visit, which had been meant to begin on 19 April, the Jordanian government announced its postponement on the grounds that certain individuals with connections to Hamas had allegedly been caught smuggling weapons and explosives into the country. Hamas vehemently denied the accusations and reiterated its position of non-intervention in the affairs of the Arab countries. The Hamas leadership said that Jordan had earlier contacted them expressing the desire to postpone the visit for other reasons, to do with the unavailability of certain senior officials in the government.

Few people found the Jordanian allegations plausible. Had Hamas been accused of using Jordanian territory to smuggle weapons into the West Bank or Gaza, some might have found this credible. However, to claim that Hamas was planning to attack Jordanian installations and personnel was farfetched; it was inconsistent with what was known about Hamas's way of thinking and style of operation. The Jordanians claimed that five Hamas agents had been caught in Jordan in possession of substantial weaponry, including rifles and explosives. The confessions of three of the alleged culprits were shown on Jordanian television, though ultimately they said little that could suggest a link to Hamas or to any criminal activity. The Jordanian Ikhwan conducted their own investigation, which revealed the identity of the three figures who made the televised confessions. The televised confessions only served to reinforce existing misgivings about the credibility of the Jordanian claims. It was shown that the three had no association with Hamas or any Islamic group, while at least one of them was a drug addict and a convicted criminal, and another had close links with Fatah. The Jordanians kept silent after these revelations were made, and the issue was not raised again. Earlier, President Mahmud Abbas had supported the Jordanian claims, saying that Jordanian officials had shown him proof of the plot. In an unambiguous display of support for the Jordanian position, he said attempts by Hamas to smuggle arms into Jordan were dangerous and surprising. His statement could not have been made at a worse time, coinciding as it did with escalating tension between Hamas and the Fatah leadership.

On Friday, 21 April 2006, President Abbas canceled the appointment of a high-level security official made by the Hamas-led government the previous day. Interior Minister Sa'id Siyam, in a bid to enforce law and order in chaotic Gaza, had appointed Jamal Abu Samhadana, a Fatah member and leader of the Popular Resistance Committees, to supervise the Interior Ministry. His brief was to set up a new police force to put an end to the lawlessness that blighted the entire Gaza Strip. Mahmud Abbas issued a decree as follows: "Security chiefs, officers, and members of the security services are ordered to disregard these pronouncements, and to proceed as if they never happened." Abu Samhadana's appointment had been a response to an attempt by Abbas to maintain exclusive control of the Interior Ministry's 60,000-strong security forces through the recent appointment of one of his own loyalists, Rashid Abu Shbak, as director-general of the Interior Ministry, without consultation with the minister. The Hamas government ignored Abbas's presidential decree and pressed on with the formation of the new force. The minister explained it would consist of serving police officers and fighters from the various armed factions, and would play an indispensable role in the restoration of order to the lawless streets of Gaza.

The issue of this decree by Mahmud Abbas was the straw that broke the camel's back. Speaking in Damascus later that same Friday, Political Bureau Chief Khalid Mish'al launched a scathing attack on the leadership of Fatah, including by implication President Abbas, though without mentioning specific names. Addressing a gathering to mark the anniversary of the assassination of Sheikh Ahmad Yassin, Mish'al accused Abbas and the Fatah organization of corruption and of plotting against Hamas. Mish'al's anger was fueled by reports that not only had the new government found the treasury empty, former ministers and top government employees had even stripped government offices of furniture and equipment. The real reason for the anger of the Hamas leadership was not actually this, however. It had become clear that the issue was not what political vision or political agenda Hamas had or was prepared to have. What was at issue was simply power and wealth, neither of which the Fatah leaders were prepared to lose.

Certain Fatah officials responded angrily to Mish'al's remarks, accusing him of seeking to provoke civil war. For 24 hours after his speech, Arab TV satellite channels and radio stations aired the views of spokespersons from both sides, and of other Palestinian commentators, thus adding fuel to the fire. The rift between the two movements seemed wider than ever. The Fatah Revolutionary Council, a key decision-making body within Fatah, said in a statement: "We view gravely the speech by Khalid Mish'al. We can only describe it as sedition intended to foment tension among the Palestinians and cause a civil war, at the orders of his masters." At rallies organized by Fatah supporters in some West Bank towns, Mish'al was accused of serving the interests of foreign powers, namely Syria and Iran, and was labeled a traitor to the Palestinian cause.

Not everyone in Fatah appeared to like what was going on. Some commentators linked to Fatah lamented that the organization was being dragged into a confrontation with Hamas at a time when the Palestinians needed to stand together, to face up to the international sanctions that were being collectively imposed on them. Others expressed their concern that Fatah was being transformed from a national liberation movement into a weapon used by the Israelis and the Americans to undermine an alternative Palestinian liberation movement that had won the confidence of the Palestinian public. Some of these disgruntled individuals leaked reports depicting aspects of the conspiracy that was being mounted against Hamas by certain Fatah leaders, in collaboration with their friends in Jordan, Israel, the US, and the EU.

Journalist Shakir al-Jawhari succeeded in obtaining exclusive information about highly confidential meetings held in Jordan around that time. In a dispatch from Amman on 16 May 2006, he wrote:

Last Friday, 12 May, Amman witnessed two important meetings that brought together the Palestinian Authority president, the Jordanian prime minister, a number of former government officials and some members of the Jordanian Parliament. The discussion at both meetings centered around the crisis raging between Jordan and the Hamas movement and how far the plans to bring down the Hamas-led government in Palestine have come. The meetings came at a time when Saudi, Egyptian, and Gulf efforts were being exerted in order to contain the dispute between Jordan and the Hamas movement. However, few details are available about these efforts so far. The second meeting was held on Friday evening. The Palestinian side consisted of Mahmud Abbas, who was accompanied by Ahmad Quri', the former Palestinian Prime minister who is also a Fatah Central Committee member. Jordan's Prime Minister Dr. Ma'ruf al-Bakhit, was accompanied by Foreign Minister Abd al-Ilah al-Khatib. The meeting took place in a suite at the Regency Palace Hotel in the center of the Jordanian capital and discussions were continued in the main restaurant on the 21st floor. According to sources, the meeting lasted between three and four hours. Apart from the main themes around which the discussion focused, no details have yet been revealed about what went on during the meeting. As for the first meeting, it took place at noon on that same day around the dining table of former Jordanian Prime Minister Abd al-Ra'uf al-Rawabidah, who closed the Hamas offices in Amman and deported its leaders from Jordan when his government was in power in August 1999. In addition to Abbas, this meeting was attended by Ahmad Quri'. Al-Rawabidah's guests included Basim Awadallah, director of the Office of King Abdullah II. As soon as he discovered the purpose of the invitation, Awadallah left al-Rawabidah's residence less than twenty minutes from his arrival so that he could not be identified with any political standpoint because of the gravity of the position he occupies. He justified his hasty departure on the grounds of having other commitments. A number of Jordanian MPs attending the meeting including

Ghalib al-Zu'bi and Mazin al-Malkawi. It was also attended by Salih al-Qal-lab, who used to be the minister of information in al-Rawabidah's government and who is well known for his extreme hostility toward Hamas as well as for his former affiliation with the Fatah movement. The sources say that a number of MPs declined the invitation by al-Rawabidah because they did not wish to embroil Jordan in inter-Palestinian disputes. Some of the participants reported that Quri's intervention during the meeting was brief and concise. As for Abbas, he said to those present: "The Palestinian Authority leadership has exhausted all efforts and has taken all possible steps to confront the Hamas movement and its government including the imposition of sanctions and disempowerment but these efforts have failed to weaken the movement. To the contrary, they have boosted the movement's popularity in the Palestinian street." He added that the Authority is no longer able to take further action against Hamas and that even if it had the ability to dismiss the Palestinian government it could not dissolve the Legislative Council. He explained that adopting a step such as dissolving the government of Isma'il Haniyah would amount to political suicide on the part of the Palestinian Authority leadership and the Fatah movement. This was because it would be perceived by the Palestinian public as an overt plot to topple the Hamas government and impose a siege upon it. Abbas added: "What is required now is for those Arab states which have been harmed by Hamas's election victory to play their own roles in confronting the movement because all the Palestinian Authority attempts to disempower it have failed." He explained that the real problem with Hamas lies with its Damascus-based leadership, which is in charge of all affairs. He pointed out that if the issue arising from these people were resolved, he would be unconcerned if Hamas inside Palestine were ten times as strong. He stressed the importance of focusing attention on the outside Hamas leadership, with the aim of besieging it and isolating it.[23]

This report illustrates the true dimensions of the war being waged against Hamas. Despite its ferocity, however, the onslaught on Hamas had little impact. As Mahmud Abbas put it, nothing seemed to be effective, and he needed further and more active assistance. As events developed, he did not have to wait long.

The Prisoners' Document

At the suggestion of the Fatah-led parliamentary Political Affairs Committee, the Palestinian Legislative Council Speaker Aziz Duwaik called for a conference to discuss national reconciliation and dialogue between the various Palestinian factions, including Fatah and Hamas, in the hope of ending the deadlock and defusing the mounting tension. President Abbas welcomed the idea and promised to address the conference's opening session. Unknown to Duwaik and his Hamas comrades, Fatah, which had so far tried but failed to cow the Hamas government, had devised a plan to undermine it.

In the opening session of the resulting National Dialogue Conference, on 25 May 2006, President Abbas stunned Hamas by giving it an ultimatum. Either Hamas reached a deal with Fatah within ten days on the basis of what had become known as the "Prisoners' Document," or it would face a referendum that the President would call in 40 days. The 18-point "Prisoners' Document," or to give it its full title, the National Conciliation Document of the Prisoners, had been written specifically to be submitted to the National Dialogue Conference. It bore the signatures of Marwan Barghouti from Fatah; Abdul Khaliq al-Natshah from Hamas; Bassam al-Sa'di from Islamic Jihad; Abdul Rahim Mallouh from the PFLP; and Mustafa Badarnah from the DFLP.

Hamas, in common with the other non-Fatah participants in the conference, would have had no objection to the inclusion of the Prisoners' Document for consideration as one of the many other proposals that were submitted to them. However, what the Fatah leaders wanted was the adoption of this document as the exclusive basis of dialogue among the Palestinians. It was not difficult for Hamas to see where this proposal was leading. The document called for acceptance of the "Arab initiative" and for submission to "international legitimacy," as well as for the recognition of the PLO as the "sole legitimate representative of the Palestinian people." These three considerations all entailed the recognition of the right of Israel to exist.

Hamas rejected Abbas's ultimatum as well as his renewed demand that it should join the PLO. Hamas said it would consider joining only after the implementation of reforms within the PLO as agreed in the Cairo talks of March 2005. Responding to the threat of a referendum, Hamas spokesman Sami Abu Zuhri said: "This threat is an attempt to put pressure and impose preconditions and a certain policy on Hamas. The idea of the referendum is an attempt to bypass the choice of the Palestinian people and the political program of Hamas, which won the support of the majority of the Palestinians in the last parliamentary election."

Hamas's leaders refused to accept that the document necessarily spoke for the entire movement merely because one of Hamas's imprisoned senior members had signed it. They argued that this was not how Hamas functioned and this was not the way it made decisions. Soon, representatives of other Hamas prisoners in Israeli jails issued a statement distancing themselves from the Prisoners' Document. They wrote: "This document does not represent the views of all the [Hamas] prisoners. It represents only those who signed it. The Hamas prisoners did not participate in the drafting of the document and we learned about it only through the media."

Although Israel dismissed the Prisoners' Document as changing little, because, among other things, it advocated continued resistance, Mahmud Abbas made it his immediate priority to force Hamas to accept it. This strategy may well have been what derailed the entire project of national dialogue and reconciliation. In the event, the conference ended without agreement. Consequently, there was no improvement on the ground. Polarization intensified, peaking in the first week of June 2006. On Saturday 3 June, Fatah deployed a new militia on the street of the West Bank town of Jenin. More than 2,000 men in black T-shirts and white headbands marched through the town in defiance of Hamas, accusing Hamas of serving foreign interests. Other slogans proclaimed that President Abbas, as the leader of Fatah, was determined to lead the Palestinians into a peace deal with Israel. A local Fatah leader by the name of Ata Abu Rmeileh told the militiamen: "You are here to protect your people and the institutions of the Palestinian Authority. We are loyal to our people, not like those who have sold themselves to Arab and non-Arab capitals." This was an allusion to Hamas's alleged links with Damascus and Tehran.

Fatah's leadership said that the formation of the new unit, comprising 2,500 members, was their response to the 3,000-strong Hamas militia that the government had mobilized a month earlier in the Gaza Strip in defiance of President Abbas's objections. With another 3,000 Fatah activists training in Gaza in preparation for possible deployment there, the prospect of a bloody conflict between the two groups became more conceivable. There was plentiful evidence that few within Fatah were prepared to recognize the legitimacy of the Hamas-led government. In their view, Hamas was an enemy, and should be treated as such. However, it continued to be questionable whether Fatah would have been capable of a military coup against Hamas. Not only was it divided and weak, but its leaders were quickly losing credibility and popular sympathy. The Israelis seemed to run out of patience and decided to do the job themselves.

The End of Truce

For many weeks, as the conflict between Hamas and Fatah continued, the Israelis had pursued the tactic of firing shells into Gaza, allegedly to deter Palestinian rocket attacks. They also continued to assassinate Palestinian activists from all factions. In what was seen as a deliberate act of provocation aimed at escalating the tension between Hamas and Israel, an Israeli air strike on 8 June 2006 killed Jamal Abu Samhadana, the chairman of the Popular Resistance Committees, who was also the coordinator of the Interior Ministry's security force.

This was apparently not enough for the Israelis, who struck again on Friday, 9 June 2006. One of several artillery shells fired that afternoon hit a crowd of Palestinian civilians picnicking on a north Gaza beach, wiping out almost an entire family.[24] The Israeli shelling, which left at least seven dead and dozens wounded, succeeded in provoking Hamas into calling off its 16-month truce, vowing to resume attacks against Israel to avenge the killing in cold blood of Palestinian civilians. Hamas could do no less than declare an end to its unilateral truce. It had to respond to the calls for revenge by the angry masses galvanized by the heartrending pictures of ten-year-old Huda Ghalia running wildly along the Gaza beach, then falling weeping beside the body of her slain father. That moment marked the resumption of operations from Gaza by the military wing of Hamas, the Izzadin al-Qassam Brigades.

For months, pressure had been mounting on the political leadership of Hamas to end the unilateral truce. Some of the commanders of the Izzadin al-Qassam Brigades had already been demanding a change of policy, believing that Israel's attacks should not go unpunished. Some of them had by then lost confidence in the viability of the political process. In addition, members of other factions that had not agreed to observe the cease-fire had begun to taunt them. Hamas's leadership had continued to urge its military commanders to exercise self-restraint and continue to observe the ceasefire. Their priority was to make the government work, despite all the obstacles in its path. However, the massacre of the Ghalia

family immediately swung public sentiment behind a resumption of resistance, and the Hamas leadership could not but heed the call.

The Israeli shell that destroyed Huda Ghalia's life and annihilated her
entire family convinced the Palestinian faction leaders to put their feuds
and their power struggle on hold, working instead for Palestinian national
unity in the face of Israeli aggression. Rather than carry out his earlier
threat to declare a date for a referendum over the Prisoners' Document,
President Abbas heeded the call by Prime Minister Haniyah for a resumption of dialogue between Hamas and Fatah. Indeed, by the beginning of
the third week of June, PLO officials began to leak information to the
media about the imminence of an agreement between the two major factions. While Hamas remained silent, Fatah and PLO spokespersons were
claiming that Hamas had agreed to recognize the right of Israel to exist
as stipulated by the Prisoners' Document. On 21 June 2006, Yasser Abed
Rabbo, a member of the PLO executive committee and a lead negotiator
on the Prisoners' Document, was quoted by the *Guardian* as saying that
Hamas had agreed to sections of the document that call for a negotiated
and final agreement with Israel to establish a Palestinian state on the territories occupied in 1967, including East Jerusalem.[25]

Speaking two days later, on the sidelines of the second Petra Conference of Nobel Prize winners in Jordan, President Mahmud Abbas suggested that Hamas might accept a two-state solution and recognize Israel.
However, Hamas sent a statement to the office of the news agency UPI in
Beirut denying any such intention. Describing Abbas's statement as "bizarre and unacceptable," the movement said that his remark "reflects only
his views, not those of Hamas, which is perfectly capable of expressing
its stance and does not need a spokesman." But Hamas's anger with Abbas
arose not only from what he said but also, even more, from what he did.
The world's television carried pictures of him hugging and kissing Israeli
Prime Minister Ehud Olmert, who also participated in the conference,
despite the continued Israeli attacks on Gaza. Hamas's statement said:
"We had expected, in the light of Zionist massacres ordered by Olmert
against the Palestinians and in view of the US-Zionist siege imposed on
our people, that the president of the Palestinian Authority would refrain
from meeting this terrorist [Olmert] until the killings stop and the siege
on the Palestinian people and its government is lifted."

Speculations about Hamas's readiness to accept Fatah's conditions continued to be fueled by similar declarations. On 24 June, a Fatah spokesman, Dr. Jamal Nazal, told the Palestinian News Agency that Hamas had expressed its readiness to drop most of its reservations concerning the Prisoners' Document. This was clarified when Hamas announced on the same day that an agreement had indeed been reached but that amendments to the Prisoners' Document had been made so that the essentials of the Palestinian position would be maintained. In other words, while continuing to refuse to recognize the right of Israel to exist, Hamas had agreed an amended version of the document acceptable to both sides. Thus, Fatah could claim success while Hamas could insist it had made no concessions. The outcome was the abandonment of the referendum. There was little time to celebrate this deal, however, because it was immediately dismissed by the Israelis as worthless. The entire region, and not just the Gaza Strip, was overtaken by an unanticipated escalation between Israel and Hamas. It would not be too much to presume that the Israelis had planned a widening of the conflict, which they triggered with the shelling of the beach that devastated the Ghalia family.

Israeli soldiers entered the Gaza Strip on the morning of Saturday, 24 June and kidnapped two brothers, Mustafa and Osama Muammar, who were both members of Hamas, after beating their father, who had to be hospitalized. This, for Hamas, was the signal for action. Less than 24 hours later, the Izzadin al-Qassam Brigades, together with the Popular Resistance Committees, and a new group called the Islamic Army raided an Israeli army outpost near the Kerem Shalom border crossing between Israel and the Gaza Strip. Seven Palestinian commandos infiltrated across the border via a 100-meter tunnel that was dug under the terminal in the Rafah area. Two Israeli soldiers were killed, four were wounded and one, a 19-year-old corporal, Gilad Shalit, was captured and taken back to Gaza. The immediate response of the Israeli government was to declare the Palestinian Authority responsible, including its president and prime minister.

Hamas soon published its demands. It asked for the release of women and children detained in Israeli prisons in exchange for the safe return of the soldier. It soon became evident that Israel was interested in more than just saving Corporal Shalit: it seemed intent on seizing the opportunity to end the threat posed to it by Hamas and other Palestinian resistance groups. On the basis of information derived apparently from sources within the Fatah organization, the Israelis pointed the finger of blame at Hamas Political Bureau Chief Khalid Mish'al and his host country, Syria. On 25 June, the *Jerusalem Post* quoted Fatah officials, including the former Palestinian Authority Minister for Prisoner Affairs Sufian Abu Zaida, who accused Mish'al of orchestrating the kidnapping operation in order to destroy the prospects of an agreement between Fatah and Hamas on the Prisoners' Document. This may have been a tactic aimed at dividing Hamas, but if so it failed this time as it had on several previous occasions. This was not a question of Hamas's outside leadership versus Hamas on the inside, but rather a matter concerning all Palestinians. The *Jerusalem Post* also quoted Sami Abu Zuhri, a prominent Hamas spokesman and member of the PLC, as welcoming the capture of Shalit. Zuhri said the operation during which it occurred was "a natural response to the Israeli crimes of killing women and children."The credence given by the Israelis to the idea that Hamas's decisions were being made in Damascus was clearly aimed at diverting attention from the real problem, which was the continued detention of thousands of Palestinians.

Issues pertaining to major matters of policy, such as whether to end or continue the cease-fire, are indeed taken at the highest level of the leadership of the Hamas movement. Decisions at this level involve whenever possible Hamas leaders in the West Bank, the Gaza Strip, and the diaspora. However, the tactics used to force Israel to release prisoners and withdraw from occupied land are local choices. The fact that Prime Minister Isma'il Haniyah and his other cabinet members knew nothing about the kidnapping operation should not have been surprising. It was agreed within Hamas before the legislative elections were held that members of the movement who were elected to the PLC or appointed to the cabinet should forfeit their leadership positions within the movement. They would, of course, continue to be members of Hamas but with no executive responsibilities. This decision was taken in order to avoid what were seen as the mistakes made by Fatah, whose members combined too many positions, at times with contradictory responsibility, with the effect of undermining their credibility and jeopardizing their ability to achieve results. Isma'il Haniyah may in the past have been a senior leader of the Hamas movement with executive powers, but while he remained in the cabinet or the legislative council he ceased to exercise such powers. It is therefore scarcely surprising that Ghazi Hamad, the spokesman for the Hamas-led government, appeared to know nothing about the operation when he appealed to the soldier's captors to keep him alive. He told reporters in Gaza City: "The occupation army says there is a kidnapped soldier. We have not received an official response from the factions of the resistance, but if this is true, then we call on the factions to protect the soldier. If the Palestinian factions are indeed holding the kidnapped soldier, we call on them to treat him well and not harm him." Appealing to Israel to refrain from carrying out attacks, Hamad added: "The Palestinian government is following the matter closely and is holding talks with the Palestinian presidency, with Egypt and other elements in a bid to resolve the issue."

There has been much speculation about the existence of two tendencies or two points of view within Hamas on this particular issue. This, however, is nothing but a myth: it is a figment of the imagination or perhaps the result of wishful thinking. It is not true to say that Haniyah is a moderate while Mish'al is a radical or an extremist. While it is only natural that different individuals have different ways of expressing or conducting themselves, when it comes to policy or strategy both Haniyah and Mish'al abide by the decisions of the collective leadership of the movement, based on *shura* (consultation).

One important factor that influences decision making within Hamas, however, is public sentiment. The streets across the Gaza Strip and the West Bank soon filled with demonstrators celebrating the capture of Corporal Shalit and urging his captors not to give him up for nothing. Families of Palestinian detainees led the rallies, holding one press conference after another to send this message to the soldier's captors as well as to the leaders of the Palestinian factions involved. But the Israelis were determined not to heed the calls for the negotiation of an exchange of prisoners. They even blocked third-party initiatives aimed at resolving the crisis. According to the Israeli press, Knesset Member Sheikh Ibrahim Sarsur, chairman of the Islamic Movement, said that Shin Bet, Israel's internal intelligence service, had prevented Hamas members from taking part in a dialogue with a group of rabbis in the West Bank, aimed at securing the release of Corporal Shalit. Hamas's Minister of Jerusalem Affairs Khalid Abu Arafah and Hamas's representative in Jerusalem, Sheikh Muhammad Abu Tir, were both detained and warned by Shin Bet not to take part in the meeting. At a press conference in Jerusalem, Sarsur was accompanied by Rabbi Menachem Fruman of the Tekoa settlement, a veteran supporter of Muslim–Jewish faith dialogue, and Rabbi David Bigman, head of the liberal Religious Kibbutz Movement's yeshiva in Ma'ale Gilboa.

In the meantime, AFP quoted Israel's minister of national infrastructure, Binyamin Ben Eliezer, who threatened that Israel could kidnap "half the Palestinian Cabinet" if need be. Another Israeli minister, Justice Minister Haim Ramon, told Israeli Army Radio that Hamas leader Khalid Mish'al was a target for assassination "for ordering the kidnapping of an Israeli soldier in the Gaza Strip."[26] It did not take long for the first threat to materialize. In the early hours of 29 June, Israelis troops kidnapped and detained 64 Hamas officials, including ministers and PLC members. Most of the Hamas officials were snatched from a hotel in Ramallah at gunpoint in what was interpreted at the time as a forceful message that Israel made no distinction between the political and military wings of Hamas. Twenty-three more Hamas members were arrested later the same day.

By 30 June, the Hamas leadership in Gaza stood made its position clear. In his weekly Friday sermon, the Palestinian Prime Minister Isma'il Haniyah vowed that his government would not give in to force, saying that Israel had to halt its offensive in Gaza if it wished to free its captured soldier. He made it clear that no concessions would be made and insisted that the Israeli offensive was intended to bring down the Hamas government, which he pledged would neither fall nor change its position. Accusing Israel of planning open warfare after failing to blackmail his administration into making concessions over the soldier's release, he said he would not trade the abducted Israeli soldier for the cabinet ministers and 56 other Hamas officials detained by Israeli troops the previous day. Defying all Israeli, regional, and global pressure on his government, he seized the opportunity to announce that there would be no referendum on a statehood initiative championed by Mahmud Abbas.

Nothing the Israelis did in Gaza seemed to be able to induce Hamas to yield, though the routine, almost daily, bombing claimed many lives and destroyed Gaza's entire infrastructure. While Israeli artillery pounded the border area, Israeli aircraft bombed the prime minister's office, the Ministry of the Economy, the Ministry of Foreign Affairs, and the Interior Ministry. Aircraft also bombed bridges and main roads across the

Gaza Strip, as well as power plants and other services, in an apparent bid to cripple completely the Hamas-led government. This confirmed suspicions that the entire operation was not about rescuing a single Israeli soldier in Palestinian captivity, but was rather a campaign aimed at destroying Hamas's ability to govern in Gaza. There was little doubt by this time that the Israelis were seeking to accomplish what their allies within Fatah had not been able to do. However, all they accomplished by making life yet more miserable for the 1.2 million people of the Gaza Strip was to unite them in defiance and in their determination to insist on an exchange of prisoners.

World attention suddenly shifted away from Gaza to South Lebanon. In what might seem to have been an operation aimed at relieving Gaza, Hezbollah carried out an attack on an Israeli military post across the border from Lebanon, capturing two Israeli soldiers and killing eight others. On several previous occasions, Israel had exchanged prisoners with Hezbollah, whose leader, Hasan Nasrallah, had vowed several months earlier that his group would do its utmost to secure the release of the remaining Lebanese prisoners in Israeli detention. The Lebanese and Palestinian populations celebrated the success of the operation and anticipated that the Israelis would agree to an exchange of prisoners. However, Israel refused to negotiate. Instead it bombed and shelled Lebanon, and also sent ground forces across the Lebanese frontier, thus triggering an international crisis. Hezbollah remained defiant, responding with rocket attacks on northern Israeli towns and settlements, and for the first time hitting the port city of Haifa with its newly acquired medium-range missiles. This caused panic not only in Haifa but also all the way to Tel Aviv, which the Israelis believed might be Hezbollah's next target.

ELEVEN

Toward the Next Intifada?

*The Mecca agreement has laid the foundations for a power-sharing proc-
ess that will produce a functioning government capable of attending to our
people's needs. It will also pave the way for rebuilding the PLO to include all
the factions and become the legitimate representative of all Palestinian people.*[1]

—Khalid Mish'al

SINCE HAMAS SCORED A CLEAR ELECTORAL WIN ON 25 JANUARY 2006,
its main rival, the Fatah movement, which has dominated the PLO and
presided over the Palestinian struggle for nearly forty years, endeavored,
with the support of a number of Arab governments, Israel, the US, and the
EU, and using every trick in the book, to force the Islamic movement out
of the political game. But, having run out of steam, the Fatah leadership
became increasingly inclined toward a compromise with Hamas based on
forming a national unity government. This was the option Hamas offered
to Fatah soon after the elections, but Fatah leaders, propped up by the
United States, said they were not interested.

The endeavors aimed at convincing Fatah and Hamas to work out their
differences and agree on a national unity government go back to August
2006, soon following the end of hostilities in Lebanon. Interest in a Palestinian national unity government as an escape route was triggered by
the failure of the measures adopted thus far to force Hamas to acquiesce
to the demands of the international community. Neither the stringent
regime of sanctions nor the series of sporadic Fatah-led industrial strikes
persuaded the Palestinian masses to rise against the Hamas-led government. Instead, Hamas seemed to maintain a satisfactory level of popular

support and sympathy. Putting pressure on Hamas seemed only to boost its popularity because Palestinians, many of whom had chosen to vote for it in the January 2006 elections, accepted that their plight was not Hamas's fault but the sin of those who were punishing the Palestinian people for exercising their democratic right.[2]

The predicament of the US-led world community was augmented by the deteriorating situation in Iraq and by Israel's embarrassing defeat in the war in Lebanon, a war whose objective of destroying Hezbollah or at least forcing it to disarm was beyond reach. The adoption of United Nations Security Council Resolution 1701 on 11 August 2006, which called for an immediate cease-fire in Lebanon, paved the way for bringing world attention back to the Palestinian arena after it had been fixated on Lebanon for more than a month.

In a bid to improve his fast-declining popularity at home because of his involvement in the war in Iraq, British Prime Minister Tony Blair volunteered to travel to the region and embarked on a mission to revive peacemaking between the Palestinians and the Israelis. More than 200 Palestinians, mostly women and children, had been killed in Israeli incursions into parts of the Gaza Strip in the weeks before his visit. Additionally, the international sanctions had not weakened Hamas but only served to augment the suffering of the Palestinian population under siege and foment more anger against Israel and its Western supporters.

On 9 September 2006, Blair arrived in the Middle East convinced that perhaps the best way to end the deadlock that ensued since Hamas was elected would be to get the Palestinians to agree on a national unity government that would adopt a formula that would, in turn, justify lifting the sanctions and would pave the way for the resumption of negotiations between Israel and the PNA. On Blair's agenda was also the case of captured Israeli soldier Gilad Shalit, whose fate lay in the hands of Hamas. Many regional and international players, including the British, had been hoping to play a part in securing his release.

However, Blair's mission did not meet much success. The day after his meeting with his Israeli counterpart, Prime Minister Ehud Olmert, in which he assured Olmert of his government's unwavering support and unyielding position on the Quartet conditions, Blair went to Ramallah for talks with PNA President Mahmud Abbas. Blair would not talk to Hamas or deal directly with any of its officials because the movement remains on the EU terrorism list. He delivered to Abbas the exit plan he had brought with him from London. The stand-off between the Palestinians and the international community, he suggested, could come to an end if Hamas were to agree to join Fatah in forming a national unity government that complied with the three Quartet conditions. In other words, Hamas would have had to recognize Israel's right to exist, renounce violence, and accept all previously concluded agreements between the PLO and Israel. That was most unlikely to happen; it amounted to political naiveté to expect Hamas to yield to such demands. After all, Hamas was elected by the majority of the Palestinians primarily because of its refusal to accept that Israel was a legitimate entity. On the other hand, and despite the fact that many Palestinians voted for Hamas as an alternative to Fatah because of the latter's reputation for corruption, Fatah lost the election primarily because its leadership was perceived as a sell-out.

Despite its lack of success, Blair's visit to the region signaled for the first time that a broader Palestinian government that still included Hamas would be acceptable to the international community. From then on much of the diplomatic effort was focused on bridging the gap between the West's insistence that such a government should meet the conditions set by the Quartet and Hamas's uncompromising position vis-à-vis recognizing Israel's right to exist. In a statement issued shortly after Blair and Abbas's news conference in Ramallah, Hamas spokesman Sami Abu Zuhri said his organization was ready to form a coalition government with the Fatah movement, but "not according to standards that are dictated" by the Quartet.

Immediately following his meeting with Blair, Abbas drove to Gaza for a meeting on Monday, 11 September 2006, with Palestinian Prime Minister Ismail Haniyah, to whom he bore the glad tidings that the suffering of the Palestinians was soon to come to an end. All that was needed was for Hamas to agree to form a national unity government that would give the impression that it had accepted the three conditions set by the Quartet and would, therefore, be a Palestinian government acceptable to the world community.

Abbas suggested to Haniyah that an implicit acceptance of the 2002 Arab initiative would be sufficient for the time being.[3] The Arab initiative recognizes Israel's right to exist within secure borders alongside a Palestinian state in the West Bank and the Gaza Strip, which Hamas had rejected at the time and continues to refuse to accept. Abbas announced later on that same day that he had reached an agreement with Haniyah to form a unity government. According to the deal, the current Hamas-led government would be dissolved within 48 hours and a new prime minister other than Haniyah would be appointed. Abbas was under considerable pressure to reach an agreement. He was to appear before the United Nations on 22 September and he wished to have something ready for the Quartet meeting that was scheduled to take place on the first of October. He desperately needed Hamas's consent before flying to New York.

It seemed later that Haniyah or some of his advisers might have given Abbas the impression that they granted him his wish. The announcement on 12 September 2006 that Abbas and Haniyah had agreed on forming a national unity government fitting the criteria set by the international community took the Hamas leadership inside as well as outside Palestine by surprise. The leadership had been in favor of forming a national unity government but not one that would consent to the Arab peace initiative. The concession had not been discussed, let alone agreed upon, by the relevant authorities within the movement. The Damascus-based Hamas leader Khalid Mish'al stepped in immediately and brought pressure to bear on the prime minister, forcing his office to announce that Haniyah had never consented to Abbas's conditions. Inevitably, the announcement dismayed Abbas and embarrassed Haniyah. It is very likely that an adviser to the prime minister had volunteered the gesture to Abbas. Some officials within Hamas suspected one or two of Haniyah's close associates: Ahmad Yusuf and/or Ghazi Hamad. The awkward episode seemed to confirm earlier rumors of a rift between the inside and the outside leaderships of the Hamas movement and played well into the hands of its critics and opponents.

President Abbas and a number of his aides accused Haniyah and other Hamas leaders of reneging on the agreement. The episode provided the Fatah movement's leaders with an opportunity to embark on a new diplomatic effort aimed at persuading the world that it was the Hamas leadership on the outside, and specifically Khalid Mish'al, that was hampering progress in reaching a deal between Fatah and Hamas. These same Fatah officials maintained that it was Mish'al who had ordered the military operation that led to the capture of Israeli soldier Gilad Shalit, which had prompted Israel to launch a twelve-week-long incursion into Gaza, purportedly to rescue its captured soldier and to halt the launching of

Qassam rockets into Israel. It is no surprise, therefore, that throughout the summer months, emissaries from around the world visited Damascus to meet Mish'al and urge him to order the release of the Israeli soldier and to stop hindering the process of negotiating a deal between Abbas and Haniyah. The one thing these emissaries returned from Damascus with was a fresh insight into Hamas. Many of them had never met a Hamas official before; some had heard only negative things about the movement and particularly about its leader, Khalid Mish'al. The summer visits were opportunities for visitors and visited alike to communicate directly and form their own impressions and issue their own independent verdicts. Undoubtedly, they were great public relations opportunities for Hamas.

In the meantime, some Fatah leaders had been claiming that the sanctions imposed on the Palestinians were having an effect on Hamas and were bound to force the movement to reconsider its position. They would cite as evidence tangible erosion in Hamas's popularity among the Palestinians. In meetings held in the US and Europe, a few Fatah and PLO officials even asked for the sanctions to remain in place. It did not take them long to discover for themselves that they had merely been indulging in wishful thinking; their counterparts in the US and Europe were discovering they were being misled. The truth was that Hamas had suffered no loss of popularity as a result of the sanctions.

Having failed to persuade the Hamas leadership to acquiesce to international demands and to convince the public to turn against its government, Fatah ordered its armed men to take to the streets in order to cripple life in the Gaza Strip by force. The presence of well-armed and well-trained members of the Interior Ministry's Executive Force frustrated the planned actions of Fatah's various military formations, the Preventive Force, Presidential Guards, and National Police. To compensate for such frustration, Fatah's militiamen went on the rampage in several West Bank towns, where Hamas had no militia to stop them, setting fire to properties housing government and Legislative Council offices and kidnapping Hamas officials or associates. Hamas officials suspected that a plot to trigger a civil war was being hatched and that these actions by Fatah militias were aimed at provoking such a conflict. Steadily, Hamas's armed wing was being drawn into the battle ground. The movement's political leadership was growing increasingly anxious that things might soon get out of control. Hamas's military commanders were beginning to show signs of impatience and it seemed a matter of time before a clan tit for tat warfare undermined discipline among their troops. In a tribal and factional society, particularly in the Gaza Strip, which had been turned into a prison for its 1.4 million inhabitants, igniting a civil war is not very difficult.

Autumn saw an unprecedented escalation between the two sides. While all parties were calling for a national unity government, Fatah and Hamas were being pushed farther apart by the day; the gap between them seemed most insurmountable. Public rallies were clear manifestations of the rising tension; a rally called for by one movement one day was responded to with a public rally organized by the other movement the following day or week. Hamas's rallies were clearly the biggest of all; the movement used these public rallies as platforms for exhibiting internal cohesion and solidarity as well as for showing strength and sending warnings to its foes. One of the most crucial rallies ever organized by Hamas was the one held in the Gaza Strip on Friday, 6 October 2006. The attendance was estimated at more than 100,000 people. Although Prime Minister Haniyah collapsed halfway through his speech from exhaustion,[4] the position he expressed was as stern and as decisive as one could be. The show was designed to assure those who fantasized about a Hamas split following Blair's September visit that the movement was as intact and as united as ever. Standing on a platform whose background bore two portraits, one his own and the other of Khalid Mish'al, Haniyah reaffirmed that his movement would never recognize Israel. He denounced what he described as the foreign dictates, especially by the Quartet, and blamed US and Israeli pressures for hindering the formation of a national unity government. He declared in unequivocal terms that Hamas would never consent to a government that recognized the legitimacy of occupation. However, he said that Hamas would agree to the establishment of a Palestinian state in the territories occupied by Israeli in the 5 June 1967 six-day war in exchange for a *hudna* (truce) "but not in exchange for a recognition or for conceding the land of the forefathers." Haniyah's speech was condemned not only by spokesmen for the Israeli government but also by spokesmen for Fatah and President Abbas.

Despite the rising tension and the deteriorating security situation in both Gaza and the West Bank, Hamas was determined to reap the fruits of its steadfastness. Opportunities seemed to open up before it to loosen the grip of isolation tightened around its neck by international and regional powers. While Mish'al was being more frequently visited in Damascus by dignitaries from around the world, Palestinian Prime Minister Haniyah embarked on a tour, his first ever outside Palestine, of a number of Arab and Islamic countries. On 28 November, he arrived in Cairo, where he was received by top Egyptian officials. After Egypt he proceeded to visit Qatar, Bahrain, Syria, Sudan, and Iran. He had planned to visit more countries, but decided to end the tour and return to Gaza on 14 December upon reports of worsening conditions in the Strip due to the escalating tension between Hamas and Fatah. Upon arriving at the Rafah crossing between Egypt and Gaza, the Israelis denied him access because he was bringing with him money he'd raised during his tour.

Haniyah's successful tour appeared to threaten the US-led sanctions regime. An increasing number of countries, Arab and non-Arab, as well as Islamic and non-Islamic, had shown signs of defiance and determination to break the embargo. Some, including Qatar, Iran, Bahrain, and Sudan, had openly made commitments to pay the salaries of Palestinian employees in the health and education sectors and to rebuild the houses and government buildings destroyed by the Israeli military.

Haniyah returned with a considerable amount of cash, and the bulk of the financial commitment promised by the countries he visited was to follow. But his return was immediately preceded by a renewed wave of lawlessness that claimed the lives of three innocent children and their driver in one incident and a judge affiliated with Hamas in another.[5] Finally, Haniyah was allowed to cross into Gaza after having agreed to leave behind the money he had brought with him. Instead of a celebratory triumphal climate, storms of factional tension blew over the Strip, instilling fear and anxiety in the minds of most of its residents. As Haniyah crossed the border from Egypt into Gaza, shots were fired at him, killing his bodyguard and wounding his son and his political adviser.

Hamas immediately accused armed men loyal to Fatah's Muhammad Dahlan of plotting to assassinate the prime minister, an accusation Fatah vehemently denied. The crisis between the two sides deepened further, prompting President Abbas to announce that negotiations between him and Hamas over the national unity government had hit a dead end.

After days of escalating tensions between Hamas and his Fatah movement that raised fears of civil war, Abbas announced on 16 December that he had decided, in view of the impasse, that presidential and parliamentary elections should be held at the earliest opportunity. He blamed Hamas for the crisis that had been triggered by the suspension of Western aid after the group's refusal to recognize Israel and renounce violence. His call was immediately rejected by Hamas, whose leadership described the move as a coup attempt against Palestinian legitimacy and against the will of the Palestinian people. The call for early elections did not help much; only hours later, armed supporters of Fatah and Hamas exchanged gunfire in the southern Gaza Strip.

For more than a week afterward, the Palestinians were immersed in discussions about whether the president had the right to dissolve the government. And not all those who agreed that he did possess such a power agreed that he also had the right to dissolve the parliament, which was due to remain in office until the end of 2010.

Hamas and Fatah supporters took to the streets to protest or to express their support for Abbas's call for early elections and battled each other with stones and bullets; in the mean time, congratulatory gestures of support landed at Abbas's front door from the three major international players that together designed and imposed the sanctions regime against the Palestinians. The White House, Tony Blair, who had been touring the Middle East at the time, and the Israeli government thought Abbas had done the right thing and urged the world community to support him in his latest bid to rid them of the Hamas-led government that had consistently refused to abide by the terms set by the international community.

Abbas's move illustrated the depth of the predicament in which his Fatah movement and its international backers found themselves. Despite many months of sanctions, Hamas had seemed to manage, though not without considerable difficulty, given the circumstances in which it had been left, to administer Palestinian affairs. The tight grip of the international community could not prevent the movement from bringing in enough money to pay, at least from time to time, civil servants some advance payments on their salaries and to keep the basic health and educational services running at a minimum. The hardship caused by the sanctions did little to convince the Palestinians that Hamas was responsible; the majority of the victims of the regime of collective punishment did not blame Hamas, which to them was equally a victim. Polls conducted by local and international bodies inside the West Bank and Gaza kept pointing to a rise in the popularity of Hamas, countered by an erosion of respect for Fatah and its beleaguered leadership.⁶ In other words, the sanctions, which had been the international community's prize awarded to the losers of the 25 January 2006 democratic elections, failed to deliver.

Following Abbas's call for fresh elections, more clashes erupted, almost on daily basis, between Hamas and Fatah. No attempt at enforcing a cease-fire or bringing the two sides to negotiate a deal succeeded. The September and December tours by Tony Blair and the multiple shuttle visits by US Secretary of State Condoleezza Rice from July 2006 to January 2007 seemed to make things worse because pronouncements of US and UK support for Abbas against Hamas only harmed his cause and undermined his credibility.⁷

Arab mediation efforts seemed to get nowhere either. Between 5 and 10 October 2006, Qatari Foreign Minister Sheikh Hamad bin Jassem al-Thani embarked on what became known as the Qatari initiative. The six-point plan was aimed at breaking the deadlock between Fatah and Hamas on the one hand, and between the international community and the Hamas-led government on the other. The Qatari minister shuttled between Syria and Palestine, meeting Hamas and Fatah officials in Damascus, Ramallah, and the Gaza Strip, but to no avail. Fatah and Hamas's disagreement on the core issue of the recognition of Israel aborted his mission.

Several times during the autumn months, Hamas and Fatah officials met in Cairo together or separately with senior officers from the Egyptian intelligence department, with its chief, Omar Suleiman, frequently presiding over the meetings. The Egyptians often seemed more interested in securing the release of Corporal Shalit than in bringing the two Palestinian factions to reconcile their differences. The Egyptians' inability to broker a deal between Fatah and Hamas as they had in March 2005 reflected a declining Egyptian influence among the Palestinians. The lack of success might have been partly caused by the Egyptian authorities' preoccupation with domestic concerns at the time: Egypt was witnessing heated debates between loyalists and critics of President Mubarak, sometimes even clashes between his opponents and the police, over plans to introduce constitutional reforms believed to pertain to Mubarak's desire to bequeath authority following his demise to his son Jamal.

On 25 December 2006, Jordan's Prime Minister Ma'ruf al-Bakhit invited President Abbas and Prime Minister Haniyah for talks in Amman. The Jordanians said the talks, which were expected to be hosted by King

Abdullah II, would be aimed at halting the political violence in Gaza. Despite acceptances from both Abbas and Haniyah, the meeting, for which a date was not set, never materialized. The Hamas leadership judged that the Jordanians were not serious about the initiative, for had they been serious enough they would have extended a proper invitation and not just made an empty gesture via the media. Furthermore, relations between Hamas and the Jordanian regime remained at the low level they had reached when the Jordanians forced Hamas to close its operations in Amman and expelled its leaders in 1999. Their relations had deteriorated further in April 2006 when the Jordanian authorities announced that they had foiled a Hamas plot to attack Jordanian installations and personnel, a claim Hamas vehemently denied at the time. From the point of view of Hamas's leadership, the Jordanians should have first sought to mend relations between them and Hamas before recommending themselves for a mediating role.[8]

On 20 January, Abbas arrived in Damascus, where the Syrian government had hoped that he and Hamas's Mish'al might meet and reach a deal on forming a national unity government. Negotiations had already been going on for a number of weeks. Two Palestinian emissaries close to Abbas, academic Ziyad Abu Amr and businessman Muhammad Rashid (known also as Khalid Salam), had been shuttling between Ramallah and Damascus to facilitate a summit meeting between Fatah and Hamas and to negotiate the terms of the deal with their Hamas counterparts. When the two emissaries arrived in Damascus on 19 January, one day before Abbas, it seemed that most of the hurdles had been removed and that an agreement was imminent. However, all Mish'al and Abbas could agree on when they finally met was to call for an end to the fighting in Gaza and for the resumption of negotiations between the two sides to form a national unity government. The Damascus meeting was no more than a photo opportunity. And the two men almost missed that opportunity because mediators failed to narrow the gap between them sufficiently. First, there was the issue of the interior ministry. Abbas had rejected the nominees proposed by Hamas. Then there was the issue of "international legitimacy." Abbas insisted that once formed, the national unity government should accept and abide by agreements signed between the PLO and Israel, whereas Mish'al maintained that what negotiators from both sides had agreed on was that such a government would only respect those agreements insofar as they did not contradict the best interests of the

Palestinian people. Initially, Mish'al thought that since a deal had not been reached there was no point in meeting Abbas. However, a meeting eventually took place upon the intervention of Syrian President al-Assad himself, who, in a private meeting with Mish'al, explained that it would not look good if Abbas left Damascus without a meeting. Al-Assad further warned that if the two men failed to meet, it would send a very negative signal and might escalate the tension between the two movements inside the territories.[9]

It was eventually the Saudis who succeeded. The Saudi initiative is believed to have been the work of Prince Bandar ibn Sultan, King Abdullah's national security adviser and the former Saudi ambassador to the US. Once all other initiatives had failed, it is assumed that the prince managed to convince the king that it was time for the kingdom to give it a shot. As a result, in mid-January, King Abdullah sent an unnamed emissary to Damascus to talk with Mish'al and to inform the Syrian government of the Saudi king's efforts, which were aimed at ending the incipient Palestinian civil war and the US-led economic blockade of the Palestinian government.[10]

Hamas and Fatah were invited to talk in Mecca, and both Mish'al and Abbas, as well as Haniyah, welcomed the initiative and accepted the invitation. A combination of good luck and patience provided Hamas with yet another opportunity to emerge out of a deep crisis with minimum losses. Only days earlier, the movement had been on the edge of civil war, a prospect its leadership had long dreaded and resisted, despite mounting pressure from within its grassroots to do what was necessary to defend its victory at the ballot box.

On Thursday night, 8 February 2007, and following two days of marathon negotiations between the leaderships of the two movements under the auspices of the Saudi royal family, the Mecca agreement was born.[11] The deal officially signaled the beginning of the end of Hamas's isolation and thus was assessed by some observers as a victory for Hamas.[12] The deal seemed on its surface to offer Fatah little more than what its leadership had already been offered and rejected weeks earlier in both Gaza and Damascus. In fact, much of the essentials of the Mecca agreement had already been negotiated and agreed upon weeks earlier, including allocating most of the cabinet portfolios. It was as though the mood, or perhaps the circumstances, had not been right for consummation to take place in Syria, Palestine, or Egypt.

Both Hamas and Fatah needed the Mecca deal; the former to avert a civil war, which—even if eventually it were to win—would have damaged its reputation among many of those who had voted for it in the last election,[13] and the latter to avoid its own total collapse, which seemed increasingly imminent due to the rapid erosion of both its credibility and its authority, particularly after Fatah security forces stormed the Hamas-aligned Islamic University in Gaza City on Friday, 2 February, setting ablaze and leaving in near total ruin the library, computer center, and other buildings.

Following weeks of gun battles across the streets and in the alleys of the Gaza Strip, the Fatah leadership concluded that the war it was waging against Hamas could not be easily won. It might have become clear to some Fatah leaders that it would be inadvisable to try to topple the Hamas government through the use of force. Other leaders, especially those commanding forces suspected of initiating trouble or prolonging the state of lawlessness, might have hoped for a break during which they would regroup before resuming the campaign. Despite full Israeli and US backing for the campaign against Hamas, the enormity of its cost for the Palestinian people, and more so for Fatah itself, deterred the Fatah leadership at this point in time from proceeding any further.

For the time being, joining a new Hamas-led national unity government had become Fatah's best option. It is not unlikely that the Saudis might have exerted a special effort to communicate to President Abbas the merits of this option. Abbas had refused the option of a national unity government eleven months earlier when the offer was first made to him by Hamas. The offer was made again, but was similarly turned down, in December 2006, as part of the mediation efforts led by Palestinian Legislative Council (PLC) member and head of the Independent Palestine List Mustafa Barghouti.[14] Had he accepted then, Abbas would have ended with a much better deal for his Fatah faction. Still under the illusion it could do better, Fatah rejected a deal that would in effect have produced a government whose premier would not have been a Hamas member and whose cabinet portfolios would have been filled by nonpartisan technocrats. This would have nearly fulfilled Abbas's own wishes, excepting only his wish to see Hamas declare unreserved commitment to abide by previous agreements between the PNA and Israel as well as full acceptance of the 2002 Arab peace initiative.

The greatest achievement of the Mecca agreement was rescuing the

Palestinians from civil war. Although sporadic clashes among Palestinian armed men did not stop completely, and although they were usually said to be between Fatah and Hamas loyalists, they were no longer seen as factional clashes but clan-related.[15]

Mecca's second most important achievement was to secure official pan-Arab recognition of the Palestinian government. Hamas's Isma'il Haniyah, who had grown ever more popular over the past few months, was named prime minister and eleven of the twenty-four cabinet portfolios went to his Hamas comrades, though two of them were appointed as independents. Fatah ended up with a deputy prime minister and five portfolios, while three portfolios went to three smaller factions, and four portfolios went to four different independents.[16]

While some analysts concluded that the Mecca deal represented a victory for Hamas and a defeat for Fatah,[17] Palestinians from all walks of life, but particularly affiliates or supporters of Fatah and Hamas, took to the streets across the Gaza Strip and the West Bank to celebrate the deal, which they saw as a victory for the Palestinians' national cause rather than for one faction over the other. Yet, it is true that Hamas ended up making few concessions if at all; it managed to get away with maintaining its longstanding position of not accepting the Quartet's conditions for lifting the sanctions against the Palestinians. Instead of agreeing to Mahmud Abbas's original demand of abiding by "Arab and international legitimacy resolutions and agreements signed by the PLO," Haniyah, as the head of the new government, vowed that his government would "respect" these resolutions and agreements in as much as the government perceived that these agreements did not contravene the best interests of the Palestinian people.[18] Hamas leaders would not let the occasion pass without making explicit statements to the effect that despite the agreement, their movement would never recognize Israel's right to exist.[19]

The Saudi Arabian success in bringing the two Palestinian rivals to Mecca took many people by surprise. The climate of doom and gloom that prevailed until the talks were underway left little room for optimism. Nevertheless, despite the success, skeptics give the Saudis little credit. They assume that Saudi Arabia would not have taken such a move unless it was given a green light by the US. The logic to this assumption is that the international community was growing weary of the deteriorating situation in Palestine, and that the US, which had been anxious that the violence in Gaza might spill over into neighboring territories, must have encouraged the Saudis to coordinate negotiating a deal between Fatah and Hamas that would eventually preserve the former and "domesticate" the latter. There have been media reports, especially in the Israeli press, about the role played by Prince Bandar bin Sultan, former Saudi ambassador to the US, who heads the Saudi National Security Council and who is said to have a very special relationship with the Bush family. By insinuating that the Mecca deal had been a US plan from the start, this theory gives the United States exclusive credit.[20]

Writing in an online publication, Ibrahim Gharaybah, a Jordanian columnist and a former member of the Jordanian Ikhwan, has gone as far as suggesting that the Mecca accord was a requirement of the Americans and Israelis. In contrast to the general perception that the US and Israel had been seeking to undermine Hamas, he suggests that both of them had willed that the Hamas government should survive. The only obstacle preventing the success of this experiment, he argues, is the Fatah movement, which would be the biggest loser were the Hamas-led government to continue.[21] In a statement released under the heading, "The National Unity Government: Palestinian Desire or American Will," banned Islamic group Hizb al-Tahrir al-Islami (the Islamic liberation party), which works for the restoration of the caliphate, similarly argued that Hamas's participation in the political process was from the start the result of an American and European plan to embroil Islamic movements such as Hamas in recognizing the legitimacy of the State of Israel.[22]

However, the US's negative response to the Mecca deal and its refusal to recognize the national unity government following its formation defeat this theory. It is highly unlikely that the US administration would have encouraged the Saudis in such an endeavor, when in October 2006 President Bush had reportedly warned President Abbas, when he received him on the sidelines of a United Nations Security Council meeting in New York, against joining Hamas in forming a national unity government. What is more plausible, however, is that the Americans did not seek to preclude the Saudi efforts, preferring, perhaps, to wait and see what would come out of them. It is certain that to the last minute the Americans and their allies were hoping that Hamas might accept the Quartet conditions.

The Hamas leadership believes that the Saudis were genuinely concerned at the mounting tension between Fatah and Hamas and that ending the strife between the two factions was the main motivation behind the Saudi move. King Abdullah of Saudi Arabia was said to have been personally concerned. According to Hamas, he had been inundated with pleas from prominent figures inside the kingdom, especially from within the business community and the religious establishment, to intervene.[23] The failure of earlier Arab initiatives to bring the two major Palestinian factions to agree on ending their strife left a vacuum in Arab diplomacy. Saudi Arabia recognized a window of opportunity to assert its regional authority and pull the rug out from underneath the Iranians, whom the Saudis believed had become too influential in Palestinian politics by virtue of their special relationship with Hamas. While there is no evidence that Iran has any leverage on Hamas, the Saudis have always feared that Hamas might be driven by the sense of isolation precipitated by the sanctions to join Saudi Arabia's rival camp, comprising Iran, Syria, and Hezbollah.

The Saudi initiative coincided with a growing anxiety within Saudi decision-making circles that the US administration's policy was undermining the kingdom's regional authority. Of particular concern to the Saudis was the disarray brought about by the US mismanagement of Iraq since the invasion and the Bush administration's unconditional support for Israel against the Palestinians.

In the end, what really mattered was that the Saudis succeeded where several regional players, including Qatar, Jordan, Syria, and Egypt, had failed. This success, it would seem, was possible because when Saudi Arabia decided to launch its initiative to reconcile Hamas and Fatah, it relinquished its demand that Hamas should first accept the 2002 Arab summit initiative. In light of Hamas's intransigence, and in a bid to maintain the validity of the Arab initiative, the Saudis did not mind repackaging it and presenting it as a potential product of a process rather than a precondition insisted upon for that process to begin. The Saudis have tried in vain more than once to persuade Hamas to announce its acceptance of the Arab initiative. The latest such attempt was made in October 2006, when, according to Hamas sources, the Saudi royal family tried to entice Khalid Mish'al, while he was on a visit to Mecca for 'umra (minor hajj), to subscribe to the Arab initiative in exchange for financial and political support. Prince Migrin was sent to see him and make him the offer but his endeavor was in vain. Eventually, the Saudis accepted that their initiative, which entails full pan-Arab recognition of Israel, could better be looked at as a reward for Israel should its negotiations with the Palestinians succeed in producing a Palestinian state in the West Bank and the Gaza Strip alongside the Jewish state.[24]

On Saturday, 17 March 2007, a national unity government headed by Hamas's Isma'il Haniyah and joined by Fatah was sworn in and given a vote of confidence by the Palestinian Legislative Council (PLC). Few people believed such a day would ever come after all that had happened. Even fewer might have thought the day would come when the Palestinian delegation to the Arab League summit conference in Riyadh on 28 March would be headed by President Abbas and Prime Minister Haniyah.

Fatah and Hamas's 15 March agreement on the national unity government was the outcome of intense negotiations that lasted for more than a month since a deal had been concluded between the two sides in Mecca on 8 February 2007. Soon after the deal was signed, Damascus-based Hamas leader Khalid Mish'al wasted no time in reaping for his movement the first diplomatic fruits of the Mecca agreement. Back in Damascus, he met with Syrian President Bashar al-Assad prior to embarking on a tour that took him to Egypt, Sudan, Russia, Malaysia, and Iran. He resumed his shuttle tour following the formation of the national unity government with visits to Qatar and Saudi Arabia, where he was received by the top leaders of the two states.

The Mecca agreement has provided an opportunity, for the first time, for a settlement between the Palestinians and Israel that does not entail a recognition of Israel but that would at the same time provide it with a safe and secure existence. Writing in the *Guardian* soon after the deal was announced, Khalid Mish'al said: "The Palestinian national accord achieved in Mecca envisages the establishment of a truly sovereign and independent Palestinian state on the territories occupied by Israel in June 1967—with Jerusalem as its capital, the dismantling of the settlements in the West Bank, the release of all Palestinian prisoners and the acknowledgement of the right of the refugees to return to their homes."[25] Such a declaration by Mish'al constitutes a departure from the traditional position of the movement as expressed in its 1988 Charter. According to the Charter, Hamas's long-term objective is the liberation of the entire land of British mandate Palestine; more precisely, the aim is to end the existence of the Jewish state. Such a radical position has been overshadowed over the years by the offer of *hudna* (long-term truce) made first in 1994 and repeatedly thereafter. When asked why he made no mention of the *hudna* in his *Guardian* piece, Mish'al said the movement had already made that offer and would make no more offers. He added that it was now up to the Israelis and their allies in the West to come up with an offer if they were at all serious about reaching a settlement.[26] It is worth noting that never before had Hamas made an unequivocal statement about its willingness to accept a Palestinian state confined to the territories occupied by Israel in the 1967 six-day war.

Such a declaration has brought Hamas criticism from various circles, some expressing reservations amicably and politely and others condemning the movement for relinquishing the struggle in the same way Fatah did before it. The most scathing comment came from Ayman al-Zawahiri, al-Qaeda's second in command, who released an audio tape accusing Hamas of having sold out.[27]

Forming a national unity government may indeed be the first step in the direction of forming such a Palestinian state. However, it is far from certain that this government will be given a chance to function. It is very likely that it will be short-lived. Several factors may cause the government to collapse and the factional fighting between Hamas and Fatah to re-ignite and spread out.

First, there is the continuing international regime of sanctions. A few members of the international community, such as Russia, Norway, Sweden, France, and Switzerland, have said they would be prepared to lift the sanctions in response to the formation of the national unity government.[28] The continuation of the sanctions will make it rather difficult for the government to perform or deliver the basic needs of the public.

Second, the insistence on the part of some governments, such as the US, the UK, and their allies, that they would be willing to communicate only with Palestinian government ministers who are not from Hamas will undermine the authority of the government. This in turn will cripple several of its public-service-oriented departments whose ministers and other senior officials need to communicate regularly with the outside world. The Hamas leadership has been rather unhappy about what Mish'al describes as "the selective and double-standard approach of some of the Western governments" in dealing with the national unity government. He insists that there should be no discrimination between one minister and another. After all, forming a national unity government has been an

Third, the unity government will suffer considerable damage if regional and international players continue to arm and provide logistical support to factional militias such as those linked to Fatah's Muhammad Dahlan or to President Abbas himself. It is widely believed within Palestinian circles that the aim of building up these forces is to topple the Hamas-led government when the moment is right. Hamas sources maintain that they have been monitoring the build-up and do keep a record of all moves, to the finest level of detail.[30] Amid growing suspicion that the Fatah leaders might have come to Mecca simply to take time out before they resume their campaign against Hamas, the United States, Israel, Jordan, and Egypt have been accused of providing Dahlan and Abbas with funds, arms, and training for their forces.[31]

The fall of the national unity government may bring down the entire Palestinian Authority. The most immediate repercussions would likely be igniting a third intifada. Having formed the national unity government, Hamas leaders maintain that the ball remains in the court of the international community: "So, will the international community seize this historic opportunity, require Israel to respect our rights and stop hindering this attempt to turn the Palestinian national agreement into a reality? Or will it remain weak and ineffective in the face of Israeli intransigence and risk alienating not only Hamas but also Fatah and all the other Palestinian factions? If the latter is the choice, the outcome will be dire indeed: the entire Middle East region will be driven towards another cycle of bloody escalation that may last for many years to come—and an entire Palestinian generation, which might not be willing to accept what we accept today, will be left profoundly embittered."[32]

In his Friday sermon in Gaza on 30 March 2007, Palestinian Prime Minister Isma'il Haniyah echoed Mish'al's earlier remarks. He declared: "We have given what we were required. We have made a unity government and a political program based on common grounds and now what is needed is to lift the siege." He then warned: "If the siege continues for two to three more months, we will study our options… and we will make a decision that will protect our dignity and will protect our interests."

An opportunity has been created by the Mecca agreement. An increasing number of observers have recognized this.[33] However, it remains to be seen whether decision makers in Israel and the United States are willing to seize it.

Postscript: As of mid-June 2007, the Palestinians seemed furthest away from a functioning national unity government. Earlier in June, after a meeting with Egyptian intelligence department officials, the Hamas leadership had concluded that the Fatah leadership could not oblige the commanders of Fatah-led security agencies in Gaza to comply with agreements made between Fatah and Hamas. Popular pressure had been mounting on the Hamas leadership to do something. After all, the Palestinians who had elected Hamas had done so based on its promise to end the lawlessness that had prevailed in the Strip for many months. Hamas had the ability to do so militarily, but had been anxious to avoid a civil war. But while it sought to avoid violence between Palestinians, sectors of the security agencies continued with total impunity to execute individuals suspected of affiliation to Hamas—many of whom had never been members of Hamas but were killed simply because they had beards and were not known to be members of Fatah. It took Hamas less than five days to bring the entire Gaza Strip under its military control. Highly trained, heavily armed, and well-funded Fatah security apparatuses fell with astonishing speed. With the top leaders fleeing the scene, many recruits had no option but to lay down their arms and surrender. Hamas maintained all the while that this was not a war against Fatah, but against those who in the name of Fatah terrorized the population and undermined the national unity government. Disempowered and bewildered, President Abbas did not seem to know how to respond. Eventually, he authorized a spokesman to announce the sacking of the national unity government led by Prime Minister Haniyah and the declaration of a state of emergency. In response, Hamas leader Khalid Mish'al held a press conference appealing to Abbas not to pursue his plan of forming another government and resume discussions, perhaps through an Arab mediator, in order to reactivate the national unity government that should be in charge in both Gaza and the West Bank. The US rushed to Abbas's aid, promising to immediately lift the sanctions imposed eighteen months earlier if he went ahead and formed a Hamas-free government. On 17 June 2007, a new government led by former World Bank official Salam Fayyad, who served as the finance minister in the short-lived national unity government, was sworn in. The Gaza Strip had by then been facing the prospect of becoming literally the world's largest prison camp. Should Israel close the passages into the Strip and cut all supply of water, fuel, and electricity, the prison inmates may find no alternative but to explode in the face of a world community that had denied them democracy and is now denying them life.

APPENDIX I

This is What We Struggle for

(Memorandum prepared by Hamas Political Bureau in the late 1990s at the request of Western diplomats in the Jordanian capital Amman)

The Islamic Resistance Movement (Hamas) is a Palestinian national liberation movement that struggles for the liberation of the Palestinian occupied territories and for the recognition of Palestinian legitimate rights. Although it came into existence soon after the eruption of the first Palestinian intifada (uprising) in December 1987 as an expression of the Palestinian people's anger against the continuation of Israeli occupation of Palestinian land and persecution of the Palestinian people, Hamas's roots extend much deeper into history.

The motivation of the movement's struggle has been expressed by its founder and leader Sheikh Ahmad Yassin: "the movement struggles against Israel because it is the aggressing, usurping and oppressing state that hoists the rifle in the face of our sons and daughters day and night."

Hamas regards itself as an extension of an old tradition that goes back to the early 20th-century struggle against British and Zionist colonialism in Palestine. The fundamentals from which Hamas derives its legitimacy are mirrored in the very name it chose for itself. Its Islamism means that it derives its guiding principles from the doctrines and values of Islam. In other words, Islam is Hamas's ideological frame of reference. It is from the values of Islam that the movement seeks inspiration in its mobilization effort and in compensating for the huge difference in material resources between the Palestinian people and their supporters on the one hand and Israel and its supporters on the other.

The prospect of the movement initiating, or accepting, dialogue with Israel is nonexistent at present because of the skewed balance of power between the Palestinians and the Israelis. In Sheikh Yassin's own words: "There can be no dialogue between a party that is strong and oppressive and another that is weak and oppressed. There can be no dialogue except after the end of oppression."

The forms of resistance adopted by Hamas stem from the same justifications upon which the national Palestinian resistance movement based its struggle for more than a quarter of a century. At least the first ten articles of the Palestinian National Charter are completely compatible with Hamas's discourse as elaborated in its own Charter and in other declarations. The same justifications for resistance were, prior to the emergence of Hamas in December 1987, recognized, or endorsed, by a variety of regional and international bodies such as the Arab League, the Islamic Conference Organization, the Non-Aligned Movement and the United Nations. Recognition that the Israeli occupation of the West Bank and Gaza in 1967 is illegal can be clearly read in UN Security Council Resolutions 242 and 338.

In spite of the initiation of peace negotiations and the eventual signing of the Oslo Accords between the PLO and Israel, Hamas continued its struggle, having recognized the failure of the peace process to bring about an end to occupation. Hamas believes that the majority of the Palestinian people have come to the same conclusion and are therefore discontented with the path taken by the PLO to create peace with Israel.

The defenders of Oslo claimed for months following its signing that it would bring an end to occupation and that the Palestinians need therefore no longer wage armed struggle against the Israelis. But years after Oslo, the following are the dividends of peace:

1. The territories occupied in 1967 are still occupied.

2. As never before, the West Bank and Gaza have been carved, mutilated, and turned into isolated densely populated islands or cantons, administered on behalf of the Israelis by the PA.

3. Existing Jewish settlements have continued to expand and new ones have been erected.

4. Jerusalem is being expanded and de-Arabized.

5. Large areas of land have been confiscated to allow for the construction of by-pass roads for the exclusive use of Israelis and especially settlers who illegally live on confiscated Arab land.

6. Thousands of Palestinians continue to be detained in Israeli prisons.

7. Various forms of collective punishment continue to be adopted, including the demolition of homes, the closure of entire areas and the enforcement of economic blockades, the destruction of Palestinian infrastructure, and the uprooting of trees and crops.

8. The economic situation is much worse than ever before.

In other words, the peace process has not improved the conditions of the Palestinians under occupation and does not seem to promise any better future. The claim that armed struggle is no longer necessary (and it should be noted here that no one within the Palestinian camp claimed it was illegal) has therefore been refuted by reality on the ground. This gives credence to the argument of Hamas (which is no different from the argument adopted before Oslo by the nationalist movement as a whole and that continues to be adopted by a score of Palestinian factions opposed to Oslo) that armed struggle is the only real means of liberation.

In spite of the overwhelmingly militant image Hamas has in the minds of many people in the West, Hamas is not a mere military faction. It is a political, cultural, and social grassroots organization with a separate military wing specialized in armed struggle against Israeli occupation. Apart from this clandestine military wing, all other sections within Hamas function through overt public platforms. The military wing has its own leadership and recruiting mechanism.

Hamas's social and educational activities in the occupied territories have become so entrenched within the Palestinian community that neither the Israelis nor their peace partners in the Palestinian Authority have been able to eradicate them. The fact is that Hamas, contrary to Israel's assessment, acts as an infrastructure for the numerous cultural, educational, and social institutions in Gaza and the West Bank that render invaluable and irreplaceable services to the public. In other words, it is Hamas that gives life to these institutions and not the reverse. The Israelis have repeatedly told the Palestinian Authority to close them down. The

Palestinian Authority has tried but failed. A crackdown on these institutions amounts to a declaration of war not against Hamas but against the Palestinian community as a whole.

Contrary to the experience of most other Palestinian factions during the 1970s, Hamas's armed struggle originates in Palestine and is restricted to its territory, which Hamas considers the legitimate battlefield. By limiting its armed struggle to resisting occupation, the movement has successfully averted Israeli attempts to drag it into battle outside Palestine. The assassination attempt on the life of Khalid Mish'al, Hamas's political head, was clearly intended to embroil the movement in a war of attrition outside Palestine, a battle Hamas has continuously tried to avoid. Hamas's adherence to this position has made it difficult for the Israelis and their allies, especially in the United States, to convince the world's public opinion that Hamas is a terrorist group. By all standards, Hamas is a national liberation movement whose military effort is directed solely and exclusively at the foreign occupiers.

Hamas's military wing, the Brigades of Martyr 'Izzadin al-Qassam, has planned and carried out a number of martyrdom operations that are usually described in the Western media as suicide operations. These operations are in principle directed against military targets. Targeting civilians is considered an aberration from Hamas's fundamental position of hitting only military targets. It represents an exception necessitated by Israel's insistence on targeting Palestinian civilians and by Israel's refusal to agree to an understanding prohibiting the killing of civilians on both sides, comparable to the one reached between Israel and Hezbollah in southern Lebanon. It is worth recalling that the first martyrdom operation was a response to the massacre of Muslim worshippers as they kneeled in prayer in al-Masjid al-Ibrahimi at dawn on the fifteenth day of the fasting holy month of Ramadan (25 February 1994).

Sheikh Yassin, who has made repeated offers of a truce to the Israelis that they have always rejected, explains that Hamas does not endorse the killing of civilians. It is nevertheless sometimes the only option open to Hamas as a response to the murder of Palestinian civilians and the cold-blooded assassination of Palestinian activists.

Notwithstanding its disagreement with the PLO and the Palestinian Authority (PA), Hamas considers all Palestinians to be victims of Israeli occupation and therefore will not be drawn into inter-Palestinian factional strife. Hamas believes that many of those who have placed their hopes in Oslo, including a large section of Yasir Arafat's own Fatah faction, have been disillusioned. They have seen the futility of the exercise, and have realized that they have no option but to resume the struggle until the occupation is brought to an end.

Hamas regards all the peoples of the world as potential friends and supporters of the Palestinian people in their legitimate struggle for freedom, which will alone guarantee the accomplishment of peace. Hamas believes that permanent peace is possible only if founded on justice and equal human dignity.

Hamas is aware of the fact that the balance of power in the world today is not in its favor, but realizes that this has always been the case whenever an oppressed people started their long-term struggle for freedom from foreign occupation and tyranny. It is therefore our firm belief that eventually the Israelis will come to terms with reality and realize that they have no option but to deliver the Palestinian people from the servitude imposed on them by occupation. This occupation violates all known international conventions and declarations, including the various UN Security Council resolutions on this issue.

Hamas would be willing to consider a cease-fire agreement with the Israelis if they agree to end their occupation of all the territories occupied in the aftermath of the six-day war in 1967. This would entail the cessation of all hostilities on the part of Hamas in exchange for the following concessions on the part of Israel:

1. the withdrawal of Israeli occupation troops from the West Bank and Gaza Strip;

2. the evacuation of all Jewish settlements illegally erected and populated by Jewish immigrants on Palestinian lands seized by force in both the West Bank and Gaza;

3. the release of all Palestinian prisoners in Israeli detention;

4. the recognition of the right of the Palestinian people to self-determination.

Hamas recognizes the importance of the role of the international community in bringing about such a settlement. It therefore extends its hand, in good faith and appreciation, to all such governments and communities that may be willing to take part in this process for the benefit of humanity and in accomplishment of a peace based on justice.

However, Hamas would enter into negotiations about the details of the settlement only once the Israelis have agreed to the aforementioned terms that are aimed at bringing about a full withdrawal from all the territories occupied in 1967.

APPENDIX II

(Memo prepared by Hamas Political Bureau in 2000 just before the eruption of the second intifada)

THE ISLAMIC RESISTANCE MOVEMENT (HAMAS)

1. DEFINITION
The Islamic Resistance Movement (Hamas) is a Palestinian Islamic struggle (*mujahidah*) movement whose supreme frame of reference is Islam and whose goal is the liberation of Palestine.

2. PHASES OF EVOLUTION AND DEVELOPMENT
A. THE MOVEMENT'S HISTORIC ROOTS: (1946–1967)
Hamas is the intellectual and dynamic successor of Jama'at al-Ikhwan al-Muslimin (the Muslim Brotherhood) in Palestine, whose foundations were laid down in the 1930s and 1940s when Ikhwan branches were founded in Yaffa, Haifa, Jerusalem, and Gaza. As the number of branches increased, the group organized a conference for the branches of the Ikhwan in Palestine, which convened in the city of Jerusalem from 29 to 30 March 1946 with the aim of unifying and coordinating the efforts of the branches to confront the Zionist project. The second conference convened in Haifa in October 1947, when the conferees declared "the determination of the Ikhwan to defend their country with all means and their readiness to cooperate with all the national associations to serve this purpose." The role of the Ikhwan reached its zenith in Palestine during the participation of the brigades of the Ikhwan volunteers from Egypt, Syria, Jordan, and Iraq in the battles against the Zionist gangs on the eve of the Nakba (catastrophe). The group continued its political and social activity in the wake of the Nakba. One of its most significant accomplishments was to foil the project to re-settle the Palestinian refugees in the north of Sinai in 1955. It also mounted a number of operations, particularly from within the Gaza Strip, across the borders against the Zionist enemy just before 1956.

B. The phase of preparation for launching the movement's
project (1967–1980)

The 1967 defeat and the consequent occupation of the West Bank, the
Gaza Strip, and other Arab lands, namely Sinai and the Golan Heights,
had numerous repercussions on the Palestinian issue. The most important of these were:

1. The role of Arab governments, as far as the Palestinian issue was concerned,
diminished in favor of popular participation, which assumed the form of military
resistance against occupation.

2. The role of the Palestinian people in confronting the occupation was strength-
ened and deepened. The entire Palestinian people with all its resources and factions came into direct contact with the occupation in the West Bank and the Gaza
Strip. In the light of this reality the movement had to face up to new challenges
at the level of thought and practice.

3. A comprehensive reappraisal of all the intellectual and political trends in this
phase opened the way for the launch of the resistance program, and for an Islamic awakening across the Arab and Islamic regions. This was an expression of
the need of the peoples of the umma (the pan-Islamic community), including the
Palestinian people, to search for their historic identity and cultural affiliation in
light of the vacuum and shock caused by the devastating 1967 defeat.

In view of these developments, the Palestinian Ikhwan inside the homeland and in the diaspora proceeded along two paths:

1. The first path: that of participation in direct military action against the Zionist occupation along the front that was available at the time, namely the Jordan
River. The Ikhwan operated from what was known at the time as the "camps of
the sheikhs" that were under the umbrella of the Fatah movement from 1968 to
1970. This activity ended as a result of the Black September events. Ikhwan volunteers from Egypt, Syria, Jordan, Yemen, the Gulf countries, and other places
contributed to the experience.

2. The second path: The establishment of the organizational infrastructure for a
jihadi (struggle) project both against the Zionist occupation in Palestine in particular and against the Zionist project in general.

To accomplish these objectives the Ikhwan undertook to work in the
following fields:

1. Arousing the enthusiasm of the members of the Ikhwan to work in the field of
da'wah (calling people to Islam) and social reform.

2. Attracting the youth, especially university graduates, to join the ranks of the Ikhwan. This group benefited from the opportunities made available to Palestinian students to pursue their university education abroad in attracting educated cadres who later provided the solid foundation as well as the leadership of the movement.

3. Revitalizing the process of building mosques in Palestine, considering that they constitute a principal source of influence in society.

4. Establishing numerous charitable and social institutions: these included al-Mujamma' al-Islami (the Islamic Center) and al-Jam'iyah al-Islamiyah (the Islamic Society) in the Gaza Strip and a number of *zakat* committees and charitable foundations in the West Bank.

5. Circulating among the Palestinian people inside Palestine and the diaspora with the aim of attracting support and membership, encouraging work for the Palestinian cause in confronting the Zionist project and reasserting the Islamic dimension of the conflict.

6. Constructing frameworks and institutions to support the Palestinian people inside Palestine and founding a number of platforms for Palestinian student activism in various arenas and around the world. The movement succeeded during that phase in building a solid organizational foundation supported by an institutional edifice that geographically extended across the West Bank and the Gaza Strip. It was also able to restore some aspects of Islamic observance in the public sphere inside Palestine.

C. The Founding Phase (1980–1987)

In this phase the process of construction continued, hand in hand with the activities of the national resistance campaign. The movement sought to attract more members, while also attending to education and specialization within the organization, and the construction of appropriate organs to provide for the needs of resistance against occupation. During this phase the "Hamas" project of comprehensive jihad was crystallized intellectually and organizationally. Some of the most significant stages of this phase were as follows:

1. The emergence of Islamic student action through the creation of Islamic blocs inside the universities of the occupied territory and in some Arab and Western countries.

2. Expanding the construction of mosques and affirming their roles in *da'wah*, guidance, and social change.

3. Preparing for the launch of military action against occupation. Some of the movement's early military formations were uncovered and disbanded, especially the military organization led by Sheikh Ahmad Yassin in 1984.

4. Proceeding in the direction of grassroots resistance action and mobilizing the internal ranks of the movement toward the same objective. This was expressed in terms of what were called the "mosque revolutions" of 1981, 1982, and 1983. The mobilization reached its zenith with the martyrdom of Jawad Abu Sulmiyah and Sa'ib Dhahab at Birzeit University in 1986. Numerous confrontations took place at the Islamic University afterward. The Israelis cordoned off the university more than once, wounding and detaining many of its students.

5. Forming specialized apparatuses within the movement such as the one called the "Munazzamat al-Jihad wa al-Da'wah" (MAJD), which constituted the movement's security apparatus in 1985, and the military apparatus called "al-Mujahidun al-Filastiniyun" in 1987, which undertook direct action against the occupation and its collaborators.

6. During this phase, the movement worked under a number of slogans and names including al-Ittijah al-Islami, al-Haraka al-Islamiyah, and others.

7. Outside Palestine, the movement and its diaspora branches continued their efforts to complete the building and founding of the movement's project of confronting the Zionist enemy in full harmony with and complementing the efforts of the movement inside Palestine. The efforts outside Palestine focused on the following:

    a. building student, intellectual, and social platforms;
    b. developing and diversifying charitable work so as to support the Palestinian people on the inside and help them remain steadfast;
    c. completing the project's vision and its general plans and formations;
    d. setting up the action committees and apparatuses needed by the project in its various fields of action;
    e. encouraging Islamic and national movements in the Arab and Islamic worlds to include in their priorities working for the Palestinian issue and confronting the Zionist threat.

The movement succeeded during this phase in achieving a marked increase in its membership. Most of the new recruits were intellectuals and university students. It also made Islamic observance a cultural norm within Palestinian society whereas it was quite rare in the 1970s and early 1980s. The movement was also able to form a powerful security apparatus thanks to the soundness of its organizational structure and the profound sense of belonging to it by its members. All of these factors contributed positively to increase the speed at which the Hamas project came to fruition in the Palestinian arena.

D. The Phase of the Launch (1987–1994)

This is the phase in which the project of the Islamic Resistance Movement (Hamas) was launched, following preparation that extended over several phases. The proclamation of the project was first made in a communiqué issued in November 1987 and distributed among the masses to warn against the danger posed by collaborators and to expose the methods used by the enemy to trap Palestinian individuals into collaboration. However, the date that acquired special symbolism was 14 December 1987. This was regarded as the day the movement was created and was associated with the eruption of the first intifada. In fact, the communiqué was not intended to declare the birth of the movement because it had already been in existence and had already been active in the field. What it did, however, was to mark the day on which the masses were informed about the existence of the movement and about the activation of its role in confronting the occupation. The communiqué signaled the start of a phase in which priorities had to be rearranged, and the dispute about which comes first, liberation or change, was settled for good in favor of the former. Resisting occupation became the basic program of the movement without any contradiction with the program of *da'wah* and the efforts pertaining to social change; it signaled a new phase in which the movement moved to the fore in the wider field of resistance.

Some of the most significant stages in this phase were as follows:

1. The movement played a leading role in triggering the intifada; it was the first organization to interact with the events and its interaction was the most intense, and it was the most capable organization to lead and mobilize.

2. During this phase, the movement ran the activities of the intifada independently of the PLO factions that functioned under the banner of United National Command.

3. The movement played a principal role in developing the intifada from a popular format to qualitative forms of resistance ranging from the kidnapping of soldiers to the war of knives and finally the martyrdom operations. The peak was in 1993 when the movement's military wing the "Martyr Izzadin al-Qassam Brigades" carried out 20 military operations in which 32 Israeli soldiers or Jewish settlers were killed.

4. The movement was subjected during this phase to several mass-detention campaigns, the biggest of which was in 1989 when Sheikh Ahmad Yassin and the leadership of the movement were detained. Major blows were repeatedly dealt to the movement in 1990 and 1991. However, the movement was able every time to surpass the crisis, rearrange its ranks, and learn from the experience.

5. The major blows dealt to the movement were associated with military operations involving the killing or kidnapping of a number of Israeli occupation troops. The 1989 blow was associated with the kidnap and killing of Israeli soldiers Ilan Sa'adon and Avi Sasportas, while the 1990 blow followed the Yaffa launch operation in which martyr Marwan al-Zayigh and struggler Ashraf al-Ba'luji killed three Zionists. One of the biggest blows dealt to the movement was the deportation of nearly 400 movement leaders and cadres to Marj al-Zuhur in South Lebanon. The background to this was the capture and killing of the Israeli officer Nissim Toledano. The movement's deportees were able to turn their deportation into a political and media protest and a heroic feat to the extent that the enemy was forced to return them to Palestine.

6. The movement rejected open or secret negotiations between the Zionist side and the PLO and expressed its position through communiqués, statements, and other forms of political expression. At the time, preparations were being made on the ground for concluding the Oslo Accords. The deportation came within that context.

During this phase, the movement assumed a leading position in resistance and military action. It greatly expanded its membership and gained considerable respect in many Arab capitals. This represented the start of the movement's external relations. That phase proved the soundness, effectiveness, and correctness of the measures and development phases of the movement's project, whose effectiveness, continuation, and ability to overcome crises, with the Grace of Allah, were guaranteed.

E. The Post-Oslo Phase (1994–2000)

This is the phase in which the movement stood against the tide of peaceful political settlement with the Zionist enemy in the aftermath of the conclusion of the Oslo Accords on 13 September 1993. The movement emerged as the principal armed faction to continue the resistance and the jihad against the Zionist occupation, a task for which it made enormous sacrifices, offering scores of martyrs and hundreds of prisoners and detainees. The campaign against the movement peaked in 1996 in the form of an alliance among local, regional, and international powers as expressed by the Sharm al-Sheikh summit – or what was called then the war on terrorism summit – convened in the aftermath of the revenge attacks carried out by the movement in retaliation for the assassination of martyr Yahya "the Engineer" Ayyash. Despite the measures adopted to undermine the movement and suppress its resistance, the movement was able to emerge from this crisis much stronger and much more effective both militarily and politically. Subsequent events vindicated the movement and proved the credibility of its position toward Oslo and the philosophy of a peaceful settlement to the conflict in the region. The movement proved capable of adapting to political and security changes, both internally and externally, in a manner that preserved the movement's jihad project and its political and social programs.

Conclusion

Since it started, the Hamas project has passed through different circumstances and several phases. At every phase since the Haifa conference of 1947, it has been absolutely clear that the Zionist project is absolutely and radically contradictory to our religious beliefs and national interests. It is both necessary and inevitable to clash with it, to do all that is possible to confront it and to provide for the proper circumstances for eliminating it. Subjective and objective circumstances prevented the Hamas project from taking shape on the ground for some time. But when the right conditions became available, the project began to construct itself, erecting its structure and crystallizing its plans and policies. 8 December 1987, the day on which the first intifada erupted, was the day the Hamas movement

was launched officially and in practice. Its first communiqué was issued on 14 December 1987 to proclaim to the public the emergence
of the movement, which had attained the full growth of its structure
and the clarity of its vision of its role in confronting the Zionist occupation.

3. THE CONFLICT WITH THE ZIONIST PROJECT IN THE THINKING OF HAMAS

Hamas considers the conflict with the Zionist project a civilizational and
existential conflict that cannot be ended without eliminating its cause,
which is the establishment of the racist colonial Zionist entity in the land
of Palestine.

The movement's view of the Zionist project is based on the following
considerations:

1. The Zionist project represents the convergence of Western colonial interests
in the region with the interests of the Zionist movement and its ambitions in
the land of Palestine, which are often justified in the name of ideological myths
espoused by Jewish and Christian Zionists.

2. The Zionist entity is a colonial settlement entity that is based on the idea of
uprooting the Palestinian people and driving them away from their land by force
to replace them with settlers using all means of terrorism.

3. The Zionist project is an expansionist one; it seeks to impose its hegemony on
the entire region and control its resources. As such, it represents a real danger
not only to Palestine but also to the entire Arab and Muslim world.

4. This project does not accept coexistence with others; it is dominated by the
inclination toward hegemony and imposing control over others to serve the interests of the Zionist movement in the region and the entire world. Therefore, it
would be futile to seek to make peace or reach a settlement with it.

5. The Zionist entity constitutes an effective colonial means of breaking the geo-
graphic contiguity among the Arab countries in Asia and Africa; it is simply aimed
at thwarting any renaissance project in the region. It seeks thus to accomplish the
colonial goals of obstructing the project of Arab and Islamic unity.

4. HAMAS'S VISION OF LIBERATION

Hamas believes that the battle for the total liberation of Palestine from
the sea to the river will not succeed unless the efforts in three main cir-

cles come together. These are:

1. The Palestinian Circle: This is the spearhead in the battle of liberation; its role is summed up in maintaining the jihad and the resistance, continuing to adhere to the national rights and fundamentals and keeping the flame of jihad alight, so as to keep the issue alive within a national program whose basis is resistance and the existential antagonism of occupation, until such time as the two other circles are ready.

2. The Arab Circle: Since the Zionist project poses a danger to the entire Arab umma, and in view of what Palestine represents in terms of ideological and nationalist dimensions, the role of the Arab Circle in liberation is fundamental and central; the Arab umma constitutes the potential force upon which the task of liberation depends.

3. The Islamic Circle: Inasmuch as the Palestinian issue is an Arab issue it is also Islamic; it is of concern to every Muslim on the face of the earth because Palestine is an Islamic endowment land that embraces within it the first of the two *qiblas* and the third most important mosque, which the Prophet, peace be upon him, visited during his night journey to the Upper Heavens. All Muslims, both as individuals as well as communities, shoulder the duty of contributing whatever they can afford to the task of liberating Palestine. The Islamic umma is considered the strategic depth and the reserve to which the Palestinian people and the Arab umma will resort in their endeavor to liberate Palestine and remove the Zionist entity from it.

5. MILITARY ACTION IN HAMAS'S PROGRAM
Military action in the Hamas project constitutes the strategic means for the liberation of Palestine and confronting the Zionist project. It is the sole guarantee for the continuation of the conflict and for preoccupying the Zionist entity to thwart its expansionism outside Palestine. The movement considers military action the real expression of the legitimacy of rejecting the occupation and resisting its existence on Palestinian soil. This legitimacy derives from Divine religions, international norms, and human history.

Military action within the movement is subject to fixed policies. The most important of these are:

1. The conflict with the Zionists is not linked to their religious affiliation but is because they occupy our land, desecrate our shrines, and violate our people.

2. Resistance, with all its forms, is aimed at ending the occupation and will not stop until it is defeated and ended.

3. Hamas's military action is confined to the land of Palestine, both that occupied in 1948 and that occupied in 1967.

4. With its military action, the movement does not target civilian Zionists; it only targets Zionist military targets. Civilians may, however, be inadvertently hit or may be targeted only in retaliation for the enemy's targeting of Palestinian civilians.

6. POLITICAL ACTION IN HAMAS'S PROGRAM

In addition to its military program, the movement possesses a political program that is based on mobilizing the resources of the Palestinian people and the Arab and Islamic umma and dedicating them to ending the Zionist project and establishing an Arab Islamic state in the whole of Palestine. It is in the light of this that the movement determines its policies and stances vis-à-vis the various issues and different developments. The following are some of Hamas's most important policies:

A. HAMAS'S STANCE TOWARD THE PALESTINIAN FORCES AND FACTIONS:

1. The movement believes in a national unity based on preserving the national fundamentals: such national unity is an important underpinning of steadfastness and liberation.

2. Hamas believes that the arena of Palestinian national action is spacious enough for all visions and opinions concerning resistance against the Zionist project.

3. Emanating from the desire to give priority to common denominators and common grounds, Hamas seeks to cooperate and coordinate with all the forces, factions, and organizations working in the Palestinian arena.

4. Hamas seeks to bolster joint national action. It believes that any formula for joint Palestinian national action must be based on the commitment to work for the liberation of Palestine and the commitment not to recognize the Zionist enemy or grant it the right to exist on any part of Palestine.

5. No matter how much difference there may be in positions or opinions as to how to act in the arena of national action, Hamas believes that no one has the right under any circumstances to use weapons or resort to violence to settle disputes or impose views or opinions within the Palestinian arena. It is for this reason that the movement has always exercised self-restraint

toward the repressive measures taken against it at certain times. It has been motivated to persevere by the desire to save Palestinian blood and to serve the supreme Palestinian interest.

6. The movement believes in the necessity of combining all efforts in the Palestinian arena in order to establish a wholesome Palestinian society that enjoys freedom, equality, and political pluralism within the framework of the basic identity and the sublime values of the Palestinian society and the Arab and Islamic umma.

B. Hamas's position regarding peaceful settlement:

1. The movement has repeatedly affirmed that it is not against the principle of peace; but the peace it seeks is that which restores to the Palestinian people their rights and guarantees their independence and sovereignty over their entire land. Such peace can only be accomplished in the light of strength and steadfastness and not in the shade of weakness and capitulation.

2. The movement considers the agreements concluded between the occupation and certain Palestinian parties to be unacceptable concessions and compromises over the national rights of the Palestinian people and the rights of the umma to its holy places.

3. The movement believes that the settlement agreements grant the enemy the right to exist, bestow legitimacy on its occupation of Palestine and give the enemy the opportunity to expand and extend by virtue of cultural, economic, and political normalization programs with the Arab and Islamic countries. As such they constitute a real danger to the presence and future of the Arab and Islamic umma.

Because of the aforementioned reasons as well as other considerations, the movement has rejected the settlement plans and what has emanated from them, such as the agreements concluded at Oslo, Wye River, Sharm al-Sheikh, and other places. The movement considers all these projects and accords to be attempts to liquidate the Palestinian issue, deny the Palestinian people the right to claim their legitimate rights in their lands and holy places, deny the refugees the right to return to their homes, and deny the Palestinians the right to resort to legitimate means to regain their rights. Additionally, they are aimed at denying the majority of the Palestinian people the right to live on their soil and in their homeland. These accords have led to the diversion of the conflict from the right direction and have had a negative impact on the relations among the various Palestinian forces and factions.

C. HAMAS'S EXTERNAL RELATIONS:

1. Hamas believes that disagreement over political developments does not bar it from communicating and cooperating with any party that is prepared to support the steadfastness and resistance of our people against the oppressive occupation.

2. Hamas does not concern itself with the internal affairs of the other countries and does not interfere in their domestic policies.

3. Hamas seeks to encourage Arab and Islamic governments to resolve their disputes and unite their positions toward pan-Arab or pan-Islamic causes. The movement refuses to take sides in disputes by standing by one party against the other and refuses to join any particular political axis against another.

4. Hamas believes in Arab and Islamic unity and would support any endeavor in this regard.

5. Hamas demands that all Arab and Islamic governments, parties, and forces perform their duty of supporting the cause of our people and assisting them in their steadfastness and confrontation of the Zionist occupation. It calls on them to facilitate the activity of Hamas and help it undertake its mission.

6. Hamas believes in the importance of establishing close ties with the umma's various Islamic and nationalist forces and movements. It has in fact been doing exactly that by means of an extensive network of close relations with the aim of mobilizing the efforts of the umma in confronting the Zionist project, which is hostile to the umma.

7. Hamas believes in the importance of dialogue with world governments and international forces and parties irrespective of their faith, nationality, or political system. Hamas does not object to cooperating with any party in the world in the service of our people's just cause and as part of the endeavor to secure their legitimate rights.

8. Hamas does not declare hostility against anyone on the basis of religious belief or racial roots; nor does it oppose any country or organization so long as it does not practice injustice against our people or support the Zionist occupation in its aggression against our people.

9. Hamas wishes to confine the arena of confrontation with the Zionist occupation to Palestine; it would not want to extend the battlefield to any other arena.

10. Hamas seeks to persuade governments and international organizations or institutions to stand by the just cause of our people and to condemn the repressive measures adopted by the occupation in contravention of the principles of international law and the values of human rights. The objective is to form an international public opinion that would put pressure on the Zionist entity in order to end its oppressive occupation of our land.

D. HAMAS POSITION TOWARD MEMBERS OF THE OTHER DIVINE RELIGIONS

Hamas believes that Islam is the religion of unity, equality, tolerance, and freedom. It is a movement with humane and civilizational dimensions; it does not adopt a hostile position against anyone except those who initiate hostility against the umma. Hamas believes that living in the light of Islam is the ideal climate for coexistence among affiliates of the Divine religions; history provides the best testimony to this fact. The movement takes guidance from the Qur'anic verse that says, "There is no compulsion in religion," and the Qur'anic verse that says "Allah forbids you not, with regard to those who fight you not for [your] Faith nor drive you out of your homes, from dealing kindly and justly with them: for Allah loves those who are just."

On the basis of these values, Hamas respects the rights of other faith communities. As for the Christians living in Palestine, Hamas considers them to be partners who share the homeland and who have been subjected to the same oppressive measures to which their Muslim brothers have been subjected at the hands of the occupation authorities; they have participated in confronting the occupation and in opposing its racist policies; and they are an inseparable part of the Palestinian people with full rights and full responsibilities.

Hamas Political Bureau
June 2000

APPENDIX III

We Will Not Sell Our People or Principles for Foreign Aid.

(Article by Hamas Political Bureau Chief Khalid Mish'al in the *Guardian*, 31 March 2006)

It is widely recognised that the Palestinians are among the most politicised and educated peoples in the world. When they went to the polls last Wednesday they were well aware of what was on offer and those who voted for Hamas knew what it stood for. They chose Hamas because of its pledge never to give up the legitimate rights of the Palestinian people and its promise to embark on a programme of reform. There were voices warning them, locally and internationally, not to vote for an organization branded by the US and EU as terrorist because such a democratically exercised right would cost them the financial aid provided by foreign donors.

The day Hamas won the Palestinian democratic elections the world's leading democracies failed the test of democracy. Rather than recognise the legitimacy of Hamas as a freely elected representative of the Palestinian people, seize the opportunity created by the result to support the development of good governance in Palestine and search for a means of ending the bloodshed, the US and EU threatened the Palestinian people with collective punishment for exercising their right to choose their parliamentary representatives.

We are being punished simply for resisting oppression and striving for justice. Those who threaten to impose sanctions on our people are the same powers that initiated our suffering and continue to support our oppressors almost unconditionally. We, the victims, are being penalised while our oppressors are pampered. The US and EU could have used the success of Hamas to open a new chapter in their relations with the Palestinians, the Arabs and the Muslims and to understand better a movement that has so far been seen largely through the eyes of the Zionist occupiers of our land.

Our message to the US and EU governments is this: your attempt to force us to give up our principles or our struggle is in vain. Our people who gave thousands of martyrs, the millions of refugees who have waited for nearly 60 years to return home and our 9,000 political and war prisoners in Israeli jails have not made those sacrifices in order to settle for close to nothing.

Hamas has been elected mainly because of its immovable faith in the inevitability of victory; and Hamas is immune to bribery, intimidation and blackmail. While we are keen on having friendly relations with all nations we shall not seek friendships at the expense of our legitimate rights. We have seen how other nations, including the peoples of Vietnam and South Africa, persisted in their struggle until their quest for freedom and justice was accomplished. We are no different, our cause is no less worthy, our determination is no less profound and our patience is no less abundant.

Our message to the Muslim and Arab nations is this: you have a responsibility to stand by your Palestinian brothers and sisters whose sacrifices are made on behalf of all of you. Our people in Palestine should not need to wait for any aid from countries that attach humiliating conditions to every dollar or euro they pay despite their historical and moral responsibility for our plight. We expect you to step in and compensate the Palestinian people for any loss of aid and we demand you lift all restrictions on civil society institutions that wish to fundraise for the Palestinian cause.

Our message to the Palestinians is this: our people are not only those who live under siege in the West Bank and the Gaza Strip but also the millions languishing in refugee camps in Lebanon, Jordan and Syria and the millions spread around the world unable to return home. We promise you that nothing in the world will deter us from pursuing our goal of liberation and return. We shall spare no effort to work with all factions and institutions in order to put our Palestinian house in order. Having won the parliamentary elections, our medium-term objective is to reform the PLO in order to revive its role as a true representative of all the Palestinian people, without exception or discrimination.

Our message to the Israelis is this: we do not fight you because you belong to a certain faith or culture. Jews have lived in the Muslim world for 13 centuries in peace and harmony; they are in our religion "the people of the book" who have a covenant from God and His Messenger Muhammad (peace be upon him) to be respected and protected. Our conflict with you is not religious but political. We have no problem with Jews who have not attacked us —our problem is with those who came to our land, imposed themselves on us by force, destroyed our society and banished our people.

We shall never recognise the right of any power to rob us of our land and deny us our national rights. We shall never recognise the legitimacy of a Zionist state created on our soil in order to atone for somebody else's sins or solve somebody else's problem. But if you are willing to accept the principle of a long-term truce, we are prepared to negotiate the terms. Hamas is extending a hand of peace to those who are truly interested in a peace based on justice.

www.guardian.co.uk/comment/story/0,,1698420,00.html

APPENDIX IV

What Hamas is Seeking

(Article by Musa Abu Marzuq in the *Washington Post* of 31 January 2006)

A new era in the struggle for Palestinian liberation is upon us. Through historic fair and free elections, the Palestinian people have spoken. Accordingly, America's long-standing tradition of supporting the oppressed's rights to self-determination should not waver. The United States, the European Union and the rest of the world should welcome the unfolding of the democratic process, and the commitment to aid should not falter.

Last week's victory of the Change and Reform Party in the Palestinian legislative elections signals a new hope for an occupied people. The results of these elections reflect a need for change from the corruption and intransigence of the past government. Since its creation 10 years ago, the Palestinian Legislative Council has been unsuccessful in addressing the needs of the people. As the occupation solidified its grip under the auspices of "peace agreements," quality of life deteriorated for Palestinians in the occupied territories. Poverty levels soared, unemployment rates reached uncharted heights and the lack of basic security approached unbearable depths. A grass-roots alternative grew out of the urgency of this situation.

Through its legacy of social work and involvement in the needs of the Palestinian people, the Islamic Resistance Movement (Hamas) flourished as a positive social force striving for the welfare of all Palestinians. Alleviating the debilitative conditions of occupation, and not an Islamic state, is at the heart of our mandate (with reform and change as its lifeblood). Despite the pressures of occupation and corrupt self-rule, Palestinian civil society has demonstrated its resilience in the face of repressive conditions. Social institutions can now be given new life under a reformed government that embraces the empowerment of the people, facilitates freedoms and protects civil rights.

Our society has always celebrated pluralism in keeping with the unique history and traditions of the Holy Land. In recognizing Judeo-Christian traditions, Muslims nobly vie for and have the greatest incentive and stake in preserving the Holy Land for all three Abrahamic faiths. In addition, fair governance demands that the Palestinian nation be represented in a pluralistic environment.

A new breed of Islamic leadership is ready to put into practice faith-based principles in a setting of tolerance and unity. In that vein, Hamas has pledged transparency in government. Honest leadership will result from the accountability of its public servants. Hamas has elected 15 female legislators poised to play a significant role in public life. The movement has forged genuine and lasting relationships with Christian candidates.

As we embark on a new phase in the struggle to liberate Palestine, we recognize the recent elections as a vote against the failures of the current process. A new "road map" is needed to lead us away from the path of checkpoints and walls and onto the path of freedom and justice. The past decade's "peace process" has led to a dramatic rise in the expansion of illegal settlements and land confiscation. The realities of occupation include humiliating checkpoints, home demolitions, open-ended administrative detentions, extrajudicial killings and thousands of dead civilians.

The Islamic Resistance Movement was elected to protect the Palestinians from the abuses of occupation, based on its history of sacrifice for the cause of liberty. It would be a mistake to view the collective will of the Palestinian people in electing Hamas in fair and free elections under occupation as a threat. For meaningful dialogue to occur there should be no prejudgments or preconditions. And we do desire dialogue. The terms of the dialogue should be premised on justice, mutual respect and integrity of the parties.

As the Israelis value their own security, Palestinians are entitled to their fundamental rights to live in dignity and security. We ask them to reflect on the peace that our peoples once enjoyed and the protection that Muslims gave the Jewish community worldwide. We will exert good-faith efforts to remove the bitterness that Israel's occupation has succeeded in creating, alienating a generation of Palestinians. We call on them not to condemn posterity to endless bloodshed and a conflict in which dominance is illusory. There must come a day when we will live together, side by side once again. The failed policies of the U.S. administration are the result of the inherent contradiction in its position.

as Israel's strongest ally and an "honest broker" in the conflict. World nations have condemned the brutal Israeli occupation.

For the sake of peace, the United States must abandon its position of isolation and join the rest of the world in calling for an end to the occupation, assuring the Palestinians their right to self-determination. We appeal to the American people's sense of fairness to judge this conflict in light of the great thoughts, principles and ideals you hold dear in the Declaration of Independence, the Constitution and the democracy you have built. It is not unreasonable to expect America to practice abroad what it preaches at home.

We can but sincerely hope that you use your honest judgment and the blessings of ascendancy God has given you to demand an end to the occupation. Meaningful democracy cannot flourish as long as an external force maintains the balance of power. It is the right of all people to pursue their own destiny.

APPENDIX V

A Just Peace or No Peace

(Article by Palestinian Prime Minister Isma'il Haniyah in the *Guardian* of 31 March 2006)

Do policymakers in Washington and Europe ever feel ashamed of their scandalous double standards? Before and since the Palestinian elections in January, they have continually insisted that Hamas comply with certain demands. They want us to recognise Israel, call off our resistance, and commit ourselves to whatever deals Israel and the Palestinian leadership reached in the past.

But we have not heard a single demand of the Israeli parties that took part in this week's elections, though some advocate the complete removal of the Palestinians from their lands. Even Ehud Olmert's Kadima party, whose Likud forebears frustrated every effort by the PLO to negotiate a peace settlement, campaigned on a programme that defies UN Security Council resolutions. His unilateralism is a violation of international law. Nevertheless no one, not even the Quartet — whose proposals for a settlement he continues to disregard, as his predecessor Ariel Sharon did — has dared ask anything of him.

Olmert's unilateralism is a recipe for conflict. It is a plan to impose a permanent situation in which the Palestinians end up with a homeland cut into pieces made inaccessible because of massive Jewish settlements built in contravention of international law on land seized illegally from the Palestinians. No plan will ever work without a guarantee, in exchange for an end to hostilities by both sides, of a total Israeli withdrawal from all the land occupied in 1967, including East Jerusalem; the release of all our prisoners; the removal of all settlers from all settlements; and recognition of the right of all refugees to return.

On this, all Palestinian factions and people agree, including the PLO, whose revival is essential so that it can resume its role in speaking for the Palestinians and presenting their case to the world.

The problem is not with any particular Palestinian group but with the denial of our basic rights by Israel. We in Hamas are for peace and want to put an end to bloodshed. We have been observing a unilateral truce for more than a year without reciprocity from the Israeli side. The message from Hamas and the Palestinian Authority to the world powers is this: talk to us no more about recognising Israel's "right to exist" or ending resistance until you obtain a commitment from the Israelis to withdraw from our land and recognise our rights.

Little will change for the Palestinians under Olmert's plan. Our land will still be occupied and our people enslaved and oppressed by the occupying power. So we will remain committed to our struggle to get back our lands and our freedom. Peaceful means will do if the world is willing to engage in a constructive and fair process in which we and the Israelis are treated as equals. We are sick and tired of the West's racist approach to the conflict, in which the Palestinians are regarded as inferior. Though we are the victims, we offer our hands in peace, but only a peace that is based on justice. However, if the Israelis continue to attack and kill our people and destroy their homes, impose sanctions, collectively punish us, and imprison men and women for exercising the right to self-defence, we have every right to respond with all available means.

Hamas has been freely elected. Our people have given us their confidence and we pledge to defend their rights and do our best to run their affairs through good governance. If we are boycotted in spite of this democratic choice — as we have been by the US and some of its allies — we will persist, and our friends have pledged to fill the gap. We have confidence in the peoples of the world, record numbers of whom identify with our struggle. This is a good time for peace-making — if the world wants peace.

www.guardian.co.uk/comment/story/0,,1743628,00.html

APPENDIX VI

Change and Reform List

(Hamas Election Manifesto for the Legislative Elections held on 25 January 2006)

In the name of Allah Most Gracious Most Merciful

> *"I only desire [your] betterment to the best of my power; and my success [in my task] can only come from Allah. In Him I trust, and unto Him I look."*

—Sura Hud 11:88

Election Manifesto for the Elections of the Palestinian Legislative Council 2006

INTRODUCTION

On the basis of the belief that we stand at one of Islam's greatest fronts; in fulfillment of our responsibility toward our struggling people and their sacred and just cause; stemming from our duty to contribute to reforming the Palestinian reality so as to ease the suffering of our valiant people, bolster their steadfastness, and protect them from the ills of corruption; and in the hope of reinforcing national unity and bolstering internal Palestinian ranks, we have taken the decision to participate in the Palestinian legislative elections of 2006.

The Change and Reform List believes that its participation in the legislative elections at this time and in the shade of the reality endured by the Palestinian cause falls within the framework of the comprehensive program for the liberation of Palestine, the return of the Palestinian people to their lands and homes, and the establishment of the Palestinian independent state with Jerusalem its capital. This participation is intended to be an act of support for the program of resistance and intifada to which our people have happily resorted as a strategic option to end the occupation.

The Change and Reform List seeks to build an advanced Palestinian civil society that is based on political pluralism and the alternation of power and seeks to direct the Palestinian political system and its political reform program in a manner that would accomplish the national rights of the Palestinian people while bearing in mind the existence of the heavy, detested, and oppressive occupation of our land and people and taking into consideration its overt interventions in every single detail of Palestinian life.

Our list's program is hereby submitted as a gesture of loyalty to our forbearing masses who see in this approach a wholesome alternative, who consider the Hamas movement a hope for a better future, and who see in this list an honest leadership for a better tomorrow, God-willing.

The Almighty Allah says: "Verily, this is My Way leading straight: follow it; follow not [other] paths: they will scatter you about from His [great] Path; thus does He command you, that you may be righteous" (Sura al-An'am 6: 153).

1. OUR ESSENTIAL PRINCIPLES

Our list (the Change and Reform List) adopts a number of invariables that stem from the Islamic frame of reference. We believe these invariables to be unanimously agreed upon not only by our Palestinian people but also by our Arab and Islamic umma. These invariables are:

1. Islam and its civilizational achievements constitute our frame of reference and way of life with all its political, economic, social, and legal dimensions.

2. Historic Palestine is part of the Arab and Islamic land; the Palestinian people's right to it does not diminish with the passage of time and no military or alleged legal procedures alter this fact.

3. The Palestinian people are united as one wherever they may be living and are an inseparable part of the Arab and Islamic umma. ("Verily, this

umma [brotherhood] of yours is a single umma, and I am your Lord and Cherisher: therefore serve Me [and no other]" [Sura al-Anbiya' 21:92].)

4. Our Palestinian people are still living through the phase of national liberation; they have the right to endeavor to regain their rights and end the occupation using all available means, including armed resistance. We must dedicate all our resources to supporting the steadfastness of our people and provide the with all the necessary means of defeating the occupation and establishing the independent Palestinian state with Jerusalem as its capital.

5. All the Palestinian refugees and deportees have right to return to their lands and properties. The right to self-determination and all our national rights are considered inalienable rights; they are fixed and cannot be compromised by any political concessions.

6. Full adherence to our people's inalterable and genuine rights to the land, Jerusalem, the holy places, water, [control of our own] borders, and a fully sovereign Palestinian state with Jerusalem as its capital.

7. Reinforcing and protecting national Palestinian unity is one of the priorities of national Palestinian action.

8. The issue of the prisoners and the detainees tops the list of the priorities of Palestinian action.

2. DOMESTIC POLICY

At the level of the domestic policy that governs Palestinian political life with all its dimensions, we aspire to accomplish the following priorities, which we believe guarantee a future befitting the struggle and sacrifices of our people and that would bolster their steadfastness in pursuit of comprehensive liberation and the aspired reform:

1. Preserving national Palestinian invariables and resisting any attempt to compromise or concede them.

2. Preserving the Palestinian presence in Jerusalem and supporting it politically, economically, socially, and culturally; resisting the enemy's

attempts to Judaize Jerusalem; and protecting the Islamic and Christian Palestinian holy cites from Zionist desecration.

3. Safeguarding political liberties, pluralism, the freedom to form political parties, resorting for arbitration to the ballot boxes, and the peaceful alternation of power are considered the best framework for regulating Palestinian political activity, and guaranteeing reform, combating corruption, and building an advanced Palestinian civil society.

4. Deepening the bonds of national unity, adopting dialogue, and resorting to logic in addressing internal disputes and prohibiting fighting and all forms of the use of force or the threat to use it within the domestic framework.

5. Establishing respect for public liberties (freedom of expression, freedom of the press, freedom of assembly, freedom of movement, freedom of work, etc.) as the living reality of the Palestinian people.

6. Palestinian blood is one of the taboos within Palestinian society; dialogue is the only acceptable method for resolving internal Palestinian disputes.

7. Prohibiting political detention and rejecting the suppression of the freedom of speech.

8. Protecting the institutions of civil society and vitalizing their role in development and in monitoring and inspection.

9. Correcting and rationalizing the role of the security agencies in protecting the security of the citizen, ending erroneous and arbitrary practices, guaranteeing the liberties of citizens, protecting private and public properties, and making these agencies accountable to the Palestinian Legislative Council.

10. Security collaboration, or so-called security coordination, with the occupation is a crime against the homeland and against religion; it should be severely punished.

11. Protecting the resistance and vitalizing its role in resisting the occupation and accomplishing the mission of liberation.

12. Building the decent Palestinian citizen who is proud of his or her religion, land, freedom, and dignity and who is willing to sacrifice the precious and the dear in the Cause of Allah.

13. Vitalizing resistance against the construction of the apartheid wall of separation until it is brought down; all available means should be employed, including international institutions and courts of justice.

14. Guaranteeing the rights of minorities and respecting them in all aspects of society as equal citizens.

15. Public funds of all types are the property of the Palestinian people and should be used in financing comprehensive Palestinian development in a geographically fair manner that would serve social justice and discourage abuse, extravagance, looting, corruption, and embezzlement.

16. Prisoners, the wounded, and martyrs are the symbols of Palestinian sacrifice; caring for them and their families and seeking the release of the prisoners top the priorities in our national agenda.

17. Raising the efficiency of the institutions that specialize in supporting prisoners and their families and the families of martyrs and the wounded. Prisoners and martyrs will be treated as if they were still employed and will be paid a stipend equivalent to the salary they would have received from employment in the civil service.

18. Preserving Palestinian Islamic and Christian endowment properties, protecting them from aggression and manipulation and developing them in a manner that would conform to the moral and material value of these endowments, which are spread across the whole of Palestine.

19. Restoring the relationship between the PLO and the Palestinian National Authority (PNA) in a manner that serves the national Palestinian objectives and respects the organizations' respective fields of specialization.

3. External Relations

1. Consolidate relations with the Arab and Islamic world in all fields for being the strategic depth of Palestine and opening up to the rest of the world's countries.

2. Revitalize the role of the Arab and Islamic masses in supporting the resistance of our people against occupation and in rejecting normalization with it.

3. Reject racial, territorial, or sectarian claims that seek to divide the umma.

4. Establish balanced political relations with the family of nations in a manner that would guarantee an active participation in the international community, preserve the unity of the umma and [achieve] its advancement, protect the rights [of the umma] and its causes, foremost of which is the Palestinian cause, and deter any aggression toward it.

5. Emphasize at all international levels in all world forums the illegitimacy of the occupation and all that comes out of it.

6. Consider occupation to be the ugliest form of terrorism and resisting it with all means a right that is guaranteed by Divine religions and internal law.

7. Call on all the good peoples and powers in the world to join together in an alliance to establish a just world peace that is based on ridding the world of all forms of occupation and of the remnants of colonialism and preventing foreign intervention in peoples' internal affairs.

8. Restore respect for the Palestinian rights in Arab and international circles, especially the right to be free from occupation, the right of the refugees to return home, and the right to establish a fully sovereign Palestinian state and to press for the issuance of resolutions and positions that support these rights.

9. Call on the international community to contribute effectively to rebuilding the towns and villages and to providing them with the necessary infrastructure.

10. Reject conditional grants that are only given in exchange for compromising our national principles and earnestly seek honorable alternatives.

4. ADMINISTRATIVE REFORM & FIGHTING CORRUPTION

1. Eliminate all forms of corruption; consider it a main contributing factor to weakening the internal Palestinian front and to undermining the foundations of national unity, and pursue investigations into administrative and financial corruption in order to bring the culprits to justice.

2. Enhance transparency, monitoring, auditing, and accountability in dealing with matters pertaining to the budget in all of its phases (planning, preparation, discussion, endorsement, and implementation).

3. Modernizing administrative rules and systems in a manner that would enhance the efficiency of administrative departments so as to provide services with ease and comfort at all levels.

4. Implement the concepts of decentralization, the delegation of authority, and shared decision making.

5. Reformulate the policy of employment in the civil service in a manner that would guarantee equal opportunities for all the children of the Palestinian people on the basis of their qualifications and would eliminate nepotism, partisan favoritism, and red tape in appointments and promotions in all government departments and public agencies.

6. Form a national parliamentary committee to inspect the dispensing of Palestinian endowment funds, both Islamic and Christian, in order to guarantee proper conduct and enable to accomplish its goals.

7. Fight slackness in government performance and the wastage of public funds and endeavor to bolster a sense of responsibility at all levels of

employment. ("Each of you is a shepherd [guardian] and each of you is responsible for his flock"—as stated in a Prophetic hadith).

8. Adopt the policy of [calling to account those in authority questioning them] "where have you acquired this from?" in order to call to account those employed in the civil service.

5. LEGISLATIVE POLICY AND JUDICIAL REFORM

1. Establish Islamic Shari'a as the main source of legislation in Palestine.

2. Emphasize the separation among the three powers: the legislative, the executive, and the judiciary.

3. Revitalize the role of the Constitutional Court.

4. Seek to enact legislations that would take into consideration the specific values and heritage of the Palestinian people.

5. Establish a judicial training institute.

6. Restructure the Supreme Judicial Council so that its members are elected from among the judges of Palestine on the basis of qualifications and experience with no consideration for political or social factionalism or personal interests.

7. Enact laws aimed at vitalizing judiciary inspection so as to achieve effective auditing within the judiciary at all levels.

8. Enact laws that would bar the politicization of the general prosecution and would ensure the observance of the parameters of qualification, inspection, review, and accountability.

9. Amend the law pertaining to civil and commercial trials and the law of penal procedures so as to prevent the prolonging of court procedures, limit the number of adjourned cases, and determine an upper time limit for each type of case and for the period of adjournment.

10. Reinforce democracy and shura in the various fields and positions and achieve effective participation.

11. End the government's encroachment on the constitution: issuing temporary laws, repetitive amendments, delaying the implementation of laws, or other forms of abuses.

12. Reject any legislations or agreement with the enemy that contravene the rights of our Palestinian people.

6. Public Liberties and Citizen Rights

1. Implement the principle that citizens are equal before the law and that they are equal in rights and duties.

2. Provide each citizen with security and with protection for his or her life and properties; no citizen should be subjected to arbitrary detention or torture or revenge.

3. End the intervention of security agencies in the issuing of licenses for publications, research centers, and public opinion polling institutions, as well as their intervention in employment.

4. Reinforce the culture of dialogue and respect for all opinions that do not contradict the people's faith or their cultural heritage and construct an information policy based on the principles of freedom of thought and expression, fairness and the accommodation of diversity, pluralism, and the right to free choice.

5. Protect the rights of people with special needs (the prisoners and their families, the families of martyrs, women, children, the disabled, and the poor).

6. Protect media institutions and guarantee the right of journalists to acquire information and to publish it.

7. Protect the freedom to form trade unions, preserve the independence of the trade unions, and avoid all forms of despotism.

8. Recognize political groups, encourage them and benefit from their role and support the various institutions of civil society.

9. Adopt the principle of equal opportunities and appointing the right person to the right position.

7. Educational Policy

Since education is the foundation necessary to build the generation capable of envisioning the future of the homeland and accomplishing the dream of freedom, liberation, and independence, our list will seek to do the following:

1. Observe the foundations on which the philosophy of education in Palestine is based. These include the principle that Islam is a comprehensive system that applies to all aspects of life and that dignifies the human being, striking a balance between individual and community rights.

2. Implement mandatory education and expand secondary education in both branches, the vocational and the academic.

3. Develop the curricula and teaching methods in conformity with the philosophy and objectives of education in Palestine and according to the needs of each age.

4. Pay attention to the humanities and focus on languages, especially the Arabic language at various levels of education.

5. Establish the ethics of the teaching profession, respect the rights of the teachers, and develop their skills.

6. Enact legislations aimed at protecting the teaching and academic process in universities and higher education institutions from abuse, unfairness, and favoritism.

7. Establish and develop institutions that specialize in providing care to the talented, high achievers, and those with extraordinary capabilities.

8. Develop the foundations of higher education and support scientific research, including the establishment of the Palestinian Scientific Research Center.

9. End the practice of using school facilities for multiple terms a day and increase the number of schools.

10. Reduce the number of students per class and the number of students per teacher at all levels of education, especially the elementary level.

11. Encourage the formation of student unions and provide them with support and with the appropriate climate so as to perform well and so as to maintain schools and universities as bastions of national action.

12. Provide all schools with athletic and cultural facilities as well as with laboratories and computers.

13. Provide schools across the homeland with the resources so as to teach various disciplines by attracting migrant Palestinian talents and training those who live inside the homeland.

14. Encourage field trips and internal tourism and include them in the educational requirements, especially as part of the national curriculum.

15. Encourage private educational institutions at all levels (pre-university) because of the savings they contribute to the state budget and the competition they provoke within the educational sector as a whole.

16. Permit the licensing of quality nonprofit private universities so as to encourage competition, which in turn results in more qualified graduates and keeps students at home, providing substantial savings to our economy.

17. Attend to vocational, technical, and agricultural education and training.

18. Develop the educational strategies that focus on qualification and shun all forms of favoritism in employment. The quality of those graduating from the educational system will be considered first and foremost.

19. Support the Needy University Students' Fund and develop its mechanisms so as to increase its transparency and objectivity and deliver aid to those who deserve it.

8. On the Subject of Preaching and Providing Religious Guidance

1. Improve the efficiency of preachers and religious guides, equate their status with that of their peers in other ministries, provide them with rewarding incentives, and formulate fair rules and guidelines.

2. End all forms of security intervention in this apparatus, enable working scholars to perform their roles, and end the policy of exclusion.

3. Review the Law of Admonition and Guidance so that those with the necessary knowledge and the qualifications may perform their religious and national duties.

4. Care for the mosques, build more of them, and reinvigorate their missionary and educational role in society.

5. Attend to the issues pertaining to hajj and 'umra [pilgrimage] in order to enable pilgrims to perform their rituals with ease and comfort.

9. Social Policy

1. Support the correct foundation and cohesion of the Palestinian family so as to constitute the solid foundation of our social values and moral ethics.

2. Establish social solidarity and encourage and expand the existing social protection network so as to guarantee the social and political stability of both the family and society and bolster the elements of steadfastness.

3. Provide social services (education, healthcare, and social security) and other public services to all citizens without discrimination, favoritism, or partisanship.

4. Unify the pension system so as to achieve equality and fairness among pensioners.

5. With regard to Personal Status Law and Shari'a Courts:

—It is necessary to enact a single law derived from Shari'a texts and from the recognized jurisprudential schools and to opt for what best suits the needs of the Palestinian Muslim society in the modern era.

—Enact legislation pertaining to the Shari'a courts of various levels, to be implemented in a unified manner (in Jerusalem, the West Bank, and the Gaza Strip), including the laws of endowment, inheritance, and non-Muslim sects.

—Seek a reasonable representation of the Shari'a courts in the Palestinian Constitutional Court.

6. Preserve the social fabric of the Palestinian people and public morality, guarantee that social principles are not violated, and prevent any measures or legislations that may undermine them.

7. Support the social institutions that care for the various marginalized sections of society such as women, children, orphans, the poor, and those with special needs.

8. Develop educational and vocational training centers and institutions to care for prisoners when still in captivity and then when freed so as to integrate them into society and enable them to contribute to the development of the homeland.

9. Provide comprehensive educational and healthcare to the families of martyrs and prisoners and all the needy segments of society.

10. Revitalize, organize, and develop the zakat committees.

11. Combat poverty by pursuing justice in wealth distribution, and encourage charitable associations and lift restrictions that may impede their activities.

12. Develop systems of social security so as to help eliminate poverty and maintain social harmony in the Palestinian society.

13. Combat narcotics and intoxicants and all forms of bad behavior through education, awareness programs, and exercising legal measures.

14. Support institutions that care for the disabled and those with special needs and develop programs to facilitate their integration into society.

15. Adopt a clear policy to care for the human element inside various departments by developing the labor force and providing workers with job security and psychological stability.

16. Revitalize reconciliation committees and support them financially, for they play an important role in resolving disputes among members of the community and in restoring climates of amicability and harmony among feuding parties.

10. Cultural and Media Policy

Because of the significant role played by cultural institutions and the media in forming the convictions and thoughts of citizens and hence the identity of the umma, our list will pursue the following:

1. Base media policy on the principles of the freedoms of thought and expression and on the value of honesty.

2. Immunize the citizens, especially young people, against corruption, Westernization, and intellectual invasion.

3. Facilitate the work of journalists and the mass media and guarantee the right of the masses to learn the truth.

4. End the intervention of security agencies in the issuing of licenses for publications, research centers, and public opinion polling institutions.

5. Elevate the level of public knowledge and awareness of rights, duties, responsibilities, and their consequences.

6. Revitalize the public sector media and liberate them from factionalism, increasing professionalism and transparency in their programs.

7. Found a public foundation, and encourage the founding of private ones, to specialize in Palestinian heritage, modern history, and holy places.

8. Direct the official media to contribute to the advancement of Palestinian society and bolster its steadfastness. These media will be turned into pulpits expressing truthfully the struggle of the Palestinian people and the nobility of their cause. They will be encouraged to provide a spacious platform for politicians, thinkers, and journalists to raise the issues freely but without infringing on the national principles.

11. WOMEN, CHILDREN, AND THE FAMILY

1. Protect and care for children, emphasizing their right to a proper upbringing, nutrition, physical and psychological care, guidance, and education.

2. The Palestinian woman is a partner in jihad and resistance as well as in building and development.

3. Guarantee women rights and establish the legislative framework for supporting them, and endeavor to enable women to contribute in social, economic, and political development.

4. Shield women with Islamic education by making them aware of their legitimate rights, and affirm women's independent personalities, based on chastity, decency, and observance.

5. Revitalize the role of voluntary women's institutions, which are a significant section of civil society.

6. Establish units in the countryside to teach women carpet and mat weaving, spinning, and other such crafts, in order to provide rural women with job opportunities.

7. Encourage the utilization of women's resources in the public sphere and highlight the role of women in building society.

8. Support the stability of the family by:

—developing legislation specific to the working woman with the aim of achieving family stability and generational protection;

—showing solidarity with families whose houses have been demolished or whose children have been detained or are on the run;

—providing adequate health clinics and hospitals so as to supply healthcare to families and attend to all the needs of maternity and childhood;

—protecting women from all forms of abuse and exploitation that demean them or treat them as if they were bodies and nothing else, as in advertising or as in the case of forcing them to perform illicit activities.

12. YOUTH ISSUES

1. Expand the founding of youth institutions and develop those that already exist so as to guarantee building a wholesome youth personality and to encourage dialogue among the youth.

2. Support sports and cultural clubs, put an end to interventions in their affairs, and combat negative phenomena within them.

3. Support and encourage the talented and the innovative among the youth in diverse fields and provide them with job opportunities in their respective fields.

4. Care for the youth and immunize them against corruption and immorality.

5. Provide the youth, especially university graduates, with honorable and appropriate job opportunities.

6. Enhance the participation of the youth in political, social, and cultural activities and in constructive arts.

7. Support sports teams' participation in local, Arab, Islamic, and international tournaments and construct sports halls and playgrounds to serve this end.

13. Housing Policy

1. Allocate certain public property lands for the establishment of residential complexes and villages to distribute them among low-earning citizens, especially those whose homes have been demolished, or impoverished families and the families of martyrs and detainees.

2. Address the shortage of housing for low earners and the crowding in housing, especially inside the Gaza Strip and some areas within the West Bank.

3. Encourage the construction of functional housing complexes that are annexed to public service institutions, such as schools, hospitals, universities, and other general facilities.

4. Distribute charitable housing equitably so as to encourage benefactors to continue funding such projects.

5. Stimulate the construction sector by funding housing projects and public building projects in order to speedily contribute to:

—solving the problem of unemployment among the
Palestinians who used to be employed in Israel, most of
whom possess experience and talents in construction;

—reduce the rent the government pays for its buildings,
and consequently alleviate some of the burden borne by
the budget and divert the resources to other priorities;

—develop social services by providing new premises or expanding
existing ones, especially in the sectors of education and healthcare.

6. Provide housing for junior civil servants and low earners
at cost price or with interest-free loans, encourage housing
contracts and remedying cases of insolvency.

7. Adopt structural and regional plans for Palestinian towns and villages.

14. Health Policy

1. Reform the health insurance system and make it available to all citizens,
starting with the poor, who are in more need.

2. Set a schedule for achieving medical sufficiency in all fields to prevent
the expenditure of public funds on treatment abroad.

3. Expand the services of primary healthcare and public health centers
to facilitate medical treatment and ease the burden on citizens in villages
and small towns.

4. Develop public health services that will surpass in quality the services
provided by the private sector.

5. Draw the necessary plans to expand the construction of fully integrated
hospitals, depending on the needs of different regions.

6. Achieve a balance in specializations and expertise in hospitals and
an equitable distribution of qualified personnel and equipment in all
regions.

7. Provide incentives that reward doctors, nurses, and other workers in the health sector who work in rural areas as well, as those with rare specializations in the health sector.

8. Encourage private and specialized health services.

9. Elevate the standard of the health sector (doctors, pharmacists, nurses, and health administrators) to meet the needs and requirements of the Palestinian society.

10. Provide appropriate health facilities to care for the wounded and disabled who were injured during the Palestinian jihad, without discrimination among the different segments of the Palestinian people.

11. Provide free and appropriate healthcare to the families of martyrs, the wounded, invalids, and captives.

12. Endeavor to provide a clean environment by developing the culture of public cleanliness, planting trees along the roads and in public parks, and encouraging private and public gardening.

13. In coordination with international agencies, protect the environment, stop Palestinian environmental deterioration, and resist the continuing pollution of the Palestinian lands as a result of the practices of the occupation and the Zionist settlements, and expose these practices at the international level.

14. Maintain the Gaza coast so that it remains clean, pleasant, and suitable for summer vacationing and tourism, stop infringements such as refuse dumping and prevent pollution caused by the pumping of household and industrial drainage into the sea.

15. Follow up the studies on getting rid of the environmental disaster caused by the existence of treatment pools to the north of the Gaza Strip, allocate new land to increase the number of "refuse dumping sites" in the Gaza Strip and the West Bank, and establish projects to make use of the refuse.

15. AGRICULTURAL POLICY

1. Develop the agricultural sector and animal resources in order first to achieve food security for the Palestinian people, and subsequently a surplus in production for export purposes.

2. Endeavor to categorize lands in Palestine, determine their agricultural uses, such as for growing citrus, grains, fruits, etc., and enacting the necessary legislation for developing them.

3. Restructure and revitalize the farmers' union across all the provinces so as to contribute to implementing agricultural policies aimed at advancing this important sector.

4. Endeavor to adopt an agricultural credit system to replace the interest-based system and encourage in-kind agricultural loaning.

5. Endeavor to improve coordination among the concerned agencies within the agricultural sector with regard to policy making, production, manufacture, and marketing, and seek to open up Arab and international markets for Palestinian agricultural produce as part of the available preferential treatment agreements.

6. Create the necessary infrastructure for agricultural development by promoting comprehensive rural development.

7. Encourage the establishment of food-processing projects that make use of leftovers; develop the quality of locally produced seeds, insecticides, and fertilizers.

8. Attend to the fishing industry and protect the rights of fishermen.

9. Regulate the import, marketing, and use of insecticides and agricultural or veterinary medications; ration the use of chemical fertilizers, and provide agricultural guidance services.

10. Encourage the reclamation of lands and support their farming and irrigation.

11. Develop animal resources and bridge the gap between demand and supply.

12. Monitor the performance of the Coastal Water Authority to ensure that it best serves the interests of the homeland and citizens.

16. Economic, Fiscal, and Monetary Policy

The Almighty Allah says: "Those who, when they spend, are not extravagant and not niggardly, but hold a just [balance] between those [extremes]" (Sura al-Furqan 25:67).

The Almighty also says: "Allah will deprive usury of all blessing, but will give increase for deeds of charity; for He loves not creatures ungrateful and wicked" (Sura al-Baqarah 2:67).

1. Achieve economic and monetary independence and disengage with the Zionist entity and its economy and currency by ending the subordination to it and issuing a Palestinian currency.

2. Review economic and fiscal legislations and regulations.

3. Foster the appropriate legal and procedural environment to encourage investment and enact additional vital economic laws, such as the law of preventing monopoly and the law of customs.

4. Endeavor to establish a "resisting economy" and encourage self-dependency; shun extravagance and abuse; avoid unproductive projects or those that damage social and moral matrices, such as nightclubs, gambling parlors, etc.

5. Thoroughly consider the wide distribution of projects so as to protect them and lessen the likelihood that the enemy will strike these projects or impose siege or sanctions.

6. Reconsider international economic agreements, taking into consideration the special circumstances of the Palestinian economy. The following are among the most important agreements that will be reviewed:

—Paris economic agreement

—Free trade agreement with the United States of America

—Partnership agreement with the European Union

—Economic cooperation agreements with Egypt and Jordan

7. Develop economic and trade relations with the Arab and Islamic world by concluding preferential trade agreements that will contribute to the development of Palestinian economy and assist it in ending its subordination to the Israeli economy.

8. Formulate economic policies (fiscal, monetary, operational, commercial, industrial, and agricultural) that seek (during the term of the PLC, which lasts four years) to accomplish balanced economic development, bolster local resources, protect vulnerable groups, preserve social solidarity, stabilize prices and wages, combat poverty, reduce unemployment, keep inflation under control, achieve economic growth, and improve individual standard of living.

9. Develop the infrastructure to meet the requirements of the industrial, agricultural, and public services sectors; concentrate on training and qualifying the Palestinian labor force so as to fulfill the needs of the Palestinian market, and consequently solve the problem of dependence on the Israeli market for employment.

10. Protect public property and assets and utilize them in a manner that brings general benefit to current and future generations. This requires implementing an ambitious program of fiscal and administrative reform in PNA agencies and departments, and using international aid to best achieve the objectives of comprehensive development, in order to end extravagance and misappropriation and thus achieve social justice.

11. Review the prices of gas and other petroleum products and of electricity, telephone, and water so as to alleviate the burden borne by citizens.

12. Attend to Palestinian production sectors by implementing the recommendations of serious scientific studies, especially those that seek to develop the internal resources of the Palestinian economy.

13. Develop the Palestinian trade and customs policy so as to correspond with the development needs of the Palestinian economy and the objectives of Palestinian foreign trade.

14. Reformulate the income tax law to make tax and therefore ease the burden on low earners; and amend indirect taxation in the Palestinian economy and reduce the value added tax so as to correspond to the Palestinian growth level.

17. QUESTIONS PERTAINING TO LABOR AND LABORERS

1. Respect, develop, and encourage the activities of trade unions and specialized professional associations.

2. Set a minimum wage for the various labor sectors so as to guarantee an acceptable standard of decent living.

3. Implement a serious national plan to deal with unemployment. The plan should rely on developing the local resources of the Palestinian economy and the appropriate use of funds (whether local or through international aid).

4. Disseminate labor culture and awareness of rights and duties among all workers in the various sectors using different legitimate means and methods.

5. Include workers in all sectors in the comprehensive health insurance system.

6. Develop labor law to guarantee the rights of laborers, including their right to form and join unions, and to ensure justice for workers in all production sectors.

7. Link workers' wages and salaries to the inflation index.

18. Transport and Passages

1. Repair and modernize all roads throughout the homeland.

2. Construct new roads connecting towns and villages; citizens displaced reserve the right to be compensated.

3. Affirm the importance of active and free communication between the West Bank and the Gaza Strip.

4. Open free passages between Palestine and Egypt and between Palestine and Jordan and reject any degree of foreign intervention in these passages.

5. Endeavor to open the port and the airport so as to contribute to the development of the Palestinian economy and facilitate communication among the children of the one people, inside and outside.

Conclusion

The blessed al-Aqsa Intifada has created new facts on the ground that have rendered the Oslo program a thing of the past, and different parties, including the Zionist occupation, have already spoken about "burying Oslo." Our people today are more united, more aware, and more invincible. Hamas is approaching the elections having, with the help of Allah and in cooperation with all the honorable ones, reinforced the method of resistance and engraved it in the minds, hearts, and souls of our people.

Brothers and sisters the voters,
This is our manifesto, which we submit to you. We share your ambition and place our hand in yours. We do not claim to create miracles and we do not possess a magic wand.

However, together we aim and proceed toward achieving our national project along the path toward our greater goals: a single, free, and guided umma.

Brothers and sisters the voters,
Responsibility is mutual; righteous deeds are rewarded by the Almighty Allah.

Our approach relies on trustworthy and qualified representatives who pledge sincerity to Allah and loyalty to Him, to the people, and to the cause. So, rest assured that they will fulfill their promises and prove to be truthful to their slogans.

Brothers and sisters the voters,
When you stand before the ballot box, remember your responsibility when you meet the Almighty Allah. You are entrusted with your vote in choosing your representative to the Legislative Council. When this representative speaks and discusses issues pertaining to religion, to the homeland, and to future, he or she acts on your behalf. So make sure you make the right choice, through which you aim to please your Lord and your Prophet, peace be upon him. "Truly the best of persons for you to employ is the [one] who is strong and trustworthy."

Yes, make the right choice for your happiness and the happiness of your people, God-willing. "Islam is the Solution."
This is our path toward change and reform.
Our program is our means to rebuild the society that has been destroyed by occupation and to protect its resistance. Our program is our course toward bolstering Islamic-national unity along the path of full liberation. Our program is the program of the entire people and the entire homeland.

(And say: "Work [righteousness]: soon will Allah observe your work, and His Messenger, and the Believers: soon will you be brought back to the Knower of what is hidden and what is open: then will He show you the truth of all that you did" [Sura al-Tawbah 9:105].)

Brothers and sisters the voters,
Your vote is a testimony, so testify nothing but the truth.

Notes

NOTE: Unless otherwise noted, all translations from the Arabic by Azzam Tamimi.

INTRODUCTION

[1] Published in 2000 by the Institute of Palestine Studies (IPS) in Washington, DC. This is a slightly updated version of his Arabic work, *Hamas: Al-fikr wa al-mumarasah al-siyasiyah,* published in 1996 by IPS in Beirut.

[2] Matthew Levitt, *Hamas: Politics, Charity, and Terrorism in the Service of Jihad* (New Haven: Yale University Press, 2006).

[3] Erlanger's review appeared in the 23 June 2006 edition of the *International Herald Tribune* entitled: "Hamas as a Terror 'Apparatus.'"

[4] Barry Rubin, "A Review that Speaks Volumes," the *Jerusalem Post* 26 June 2006.

[5] Hassam al-Banna, *Baynal-'ams wal-yawm* (Between yesterday and today) (Beirut: Al-Risalah, 1975), 250–251.

1. THE BEGINNINGS

[1] Sheikh Ahmad Yassin's testimony was broadcast by Aljazeera Arabic satellite channel between 17 April and 5 June 1999. The interviews were recorded with the sheikh during his visit to Qatar in the spring of 1998. This reference is henceforth referred to as "Yassin's Aljazeera testimony." The series of eight recorded interviews were conducted by Aljazeera anchor Ahmad Mansur for his weekly program "Shaid 'Ala Al-'Asr" (Witness To the Age). The full transcript is also available in a book edited by Ahmad Mansur, *Al-Shaykh Ahmad Yassin, shahid 'ala 'asr al-intifada* (Sheikh Ahmad Yassin, a Witness to the Age of the Intifada) (Beirut: Arab Scientific Publishers and Dar Ibn Hazm, 2003).

[2] The first three leaders named have already been assassinated by the Israelis. The first to be liquidated was Salah Shihadah, in the early hours of 23 July 2002. An Israeli F-16 dropped a 1,000-pound bomb on the apartment building where he lived in the densely populated neighborhood of al-Daraj, killing him, his wife, and several others. Sheikh Ahmad Yassin was killed on 22 March 2004 as he left a mosque after dawn, when an Apache helicopter fired rockets, killing him, his guards, and several

worshippers. Dr. Abd al-Aziz al-Rantisi was killed on 17 April 2004, when Israeli helicopters fired rockets at the car he was traveling in, killing him, and three of his associates. What is significant about this group of seven is that they were all refugees (born either prior to the Nakba or afterward). Until the 1967 war, which saw Gaza come under Israeli occupation, the leadership of the Ikhwan in Gaza came from among the traditional affluent and influential families of the Strip. Thereafter, however, the leadership has almost always come from among the refugees.

3   In the aftermath of the creation of the State of Israel on nearly two-thirds of British Mandate Palestine in 1948, the West Bank and the Gaza Strip became distinct and separate geographical units. An armistice concluded in 1949 between the newly founded Israeli state and the neighboring Arab countries placed the West Bank, including East Jerusalem, under Jordanian Hashemite rule while the Gaza Strip was put under Egyptian military administration. The West Bank was eventually annexed to Jordan in 1950 and Jordanian citizenship was extended to its Palestinian inhabitants.

4   Until Egypt lost control of the Gaza Strip, Palestinian political activists suffered the same fate as their comrades in Egypt. In the mid-sixties, when Abd al-Nasir clamped down on the Ikhwan of Egypt, executing several of its leaders, including Sayyid Qutb, Gaza witnessed a heavy suppression of Islamic activities and the arrest of individuals suspected of affiliation to the Ikhwan. Such suspects were usually banned from entering Egypt. Ahmad Yassin was detained for a month from 18 December 1965 and then banned from entering Egypt. He was thus prevented from sitting for his examinations at 'Ain Shams University in Cairo where he was an external student at its Faculty of English Literature.

5   When Israel was created in 1948, two-thirds of the Palestinians were expelled from their homes and have since been living in refugee camps or elsewhere in the diaspora. However, some 156,000 remained in what had become the State of Israel, constituting around 17 percent of the total population of the newly founded state. To the Arabs, these Palestinians, who in 2002 had grown to about 1.23 million, are known as "1948 Palestinians," while the Israelis call them "Israeli Arabs."

6   It was primarily the Battle of al-Karamah, in the Jordan Valley, on 21 March 1968, that rekindled Palestinian national fervor, restoring confidence and hope among Palestinians worldwide. This was trumpeted as a miraculous victory, inflicted by ill-trained and ill-equipped Palestinian resistance fighters against Israel's powerful army. However, it became apparent in time that the credit for victory against the Israelis was due to the Jordanian army units commanded by Mashhur Hadithah al-Jazi, who ignored orders from the Palace to stop firing at the advancing Israelis. Instead, he seized the opportunity to avenge the humiliation of the Arab Jordanian Army in 1967. The units under al-Jazi's command brought delight to the hearts of millions of Arabs. For the first time since the conflict with the Zionists over Palestine had begun, Arab troops charged forward rather than retreating, battering the Israelis, destroying many

[pp. 12–16]

of their armored vehicles and forcing them to retreat. The Palestinians believed, and some may still be under this illusion, that it was al-Fatah under the leadership of Yasir Arafat that accomplished the victory. In fact, Yasir Arafat's main achievement on the day was to claim the victory for himself and his guerrillas. As a consequence, he was decorated by a number of Arab leaders, from Saudi Arabia's King Faysal to Egypt's al-Nasir and Algeria's President Boumedienne. He emerged as the leader of al-Fatah and eventually assumed the chairmanship of the Palestine Liberation Organization (PLO). For more details see the text of the testimonies given by Mashhur Hadithah al-Jazi and then Ahmad Jibril to Aljazeera television's program, "Shahid 'ala al-'Asr." The full texts may be found on <www.aljazeera.net>

[7] On 17 May 1977, under the leadership of Menachem Begin, Likud won its first electoral victory, which represented a major landmark in Israel's history and brought to an end three decades of Labor rule. Likud ruled for fifteen years until it was voted out of power in June 1992.

[8] A number of other Islamic organizations were active at the time, apart from the Ikhwan. Among these were Tablighi Jamaat, an apolitical group that originated in India, and Hizb al-Tahrir al-Islami, a group with the political objective of restoring the caliphate that originated in Palestine in the fifties. There were also several Salafi tendencies, mainly but not exclusively linked with Saudi Arabia, which focused primarily on doctrinal and behavioral aspects of Islam and took little interest in politics.

[9] Izzadin al-Qassam was born in the village of Jabalah, near the Syrian port city of Latakia in 1871. In his youth he traveled to Egypt, where he studied under Sheikh Muhammad Abduh. Back home in Syria, while working as a teacher at Sultan Ibrahim Mosque, he took part in the 1920 revolution against the French occupation. He was sentenced to death but fled to Haifa in 1922, where he presided over the local chapter of the Young Muslims Organization until 1935. He was killed in November 1935 as he led an armed assault on British troops in Palestine. Since then, he has been an emblem of struggle against colonialism across the region.

[10] Dr. Salman Abu Sitta maintains that 531 Palestinian towns and villages were depopulated by Israel in 1948. Salman Abn Sittah, *Haq al-'awdah muqaddas wa qanuni wa mumkin* (The right of return is sacred, legal, and possible) (Beirut: Al-Mu'assah al-'Arabiyahli al-Dirasat wa al-Nashr, 2001), 9.

[11] Yassin's Aljazeera testimony.

[12] Early in the morning of 9 April 1948, commandos of the Irgun (headed by Menachem Begin, who in 1977 became Israel's prime minister) and the Stern Gang (headed by future Israeli Prime Minister Yitzhak Shamir) attacked Deir Yassin, a village with some 750 Palestinian residents. Over 100 men, women, and children were systematically murdered. Israeli apologists have always claimed that the Arabs have exaggerated the massacres. Al-Dawayima was the site of another massacre perpetrated this time not by militiamen but by Israel's army after the state was founded. On 29 October 1948,

as part of an Israeli army operation called Yo'av, 80 to 100 Palestinians, including women and children, were killed by what was described at the time as "the first wave of conquerors." The Israeli daily *'Al Ha-Mishmar* described what happened: "The children they killed by breaking their heads with sticks. There was not a house without dead... One commander ordered a sapper to put two old women in a certain house ... and to blow up the house with them [in it]. One soldier boasted that he had raped a woman and then shot her..." Another description of the massacre was given by the former *mukhtar* (head) of the village, interviewed in 1948 by the Israeli daily *Hadashot*. "The people fled, and every one they saw in the houses, they shot and killed. They also killed people in the streets. They came and blew up my house, in the presence of eye-witnesses." About 75 old people gathered in the mosque to pray. They were all killed. About 35 families were hiding in caves outside al-Dawayima, including some from the previously occupied village of al-Qubayba. When the Israeli forces discovered them, "They told them to come out and get into line and start to walk. And as they started to walk, they were shot by machine guns from two sides... The unit responsible for the massacre was the Eighty-Ninth Battalion, which was part of the Eighth Brigade, commanded by General Yitzhak Sadeh, the founder of the Palmach. In December 1948, during a general discussion of atrocities by an Israeli ministerial committee, the issue of al-Dawayima was raised. Agriculture Minister Aharon Zisling was probably reacting to a letter he had received about the massacre when he said: "This is something that determines the character of the nation... Jews too have committed Nazi acts." Although he complained that the investigation was not proceeding as it should, he agreed with other ministers that Israel should admit nothing outwardly, in order to preserve its image. See Walid Khalidi, *All That Remains: The Palestinian Villages Occupied and Depopulated by Israel in 1948*. (Washington, DC: Institute for Palestine Studies, 1992).

13   When on 15 May 1948 the last British soldier left Palestine, David Ben Gurion announced the establishment of an independent Jewish State, to be known as Israel in two-thirds of the land of Mandatory Palestine. In response, Arab armies invaded from five Arab states—Egypt, Jordan, Lebanon, Syria, and Iraq—ostensibly with the aim of helping the Palestinians and preventing the Zionists from turning Palestine into Israel. But in reality they were neither capable nor serious. More than 750,000 Palestinians became homeless.

14   Yassin's Aljazeera testimony.

15   This hemorrhage of members was what prompted leading Palestinian Ikhwan members outside Palestine to organize a meeting in Cairo in 1960 to set up a clandestine Palestinian Ikhwan organization, to include Palestinian Ikhwan members who were not affiliated to the Jordanian Ikhwan organization. The initiative was intended to shield the movement from the threat of Fatah's encroachment on its cadres. Twelve students and a senior Palestinian Ikhwan member who had come from the Gulf region, where he had been residing, attended the meeting, held in an

apartment overlooking the Nile. Hani Bsisu, who had been working at al-Zubair in Iraq, joined the group and was requested to go to Cairo to head the new organization. In Cairo, Bsisu was arrested by the Egyptian authorities as part of the campaign against the Egyptian Ikhwan in 1965 and soon afterward died in prison. (Source: interview with Ibrahim Ghosheh in Amman, 17 August 2003: Ghosheh was one of the 12 students who attended the founding meeting in Cairo).

16 Kamil al-Sharif, who had been a leading member of the Ikhwan until the mid-1950s and then joined the Hashemite regime as ambassador and then minister, arrived in Kuwait in 1965 with an offer to the leadership of the Palestinian Ikhwan. He met with Hasan Abd al-Hamid, Omar Abu Jbarah, Muhammad Siyam, and Ibrahim Ghosheh, proposing that the Ikhwan should merge with Fatah. After deliberation, the Palestinian Ikhwan responded with a conditional acceptance of the offer. They requested that Fatah commit itself to Islamic ideology and adhere to Islamic values. They were told Fatah could not, and would not, make such a commitment. (Ibid.)

17 Yassin's Aljazeera testimony. Ahmad Yassin reports that a friend who once lived in the neighborhood, a Palestinian officer in the Iraqi army by the name of Muhammad al-A'raj, came to invite him to join Fatah. After a discussion Yassin told al-A'raj: "I object and refuse to work in this manner because it would only embroil the Arab states who are not ready to resist at this stage." Al-A'raj responded by offering a prayer that these states be so embroiled. Yassin responded: "I am not prepared to cause harm to any other Arab country to the benefit of Israel. This approach will not liberate the land seized by Israel."

18 The former Ikhwan founders of Fatah included Khalil al-Wazir (Abu Jihad), Abd al-Fattah al-Humud, Yusuf 'Umayrah, and Sulayman Hamad. They were soon joined by other Ikhwan members, including Muhammad Yusuf al-Najjar, Kamal 'Adwan, Salim al-Za'nun, Fathi al-Bal'awi, Rafiq al-Nathshah, and Salah Khalaf.

19 Yassin's Aljazeera testimony.

20 Ibid., 69–70

21 Ibid., 70.

22 In the aftermath of the June 1967 war, Israel established a military administration to govern the Palestinian residents of the occupied West Bank and Gaza. Under this arrangement, all aspects of Palestinian life were regulated and often severely restricted.

23 Both Abd al-Aziz Awdah and Fathi al-Shiqaqi (b. 1951) were later expelled from the Ikhwan while studying in Egypt; the first in 1974 for alleged misconduct and the other in 1979 for publishing a booklet praising Khomeini, despite a banning order from the leadership of the Ikhwan. The two men later joined forces to form the Palestinian Islamic Jihad. Al-Shiqaqi was assassinated by an Israeli hit squad in Malta on 26 October 1995. Ibrahim al-Maqadmah (b. 1952) and Isma'il Abu Shanab (b. 1950) became leading Hamas figures in Gaza and were both assassinated by the Israelis, the first on 8 March 2003 and the second on 21 August 2003. Musa Abu

Marzuq became Hamas's first Political Bureau chief and has been deputy leader from 1997 until time of writing (2006).

24 Moshe Dayan, Israel's defense minister, proposed the "open bridges" policy following the occupation in 1967 of Jerusalem, the West Bank, and Gaza. The purpose was to allow a route to be opened between the newly occupied territories and the Arab World via Jordan. According to an article by T. Q. Shang in the *Stanford Journal of International Relations*, Dayan's strategy was the employment in Israel of large numbers of Palestinian refugees languishing in camps in the West Bank and the Gaza Strip. Dayan assumed that a rise in living standards would compensate for the loss of political freedoms suffered by Palestinians under permanent Israeli rule, while enabling the Israeli economy to exploit the advantages of a large reservoir of cheap labor. In this manner, Dayan hoped to create an economic foundation for Palestinian participation in the status quo. (See <www.stanford.edu/group/sjir/3.1.03_shang.html>) However, the policy was condemned by the PLO, who suspected that it was mainly intended to normalize the occupation of the territories and pave the way for their annexation. Palestinian nationalists saw the policy as nothing but a safety valve for the jobless and homeless that effectively decreased the resistance of the population against Israeli occupation. With the reopening of the two bridges across the Jordan River (the Damia Bridge and the Allenby or Hussein Bridge), the policy was applied for over twenty years with the dual aim of allowing:

1. the export of surplus Palestinian farm products, potential competition for Israeli produce, to Arab markets, and

2. the passage of Palestinian workers, mainly to the Gulf countries, in order to permit a flow of capital to the occupied territories, which had become an essential market for Israeli goods. With this policy, the Israeli authorities also encouraged Palestinian emigration. Palestinians aged between twenty and forty crossing the bridges were not authorized to return for nine months and could lose their right of residence if they did not return within three years. The reinforcement of border checks and the enforcement of internal blockades on the autonomous enclaves created by the Oslo agreements (1994–1999) have considerably reduced the movements of people and have weakened the "open bridges" policy. See the European Institute for Research on Mediterranean and Euro-Arab Cooperation, November 2001, <www.medea.bc>.

25 Bashir Nafi, interview with the author, London, 15 September 2003.

26 Musa Abu Marzuq, interview with the author, Damascus, 17 July 2004.

27 Ibid.

28 The Ikhwan of Jordan had played an active part in the guerrilla warfare against Israel conducted from Jordanian territory. However, when they saw an imminent clash between the PLO and the Jordanian regime, they decided to disband their own *fidayeen* (guerillas) and close down their bases, known at the time as *Qawa'id al-Shuyukh* (bases of the sheikhs), eight months before the tragic September civil war broke out. Of the prominent Ikhwan members that operated out of these bases were

[pp. 25–26]

Abdullah Azzam and Ahmad Nawfal, who both later left for Egypt to pursue their postgraduate education. In the 1980s, Abdallah Azzam settled in Peshawar as part of the pan-Islamic effort to aid the Afghan cause and was mysteriously assassinated together with two of his sons in 1989.

29 Bashir Nafi is today a British academic. In February 2003 the US authorities accused him of being the UK head of Islamic Jihad. In fact he has never been a member of Islamic Jihad and has strongly opposed the idea of setting up such an organization. Fathi al-Shiqaqi, the founder of Islamic Jihad, its late secretary general, and a fellow student in Cairo in the early 1970s, had claimed Nafi was linked to his organization. (Source: Bashir Nafi, interview with the author in London, 15 September 2003.)

30 Sayyid Qutb (1906–1966), who was given a ten-year prison sentence in 1954 and executed in 1966, joined the Muslim Brotherhood in Egypt after the assassination of its founder Hasan al-Banna in 1949. He soon became the leading ideologue of the group, inspiring its members for no less than 30 years from the mid-1950s to the mid-1980s, long after his execution. In 1953, he was appointed editor of the Ikhwan publication *Al-Ikhwan al-Muslimun*. He then became the director of the Ikhwan's Media Section, soon afterward becoming a member of the Ikhwan's Guidance Council and Executive Committee, the two highest bodies in the organization. Qutb was initially imprisoned for three months in 1954 after Nasir accused the Ikhwan of attempting to assassinate him. As a result of severe torture he was transferred in May 1955 to the prison's hospital and was released due to bad health, only to be rearrested in July 1955 and sentenced to 15 years, most of which he spent in hospital. While in prison he witnessed the persecution of his colleagues. He was particularly affected by the Turrah prison massacre in 1957, when no less than ten of his comrades where killed and many more wounded as prison guards opened fire on them in their cells. That is believed to have been the moment when Qutb began to think of the creation of a disciplined secret cadre of devoted followers. Although he did not explicitly advocate the use of force against the state, self-proclaimed disciples have since extrapolated his theory to justify a belief in the use of violence against authorities that impose un-Islamic laws or modes of behavior on Islamic societies. After an appeal for clemency by Iraqi President A. Arif, Qutb was released from prison in 1964 only to be rearrested in August 1965 and charged with terrorism and sedition. His reaction to the detention, torture, and execution of leading Islamic activists in Egypt was to anathematize everything other than Islam. Democracy and all it entailed was deemed alien and un-Islamic and the other had become the enemy. This rejection was based on the categorization of modern societies, including those in majority-Muslim countries, into Islam and *jahiliyah* as Sayyid Qutb had asserted in *Ma'alim fi al-tariq* (translated into English as *Milestones*), the book for which he was executed in 1966.

31 Musa Abu Marzuq, interview with the author, Damascus, 17 July 2004. On his release from prison, Barud resumed his studies and when awarded the doctorate left

Egypt and settled in Saudi Arabia.

32 Al-Maqadmah was born in Jabalia Camp in the Gaza Strip in 1952 and was assassinated by the Israelis on 8 March 2003. Shihadah was born in Beit Hanun in the Gaza Strip on 3 February 1953 and was assassinated by the Israelis on 23 July 2002.

33 Abu Marzuq, ibid. When the author interviewed Bashir Nafi in September 2003, Nafi continued to insist that he was expelled from the movement as long ago as 1974. It would seem that in fact he simply left out of sympathy for Awdah, who was the Ikhwan's student leader when he gave his *bay'ah* (oath of allegiance) to the group and for whom he had great respect. He could not accept the Ikhwan's reasons, allegedly a misdemeanor of some sort, for terminating Awdah's membership.

34 Bashir Nafi, interview with the author, 15 September 2003. Al-Tayyib apparently never finished his studies. Instead he returned to Lebanon in the mid-1970s and established a publishing house called Al-Dar al-Ilmiyah. He was associated with the distinguished Islamic intellectual publication *Al-Muslim al-mu'asir*. The first issue of this publication, labeled as the "introductory" edition, appeared in November 1974 and included another paper by al-Tayyib entitled "The Islamic Movement's Absolute and Necessary Characteristics and its Acquired Characteristics"; the second issue numbered as issues 1 and 2 combined, appeared in April 1975.

35 Tawfiq al-Tayyib, "Al-Hal al-Islami ma ba'da al-nakbatayn" available online at <www.qudsway.com/Links/Islamyiat/6/Html_Islamyiat6/6hisl1.htm>.

36 Ibid.

37 The caliphate is the name of the political system that came into existence immediately following the death of Prophet Muhammad in 632 and lasted until 1924, when the Ottoman state came to an end. In its golden era, which lasted for only a brief period, the bases of the caliphate included the principles that authority belongs to the umma (people), that decision-making should take place through *shura* (a process of consultation), that rulers and ruled are equal before the law, and that law-making must not contradict the fundamentals of Shari'a, the set of revealed guidelines embodied in the Qur'an. While Shari'a continued to be respected for much of history, *shura* was compromised quite early in the history of Islam.

38 Azzam S. Tamimi, *Rachid Ghannouchi: A Democrat within Islamism*, New York: Oxford University Press, 2001, 18.

39 See chapter eight for a detailed discussion of the concepts of jihad and martyrdom.

40 Imad al-Alami, interview with the author, Damascus, 13 August 2003.

41 According to Khalil al-Wazir (Abu Jihad), the co-founder of al-Fatah, the founding meeting was held in Kuwait in the second half of 1957. Five Palestinians, who came from different locations in the Arab world, attended the meeting. They represented four major groupings of Fatah's founders: the Kuwait group, which included Yasir Arafat, Khalil al-Wazir, and Salah Khalaf; the Qatar group, which included Muhammad Yusuf al-Najjar, Kamal 'Adwan, Mahmud Abbas, and Rafiq al-Natshah; the Saudi Arabia group, which included Sa'id al-Muzayyin, Mu'adh 'Abid, and

Ahmad Wafi; and the Gaza group, which included Fathi al-Bal'awi, As'ad al-Saftawi, Salim al-Za'nun, and 'Awni al-Qishawi.

42 Khalid Mish'al, interview with the author, Damascus, 13 August 2003.

43 Ibid.

44 Hizb al-Tahrir al-Islami was established in Jerusalem in 1953 by Taqiy al-Din al-Nabhani (1909–1977). The party declares itself to be a political party with Islam as its ideology and the revival of the Islamic umma as its goal. It seeks to achieve this goal by creating a single Islamic state, erected on the ruins of existing regimes. It is currently banned in most of the Arab countries, but has lately been active in several Western countries among the Muslim youth.

45 Khalid Misha'al, interview with the author.

2. FROM DA'WAH TO JIHAD

1 Yassin's Aljazeera testimony.

2 From the time of Israel's occupation of the West Bank and the Gaza Strip in 1967, it has relied on an army of Palestinian collaborators. These have supplied its security agencies with valuable information leading to the detention or liquidation of anti-Israel activists or to the foiling of potential attacks against Israeli targets. Collaborators operate in exchange for rewards ranging from small cash payments to the promise of an exit visa to somewhere in America or Europe. One of the main tasks of the collaborators is to recruit others, which they do mainly through blackmail, after embroiling their potential recruits in pornography, sex scandals, drugs, or similar conduct that would disgrace them in the eyes of the Palestinian community.

3 See chapter 1, note 30.

4 The Prophet Muhammad is reported by al-Bukhari as saying: "Islam is based on five [principles]. These are: to testify that there is no deity but Allah and that Muhammad is Allah's Messenger; to perform the *salah* [compulsory prayer]; to pay *zakat* [obligatory charity]; to perform *hajj* [the pilgrimage to the Ka'bah in Mecca]; to perform *saum* [the fast during the month of Ramadan]." The root meaning of the word *zakah* in Arabic relates to growth, and it is used to describe this act of charity because Islam promises the growth of an individual's wealth after giving donations from it to those in need. A Muslim individual is required to pay *zakat* as an expression of obedience to Allah. This goes hand in hand with *salah* (prayers); one is the bodily expression of submission to the Creator, the other is the financial expression of the same.

5 Despite Israeli efforts to prove these charities have funded acts of violence, no evidence to prove such allegations has ever been provided. In the wake of the outbreak of the intifada of 1987, in order to avert any legal sanction, it was ensured that zakat committees and the institutions that supported them abroad were properly licensed. Meticulous care was taken to ensure their activities were absolutely legal and transparent; and not a single penny of the money received by these charities was allowed to slip into other projects, especially not to the military effort, which had its

own discrete sources of funding.

6 The Ikhwan members of the founding committee included Musa Abu Marzuq, who had been working in the United Arab Emirates and was at the time head of the Palestinian Ikhwan chapter there, and a number from Jordan, including Qandil Shakir and Ishaq al-Farhan.

7 Ikhwan sources say that a hit list endorsed by the late Khalil al-Wazir (Abu Jihad), Fatah's second in command under Yasir Arafat, was sent to Gaza in the early 1980s. The persons intended for liquidation were mostly individuals suspected of collaboration with Israel. However, the list included the names of some Islamists working for or associated with the Islamic University but who were not members of the Ikhwan organization. These included Dr. Isma'il al-Khatib, dean of the Arabic Language faculty, who was murdered in his own car in front of his house and in the presence of his nine children. The Ikhwan believed that others would also have been assassinated had the organization not threatened determination to use force if necessary against Fatah, thus obliging it to desist. The temporary president of the university, Riyadh al-Agha, who was Arafat's favorite, had to resign and was replaced by Muhammad Saqr, the Ikhwan's choice. Fatah's plan to impose a new university board was abandoned as Fatah's leaders concluded that this would lead to serious repercussions. One further consideration was that Fatah still had some unfinished business in its fight against the left, represented by the Communist Party and the PFLP, in which it needed the collaboration of the Islamists.

8 The massacre of Sabra and Shatila took place over a period of 40 hours between sunset on Thursday, 16 September and midday on Saturday, 18 September 1982. Sabra Street and Shatila Camp lie in a working-class residential area of Beirut. Unofficial estimates of the number of the victims, by the Lebanese government, the International Committee of the Red Cross, and the Lebanese Red Cross reached around 2,000, 2,750, and 3,000 respectively. These statistics, never officially announced, were communicated in confidence to foreign investigators and writers. The Palestinians believed that the actual figure was much higher. PLO Chairman Yasir Arafat announced at the time that the number of the Sabra and Shatila victims was between 5,000 and 6,000. See Bayan Nuwayhed al-Hout, *Sabra and Shatila: September 1982* (London: Pluto Press, 2004).

9 Abdallah Ramadan Shallah, interview with Ghassan Sharbal, *Al-Hayat* (London), 10 January 2003.

10 The *Christian Science Monitor* of 8 May 1980 reported that among those killed was Elia Hazeev, who had been convicted a year before of breaking into Arab houses in Hebron, beating residents, smashing furniture, and ordering the Arabs to leave Hebron. The Palestinian attack on the settlers, according to the *Christian Science Monitor* report, came a day after the murder of a Palestinian youth who had allegedly attempted to take a rifle away from an Israeli soldier. The attack on the settlers took place in the city center in an area known to the people of Hebron as al-Dabbuya and

[pp.44–50]

called Beit Hadassah by the Israelis. Tension had been mounting there since 1979, when a group of settlers from Kiryat Arba led by the wife of Rabbi Levinger seized a building in the center of the city, making it into a colony. The colony received Israeli army protection since the day it was founded. In the wake of the Palestinian attack on the settlers, however, the Israeli government under Menachem Begin gave its official authorization for what had become in effect a fortified Jewish settlement in the midst of the Arab population of the city center.

[11] Abdullah Azzam was assassinated on 24 November 1989 in Peshawar, Pakistan, aged 48. His assassination remains a mystery and various agencies have been accused of carrying it out, but no one has ever claimed responsibility.

[12] The Fatah leaders of Saraya al-Jihad, Bassim (Hamdi) Sultan, Marwan al-Kayyali, and Muhammad Hasan Bhais were assassinated by the Mossad on 14 February 1988 in the Cypriot port city of Limassol. The three had just entered al-Kayyali's car when a bomb planted in the car was triggered from a distance by remote control, killing all three of them.

[13] Khalid Mish'al, interview with the author, Damascus, 13 August 2003.

[14] This committee, which began as a small group of operatives attached to the department of the Secretariat of the Ikhwan's Executive Office, was in a few years time to grow into the massive network of organizations that collectively became known as the Islamic Resistance Movement (Hamas). As will be seen in chapters four to six, the child outgrew its parent. The failure of both parties to accommodate to the rapid changes within and between them was one of the main factors leading to the tension that strained relations between Hamas and the Ikhwan in Jordan. This was to the advantage of the Jordanian authorities, whose plan to expel Hamas from the country was thus made much easier.

[15] Mu'in Shabib (former student leader at Birzeit University): interview with the author, Manchester, 18 May 2005). The term "harem" may refer to the private quarters of an Arab household where no access is permitted to male strangers; it may also refer to a group of women, wives, and/or concubines in a household.

[16] The two students killed on that day were both from the Gaza Strip. One of them was Jawad Abu Sulmiyah from the Khan Yunis refugee camp; the other was Sa'ib Dhahab from al-Shuja'iyah in the city of Gaza.

[17] Both men were apprehended by the Israelis and are still serving long-term sentences in Israeli detention. Yahya al-Sinwar was arrested on 20 January 1988 and in 1989 was sentenced to a long period in prison. Rawhi Mushtaha was arrested on 13 February 1988 and was sentenced to seven years. However, his sentence was later revised and altered to four life terms plus twenty years.

3. AN ALL-OUT WAR

[1] Yitzhak Rabin, statement attributed to him when he was Israel's minister of defense in the unity government of the late 1980s. Bone-breaking was the policy authorized

by him in a bid to to break the first intifada, whose main weapons for months had been civil disobedience, in the form of strikes, and throwing stones at Israeli occupation troops.

2   From statement in the Knesset by Israeli Prime Minister Rabin, 21 December 1992.

3   Quoted in a booklet entitled *Al-Hurriyah li-shaykh al-intifada al-mubarakah al-mujahid Ahmad Yassin* (Freedom for the Sheikh of the blessed intifada struggler Ahmad Yassin) published by the al-Ikhwan al-Muslimun (Muslim Brotherhood) in Amman, Jordan in 1995 on the anniversary of Sheikh Yassin's detention on 18 May 1989.

4   One of several instances of mass expulsion was that of the 50,000 Palestinian inhabitants of the towns of Lydda and Ramle. Massacres continued even after Israel was established. One notorious case is that of the village of Qibya. The operation at Qibya was carried out in October 1953 by two Israeli units: a paratroop company and Unit 101, a Special Forces unit of the IDF founded and commanded by Ariel Sharon. The Qibya raid led to the deaths of over 60 Palestinians and the demolition of most houses in Qibya, a village in the western part of the West Bank, then under Jordanian control. Many Qibya residents fled, but some stayed, hiding in their homes. On 18 October 1953, the US State Department issued a bulletin denouncing the Qibya raid and demanding that those responsible be "brought to account."

5   Yassin's Aljazeera testimony.

6   Ibid.

7   Ibid. The letter "h" was the first Arabic letter in the word *haraka* (movement), "m" the first letter of the word *muqawama* (resistance) and "s" the second letter of the word *islamiya* (Islamic). Then someone suggested in a leadership meeting that it would be better if the letter "a" was added before the last letter so as to make the abbreviation meaningful on its own. "Hamas" in Arabic means zeal, enthusiasm, or vigor.

8   Born in 1947, al-Quqa was one-and-a-half years old when his family was forced to flee Palestine for safety in the Gaza Strip when Israel was created in 1948. He lived most of his life as a refugee in al-Shati' (Beach) Camp until deported by the Israelis to South Lebanon on 11 April 1988. He was a renowned orator and an influential leader of the Ikhwan in Palestine until his deportation. He was never allowed back into Gaza and died in the United Arab Emirates on 26 October 2005, where he had lived for much of the seventeen years of his exile.

9   He was arrested again on 4 March 1988 and detained until 4 September 1990. Not long afterward, on 14 December 1990, he was re-arrested and then deported straight from prison to South Lebanon on 17 December 1992.

10   Hamas's Charter will be discussed in detail later (See chapter seven).

11   The festival of Id al-Adha (the festival of the sacrifice) falls on the tenth day of the twelfth month (Dhul-Hijjah) of the Islamic (lunar) calendar. For pilgrims performing the rituals in Mecca, the tenth day of Dhul-Hijjah is the culmination of the pilgrimage, when they circumambulate the Ka'bah (the ritual known as *tawaf*), and offer their

sacrifices. For Muslims elsewhere in the world the custom on the day of the Id is to sacrifice an animal to eat and feed the poor. In doing so, they revive the tradition of Abraham, who initiated the ritual of sacrifice when he was excused from the Divine Order to slaughter his only son, Isma'il.

12 Al-Sharatiha was twice detained by the Israelis before but never confessed to anything or informed against anyone, despite the use of torture. On this occasion, however, he could not bear the suffering. The Israeli interrogators told him and his fellow Hamas detainees that they had orders to kill them but that they would do so only very slowly. Al-Sharatiha is serving a sentence of several life terms in solitary confinement.

13 Yassin's Aljazeera testimony. Isma'il Haniyah, who was one of the members of Hamas closest to Sheikh Yassin, reported that he saw the sheikh in detention being severely abused by his interrogators and by the prison guards. He was one of several Hamas detainees who were brought from their cells to see that the sheikh had been apprehended and that therefore the movement had been broken. He saw prison guards turn the sheikh around in his wheelchair and push him forward until he fell. He was left on the floor for hours before he was picked up again and restored to his chair. Haniyah also reported that the sheikh had the hair of his beard plucked and his testicles squeezed until they were swollen.

14 Khalid Mish'al, interview with the author, Damascus, 14 August 2003.

15 Musa Abu Marzuq, interview with the author, Damascus, 17 July 2004.

16 The Temple Mount and Land of Israel Faithful movement was established in 1967. It was founded and is led by Gershon Salomon, a former officer in the Israeli armed forces who claims that he heard the voice of God speaking to him, calling him to continue the work for the redemption of the people of Israel. This, he believes, was a divine call to consecrate himself to the redemption of the Temple Mount.

17 Imad al-Alami is now a member of Hamas's Political Bureau. For a while he was the Hamas representative in Iran but is now stationed in Damascus. Fadl al-Zahhar is the only one of these four deportees to return to Gaza. He returned in 2005 following Israel's withdrawal from the Strip.

18 The charges included the following: 1) Founding the Islamic Resistance Movement (Hamas) and setting up its security apparatus "Majd" and its military apparatus "Al-Mujahidun al-Filastiniyun." 2) Issuing orders for the assassination and liquidation of six persons for their collaboration with the (occupation) authorities. 3) Issuing orders for the assassination of residents involved in crime or immoral acts. 4) Ordering members of "al-Mujahidum al-Filastiniyun" to throw explosive devices at Israeli military vehicles. 5) Ordering elements of "al-Mujahidum al-Filastiniyun" to set fire to a number of fields in Israeli territory. 6) Members of the same organization to fire on an Israeli as he was drilling a well in the south of the Gaza Strip and at an Israeli vehicle that was being driven in the Gaza Strip. 7) Responsibility for eighteen types of weapons found in the possession of elements of "al-Mujahidum al-Filastiniyun"

apparatus, including pistols, an M16 automatic rifle, a Carl Gustav, and a Kalashnikov. 8) Responsibility for the kidnapping and killing of the two Israeli soldiers, Avi Sasportas and Ilan Sa'adon. 9) The illegal transfer of $600,000 to officials within the Hamas movement. 10) Involvement in an attempt by certain prisoners to escape from Israeli prisons.

[19] This refers to the official Israeli–Palestinian talks in Washington, DC, which began in December 1991 in the wake of the October 1991 Madrid conference between Israel and the Arabs. The PLO was not officially involved, but the Palestinian team that took part in both the conference and the talks had its approval and received instructions from it. The talks went through ten rounds without arriving at an agreement. They ended when, to the astonishment of the Palestinians delegates to the Washington talks, it was revealed in August 1993 that Israel and the PLO had initialled an agreement negotiated in secret talks in Norway. A month later, the PLO and Israel signed the "Oslo Accords" in a ceremony held at the White House in Washington, DC.

[20] Ghassan D. al-Jarban, *Usud Hamas, harb al-ayyam al-sab'ah* (Hamas lions, the war of the seven days), Part I. Amman: Filastin al-Muslimah Publications, 1993, pp. 186–187.

[21] The Fourth Geneva Convention was concluded on August 12, 1949. Article 33 states: "No protected person may be punished for an offence he or she has not personally committed. Collective penalties and likewise all measures of intimidation or of terrorism are prohibited. Pillage is prohibited. Reprisals against protected persons and their property are prohibited." Article 49 states, in part: "Individual or mass forcible transfers, as well as deportations of protected persons from occupied territory to the territory of the Occupying Power or to that of any other country, occupied or not, are prohibited, regardless of their motive."

[22] Ibn Taymiyah (AH 661–728/1263–1328 CE), more fully Taqi al-Din Abu al-'Abbas Ahmad Ibn 'Abd al-Halim Ibn 'Abd al-Salam al-Harrani al-Dimashqi, was a jurisconsult, theologian, and Sufi. He was born in Harran, and at the age of six he fled with his father and brothers to Damascus during the Mongol invasions. Ibn Taymiyah devoted himself from early youth to various Islamic sciences (Qur'an, hadith, and legal studies), and was a voracious reader of books on sciences that were not taught in the regular institutions of learning, including logic, philosophy, and *kalam*.

[23] Musa Abu Marzuq, interview with the author, Damascus, 17 July 2004.

[24] Ibid.

4. INTO JORDAN

[1] Khalid Mish'al, interview with the author, Damascus, 14 August 2004.

[2] The government of the State of Kuwait continued to give financial support to the PLO, and especially to the Fatah organization, until the early 1980s, either directly or through the Arab League. There was then a change in policy, prompted by charges

[pp.67–74]

of corruption and misappropriation of funds leveled at the PLO leadership. Public pressure led to a new system, whereby funds raised by the government or donated by it began to be transferred directly to projects or institutions such as universities in the Palestinian territories without reference to the PLO. This shift in policy soured relations between the PLO leadership and the Kuwaiti government. By the late 1980s the PLO and its secular factions had lost much of their support within the Palestinian and Kuwaiti communities to Hamas. This, some believe, explains why Yasir Arafat was so overt in his support of Saddam Hussein's annexation of Kuwait. It was a miscalculation for which he, and half a million Palestinians in Kuwait, paid dearly.

3   The second year of renewed democracy in Jordan began in November 1990 in the midst of the Gulf crisis, at a time when the country had never enjoyed such a degree of national unity and mutual understanding between the regime and its opponents. The head of the Ikhwan's parliamentary bloc, Dr. Abdullatif Arabiyat, was elected to the post of speaker of Parliament, and the Ikhwan accepted an offer by Prime Minister Mudar Badran to hold five cabinet positions. They asked for and were given the portfolios for Awqaf and Islamic affairs, education, health, justice, and social affairs. The four months of honeymoon and power sharing came to an abrupt end when the prime minister was replaced in preparation for the launch of the US-sponsored Middle East peace process.

4   Ghosheh was appointed as a representative of Hamas for the first time in September 1990, and became Hamas's representative in Jordan a few months later. One of his early missions in this capacity was to represent Hamas in the Islamic delegation that mediated between Iraq and Saudi Arabia after Saddam Hussein invaded Kuwait in August 1990. The delegation, which comprised leading Islamic figures from around the world, visited Iraq, Iran, and Saudi Arabia in the hope of preventing the US war on Iraq, though to no avail. He was officially appointed official spokesman of Hamas by its Political Bureau upon its formation in 1992, at which time Muhammad Nazzal was named Hamas's representative in Jordan.

5   Ibrahim Ghosheh, interview with the author, Amman, 17 August 2003

6   Musa Abu Marzuq, interview with the author, Damascus, 17 July 2004.

7   According to some reports Ibrahim Ghosheh also took part in the meeting.

8   Muhammad Nazzal, interview with the author, Amman, 16 February 2004.

9   Ibid.

10   Musa Abu Marzuq, interview with the author.

11   Khalid Mish'al, interview with the author, Damascus, 14 August 2003.

12   Muhammad Nazzal, interview with the author.

13   For the full text of the agreement, see <www.kinghussein.gov.jo/peacetreaty.html>.

14   The Israelis have constantly failed to understand that these young men do not see martyrdom as a defeat. For them, it is a positive achievement no less in value

than victory itself. This concept derives from verse 52 of Sura (al-Tawbah) of the Qur'an (Say: Can you expect for us [any fate] other than one of two glorious things [martyrdom or victory]?).

15 Musa Abu Marzuq, interview with the author.

16 Ibid.

17 Ibrahim Ghosheh, interview with the author.

18 M. Nazzal, interview with the author.

19 Musa Abu Marzuq, interview with the author.

20 The US first designated Hamas as a terrorist organization and banned any transactions with it when President Clinton issued Executive Order 12947 of 23 January 1995: "Prohibiting Transactions With Terrorists Who Threaten To Disrupt the Middle East Peace Process." Hamas was the fifth organization on the list annexed to the executive order, which described it and the others as "terrorist organizations which threaten to disrupt the Middle East peace process." In addition to Hamas, the list also included the Abu Nidal Organization (ANO), the Democratic Front for the Liberation of Palestine (DFLP), Hezbollah, Islamic Gama'at (IG), Jihad, Kach, Kahane Chai, Palestinian Islamic Jihad-Shiqaqi faction (PIJ-S), Palestine Liberation Front-Abu Abbas faction (PLF-Abu Abbas), the Popular Front for the Liberation of Palestine (PFLP), and the Popular Front for the Liberation of Palestine-General Command (PFLP-GC).

21 Reporting to the leadership in Amman on the proceedings of a special rally held in Beirut in support of Musa Abu Marzuq days after his arrest, Hamas official Mustafa al-Liddawi spoke of the resentment of leading figures within the Lebanese and Palestinian national movement.

22 According to the US State Department, foreign terrorist organizations are foreign organizations that are designated by the secretary of state in accordance with section 219 of the Immigration and Nationality Act (INA), as amended. Section 212 (a) (3) (B) of the INA defines "terrorist activity" to mean: "any activity which is unlawful under the laws of the place where it is committed (or which, if committed in the United States, would be unlawful under the laws of the United States or any State)." Section 140 (d) (2) of the Foreign Relations Authorization Act, Fiscal Years 1988 and 1989, defines "terrorism" as "premeditated, politically motivated violence perpetrated against noncombatant targets by sub-national groups or clandestine agents."

23 Musa Abu Marzuq, interview with the author.

24 Ibid.

25 Peres's failure to be re-elected was also connected to another blunder, when, as part of a 17-day bombardment of Lebanon codenamed "Operation Grapes of Wrath," Israeli forces shelled a UN base at Qana on 18 April 1996, killing about 100 of 800 civilians sheltering there. The UN has always maintained that the attack was intentional.

[pp.85–93]

26 Bassam al-'Umush ceased to be a member of the Ikhwan after he rebelled against the movement's decision to boycott the 1997 parliamentary elections. He contested the election and was appointed by King Hussein as minister of administrative development. He then served as Jordan's ambassador to Iran before returning to academic life, teaching Islamic theology at Zarqa University.

27 From the joint statement read by President Clinton during his joint press conference with Egyptian President Hosni Mubarak at the conclusion of the Sharm al-Sheikh summit on 13 March 1996. For a transcript see <www.presidency.ucsb.edu/us/index.php?pid=52537>.

28 Five of these men considered suing the GID officers for abusing them and using torture on them during interrogation but were prevented from doing so because Jordan does not permit the GID or any of its officers to be sued.

29 Mish'al was Abu Marzuq's deputy when the latter was apprehended in the United States. When Abu Marzuq left for the United States, his term as head of the Political Bureau was nearing its end. Hamas's Majlis al-Shura (its highest authority) elected Mish'al as head. However, he insisted on not claiming the title in public out of courtesy and in sympathy with his colleague Abu Marzuq.

30 Ibrahim Ghosheh, interview with the author, Amman, 17 August 2003.

31 Ibid.

32 This story was reported to the author by Muhammad Nazzal, interviewed in Amman, on 16 February 2004. The allegations were referred to in the US State Department's report entitled: "Jordan Country Report on Human Rights Practices for 1996," Bureau of Democracy, Human Rights, and Labor, 30 January 1997. According to the report, "Opposition deputies charged the government with detaining and torturing Essam al-Najjar, a Hamas supporter, for two weeks. They alleged that al-Najjar was beaten in the stomach, throat, and on the soles of his feet, was cursed by guards, and had excrement wiped in his face."

5. THE MISH'AL AFFAIR

1 Yassin, following his release from an Israeli detention center on 1 October 1997.

2 Saudi Crown Prince Abdullah Ibn Abd al-Aziz, greeting Yassin when he received him after the hajj in April 1998.

3 Yassin's Aljazeera testimony.

4 The full title of the book is *Al-Majmu' sharh al-muhathab*. *Al-Muhathab* was authored by Abu Ishaq al-Shirazqi (d. AH476/1083CE). As it stands today, *Al-Majmu'* is a comprehensive manual of Islamic law according to the Shafi'ite school of jurisprudence. The 23-volume elucidation of *Al-Muhathab* was begun by Abu Zakariyya Yahya Ibn Sharaf al-Nawawi (1233–1278 CE). The work was continued but not finished by Taqiy al-Din Ali bin Abd al-Kafi al-Subki (d. AH756/1355CE). It was finally completed by Muhammad Najib al-Muti'i, who died recently.

5 As an act performed by the tongue, *dhikr* is the utterance of expressions that stand for

tasbih, *tahmid*, and *tamjid* — exaltation, praise, and glorification.

6 The Qur'an is divided into 30 *juz'* (pl. *ajza'*). The recitation of a single *juz'* at moderate speed would take at least an hour.

7 Some officers in the Shin Bet, Israel's domestic intelligence agency, were reportedly quoted as saying that they would celebrate Sheikh Yassin's release as much as his supporters in Gaza.

8 Islamic Jihad claimed responsibility for the attack carried out by two of its members. Anwar Sukkar blew himself up first, killing four Israeli soldiers at a bus stop used mostly by Israel army conscripts. Three minutes later Salah Shakir detonated his bomb, killing many more troops.

9 Yassin's Aljazeera testimony.

10 The Kidon unit, named for the Hebrew word for bayonet, is part of Israel's overseas intelligence service, Mossad, and specializes in assassinating Israel's enemies. Although their operations are illegal under international law, they act under orders from the highest political leadership in Israel. The unit has been responsible for killing scores of Palestinian leaders around the world. These have included Khalil al-Wazir (Abu Jihad), assassinated in Tunis on 16 April 1988; Salah Khalaf (Abu Iyad), assassinated in Tunis on 15 January 1991 together with his adviser Fakhri al-Umari (Abu Muhammad) and the PLO security chief Hayil Abd al-Hamid (Abu al-Hawl); Islamic Jihad's Fathi al-Shiqaqi, gunned down in Malta on his way back from a conference in Libya on 26 October 1995; and Hamas's Yahya "Engineer" Ayyash, assassinated using a booby-trapped mobile phone on 6 January 1996. Scores of Palestinian activists were eliminated by Mossad throughout the 1970s and the 1980s in Europe and the Middle East.

11 Muhammad Abu Sayf, interview with the author, Damascus, 16 July 2004.

12 Muhammad Nazzal, interview with the author, Amman, 16 February 2004.

13 According to press reports published in Israel at the time, four Arab collaborators were involved in the plot. One of these was the tenant of an office on the second floor of the same building where Mish'al's office was on the fifth floor. This office, whose actual purpose was to spy on Mish'al and his office employees, was ostensibly the headquarters of a branch of a Jordanian-Israeli diamond company owned jointly by this person, together with an Israeli partner. While the latter fled to Israel after the attempted assassination, the Arab suspect was arrested by the Jordanian police and interrogated. He was later released and allowed to go to Tel Aviv. Press reports also spoke of two Mossad agents of Jordanian nationality, who helped to monitor Mish'al's movements and observe his daily routine for the hit squad. In total, the Kidon unit that carried out the assassination attempt comprised 13 agents and collaborators excluding the Mossad station manager in Amman, who also played an active and crucial role in the plot.

14 According to Ibrahim Ghosheh, it was reported in the press at the time that the idea of demanding the release of Sheikh Ahmad Yassin came from a senior Mossad

official. Efraim Halevy, who was well acquainted with King Hussein, was reported to have suggested it to the king. Halevy made this claim in his book entitled *Man in the Shadows: Inside the Middle East Crisis with a Man Who Led the Mossad* (New York: St. Martin's Press, 2006). This lends credence to the claim that senior Israeli intelligence officers had indeed been for years in favor of releasing Sheikh Yassin. In 1998, Halevy succeeded Danny Yatom as head of Mossad and served until 2002. Since 2003 he has been head of the Center for Strategic and Policy Studies at the Hebrew University of Jerusalem.

15 Following his visit to the sheikh, Yasir Arafat claimed in a press statement that Sheikh Yassin told him he accepted the Oslo Accords and supported the peace process as conducted by the PLO. Asked about this, Musa Abu Marzuq, who had been present, denied categorically that the topic was raised during the brief visit. During the following months, several attempts were made to create the illusion that two currents of opinion on the matter had existed within Hamas, one moderate and pragmatic, led by Sheikh Yassin, and the other dogmatic and extremist, led by Khalid Mish'al.

16 BBC News, "Israel Spy Chief Blames PM," 4 November 1997 <news.bbc.co.uk/1/hi/world/middle_east/21858.stm>.

17 The Jordanian government responded with a statement welcoming Danny Yatom's resignation. The Jordanian foreign minister, Jawad al-Anani, said he hoped the resignation would lead to better relations between the two countries. As if accepting that Prime Minister Netanyahu was completely innocent, al-Anani told an Israeli radio station that the move was a step in the right direction toward the resumption of cooperation on security intelligence, which had been suspended by King Hussein after the attempted assassination.

18 The convicted spy Jonathan Pollard, serving a life sentence for espionage on behalf of Israel in the US, complained about Israel's success in obtaining the quick release of its Mossad hit men from Jordan while failing to secure his release for 13 years. On 28 October 1997 he was quoted as saying: "Clearly this Mish'al affair shows that the [Israeli] government knows how to get its agents out." (Lucille Barnes, "Arafat Reported 'Close to Despair,'" *Washington Report on Middle East Affairs* [Jan/Feb 1998]: 66–68 <www.washington-report.org/backissues/0198/9801066.htm>).

19 Khalid Mish'al, interview with the author, Damascus, 14 August 2003.

20 Ibrahim Ghosheh, interview with the author, Amman, 17 August 2003.

21 Commenting on the significance of Sheikh Yassin's hajj, the present author was quoted as saying at the time: "The hajj presented a golden opportunity for someone like him to receive invitations from so many Arab capitals and to talk to people—not only about Hamas, but to talk to them about the Palestinian problem because what Sheikh Yassin represents is a symbol of Palestinian resistance, rather than just one faction within Palestine. This is what distinguishes him from anybody else. His presence does not mean a partisan affair. That is why he was met with a sort of veneration and

respect. His visits came at a time when the governments and people were becoming increasingly frustrated with the peace process. The way in which they received him and the statements they made gave greater legitimacy to Palestinian armed resistance as exemplified by Hamas." Grace Halsell, "Palestinian Islamist Azzam Tamimi Defines Hamas, PLO Differences and Calls for Dialogue With Both," *Washington Report on Middle Eastern Affairs* (December 1998): 23–24. <www.washington-report. org/backissues/1298/9812023.html>.

22 The channel broadcast the eight recorded episodes between 17 April and 5 June 1999.

23 The killers of Muhyiddin al-Sharif sought to camouflage the murder by staging an explosion in the warehouse where his body was found. According to a report prepared by al-Raqib, the Palestinian Human Rights Monitoring Group, an explosion occurred at 8:30 PM on 29 March 1998 in a warehouse in the industrial zone of Ramallah. A naked body was found at the scene of the incident with one severed leg and fractures in the other. However, the injuries were inflicted on the victim prior to the explosion. According to the coroner's report at least four hours had elapsed between shooting the victim and the car explosion that took place inside the warehouse. The cause of death was said to be hemorrhage in the chest and loss of blood from the wounds caused by the three shots. Fire was not the cause of death. When the body of the victim was identified two days later, and it became clear that it was Muhyiddin al-Sharif, Jibril al-Rujub, the PA top security man in the West Bank, insinuated that al-Sharif was liquidated by his own colleagues in Hamas and not by Israel. He went further to claim that al-Sharif would not be the first to be liquidated by his own organization.

24 Imad Awadallah, 29, and Ghassan al-Addassi, 19, were accused of killing al-Sharif. Both of them were arrested on the day of his murder, 29 March 1998. The first was severely tortured until he mysteriously escaped from Jericho Prison around 15 August 1998. He published a letter dated 18 August detailing what happened to him and naming the Palestinians officials who were directly involved in interrogating him, who offered him various deals in exchange for his confession to the murder. Yasir Arafat's aides and top security chiefs al-Tayyib Abd al-Rahim, Jibril al-Rujub, Amin al-Hindi, al-Haj Isma'il Jabr, Tawfiq al-Tirawi, and Muhammad al-Jabarni feature in his letter. They first wanted him to confess that he killed al-Sharif by mistake. When he refused, they offered to release him if he said that al-Sharif was executed for collaborating with the Israelis or for some act of indecency. On 10 September 1998 both Imad and his brother Adil Awadallah, who had been on the run, were ambushed by Israeli armed units and liquidated. As for Addasi, he was similarly tortured and offered various deals. The Palestinian Authority stated that he had willingly confessed to killing al-Sharif. However, he denied this in a statement released in the West Bank and the Gaza Strip. This prompted the Palestinian High Court to order his release on 6 October 1998 due to the illegality of the measures adopted during his detention in violation of articles 100 and 103 of the Court Penal Sentences No. 9/1961.

[pp.113–123]

6. OUT OF JORDAN

1   Khalid Mish'al, speaking on the Aljazeera satellite channel from Doha, Qatar, 26 November 1999.

2   Ibrahim Ghosheh, rejecting a demand from the GID deputy director to write a statement asking King Abdallah of Jordan for pardon. Bangkok Airport, 29 June 2001.

3   State Department spokesman James P. Rubin, press statement, 20 October 1998 <telaviv.usembassy.gov/publish/peace/october98/102098a.html>.

4   For the text of the Wye River Memorandum see <www.state.gov/www/regions/nea/981023_interim_agmt.html>.

5   *Jordan Times*, Amman, Jordan, 23 April 1998.

6   Ibrahim Ghosheh, interview with the author, Amman, 17 August 2003. Ghosheh said he had been warned by Ikhwan officials at the seminar before he spoke that if he criticized the Wye River Memorandum he might be detained by the GID. They knew this was a very sensitive issue over which the regime was unlikely to tolerate any dissent.

7   *Assabeel*, Amman, 2 November 1998.

8   Khalid Mish'al, quoted by *Arabicnews,* 18 November 1998.

9   *Al-Majd* (Amman), 9 November 1998.

10 Muhammad Nazzal, interview with the author, Amman, 16 February 2004. What the Hamas leaders in Jordan heard from Abu Dayyah at this meeting was in due course reiterated by the Jordanian Authorities to justify the deportation of Hamas leaders and the insistence on denying them the right to return to Jordan until they decided where their loyalties were.

11 Ibrahim Ghosheh, interview with the author.

12 He was eventually retired by King Abdullah as GID director on 9 November 2000. This followed the king's appointment of Ali Abu al-Raghib as prime minister on 19 June 2000. Apparently, Abu al-Raghib and al-Battikhi did not see eye to eye on a number of issues. Other observers in Jordan speculated that the king wanted to get rid of al-Battikhi before he turned against the king himself. This is evident by the fact that al-Battikhi, who had held the post of adviser to the king since October 1999, had to give up his palace job when the king appointed him to the Senate. In March 2002, al-Battikhi was officially indicted in a massive fraud operation. He was accused of illegally using his credentials as the head of intelligence to sign orders for a company called "Global Business," which allowed the company's manager, 31-year-old Majd al-Shamayleh, to obtain loans amounting to $130 million from four Jordanian banks. In July 2003 al-Battikhi was found guilty and sentenced to eight years' imprisonment, reduced by his former deputy and successor as GID Chief Sa'd Khayr to four years and transmuted from imprisonment to house arrest at his private seaside villa in the Jordanian port city of Aqaba.

13 The writer used a pseudonym but many people thought he was Ibrahim Gharaybah,

a former Ikhwan member who was later expelled from the organization. He was a leading voice in the campaign from within the Ikhwan against Hamas. He was believed to speak for the trend within the Ikhwan that believed that there was no room in Jordan for a Palestinian Islamic movement and that Hamas Jordanian leaders must choose whether they wanted to be Jordanian or Palestinian.

[14] The GID seemed to favor action against the leaders of Hamas when they were in Tehran, thinking that cracking down on them while in Iran would draw less condemnation from the world's public opinion because of Iran's reputation of association with extremism and Hamas with terrorism. A BBC correspondent in the region reported that the timing of the office closure might not be coincidental. He added that Israel — which had been pressing Jordan to expel Hamas — would be pleased, but the move could cause difficulties for the Palestinian leader, Yasir Arafat, who was trying to mend fences with Hamas. (BBC World Service on 30 August 1999)

[15] Muhammad Nazzal, interview with the author.

[16] Ibrahim Ghosheh, interview with the author, Amman, 21 August 2003. Ghosheh said he could not imagine himself living permanently away from Jordan. He said he would rather be in Jordan without the freedom to travel abroad than be abroad and free to travel anywhere except to Jordan.

[17] The media and the security agents were waiting for Nazzal to speak because this had been leaked earlier. His arrest would have made headlines but it never happened. The following day it was reported in the press that Nazzal attended the rally and that he was disguised in Arab traditional robes. In fact he never entered the hall where the rally was being held, but someone, seemingly, spotted him leaving the premises in his traditional Arab costume, which he put on just before he departed in order to evade the authorities.

[18] Muhammad Nazzal, interview with the author.

[19] Ghosheh was convinced that it was the GID that tried to convince the Jordanian Ikhwan to dissuade the Hamas leaders from returning. However, this is vehemently denied by the Ikhwan.

[20] When the Hamas officials and their companions were handed over the police, they were handcuffed. Ghosheh tried to resist; he did not want to be handcuffed with his hands behind his back. His resistance was in vain. Before boarding the van that took him and the others to court he spoke to one of the officers saying: "Shame on you; you are detaining the most honorable people in Jordan, those that resist Zionist occupation. You know well that as a result of our incarceration the Zionist ambassador in Amman must be celebrating in jubilation." He recalls that several Jordanian police officers lowered their heads and remained silent. He could tell that they were ashamed but could not disobey orders. Someone came forward and ordered them angrily to take the prisoners away.

[21] He was put on the same plane which took him back to Dubai, where he stayed for a

couple of days and then left for Damascus.

22 Ghosheh denied that he had any weapons in his office, and that whatever the GID claimed they found there must be something they planted to frame him, as they had done when they arrested him in 1997. The military prosecutor then shouted at him and abused him. His lawyer, Salih al-Armuti, rose to protest, saying to the prosecutor: "Lower your voice: the person you are speaking to is a *mujahid* [struggler] who is respected by the entire people of Jordan."

23 Ghosheh, who is an engineer, wrote a memorandum to the prison warden suggesting a better design for the beds, attaching a drawing of his proposed design.

24 They complained that they were treated badly in the hospital. While receiving intravenous nutrition in one arm, each hunger striker would have the other arm chained tightly to the bed.

25 Ghosheh is not usually comfortable with government officials but was impressed by the politeness and compassion shown by Minister Haddad. His kind gesture was critical in persuading the group to call off its hunger strike. Hamzah Haddad is a highly respectable lawyer in the Arab world. No longer a minister, he is now the president of the Law and Arbitration Center and the assistant secretary-general of the Arab Union of International Arbitration (AUIA) for the Arab Eastern Region.

26 Some people speculated at the time that al-Ma'aytah might have been collaborating with the authorities when he arranged to meet al-Rishiq. However, Hamas leaders, including al-Rishiq and Nazzal, did not agree. Apparently al-Ma'aytah had just met a US diplomat in Jordan and wished to tell al-Rishiq what he had learned that was relevant to Hamas. The telephone calls between al-Rishiq and al-Khatib had led the GID agents to them.

27 Al-Khatib, who was later released on bail together with al-Ma'yatah, reported hearing al-Rishiq being tortured. He heard him shout at his interrogators in pain: "You cannot be Arabs or Muslims; you are Israelis." Al-Rishiq later described how they tried various tools of torture on him and applied the most excruciating punishment in order to confess the whereabouts of Nazzal. (Both statements made to the author in interviews in 2005.)

28 The absence of Imad Abu Dayyah from the meeting confirmed the existence of the split. Soon after the return of the Hamas leaders from Tehran an argument had erupted between him and the other Ikhwan leaders, and he decided to step down from the leadership. Some Hamas circles attribute his decision to the fact that he believed that the Ikhwan's leadership had the leverage to compel Hamas to comply but did not make use of it. However, his Ikhwan colleagues believe he was distraught because of the circulation within Ikhwan ranks of rumors that he might have been collaborating with the Jordanian authorities, something categorically denied by his close associates within the movement.

29 Ibrahim Ghosheh, interview with the author.

30 Al-Jafr is a notorious Jordanian prison in the middle of the desert. It was closed in

the 1970s, but it reopened in the 1990s as a maximum-security jail where terrorism suspects are detained. In the aftermath of 9/11 and as part of the US war on terror, the CIA has used al-Jafr as a secret interrogation center. According to US and Jordanian intelligence sources, as many as 100 al-Qaeda prisoners have passed through al-Jafr. Most suspects stay just a few days before being transferred to longer-term facilities. The reference to Yasir Arafat was prompted by some remarks in the semi-official Jordanian media during the early days of the crisis that if these Jordanian Hamas officials wanted to stick with Hamas they should be shipped to Gaza or Ramallah.

31   Ibrahim Ghosheh, interview with the author, Amman, 21 August 2003.

32   It was reported in the Arabic press that when the amir of Qatar met Israeli Prime Minister Ehud Barak in New York during the Millennium Summit in September 2000, the latter demanded that the Qatari authorities impose restrictions on the movement and activity of Hamas leaders. The same reports added that Qatar dismissed the Israeli request, insisting that the Hamas leaders were the guests of Qatar and that no restrictions would be imposed on them.

33   Jordanian lawyer Hani al-Dahlah, who was traveling on the day, was asked by Ghosheh's family to search for him in the airport. He looked for him in the transit and duty-free lounges but could not find him. The airport security authorities immediately removed him from the public zone and incarcerated him in an empty office.

34   Ibrahim Ghosheh, interview with the author.

35   Muhammad Nazzal, interview with the author.

36   Initially, Khalid Mish'al issued a statement holding the Jordanian authorities responsible for the safety of Ghosheh. In the meantime, lawyer Salih al-Armuti launched a scathing attack on the government. When it became known to him that Ghosheh was taken to Bangkok, he accused the GID of risking his life because Thailand, according to him, was infested with Mossad agents who might harm the Hamas official. He later blamed Khalid Mish'al and Nazzal for not informing him about the deal with the GID; he was embarrassed that he had criticized the government while not knowing the full details of the operation.

37   Ibrahim Ghosheh, interview with the author, Amman, 21 August 2003.

38   The Jordanian Ikhwan's *Assabeel* newspaper criticized Ghosheh for what they perceived as a compromise. Ghosheh dismissed the criticism as uninformed. He maintained that all he did was to comply with the decision of his fellow Hamas Political Bureau members. The statement to which he put his name, he maintains, did not alter his position in Hamas or his commitment to the cause.

39   Both *'umra* and hajj are Islamic acts of worship performed in and around the holy places in Mecca. The difference between them is that the first is optional and can be performed any time of the year, whereas the second is compulsory once in a lifetime for every adult Muslim that can afford it. Hajj can only be performed during the twelfth month of the Islamic *hijra* (lunar) calendar.

[pp.142–149]

7. THE LIBERATION IDEOLOGY OF HAMAS

1   Sheikh Ahmad Yassin, speaking to students at the Islamic University in Gaza, 22 October 1997.

2   See Appendix I for the full text of the document. Appendix II is the English translation of another more recent Hamas document written in early 2000 with the aim of introducing the movement to the world.

3   *Al-Mithaq Hamas* (the charter of Hamas), Palestine, 18 August 1988, 3.

4   Khalid Mish'al, interview with the author, Damascus, 14 August 2003.

5   Ibrahim Ghosheh, interview with the author, Amman, 21 August 2003.

6   In 2002 the present author wrote: "Hamas has come along way since the Charter was first published. In fact, within Hamas circles the Charter has been long forgotten and even distanced. These circles would attest that the Charter was written in haste, that those who wrote it were influenced by conspiracy theory and were lacking in their knowledge and comprehension of world history and international politics. Rather than seek to enlighten the public, the authors of the Charter sought to affirm the publicly perceived notions regarding the Jews and Judaism. It is not unlikely that a number of Hamas's most influential and senior personalities would today admit that the Charter was a big mistake. The current position of the movement is much more sophisticated; it is well-informed and enlightened. Statements made by leading figures within the movement over the past ten years, including Sheikh Ahmad Yassin, Khalid Mish'al, Musa Abu Marzuq, and Mahmud al-Zahhar, prove beyond doubt that the Charter is no longer their frame of reference. Nevertheless, a growing trend within the movement believes that this is clearly not enough. The leaders of Hamas have been urged to officially repudiate the Chapter and authorise the writing of a new one." For the full article, see<www.ii-pt.com>.

7   Khalid Mish'al, interview with the author.

8   During a visit by former Israeli Prime Minister Yitzhak Rabin to Washington in the early nineties he demanded that the United States should support Israel in its war against the Islamists, "the enemies of peace, who threaten the regimes of Algeria, Egypt, Tunisia, and other countries in the region." Addressing the Federation of Jewish Organizations in Washington, Rabin said: "We are not sure that President Clinton and his team fully realize the threat of Islamic fundamentalism and the decisive role Israel plays in combating it. The Arab world and the entire world will pay dearly if this Islamic cancer is not stopped.... By fighting Muslim terrorists we aim to awaken the world that is sleeping, unaware of an important fact, namely that this danger is serious, real, and threatens world peace. Today, we the Israelis truly stand in the firing line against fundamentalist Islam. We demand all states and nations to focus their attention on this huge threat inherent in Islamic fundamentalism." Similar remarks were made at different occasions and different places by other Israeli leaders, including former Israeli foreign minister Shimon Peres, who in February 1993 addressed a group of U.S. officials inside the White House, saying: "The U.S.

should increase its aid to Israel instead of reducing it because Israel is waging a ferocious war against Islamic extremism." Former Israeli Prime Minister Binyamin Netanyahu surpasses all others in his campaign against Islamists around the world. For a more detailed treatment of the Israeli warmongering attitude see chapter six of the present author's book *Rachid Ghannouchi: A Democrat within Islamism* (Oxford: Oxford University Press 2001).

9   Abd al-Fattah Dukhan was born around 1937 in the village of 'Iraq-Suwayd in al-Majdal District (Ashkelon). He was caught up in the deportation of Hamas and Islamic Jihad leaders and activists to South Lebanon in 1992, together with 400 others, and was imprisoned by the Israelis several times. When the Palestinian parliament opened after the 25 January 2006 elections, he was the oldest elected member of the Palestinian Legislative Council. He worked as a teacher for about 40 years and was one of the most prominent orators and preachers in the Gaza Strip. He was a member of Hamas's negotiating team with the PLO at the Cairo talks in December 1995.

10   *Al-Mithaq*, p. 12–13.

11   *Al-Mithaq*, Article 11.

12   For a personal eyewitness account of the way many Iraqi Jews were tricked into migrating to Palestine, see Naeim Giladi's book *Ben Gurion's Scandals: How the Haganah & the Mossad Eliminated Jews* (Glilit Pubishers, 1995).

13   Sephardic and Mizrahi Jews have suffered decades of discrimination in Israel. They have been treated as second-class citizens and had to settle for inferior housing and much lower standards of services in education and health. According to Phyllis Bennis, head of the Middle East Project at the Institute for Policy Studies in Washington, D.C., "within Israel there are four levels of citizenship, the first three being various levels of Jewish participation in Israeli society, which are thoroughly racialized. At the top of the pyramid are the Ashkenazi, the white European Jews. At the level of power the huge contingent of recent Russian immigrants — now about 20 percent of Israeli Jews — are being assimilated into the European-Ashkenazi sector, though they retain a very distinct cultural identity. The next level down, which is now probably the largest component of the Jewish population, is the Mizrahi or Sephardic Jews, who are from the Arab countries. At the bottom of the Jewish pyramid are the Ethiopian Jews, who are black. You can go into the poorest parts of Jewish West Jerusalem and find that it is predominantly Ethiopian. This social and economic stratification took shape throughout the last 50 years as different groups of Jews from different parts of the world came, for very different reasons, to Israel. So while the divisions reflected national origins, they play out in a profoundly racialized way. The Yemeni Jews in particular faced extraordinary discrimination. They were transported more or less involuntarily from Yemen to Israel. On arrival, they were held in primitive camps, and many Yemeni babies were stolen from their mothers and given for adoption to Ashkenazi families. In the early 1990s, a high-profile campaign began to try to reunite some of those shattered families. Beneath all these layers of

Jews come the Palestinian citizens." Source: "For Jews Only: Racism Inside Israel," an Interview with Phyllis Bennis by Max Elbaum <www.zmag.org/meastwatch/for_jews_only.htm>.

[14] For the secular origins and biblical justifications of political Zionism, see the following: Abdelwahab Elmessiri, *The Land of Promise: A Critique of Political Zionism* (New Brunswick, NJ 1997); Michael Prior, *The Bible and Colonialism: A Moral Critique*, (Sheffield: Sheffield Academic Press, 1997); and John Rose, *The Myths of Zionism* (London: Pluto Press, 2004).

[15] In an unprecedented event on an Arab television station, on 1 May 2002 Aljazeera satellite channel hosted Rabbi Yisroel Dovid Weiss, spokesperson for the "Neturei Karta International — Jews against Zionism." His 90-minute live appearance on Ahmad Mansour's *Bila Hudud* (Without frontiers) weekly show shocked many viewers. Some of them were extremely skeptical, suggesting that perhaps the guest was a Hamas member disguised as a rabbi. The program can be accessed on <www.aljazeera.net/programs>. It would have been unthinkable at the time when the Hamas Charter was published that a leading Hamas figure would meet with a Jewish rabbi. On 21 March 2006, newly elected PLC speaker Dr. Aziz Duwayk received at his office at the Palestinian Legislative Council in Ramallah a delegation from Neturei Karta International led by Rabbi Moshe Hirsh. At the meeting, reported on the PLC website, Duwayk stressed that the Palestinian people can never be against the Jews and the Jewish people. He added: "Our people are against the Zionist movement and not against the Jews." He explained that the Muslims would never contemplate inflicting harm on the Jews or the Christians and that the Jews had lived in the Arab and Muslim states for centuries in peace and mutual understanding. He went on to affirm that the Palestinian people's problem is with the Zionist movement, which refuses to recognize our people and their legitimate national rights. The meeting is reported on at <www.pal-plc.org/news/MainAnnounce2.asp?key=190>.

[16] This paradigm is referred to in the Qur'an in two verses. The first is verse 251 of al-Baqarah (Sura 2, "The Cow"): "Had Allah not checked one set of people by means of another, the earth would indeed be full of mischief: but Allah is full of bounty to all the worlds." The second is verse 40 in al-Hajj (Sura 22, "The Pilgrimage"): "Had Allah not checked one set of people by means of another there would surely have been pulled down monasteries, churches, synagogues, and mosques, in which the name of Allah is commemorated in abundant measure. Allah will certainly aid those who aid His [cause]; for verily Allah is Full of Strength, Exalted in Might, [able to enforce His Will]."

[17] This is what Muslims are supposed to believe in. In the Qur'an, verse number 26 of al-'Imran (Sura 3, "The Family of Imran") reads: "Say: O Allah! Lord of Power [and Rule], you give Power to whom you please and you strip off Power from whom you please: you endue with honor whom you please, and you bring low whom you please: in your hand is all Good. Verily, over all things you have power."

[18] In the early hours of Monday, 22 March 2004, an Israeli helicopter fired a missile at Sheikh Ahmad Yassin as he was being pushed in his wheelchair outside the neighborhood mosque where he had just performed dawn prayers after a night of *qiyam* (vigil). The sheikh and several worshippers were blown to pieces.

[19] Khalid Misha'l, interview with Olivia Ward, Beirut, December 2004. Parts of this filmed interview were incorporated into a documentary produced by Shelley Saywell entitled "Hamas Behind the Mask."

[20] Ibrahim Ghosheh, interview with the author, Amman, 21 August 2003.

[21] Sheikh Yusuf al-Qaradawi, interview with al-'Azab al-Tayyib al-Tahir, *Al-Rayah* (Doha), 27 January 1999. No dates for the conferences are given in the interview.

[22] Ibid.

[23] On 5 June 1967, Israel launched what it claimed was "a pre-emptive defensive strike" against Egypt, Syria, and Jordan, starting a war that lasted six days, during which it occupied what had remained of Palestine (the Gaza Strip and the West Bank), the Sinai Peninsula, and the Golan Heights. More than 250,000 Palestinians were made homeless.

[24] Jewish settlements in the Gaza Strip had already been evacuated and dismantled. On 15 August 2005 Israel began to implement the plan that ended Israeli occupation, though not overall control, of the Gaza Strip. The former Israeli Prime Minister Ariel Sharon opted for a unilateral withdrawal plan after Israel's occupation of the Gaza Strip became too costly for his administration to maintain, in both economic and political terms. After the completion of Israel's withdrawal, Hamas proclaimed victory, attributing the Israeli decision to the success of Hamas's military strategy. Sharon's successor, Ehud Olmert, announced that he would pursue a similar course of action in the West Bank with the aim of effecting a total separation from the Palestinians along lines that fall well short of the pre-1967 war borders.

[25] Settling Jewish immigrants on land confiscated from the Palestinians within the areas occupied by Israel in 1967 was meant to enhance Israel's security. However, Jewish settlements have proved to be a heavy burden on Israel and a source of constant provocation for the Palestinians. One of the main reasons for the failure of efforts to make peace between the Palestinian Authority and successive Israeli administrations has been the existence of these settlements.

[26] For full details of the poll and its results, visit <www.fafo.no/gazapoll/summary. htm>.

[27] <www.pcpsr.org/survey/survey.html>

[28] <www.sis.gov.ps/english/index.html>

[29] Abd al-Aziz al-Rantisi, interview with al-Qassam website,7 March 2004.

[30] Khalid Misha'l, interview with Olivia Ward, Beirut, December 2004.

[31] BBC News, 7 October 1997.

[32] BBC News, 12 October 1999.

[33] Graham Usher, "Hudna, Resistance and War on Islam," *Al-Ahram Weekly*, 6–12

November 2003.

[34] BBC News, 14 November 2003.

8. JIHAD AND MARTYRDOM

[1] Sheikh Sayyid Tantawi, the grand sheikh of al-Azhar. *Al-Hayat* (London), 4 August 1997.

[2] According to al-Imam al-Shatibi (d.1388), Islamic shari'a is aimed primarily at protecting the five essentials: life, faith, progeny, property, and reason.

[3] See Mohamed S. el-Awa, *Punishment in Islamic Law* (Indianapolis: American Trust Publications, 1993).

[4] Sheikh Yusuf al-Qaradawi, interview with the author in Doha, Qatar, 19 October 2005.

[5] Prominent commentators (scholars of Qur'anic exegesis) al-Tabari and al-Qurtubi both agree in their commentaries on this verse that Prophet Muhammad was instructed to challenge the unbelievers with the Qur'an and to perform jihad against them by reading it and conveying its message to them. Al-Qurtubi goes further and criticizes "those who claimed that the Prophet was ordered in this verse to perform jihad against the unbelievers of Quraysh with the sword." He argued that this was a Meccan verse; fighting with the sword had not yet been allowed.

[6] Esther Mitchell, "History of the Crusades a Holy War," Essortment 2002 <vt. essortment.com/crusadesholywa_rhvy.htm>.

[7] M. Sharif Basyuni, *Al-Watha'iq al-dawliyah al-ma'niyah bi huquq al-insan, vol. II* (International documents on human rights) (Cairo: Dar al-Shuruq, 2003).

[8] For more discussion of the opinions of both thinkers on this issue, see chapter three of my book *Rachid Ghannouchi: A Democrat within Islamism* (New York: OUP, 2001).

[9] See the Qur'an: verse 111 of Surat al-Tawbah (Chapter of the Repentance or chapter 9) and verses 1–6 of Surat al-Saff (Chapter of the Ranks or chapter 61). Both al-Tirmidhi and Ibn Majah reported that the Prophet (peace be upon him) said that a martyr receives six rewards: he will be forgiven for all his sins, he will be able to see his place in Paradise, he will be saved from the ordeal of the grave, he will be secured from the Day of Great Fear (Day of Resurrection); on his head will be placed the crown of dignity in which a single gem is better than life and what exists in it; he will be married to seventy-two wives of the Hur al-'In; and he will be granted permission to intercede on behalf of seventy of his relatives.

[10] The fatwas of both Sheikh al-Shu'aybi and al-Qaradawi are quoted in *Filastin al-Muslimah* (March 2002).

9. HAMAS, THE PLO, AND THE PALESTINIAN AUTHORITY

[1] Khalid Mish'al, interview with the author in Damascus, 14 August 2003.

[2] The PLO was established by the first Arab Summit Conference, which convened in Cairo on 13 January 1963. Ahmad al-Shuqayri, who was appointed by the Egyp-

tians to represent Palestine in the Arab League, was commissioned to convene the General Palestine Conference in Jerusalem between 28 May and 2 June 1964. This conference, inaugurated by King Hussein of Jordan, constituted the First Palestinian National Council, which decreed the foundation of the Palestine Liberation Organization and elected al-Shuqayri as the PLO chairman. Yasir Arafat took over when he was elected PLO chairman by the Fifth Palestine National Council, which convened in Cairo from the 1 to 4 February 1969. This followed the decision of the Fourth Palestinian National Council, which convened in Cairo from 7 to 17 July 1968 to welcome into the PLO the various Palestinian factions that existed at the time, including Arafat's Fatah movement. The PLO was recognized by the Arab states as the "sole legitimate representative of the Palestinian people" during the Rabat Arab Summit conference in October 1974. That decision paved the way for the United Nations to grant observer status to the PLO the following month. By 1988, and following the Algiers Declaration of Independence, more than 120 countries had recognized the PLO.

3   Munir Shafiq, interview with the author, London, 9 May 2006.

4   For an excellent account, see Said K. Aburish, *Arafat: From Defender to Dictator* (London: Bloomsbury, 1998).

5   This was a reference to the story of King Solomon with the ants, referred to in verse 18 of Surat al-Naml (Qur'an, chapter 27).

6   The Palestinian National Council (PNC) is the parliament in exile of the Palestinian people. The first PNC, composed of 422 representatives, met in Jerusalem in May 1964 and adopted the Palestinian National Charter (also known as the Palestinian National Covenant). At this conference, the PLO was established as the political expression of the Palestinian people. The PNC elects the Executive Committee of the PLO, which constitutes the leadership between sessions. The participants in the founding conference were meant to represent the Palestinian communities in Jordan, the West Bank, Gaza, Syria, Lebanon, Kuwait, Iraq, Egypt, Qatar, Libya, and Algeria. Ahmad al-Shuqayri was elected the first chairman of the PLO Executive Committee. Later sessions were held in Cairo (the second, in 1965), Gaza (the third, in 1966), Cairo (from the fourth to the thirteenth, between 1968 and 1977), Damascus (14th and 15th, in 1979 and 1981), Algiers (16th, in 1983), Amman (17th, in 1984), Algiers (from the 18th to the 20th, between 1987 and 1991), and Gaza (the 21st in 1996, and the 22nd in 1998). At its 19th session in Algiers in November 1988, the PNC unilaterally declared the independence of the State of Palestine. After the signing of the Oslo Accords in September 1993, the PNC convened in Gaza in April 1996 and repealed the articles of the Palestinian National Covenant that denied Israel's right to exist by a majority of 504 to 54. In accordance with of the conditions of the Wye River Memorandum, signed by the Palestinian Authority and Israel in October 1998, the PNC convened again in Gaza in December 1998, in the presence of US President Clinton, to reaffirm the deletion of those articles of the Charter that denied Israel's

right to exist. By the end of the 1990s the PNC had 669 members. It consisted of the 88 members of the Palestinian Legislative Council (PLC) directly elected in January 1996, 98 other members from inside the Palestinian territories who represent the Palestinian population living in the Palestinian territories occupied in 1967, and 483 members representing the Palestinian diaspora. The Council normally meets every two years but has not met since 1998. Resolutions are passed by a simple majority; two-thirds of the members must attend for a quorum.

[7] Ibrahim Ghosheh, interview with the author, Amman, 17 August 2003.

[8] Ibid.

[9] Khalid Mish'al, interview with Ghassan Sharbal in *Al-Hayat* (London), 5 December 2003, part II.

[10] Yasir Arafat regarded himself as the father of all the Palestinians and the leader of the entire people. It would therefore not have been appropriate for him to lead a Palestinian Authority team in negotiations with Hamas unless agreement had already been achieved.

[11] For a summary of the report, visit <www.amnestyusa.org/countries/israel_and_occupied_territories/document.do?id=19024C93E884246A80256A0F005BCC96>.

[12] Khalid Mish'al, interview with *Al-Hayat*, 6 December 2003, part III.

[13] BBC News quoting Israeli TV, 24 January 1998.

[14] BBC News: 19 April 1998.

[15] Sheikh Ahmad Yassin, interview with *Al-Ahram Weekly*, no. 428 (6–12 May 1999).

[16] For an analysis of what occured and what went wrong at Camp David, see Hussein Agha and Robert Malley, "Camp David: The Tragedy of Errors," *New York Review of Books*, 9 August 2001, <www.nybooks.com/articles/14380?email>. See also: Robert Wright, "Was Arafat the Problem?", 18 April 2002 <www.slate.com/?id=2064500#ContinueArticle>. For an excellent documentation of the various stages of peacemaking between the Palestinians and Israel between 2000 and 2004, see the 3-part BBC documentary, "Israel and the Arabs, Elusive Peace," produced for the BBC by Brook Lapping Production, 2005.

[17] Nabil Amr, a former minister in the PA and a member of the negotiating team, accused his boss, Yasir Arafat, of "scuttling the talks." After returning to Palestine, Amr received a bullet in the leg in a mysterious shooting incident that some people believe was in reprisal for his remark. Both the United States and Israel supported challenges to Yasir Arafat and appeared to encourage dissent by such senior figures within the Palestinian security apparatus such as Muhammad Dahlan, based in Gaza, who was also at the Camp David meeting, and Jibril al-Rajub, based in the West Bank.

[18] BBC News, 11 October 2000.

[19] Quds Press, 9 October 2000.

[20] BBC News, 13 October 2000.

[21] BBC News, 11 August 2001.

22 The first was a double suicide bombing carried out in Jerusalem by Nabil Mahmud Halbiyah and Osama Muhammad Bahar, killing 10 Israelis and wounding more than 150. The second was a bus bombing executed by Mahir Muhammad Hubaysh, killing 18 Israelis and wounding more than 40.

23 BBC News, 20 December 2001.

24 See Chris McGreal, "No Independent Palestine, Sharon Insists," *Guardian*, 17 March 2003 <www.guardian.co.uk/israel/story10,,915690,00.html>.

25 Khalid Mish'al, interview with the author, Damascus, 20 April 2006.

26 During Sharon's tenure in office, the Israelis assassinated several of Hamas's founders and some of its most senior figures, including, in chronological order, Jamal Salim and Jamal Mansur on 31 July 2001, Mahmud Abu Hannud on 23 November 2001, Salah Shihadah on 22 July 2002, Ibrahim al-Maqadmah on 8 March 2003, Isma'il Abu Shanab on 21 August 2003, Sheikh Ahmad Yassin on 21 March 2004, and Abd al-Aziz al-Rantisi on 17 April 2004.

27 "Israel and the Arabs, Elusive Peace," part III, produced for the BBC by Brook Lapping Productions, 2005.

28 A British MP and former minister informed the author that he heard Sharon say that Gaza had become too costly for Israel to remain there.

29 *Haaretz*, 18 July 2005

30 "Israel and the Arabs," op. cit.

31 Many Palestinians believe that Yasir Arafat was poisoned. The accusation is that Israel poisoned him with the help of some of his close associates. Controversies over the medical report on the causes of his death have fueled the belief in a plot of some sort. Hamas's Khalid Mish'al is adamant that Arafat was poisoned.

32 Ra'id Karmi, commander of Fatah's al-Aqsa Martyrs Brigades, was assassinated in Tulkarm on 14 January 2002. An earlier attempt on his life in September had failed, but killed two of his comrades. Marwan Barghouti, a top Fatah leader in Ramallah, was arrested by the IDF on 14 April 2002. He was tried before a military court and was sentenced to several terms of life imprisonment for his role in the al-Aqsa intifada.

10. HAMAS IN GOVERNMENT

1 Khalid Mish'al, interview with *Al-Hayat* (London), 9 December 2003, part IV.

2 According to Palestinian Authority official figures, 70 percent of the registered voters (775,000 out of 1.1 million) cast their votes. Mahmud Abbas won 62.32 percent, Mustafa Barghouti 18 percent, and Taysir Khalid of the DFLP 3.5 percent.

3 Izzat al-Rishiq, interview with the author in Doha, 28 April 2006.

4 *Al-Ahram Weekly*, no. 735 (24–30 March 2005).

5 Ibid.

6 *Al-Hayat*, London, 1 April 2005.

[pp.201-214]

7   *Al-Hayat*, London, 26 May 2005, quoting Palestinian Information Minister Nabil Sha'ath, who announced on 25 May that the elections were to be postponed until further notice.

8   The number of seats allocated to each electoral district was determined by its population; the breakdown for local constituencies was as follows: Jerusalem 6 seats, with 2 seats reserved for Christians; Tubas 1 seat; Tulkarm 3 seats; Qalqilya 2 seats; Salfit 1 seat; Nablus 6 seats; Jericho 1 seat; Ramallah 5 seats, with 1 seat reserved for Christians; Jenin 4 seats; Bethlehem 4 seats, with 2 seats reserved for Christians; Hebron 9 seats; North Gaza 5 seats; Gaza City 8 seats, with 1 seat reserved for Christians; Deir al-Balah 3 seats; Khan Yunis 5 seats; and Rafah 3 seats. The total would be 66 seats including 6 seats for the Christians.

9   Donald Macintyre, "Fatah Invokes Memory of Arafat as Campaign Closes," *Independent*, 24 January 2006 <news.independent.co.uk/world/middle_east/article340625. ece>.

10   The Palestinian Central Elections Commission reported a turnout of 74.6–76 percent in the Gaza Strip and 73.1 percent in the West Bank.

11   Hussein Agha and Robert Mattey, "Hamas Has Arrived, but There Are Limits to Its Advance," *Guardian*, 24 January 2006 <www.guardian.co.uk/israel/Story/0,,1693354,00.html>.

12   Ibid.

13   Chris McGreal, "Fatah Struggles with Tainted Image," *Guardian*, 24 January 2006 <www.guardian.co.uk/israel/Story/0,,1693433,00.html>.

14   Chris McGreal, "Surge in Support for Hamas as Voters Prepare to Reject Fatah at Polls," *Guardian*, 25 January 2006 <www.guardian.co.uk/israel/Story/0,,1694141,00. html>.

15   Donald Macintyre, "Divisions in Fatah Give Hope to Hamas as Palestinians Go to Polls," *Independent*, 25 January 2006 <news.independent.co.uk/world/middle_ east/article340810.ece>

16   Izzat al-Rishiq, interview with the author in Doha.

17   The Syrian authorities had not been allowing Hamas officials any public activities in the city, where they were allowed to reside since they were expelled from Jordan in 1999. Things changed immediately following the election; the Syrians felt they were vindicated in hosting a movement that had been proven to be democratically the most representative party of the Palestinian people. From then on, the Hamas leaders were given the green light to conduct political and media activities more openly than they had been permitted in the past. More restrictions on the Hamas officials were imposed soon after the fall of Baghdad, when the US administration seemed to be looking for more reasons to impose sanctions on Syria or even authorize invading it as Iraq was.

349

18 Hamas Political Bureau Chief Khalid Mish'al and his Deputy Musa Abu Marzuq responded to the US demands with articles published in the UK and the US. See the appendices.

19 A Hamas delegation headed by Khalid Mish'al, Political Bureau chief, arrived in Ankara for talks with Turkish foreign minister and other officials on Thursday, 16 February 2006.

20 Khalid Mish'al led the Hamas delegation that arrived in Moscow on Friday, 3 March 2006.

21 Khalid Mish'al, interview with the author in Damascus, 20 April 2006.

22 Almustaqbal Research Center, 8 May 2006 (Gaza, Palenstine) <www.mustaqbal. net>.

23 Shakir al-Jawhari, "Abbas in Amman," 16 May 2006 <www.palestine-info.info/arabic/palestoday/press/2006_2/21_5_06_11.htm>.

24 This is how Anne Barnard, a *Boston Globe* journalist, reported the incident: "Ali Ghalia, 55, a farmer, had taken his two wives and 10 of their children, ranging in age from his 6-month-old son Haitham to his daughter Alia, 25 — from their home in Beit Lahiya to the nearby beach for their first seaside outing of the summer. It was an appealing spot in an overcrowded area with little entertainment, cleaner than the sewage-tinged shoreline of Gaza City and newly open to Palestinians after Israelis evacuated a nearby settlement in the Gaza pullout last summer. Around 4 PM, as the heat was breaking and the light was turning gold, the shell crashed down near the beach with a boom that could be heard several miles down the coast in Gaza City. A second shell hit near the road, said beachgoers who gathered at the hospital, some wearing bloody swimming gear. 'It landed right among us,' Hamdiya Ghalia, Ali's surviving wife, said from her hospital bed, which was soaked with blood. 'What was the crime of these babies?' she wailed. Two of Hamdiya's children were killed in front of her, said a cousin, Yunis Ghalia. The baby, Haitham, was blasted from her grip by a piece of shrapnel that also severed her hand, he said. 'It took her hand and the baby.' But the mother, he said, had not yet been told how many from her family were dead — her husband, his other wife, Raisa, and four daughters: Alia, 25, Sabrina, 22, Ilham, 15, and Hanadi, 1, according to hospital records. A son, Ayham, 18, was in critical condition and two daughters, Amina, 22, and Latifa, 7, were among the 30 other people injured in the beach shelling. 'They just wanted to swim on the beach, that's all,' Yunis Ghalia said, standing in the dingy, fluorescent-lit hospital hallway with dazed male relatives as their wives crouched in silence by Hamdiya Ghalia's bed." See "Shell Kills 7 in Gaza Family," *Boston Globe*, 10 June 2006 <www.boston.com/news/world/middleeast/articles/2006/06/10/shell_kills_7_in_gaza_family/>.

25 At around the same time, the US Senate adopted a bill to isolate the Hamas-led Palestinian government and to ban contacts with Hamas. The legislation, approved by voice vote, was similar to a bill the House passed a month earlier. Democratic Senator Joseph Biden, number two on the Senate Foreign Relations Committee, told

the press: "None of us want to see a penny of American taxpayer money going to a Hamas-led government that refuses to meet the basic demands not just of the United States, but of the international community." However, the bill allows for continued assistance for food, water, health, and medicine, as well as for democracy promotion, human rights, and education to help Palestinian President Mahmud Abbas in "fulfilling his duties."

26   Mossad tried to kill Mish'al in a botched assassination attempt in Jordan in 1997. See chapter five.

11. TOWARD THE NEXT INTIFADA?

Khalid Mish'al, "Our Unity Can Now Pave the Way for Peace and Justice," *Guardian*, 13 February 2007 <www.guardian.co.uk/comment/story/0,,2011657,00.html>.

2
1   See for instance, Ian Fisher, "Israel Squeezes, and Gaza Residents Adapt to the Vise," *New York Times*, 2 July 2006.

3   This was originally a proposal from Saudi Arabia that was then adopted by the Arab summit in Beirut on 28 March 2002. The initiative stated that should Israel withdraw from all territories occupied since the 1967 Arab–Israeli war, provide a just solution to the Palestinian refugee problem, and recognize the establishment of a sovereign and independent Palestinian state in the West Bank and Gaza Strip; then the Arab countries would in turn recognize Israel, enter into peace agreements with it, and establish normal relations with it.

4   Haniyah's doctors attributed his collapse to exhaustion because of heat and fasting; it was the fasting month of Ramadan, during which Muslims refrain from eating and drinking everyday from dawn to sunset.

5   Fatah officials accused Hamas of murdering the three children and their driver in a strike intended to liquidate their father, Officer Ba'luchi, a strongly anti-Hamas Fatah official. Hamas denied any connection with the murder, blaming it on an internal Fatah feud. Apparently, the judge was murdered to avenge the killing of the children.

6   A poll conducted by the Palestinian Center for Policy and Survey Research in the West Bank and the Gaza Strip 14–16 September 2006 concluded that "despite dissatisfaction with the performance of the Hamas government, especially regarding salaries, and despite public preference for a National Unity Government in which Fatah and Hamas are equal, Hamas's popularity remains largely unchanged and the majority does not think it should recognize Israel." For more details of the poll, visit <www.pcpsr.org/survey/polls/2006/p21epressrelease.html>.

7   Take, for instance, Rice's 4 October meeting with Abbas in Ramallah when, as the BBC reported, upon his declaration that talks with Hamas on forming a national unity government had collapsed, the US secretary of state pledged the US's support for

him. She was quoted as saying that the US had "great admiration" for his leadership. ("Rice Pledges US Support for Abbas," BBC News, 5 October 2006 <news.bbc. co.uk/go/pr/fr/-/2/hi/middle_east/5404998.stm>.)

8   Khalid Mish'al, interview with the author, Damascus, 11 April 2007.

9   These details were divulged to the author by a member of Hamas Political Bureau who insisted on anonymity.

10 Alastair Crooke and Mark Perry, "How the Saudis Stole a March on the US," *Asia Times Online*, 6 March 2007 <www.atimes.com/atimes/Middle_East/IC06Ak04.html>. Hamas sources deny, however, that Prince Bandar had anything to do with initiating the process. They maintain that it was entirely the idea of the king himself and that Bandar, like other Saudi officials, was instructed to implement the proceedings that led eventually led to the agreement in Mecca.

11 The text of the Mecca agreement for National Palestinian Accord:

In the Name of Allah Most Gracious Most Merciful. Glory be to Him Who did take His Servant for a journey by night from Sacred Mosque [in Mecca] to the Furthest Mosque [al-Aqsa in Jerusalem] whose precincts We did bless. Upon the good initiative announced by the custodian of the two noble sanctuaries King Abdullah ibn Abd al-Aziz of the Kingdom of Saudi Arabia, and under his majesty's honorable auspices, national Palestinian accord and concord dialogues took place between the movements of Fatah and Hamas during the period from 19 to 21 Muharram 1428 of hijra, [which corresponds to] 6 to 8 February 2007. By the Grace of the Almighty Allah, these dialogues have been crowned with success. The following has been agreed upon: First: Affirming the prohibition of [shedding] Palestinian blood and taking all measures and [making] all arrangements that would prevent this [from happening], while stressing the importance of national unity as a basis for national steadfastness and confronting occupation and for accomplishing the legitimate national objectives of the Palestinian people and resorting to dialogue as the sole basis for resolving political differences in the Palestinian arena. Within this framework, we extend profound gratitude to the brothers in sister Egypt and to the Egyptian security delegation [based] in Gaza, who exerted considerable efforts in order to calm the situation in the Gaza Strip during the previous period. Second: Agreeing, finally and absolutely on the formation of a Palestinian national unity government in accordance with a detailed agreement endorsed by both sides and proceeding immediately with adopting the constitutional measures [necessary] for establishing it. Third: Going ahead with the measures [necessary] for improving and reforming the

Palestine Liberation Organization and expediting the work of the preparatory committee based on the Cairo and Damascus concurrences. Detailed steps have been agreed in this regard between the two sides. Fourth: Affirming the principle of political partnership on the basis of the laws of the Palestinian National Authority and on the foundation of political pluralism in accordance with an agreement endorsed by both parties. As we send the glad tidings of this agreement to our Palestinian masses and to the masses of our Arab and Islamic umma as well as to all [our] friends in the world, we confirm our commitment to this agreement in letter and spirit so as to concentrate on the accomplishment of our national goals, get rid of occupation, regain our rights, and attend to the basic issues, foremost of which are the issues of Jerusalem, the refugees, al-Aqsa Mosque, and the issues of the war prisoners and the detainees and confronting the wall and [the building or expanding of Jewish] settlements. Allah provides success. Mecca, 21 Muharram 1428 of hijra, [which corresponds to] 8 February 2007.

From the Saudi daily newspaper *Al-Sharq al-Awsat*, 9 February 2007.

[12] The Israeli media invariably saw Hamas as the main, if not the sole, beneficiary of the Mecca agreement. See, for example, Khaled Abu Toameh, "Why Hamas Came Out Clear Winner from Mecca Summit," *Jerusalem Post*, 11 February 2007, <www.jpost.com/servlet/Satellite?cid=1170359828092&pagename=JPost%2FJPArticle%2FShowFull>. Similar comments appeared in other Israeli media. In a 10 February 2007 article in the Israeli newspaper *Ynetnews* under the title "Hamas Won the Jackpot," Ronny Shakel wrote, "The unity agreement signed in Mecca last Thursday marked a major victory for Hamas." (See <www.ynetnews.com/articles/0,7340,L-3363256,00>) There could be no better indication of the beginning of the end of Hamas's isolation than the assertion by former Mossad head Ephraim Halevy on the day of the Mecca agreement that he believed it was impossible to hold talks with the Palestinians without holding talks with Hamas. See "Talks with Palestinians sans Hamas not Possible," Jerusalem Post, 8 February 2007 <http://www.jpost.com/servlet/Satellite?cid=1170359814830&pagename=JPost%2FJPArticle%2FShowFull.>

[13] Many Palestinians who were not members of Hamas or even supporters of the organization voted for it on the basis of its perceived reputation as an honest and responsible group. It is believed that many Fatah members and supporters may have also voted for Hamas as a protest against the Fatah leadership, which was smeared by charges of corruption.

[14] Barghouti was appointed information minister in the first national unity government.

[15] The leaders of both sides continued to be commitment to ending the strife. Much of the fighting in the aftermath of the Mecca agreement amounted to no more than family feuds, individual acts of revenge, or some criminal activities.

[16] The composition of the cabinet as submitted by Prime Minister Designate Isma'il Haniyyah to PNA President Mahmud Abbas on 14 March was:

Azzam al-Ahmad (Fatah), deputy prime minister;

Ziyad Abu Amr (independent), foreign minister;

Salam Fayyad (the Third Way Bloc), finance minister;

Hani Talab al-Qawasimah (independent), interior minister;

Mustafa al-Barghouti (independent), information minister;

Ridwan al-Akhras (Fatah), health minister;

Bassam al-Salihi (the People's Party), culture minister;

Salih Zaydan (DFLP), social affairs minister;

Mahmud al-'Alul (Fatah), labor minister;

Sa'di al-Karnaz (Fatah), transport minister;

Taysir Abu Sunaynah (Fatah), captives' (prisoners in Israeli detention) affairs minister;

Samih Shabib (Fatah), public works minister;

Nasir al-Sha'ir (Hamas), education minister;

Muhammad al-Barghouti (Hamas), local government minister;

Samir Abu 'Ayshah (Hamas), planning minister;

Basim Na'im (Hamas), youth and sports minister;

Muhammad al-Agha (Hamas), agriculture minister;

Yusuf al-Mansi (Hamas), telecommunications minister;

Ziyad al-Zhazha (Hamas), economics minister

Isma'il Shindi (Hamas), endowments and religious affairs minister;

Ali al-Sartawi (Hamas), justice minister;

Wasfi Qubbaha (Hamas), state minister;

Khulud Hudayb (independent), tourism minister; and

Mariam Salih (Hamas), as women's affairs minister.

[17] One of these is Mohammad Yaghi. In an analysis written for the Washington Institute for Near East Policy, he considered Fatah's failure to rout out Hamas to be the main factor that brought its leadership to Mecca and persuaded it to negotiate the Mecca agreement. He also provides a list of arguments as to why he believes Hamas emerged out of Mecca a winner. See "Hamas's Victory: From Gaza to Mecca," 16 February 2007 <www.washingtoninstitute.org/templateC05.php?CID=2569>.

[18] The following is the text of Abbas's letter of designation to Haniyah:

In the name of Allah Most Gracious Most Merciful. A letter of designation to form a government. His Excellency Mr. Isma'il Abd al-Salam Haniyah. Greetings. In our capacity as chairman of the PLO's Executive Committee and president of the Palestinian National Authority, and having had a look at the statute, and in accordance with the powers assigned to me, we hereby first: designate you to form the next Palestinian government within the period stated in the statute; second: once the government is formed and is submitted to us, it should be submitted to the Legislative Council for obtaining a vote of confidence; third: I call on you as prime minister of the next government to abide by the supreme interests of the Palestinian people, to safeguard their rights, to preserve their gains and improve them and to work for the accomplishment of their national goals as endorsed by the resolutions of the national councils, the articles of the statute, the national accord document and the resolutions of the Arab summits. On that basis I call on you to respect the resolutions of the international legitimacy and the agreements signed by the PLO. May Allah provide you with success and guide your steps along the path of good. Mahmud Abbas. PLO Executive Committee Chairman. PNA President.

The Arabic text was published in the Saudi daily newspaper *'Ukaz*, 9 February 2007.

[19] On 10 February 2007, Reuters quoted Ahmad Yusuf, the political adviser to Prime Minister Haniyah as saying that "a new Palestinian unity government to be formed in accordance with the Mecca between Fatah and Hamas will not recognize Israel." He said the unity government, which he expected Haniyah to unveil within ten days, would "respect" previous Palestinian peace accords with Israel but would not be committed to them, nor to recognizing the Jewish state. He further insisted that "the issue of recognition was not addressed at all [in Mecca]."

[20] See Aluf Benn, "Israel's Liaison to its Neighbors: Prince Bandar," *Haaretz*, 2 March 2007 <www.haaretz.com/hasen/spages/832361.html>. This article claims that Prince Bandar bin Sultan, Saudi Arabian national security adviser—who is said to be the key figure in Middle Eastern diplomacy—was the man behind the Mecca agreement between Fatah and Hamas for the establishment of a Palestinian national unity government. The report also gives him credit for being active in calming the rival parties in Lebanon, as well as for mediating between Iran and the US administration. Benn claims that "two weeks ago he [Bandar] brought President George W. Bush up to date on his efforts" just one week before Bush participated in a meeting of intelligence chiefs from three other Arab states with Secretary of State Condoleezza Rice in

Amman. It is assumed that Bandar's endeavors are fully coordinated with his country's ally, the US, all the way up to the highest decision-making circles in the White House.

[21] "What the moment necessitated was a real and sincere partnership between Fatah and Hamas because the latter needs [the partnership] and is ready to accept it. It was clear from the beginning that the United States and Israel did not wish to finish Hamas or its government off despite the tight grip and the severe embargo. What they wanted was to integrate Hamas in the political process and force it to participate in it according to the rules and conditions of the game." Ibrahim Gharaybah, "Ma ba'da ittifaq Makkah" (Post-Mecca agreement), Al-'Asr online, 21 February 2007 <www.alasr.ws>.

[22] See Hizb al-Tahrir al-Islami's argument at <www.hizb-ut-tahrir.info/arabic/index. php/polycomment/single/1911 >.

[23] Khalid Mish'al, interview with the author, Damascus, 11 April 2007. Mish'al said that King Abdullah warmed up to him from the moment he met him in Mecca despite having earlier expressed dismay over Hamas's refusal to accept the 2002 Arab (Saudi) peace initiative.

[24] The Arab initiative was adopted once again, this time unanimously, by the Arab summit that was hosted by the Saudis in Riyadh on 28 and 29 March 2007. Israel responded with a rejection.

[25] Mish'al, "Our Unity."

[26] Khalid Mish'al, interview with the author, Damascus, 11 April 2007.

[27] In his audio message, aired by Aljazeera Arabic satellite TV, on 11 March 2007, al-Zawahiri, accused Hamas of capitulation for agreeing to form a Palestinian national unity government. He said Hamas had fallen into the swamp of surrender by accepting a Saudi-brokered deal with the US-backed Fatah faction. The leadership of Hamas, he asserted, "surrendered to the Jews most of Palestine." Hamas, according to him, sold out so that it can keep a hold of a third of government; a government, he continued, that doesn't even have the right to enter or leave Palestine without Israeli permission. He poured his scorn on the leadership of Hamas, which he said had committed an aggression against the rights of the Islamic nation by agreeing to respect international agreements. He lamented: "I am sorry to have to offer the Islamic nation my condolences for the [virtual demise] of the Hamas leadership as it has fallen in the quagmire of surrender." See <english.aljazeera.net/NR/exeres/E63EA439-C428-4914-9985-C51D3F2118A7.htm>.

[28] In his Guardian article, Mish'al expressed hope that the agreement to form a national unity government would bring an end to the sanctions. He wrote: "Now that Hamas and Fatah have agreed to form a national unity government, the international community has no excuse to maintain the siege against our people. We know that

many governments around the world are unhappy with these sanctions and want to see an end to them." Mish'al, "Our Unity."

29 Ibid.

30 Khalid Mish'al, interview with the author, Damascus, 11 April 2007.

31 These remarks were divulged to the author by a member of Hamas Political Bureau who insisted on anonymity.

32 Mish'al, "Our Unity."

33 A number of prominent British figures published a statement in the Guardian on 14 February 2007 in support of Khalid Mish'al's call on the world to seize the opportunity created by the Mecca agreement. Former senior politician Tony Benn, writer Victoria Brittain, Member of Parliament Jeremy Corbyn, and Betty Hunter from the Palestine Solidarity Campaign wrote:

It is to be hoped that the British government heeds the words of Khalid Mish'al (Comment, February 13). Since the Oslo accords more than a decade ago, the Palestinian people have expected the world's leaders to help them to achieve their national and human rights. Instead collective punishment has been imposed and war crimes, documented by Amnesty International and others, have been ignored.

The Commons select committee on international development urged in its January report on the occupied territories that Israel be held to account for its violations of the rights of the Palestinian people. If, as Tony Blair says, he seeks a just solution to the situation, the government should end its partisan approach. The democratically elected Palestinian government must be recognized and the economic siege imposed on the already impoverished Palestinian people lifted immediately.

Index

Barghouti, Marwan 206, 208–209, 237, 348
Barghouti, Mustafa 257, 348
Barud, Abd al-Rahman 26, 323
Basyuni, M. Sharif 312
Battikhi, Samih al- 76, 87–89, 92, 98, 105, 106, 111, 123–124, 133, 135–138, 337
BBC 114, 335, 338, 345, 347, 348
Beads, Barry 104
Begin, Menachem 12, 319, 327
Beirut ix, 29, 42, 68, 145, 150, 162, 240, 317, 326, 332, 344
Beit Hadassah 327
Beit Hanun 56, 324
Beit Lahia 64, 213
Beit Lid 100, 102
Ben Eliezer, Binyamin 244
Ben Gurion, David 320, 342
Bennabi, Malik 178
Bennis, Phyllis 342–343
Bethlehem 39, 349
Bhais, Muhammad Hasan 327
Bigman, Rabbi David 244
Bir Nabala 81
Birzeit University 39, 49, 113, 218, 274, 327
Bishat, Ahmad 129
Black September 24, 111, 272
Blair, Tony 113, 247, 248, 251, 253, 254
British Mandate 318
Bsisu, Hani 321
Bukhari, al- 181, 325
Buraij, al- 213
Buraq (Wailing Wall), al- 44
Bush, George W. 199, 200, 202–203, 206, 214, 225, 260
Byzantines 177

Cairo 5, 16, 19, 24, 25, 29, 43, 111, 115, 141, 157, 189, 296, 298–299, 301, 323–325; talks 166, 192–194, 211–215, 237, 342; declaration 212

Calcutta 144
Caliph Abu Bakr, 177
Caliph Omar 151
caliphate x, 28, 169, 319, 324
Camp David, Accords 12; Summit 198–199, 347
Canada 104–106; Canadian TV 156, 165
Cape Town 113
Carter, Jimmy 12
Center for Strategic and Policy Studies 335
Change and Reform List 9, 217–218, 292
Charter, Hamas 7, 56, 147–156, 189, 261, 266
Charter, Palestinian National (PLO) 61, 120, 122, 266, 346
Children of Israel 172
Christian Lebanese Forces 42
Christian Science Monitor 326
CIA (Central Intelligence Agency) 85, 200, 340
civil society, Palestinian 38, 293, 295
Clinton, Bill 85, 88, 102, 106–107, 116, 119, 122, 198, 200, 333, 341, 347
CNN 69
collaborators 15, 35, 47, 50, 56–57, 59, 96, 205, 222, 275–276, 325, 334
colonialism 4, 20, 169, 265, 319
Communist Party (Palestinian) 326
Cordova 27
Covenant, divine 15, 153, 177, 179, 285; Hamas (see Charter); National or PLO (see Charter)
Crooke, Alastair 166
Crusade, Holy 176; Third 159
Crusaders 27, 158–159; Kingdoms 220

da'wah 5, 35, 272–275
Dabbuya, al- 326
Dahlah, Hani al- 340
Dahlan, Muhammad 102, 190, 228, 252, 263, 347

Wihdat Refugee Camp, al- 131
Wye River 119–123, 281, 337, 347

Yaffa 271, 276; street in Jerusalem 163
Yahya, Abd al-Razaq al- 82, 191
Yassin, Sheikh Ahmad 6, 10–11, 35–37,
    39, 50, 52, 60, 99–104, 107–110,
    120, 126, 136, 141, 147, 150–152,
    155, 168, 192, 221; assassination at-
    tempt on 167; murder of 206; child-
    hood to adolescence 15–19; PLO
    central council meeting controversy
    196–198; under house arrest 201;
    campaign for his release 64, 81, 100;
    first detention 46–48; first military
    project 44–45; *hudna* (truce) offer
    158–160, 165–166; Ikhwan connec-
    tion 20–25; in Jordan 103, 107–108,
    110; Israeli TV interview 65–66;
    military trial and imprisonment 63;
    prison life 101–102; release from
    prison 103, 112; second detention
    58; second military project 55–57;
    world tour 111–117
Yatom, Danny 108–109
Yazuri, Ibrahim, al- 10, 56
Yemen 28, 46, 78, 84, 114–115, 140–
    143, 145, 153, 189–190, 227, 272,
    342
Young Muslims Organization 319
Yubnah 23
Yusuf, Hassan 192
Yusuf, Nasr 190

Za'nun, Salim al- 190, 193, 321, 325
Zahhar, Fadl al- 63, 329
Zahhar, Mahmud al- 69, 89, 116, 168,
    192, 195, 232, 341
Zakarnah, Ra'id Abdullah 160
zakat 38, 325; committees 273, 304
Zaqaziq 25
Zarqa 90, 107, 132; University of 94, 333
Zawahiri, Ayman al- 262

Zayigh, Marwan al- 62, 276
Zinni, General Anthony 202
Zionism 153–154, 343; and anti-Semitism
    152; and Islamists 37, 154–155; and
    Jewish state 15, 17, 151, 153–154;
    political 154, 169
Zisling, Aharon 320
Zubair, al- 321
Zumriyeh crossing 67